VOLUME 9   SINCE THE SECOND WORLD WAR

The Cambridge Guide to the Arts in Britain

The Cambridge Guide to the Arts in Britain

edited by
BORIS FORD

VOLUME 9
SINCE THE SECOND WORLD WAR

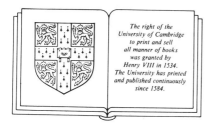

The right of the
University of Cambridge
to print and sell
all manner of books
was granted by
Henry VIII in 1534.
The University has printed
and published continuously
since 1584.

CAMBRIDGE UNIVERSITY PRESS
CAMBRIDGE
NEW YORK   NEW ROCHELLE   MELBOURNE   SYDNEY

Published by the Press Syndicate of the University of Cambridge
The Pitt Building, Trumpington Street, Cambridge CB2 1RP
32 East 57th Street, New York, NY 10022, USA
10 Stamford Road, Oakleigh, Melbourne 3166, Australia

First published 1988

Printed in Great Britain at the University Press, Cambridge

British Library cataloguing in publication data

The Cambridge guide to the arts in Britain
  Vol. 9 : Since the Second World War
  1. Arts – Great Britain – History
  I. Ford, Boris
  700'.941   NX543.A1

Library of Congress cataloguing in publication data

The Cambridge guide to the arts in Britain.
  Includes bibliographies and indexes.
  Contents: – v. 2. The Middle Ages, 1100–1500
  – v. 9. Since the Second World War.
  1. Arts, British.   I. Ford, Boris.
NX543.C36   700'.942   87–11671

ISBN 0 521 32765 2

VN

Contents

Notes on Contributors

Boris Ford: see inside back cover.

Christopher Frayling is Professor of Cultural History at the Royal College of Art. He has published numerous articles on design and craftsmanship in *Crafts*, *Design*, *Designer* and *Blueprint*, and three books on the history of popular culture.

Peter Fuller is a writer and art critic, and has written numerous books on art, among them *Art and Psychoanalysis*, *Images of God*, and *The Australian Scapegoat*. He is the editor and publisher of a new quarterly journal of the fine arts, *Modern Painters*.

Paul Griffiths is the music critic of *The Times*. He has written books on Bartók, Boulez, Ligeti, and Messiaen, a *Concise History of Modern Music from Debussy to Boulez*, and *New Sounds, New Perspectives*.

Fernau Hall, doyen of ballet and dance criticism in the English-speaking world, was dance critic for *The Daily Telegraph* for eighteen years. His books include *Modern English Ballet*, *An Anatomy of Ballet*, and *The World of Ballet and Dance*.

John Heskett is Head of Historical and Theoretical Studies at Ravensbourne College of Design and Communication. He is the author of *Industrial Design* and *Design in Germany 1870–1918*.

Alan Munton is Senior Lecturer in English at the College of St Mark and St John, Plymouth. He edited *Wyndham Lewis: Collected Poems and Plays*, and with Alan Young compiled *Seven Writers of the English Left: A Bibliography of Literature and Politics, 1916–1980*.

Simon Pepper is Senior Lecturer at the Liverpool University School of Architecture, where he teaches design and architectural history. His books include *Housing Improvement* and *Firearms and Fortifications: Military Architecture and Siege Warfare in Sixteenth Century Siena*.

Gilbert Phelps was formerly a producer with the BBC Third Programme, and is now a full-time writer, lecturer and broadcaster. He is the author of *The Russian Novel in English Fiction*, *A Survey of English Literature*, and a short history of world fiction. His novels include *The Winter People*, *The Old Believer* and *The Low Roads*.

Joseph Rykwert is Reader in the History of Architecture at the University of Cambridge, and Visiting Professor of Architecture at the University of Pennsylvania. Among his publications are *First Moderns*, *Necessity of Artifice*, and, with his wife, Anne, *Brothers Adam*.

Andrew Saint is a historian with the London Division of the Historic Buildings and Monuments Commission. His most recent book, *Towards a Social Architecture*, is about the post-war school-building movement in England.

Sir Roy Shaw was Secretary General of the Arts Council from 1975 to 1983, and before that was Professor of Adult Education at Keele University. He is the author of *The Arts and the People*. *Gwen Shaw* was an economist who switched to the arts and became an Open University tutor in the humanities.

Neil Sinyard is a freelance writer and lecturer on film and literature, in particular Victorian fiction. His books include *Filming Literature: the Art of Screen Adaptation* and studies of Billy Wilder, Richard Lester, Alfred Hitchcock and Woody Allen.

General Introduction

BORIS FORD

If English literature is, by common consent, pre-eminent in the world, the same would not often be claimed for Britain's arts as a whole. Indeed, the British people sometimes strike foreigners, and even themselves, as rather more philistine than artistic. And yet, viewed historically, Britain's over-all achievements in the visual and applied art and in architecture and music, as well as in drama and literature, must be at least the equal of any other country.

The Cambridge Guide to the Arts in Britain, to give it its full title, is not devoted, volume by volume, to the separate arts, but to all the arts in each successive age. Histories of the independent arts are legion. But being of their nature self-centred, they provide a very poor impression of the cultural richness and vitality of an age. Moreover, these separate histories obscure the ebb and flow of artistic creation from one age to the next.

When the arts in Britain are viewed collectively, it can be seen how often they reinforce each other, treating similar themes and speaking in a similar tone of voice. Also it is striking how one age may find its major cultural expression in music and drama, and the next in architecture or the applied arts: while in a later age there may be an almost total absence of important composers compared with a proliferation of major novelists. Or an age may provide scope for a great range of anonymous craftsmen. These contrasts in the degree to which the individual arts have flourished are not fortuitous, but are bound up with the social aspirations and characteristics of the age, with its beliefs and preoccupations and manners, which may favour expression in one art rather than another.

The Cambridge Guide is planned to reveal these changes and the resulting character of the arts and the balance between them. Thus these volumes do not consist of a sequence of mini-surveys of the separate arts. Rather, they are designed to help readers find their bearings in relation to the culture of an age: identifying major landmarks and lines of strength, analysing changes of taste and fashion and critical assumptions. And these are necessarily related to the demands of patrons and the tastes of the various overlapping publics.

These volumes are addressed to readers of all kinds: to general readers as well as to specialists. But virtually every reader is bound to be a non-specialist in relation to many of the arts under discussion, and so the chapters on the individual arts do not presuppose specialist knowledge. On the other hand, these volumes are not elementary nor naive; they assume a measure of familiarity with the arts, and above all a wish to understand and appreciate the artistic achievements of successive ages in Britain.

This final volume deals with a comparatively short period of time, not because the years since the Second World War have been an exceptionally rich age artistically so much as a very voluminous one: an astonishing and even unnerving volume of books are written, pictures are painted and music is composed every year. And unlike the art of pre-Conquest and medieval Britain, all of it is extant; we are living in its midst and so are rightly interested in it. Even though much of it may not be of great calibre, it has a contemporary significance. And some of it is indeed distinguished art by any standard.

Each of the nine volumes in this series contains five kinds of material:

The Cultural and Social Setting

This major introductory survey provides a map of the cultural landscape, and an examination of the historical and social developments which affected the Arts (both the 'high' and popular arts):

(a) The shape and pattern of society; its organisation, beliefs, ideals, scepticisms.
(b) How the concerns of society were embodied or reflected in the individual arts, and in the practical arts and crafts; the notion and 'function' of art at that time.
(c) The character and preoccupations of the separate arts, and of patrons and audiences. Why particular arts tended to flourish and others to decline in this age.
(d) The organisation and economic situation of the arts.

Studies in the Individual Arts

These studies of individual artists and themes do not aim to provide an all-inclusive survey of each art, but a guide to distinctive achievements and developments. Thus the amount of space devoted to the individual arts differs considerably from volume to volume, though it is interesting that literature is very strong in almost every volume.

In this section, one chapter will focus on a single town and one on a particular house or group of houses, as microcosms of the period.

Appendix

Bibliographies for further reading and reference.

   The Appendix in this volume does not have space to include short
biographies of artists; and anyway such information would very soon be out
of date.

Illustrations

The volumes are generously illustrated, though it has been decided not to
include pictures of individual artists.

Index

This is the key to making good use of each volume. Many chapters naturally
refer to the same historical developments and works of art. These have not
been cross-referenced in the texts, because material common to various
chapters has been fully noted in the Index.

   Where the contributors to these volumes have been obliged to use specialist
terms, they have for the most part explained these in the text. But they have
also assumed that readers will use their dictionaries. The following are among
the most useful dictionaries for readers: *The Oxford Illustrated Dictionary*,
The Penguin Dictionary of Architecture, *The Penguin Dictionary of Art &
Artists*, and *The Penguin Dictionary of Music*.

   In conclusion, I am greatly indebted to Professor Donald Mitchell and Dr
Joseph Rykwert for their generous and detailed advice during the
preliminary stages of this project; and to the staff of the Cambridge
University Press, especially Sarah Stanton, Ann Stonehouse and Penny
Wheeler for their sympathetic collaboration and unfailing patience.

PART I
The Cultural and Social Setting

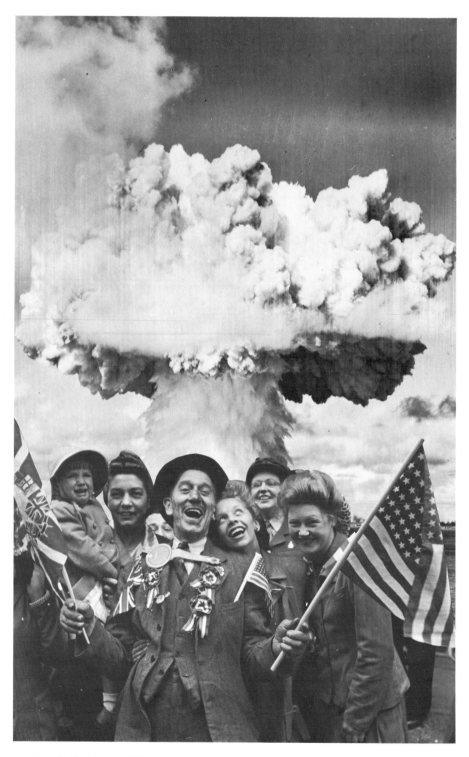

Revellers in London on VE Day, 19 May, 1945; and the fifth atomic explosion in tests at Bikini, 24 July, 1946.

The Cultural and Social Setting

ROY AND GWEN SHAW

In the years following the Second World War there was a vast increase in artistic activity of all kinds; more books published, more plays performed, more and more varied visual artefacts, more photography, still and moving, more concerts, operas and dance, more design and more new buildings. Yet although a handful of major artists emerged, few commentators saw the period as one of outstanding creative achievement. However, the period was outstanding for the attempt, mainly through public subsidy, to make artistic experience accessible to more than a cultivated elite.

If few artists are judged to have confronted adequately the human condition in the post-war years, the reason for this must in part lie in the fact that at a time when the spiritual resources of society were at a low ebb, as partly evidenced in a marked decline in religion, we had to come to terms with evil on an unprecedented scale. 1945 saw first the opening up of the concentration camps in Germany and occupied Europe, camps in which millions of men, women and children had been systematically murdered in circumstances of inhuman degradation. Soon after came the dropping of atomic bombs on the Japanese cities of Hiroshima and Nagasaki, a further horrifying slaughter of innocents which had apocalyptic implications for humanity. In the 1980s one word, 'holocaust', linked these two events in the common mind; before 1945, few Britons would have had the word in their vocabulary.

In the long historical perspective, the discovery of nuclear energy and its destructive potential may be the most significant event of the period, if not the most significant event in all history. But in a time of remarkable scientific and technological advance on many fronts, it would be foolhardy to be dogmatic. The years 1945–85 saw a Wellsian opening up of space and the consequent use of spy and communications satellites, and rumours of 'star wars'; immensely significant advances in micro-biology, molecular biology, genetic engineering and immunology, whose implications projected mankind into Aldous Huxley's *Brave New World* and beyond; and the development of fibre optics and laser technology. A communications revolution took place, whereby a televisionless post-war Britain was transformed by 1985 by the presence of a set in every home, watched on average for more than three hours a day. Further, the development of computers seemed set to change the lives of large numbers of people by making many workers redundant and enabling others to work and to communicate their needs without leaving the home (a situation prefigured before the First World War by E.M. Forster in his short story *The Machine Stops*).

The extent of the scientist's moral responsibility for his inventions, and the relation between the scientists and society, insufficiently debated in public, nevertheless haunted the popular mind in the forty years after the war. The popularity of the catastrophe movie and of science fiction reflected a widespread anxiety and a desire to explore, if obliquely, the problems of responsibility and control which often form the subtext of the best science fiction.

For the serious artist the difficulty of making a positive affirmation in a world which was systematically stockpiling the means for its own destruction could be overwhelming. Certainly, one feature common to almost all arts in our period was an inward-turning concentration on art itself as a subject for art. The autonomous development of form, to the neglect of content, was a striking feature of much post-war visual art, architecture, music and literature.

Wartime beginnings

If 1945 marked a watershed in the history of the whole world, the war years were significant years of change in British society. The great shake-up of population, through evacuation and military and industrial conscription, forced the more privileged to come face to face with the poverty and injustice of pre-war British society. The consequent stirring of conscience led to vigorous public debate at all levels, including members of the armed forces through the work of the Army Bureau of Current Affairs (ABCA). The popular campaigning photo-journalism of *Picture Post* focused criticism of conditions at home and at the front, and the paper involved such people as Julian Huxley in plans for a future Britain, preparing the way for the *Beveridge Report* and other wartime government planning. On radio, the writer J.B. Priestley reinforced the sense of unified national will which the fall of France had precipitated by speaking of Britain's historic past, its countryside, and its future. Indeed, the main contribution of creative artists during the war was a celebration of 'Britishness'. The First World War had elicited remarkable poetry out of a sense of outrage at the futile waste of life. When Benjamin Britten composed his *War Requiem* (1960) to lament 'the pity of war', at a time when anxiety about nuclear weapons was at its peak, he set to music the poetry of that earlier war rather than the one he had lived through. The Second World War seemed to most people necessary and inevitable, so that outrage was inappropriate. Instead there were Henry Moore's reticent but powerful shelter drawings speaking of British endurance (their sales in reproduction far exceeded expectations); the popular British folk song settings by Benjamin Britten, and his settings of English poetry in the Serenade for tenor, horn and strings (1943), and the pastoral yearnings of Henry Reed's poem 'The Naming of Parts'. The Pilgrim Trust funded a *Recording Britain* project, of which the artist John Piper was a member. The film industry, in a great burst of wartime creativity, celebrated for the first time the ordinary British citizen, both in outstanding semi-fictional documentaries such as *Fires were Started*, and in entertainment films: *Love on the Dole*, based on Walter Greenwood's bitter pre-war pay, Noel Coward's *In Which We Serve*, and Sidney Gilliat's *Waterloo Road* among others.

Direct government patronage of visual artists through the War Artist's Commission produced some fine paintings from established artists like Paul Nash, Sutherland, Piper and Spencer, but as the critic Kenneth Clark was later to admit, it did not elicit any great work from new painters, although 15,000 works of art were produced. 'Art obeys its own laws', said Clark, 'and at the time the artistic impulse was moving away from illustration.' Untypically, the wartime paintings of Edward Burra express a sense of outrage at the dehumanising effects of war, in paintings which form a continuum with his paintings of the Spanish Civil War. The disgust in Francis Bacon's controversial *Crucifixion* (1945) (see page 123) may have similar origins. But these painters were not commissioned war artists.

However, Government intervention on behalf of *audiences* for the arts was spectacularly successful. Full employment and the shortage of consumer goods meant people had money to spare, and the Government, realising that the arts could have a role in maintaining morale, funded from 1940 the newly formed and oddly named Council for the Encouragement of Music and the Arts (CEMA). This furthered the work already being done by the Old Vic and Pilgrim Players and brought into being other non-profit-making companies to take theatre to regions where live performances had never been seen: to miners' welfare halls, and church halls in small towns and villages. Exhibitions of paintings were also toured, and fine prints by Degas, Renoir and Cézanne were made available at modest prices. There were concert tours, and (to avoid the blackout) lunch-time music and ballet performances in London, which by their informality attracted a new audience. In addition the commercial firm of H.M. Tennent Ltd co-operated with CEMA on a non-profit-making basis to send some outstanding theatrical productions (including John Gielgud in *Macbeth*) on long and highly successful provincial tours. Opera and ballet were taken to the provinces by the Sadler's Wells company which needed respite from the bombing of London, and some large regional orchestras, the Hallé, the Liverpool Philharmonic and the City of Birmingham Symphony Orchestra, were put on a more solid basis. Under other government auspices, travelling film vans took the exciting new products of the British cinema to factories, village halls and Women's Institutes. The result of all this activity was the creation of new audiences and a sharpening of public taste, with important post-war consequences.

Nor were the armed forces forgotten. ENSA (the Entertainments National Service Association) and Army Education sent shows to all parts of the world – not only popular entertainers such as Gracie Fields and George Formby, but also theatre companies including The Old Vic Company, and concert artists, among them the violinist Yehudi Menuhin. As an integral part of army education, the Army Bureau for Current Affairs sponsored a company to produce dramatic documentaries dealing with political issues of the day.

Both in the forces and among civilians the war created a huge demand for reading matter. There were long periods of boredom when little was happening, and the air raids and black-outs kept people indoors. With paper supplies at only forty percent of pre-war, publishers were faced with difficult choices. Predictably, books explaining the origins of Nazism and the current conflict, and others discussing planning for the future were in great demand. More interestingly, the writer of a British Council booklet published at the end of the war noted a remarkable interest in writing which discussed agricultural planning, and which often went far deeper than the practice of agriculture into a kind of 'religion of the soil' which, he surmised, might arise from 'a subliminal fear . . . of the destructive potential of modern technology'. Edwin Muir was to touch the same chord in his great fifties poem of the nuclear age, 'The Horses'. In the eighties, the rise of the ecological ('green') movement was evidence of a similar intuition.

Paperback publishing played an important part in the wartime trend towards the democratisation of culture. Penguin books helped contemporary artists to find a new audience with such series as *Penguin New Writing* and *Penguin Modern Painters*, the latter aiming, said the editor, Kenneth Clark, to dispel 'the current idea that modern painting is unintelligible and that modern Art Galleries are for the few selected initiates'. The low-priced Puffin Picture Books, first published in 1940 and inspired by Soviet Russia's colourful children's books, set a new standard in children's books through the quality of their text and illustration.

Post-war achievements and disillusion

The war ended in 1945 with the election of a Labour government by a resounding majority and the ousting of the great wartime leader, Winston Churchill. This was not, as one Home Counties' elector wrote, 'the greatest act of treachery since Christ', but a sign of the rejection by the electorate of the unjust society of the pre-war years. In the event, many leading Tories were as committed to change as their opponents, and a period of consensus politics began. The war had been a people's war, with the killing of 60,000 civilians and 35,000 merchant seamen, in addition to 300,000 combatants. Now the people were to be thanked, by legislation for a fairer deal 'for all' – key words of the new Welfare State. Despite a warning from Lord Keynes that Britain faced a 'financial Dunkirk' because of its war debts, the Labour government pressed ahead. An Education Act had already been passed in 1944, guaranteeing secondary education to the age of fifteen. Measures setting up a free National Health Service for all, and contributory National Insurance to provide security at all stages of life, followed, together with the nationalisation of coal, steel and the railways, housing legislation, and environmental planning through the New Towns Act and Town and Country Planning Act. At the same time, the granting of Indian independence immediately after the war heralded the gradual dissolution of the empire.

Although many young National Service conscripts were involved in the process, the loss of empire was to impinge upon the national consciousness to a remarkably small degree, as most people had had little understanding of the benefits which the empire had conferred. However, a latterday, somewhat detached interest in India surfaced in the early eighties, with the televising of Paul Scott's *Raj Quartet* as *The Jewel in the Crown*, and the film *Gandhi* (see page 250).

But for the extensive planning which had taken place during the war, it is doubtful whether the sweeping post-war legislation could have been carried through, for the war had left both people and leaders in a state of exhaustion exacerbated by persistent financial crises and continued austerity. (Rationing did not completely end until the mid-fifties.) The British people, for a brief period after the fall of France in 1940 and before Russia and America entered the war in 1941, had stood alone against Germany. In the years following the war, feelings of a new isolation grew. The sudden ending of American aid and the knowledge that America looked with suspicion at a Labour government's socialism, together with fears of being swamped by American culture, engendered anti-American feelings, whilst fear of Russia's intentions quickly gave rise to a 'cold war' atmosphere. In 1947 Churchill was to speak of an 'Iron Curtain' which divided eastern and western Europe.

The tension between the conflicting pulls of egalitarianism and freedom were to become a major theme of British politics. In 1949 George Orwell, himself a democratic socialist, published his warning vision of a totalitarian future in the novel *Nineteen Eighty-Four*. In the same year, against the background of the Russian-backed Czechoslovak coup and the Berlin airlift, America was given permission to station atomic bombers in Britain. The cold war became a dominant theme of popular fiction, notably in the spy stories of Ian Fleming, and in science fiction. In the cold war atmosphere, fear became a threat to objectivity. Tom Hopkinson of *Picture Post* resigned in 1950 after twelve years as editor, because his proprietor refused permission to print a story by two highly respected journalists, James Cameron and the photographer Bert Hardy, about the ill-treatment, with American connivance, of North Korean prisoners by the South Koreans. The objectivity of the quality journal of politics and culture *Encounter*, was compromised by secret funding from the American CIA (Central Intelligence Agency). In the popular press, anyone on the left might incur the slur of being a 'fellow-traveller' and 'soft on Russia', and of course a few were, often sincerely believing the evidence of Stalinist brutalities to be Western propaganda.

In this atmosphere of suspicion, the more abstract arts fared best. The new generation of visual artists were eager to re-establish European contacts, stimulated by post-war exhibitions of the work of Picasso, Braque and Van Gogh. The tendency to abstraction reduced the possibility of ideological conflict, although the Marxist art critic John Berger, writing in the *New Statesman* in the early fifties was vilified as a 'fellow-traveller'. In the eighties, not untypically, he was to be criticised from the left for his bourgeois tendencies. Music flourished, especially through the influence of the BBC, its orchestras, its daring new Third Programme, and its support of the popular annual series of Promenade Concerts. Annual festivals were established at Edinburgh and Aldeburgh, and English-language opera found a home at Sadlers Wells, opening with Benjamin Britten's new opera, *Peter Grimes*, the first major English opera since Purcell. The two outstanding young composers, Britten and Tippett, were both pacifists but this had not entirely shielded them from the trauma of war: Tippett had been head of Morley College through the bombing, and was given a three month prison sentence for his conscientious objection to military service; Britten played in the concentration camps in 1945 with Yehudi Menuhin, in the wake of which he composed his *Holy Sonnets of John Donne*. But they had not shared in the passions of war and the euphoria of victory, and so perhaps were less disorientated and better able to tackle major themes despite the uncertainties of the post-war period. Whilst the work of novelists and playwrights explored the rather parochial subject of social class, Britten's exploration of the theme of innocence and corruption, and Tippet's of 'light' and 'dark' forces, showed a deep awareness of the moral dilemma of the times (an awareness which Tippett made explicit in his autobiographical *Moving into Aquarius*, 1959).

With less profound treatment the theme of innocence and corruption could become a rejection of experience and therefore of life. P.H. Newby, writing in 1951 on the state of the novel in the post-war years, commented on the number of young writers who were writing about childhood in this negative way. He attributed this to 'the state of unbelief or bewilderment in which they live. The atmosphere was threatening, so that the war seemed, in spirit, to go on and on.' Forty years later, it could be argued, this feeling still prevailed. In 1954 when nuclear anxiety was resurfacing after the testing of a British A-bomb, William Golding gave the same theme of childhood innocence and corruption its full symbolic force in his fable *The Lord of the Flies*, a powerful parable of the origins and nature of evil in society. A most moving semi-autobiographical treatment of the theme came only after forty years' assimilation with J.G. Ballard's *The Empire of the Sun* (1984), a novel in which he confronted his childhood experience of the war in Shanghai with a triumphant affirmation in the face of appalling events. It may be significant that Ballard had previously written science fiction 'catastrophe' novels, such as *The Drowned World* (1962).

Cultural democracy: a mixed blessing?

The wartime fillip to the cultural life of the provinces carried over into peacetime. Government commitment to the arts was endorsed by the setting up of the Arts Council of Great Britain in 1946, and the National Film Finance Corporation in 1949. The Coventry Municipal Theatre (1956) was the first of many civic repertory theatres to be established, some initially with the support of distinguished local amateur groups. However, most new writing for the theatre in the ten years after the war shared the parochial drift of the novel. Poetic drama was thought by the critics to be an important trend, but although in the hands of T.S. Eliot it produced some significant works, as a form it was short-lived. Conversely, a little remarked theatre workshop collective established in 1945 by two left-wing artists, Joan

Littlewood and Ewan McColl, to tour small northern venues and perform documentaries with ballads was to have a significant influence on the theatre from the late fifties onwards.

Nevertheless, in spite of this and other moves to democratise the arts, such as the gradual extension of the library services, the bulk of the population still remained on the outside, although they were not forgotten by the organisers of the Government-inspired Festival of Britain in 1951 at Battersea Park, which had a fun-fair as well as a sculpture park. The cinema in the immediate post-war years had record attendances, peaking in 1946, and the British film industry continued to make outstanding films with popular appeal, including *The Third Man* and *The Fallen Idol*, scripted by the novelist Graham Greene, both of which also explored the theme of innocence and experience. Football crowds were never larger. But television, becoming more widespread from the early fifties, was set to change much in British life, perhaps most of all for the 'common man'.

Although working-class standards of living in the ten years after the war left much to be desired, with a third of houses still without bathrooms in 1950, and few homes possessing washing machines, let alone cars or telephones, the war, full employment, a better diet and a general sense of being needed had given greater confidence to people from the working class.

The development of mass communications had already, particularly through radio, lowered social and cultural barriers. George Formby, the Lancashire comedian, was popular with the Royal Family as well as in northern homes. The entire nation had united in tuning in to the mildly satirical wartime radio show, ITMA. But the greater confidence and participation of the working class and lower middle class caused anxiety too. Evelyn Waugh's *Sword of Honour* trilogy, a satire on British society in wartime, embodied fears of a decline in social standards, whilst some influential social critics feared a serious undermining of cultural standards through a general levelling down, particularly through the spread of American cultural influence. In later years, a more discerning approach to American culture gave recognition to the richness that American jazz, the American musical, and the best of American films had added to Western society, to be set against the TV quiz games and soap operas. The work of the British Film Institute, established before the war, contributed largely to this process, particularly through its education department, as did the new schools of American Studies in some universities after 1970; and in the late 1970s the Arts Council itself added jazz to its departments, and helped to fund touring productions of the American musicals *My Fair Lady* and *Oklahoma*.

But in the 1950s the development of television gave a new urgency to fears which had already been expressed in the thirties and forties by such writers as F.R. Leavis and T.S. Eliot. Leavis believed, in the tradition of nineteenth-century thinkers such as Matthew Arnold, that 'the imagination in great writers is moral', and he was concerned that this moral quality would be lost in a levelling down of civilisation. His influence was considerable in the post-war years through the journal *Scrutiny*, through such books as *Mass Civilisation and Minority Culture* (1931), and through the many distinguished students who passed through his hands at Cambridge (among others Peter Hall, Trevor Nunn, John Barton and Peter Wood, later to be highly influential in the theatre). For Leavis, the problem of reconciling democracy with high cultural standards could only be tackled through education, and already with Denys Thompson in 1933 he had written an educational handbook, *Culture and Environment*, urging teachers to discuss with their pupils such subjects as newspapers, advertising, mass production and standardisation. This enlightened advice was only slowly adopted even during the post-war period, and it was unlikely to affect the most vulnerable and least educated section of the population, whose secondary education in the thirties and forties was negligible, and in the post-war years generally second-rate. But Leavis' concern was not with the educationally underprivileged so much as with the preservation of excellence in British cultural life. For this reason, although he favoured an extension of higher education, he believed university growth should be restricted in the interests of the highest standards, and he was opposed to the Open University and the conversion of colleges of advanced technology into universities.

Leavis' insistence on the moral quality of art, and the danger that mass culture could undermine the moral values of society was an important influence on two seminal critics of the fifties, Richard Hoggart and Raymond Williams, both of whom, significantly, were then lecturers in adult education, and both of whom came from working-class backgrounds. Hoggart's detailed description, in *The Uses of Literacy* (1957), of the working-class world of Hunslet, in Leeds, which he knew from his childhood: its strengths and its failings, its attitudes to work, to sex, to money, and to education, had a special poignancy because he was describing it at a point of change. For his middle-class readers he opened the window on a world hitherto largely glimpsed only in caricature. Hoggart analysed the current trivialisation, mainly through American influence, of the women's magazines, the comics, the popular weeklies, the newspapers and cheap novels which were the principal reading matter of the working class, and which had once reflected solid if limited values. He saw the new products as enervating in their effect: they made it 'harder for people without an intellectual bent to become wise in their own way'. Anticipating the hedonism to come, he warned of the 'corrupt brightness' of a synthetic culture, a 'candyfloss world' in which 'progress is conceived as a seeking of material possessions, equality as a moral levelling, and freedom as the ground for endless irresponsible pleasure'.

These were hard sayings, perhaps, for a working class which had hitherto shared few of society's possessions or pleasures. For Hoggart, as for Leavis, art, especially literature, was central to the cultural problem, and good art, whether 'serious' or 'popular', should embody a moral sense. Like Leavis, he did not seek to change the structure of capitalist society, but to modify its influence through education. This stance was shared by Raymond Williams in his early work, *Culture and Society* (1957) and *The Long Revolution* (1961), although he rejected Leavis' hierarchical view of culture. Like Hoggart, Williams' chief concern was with the culturally disinherited masses, and he criticised those who concentrated their energies on the presentation of an elitist tradition. In *The Long Revolution*, a searching inquiry into the relation between art, democracy and industry, he identified with remarkable precision most of the problems which were to beset British society in the ensuing years: the precariousness of Britain's apparent economic recovery; the threat to the provision of social needs in schools, hospitals, libraries and the infrastructure from a consumer-orientated society; the moral decline of the Labour movement with the growth of sectional self-interest, and the perpetuation of a confrontational style; the institutionalised persistence of class division despite the optimistic claims of the period that British society was becoming classless; and the failure to involve people in work and community decisions. Like Hoggart he deplored the widespread dissemination of bad art and the failure to make the best art available to the majority of the people. Williams, in 1961, wanted these problems to be tackled through education and through politics. There should be a widening of syllabuses to take in social studies, art history and criticism, including film, television drama and jazz as well as the traditional arts. Students should be coached in the critical reading of the press, and should study the social implications of science. He also urged a livelier approach to language teaching. Politically, he stressed the importance of developing a participating democracy with people more involved in decisions about work, housing and community matters, and with greater access to the channels of communication. In the seventies, although some progress had been made in achieving these ends, partly through Williams' own considerable influence on the ideas of the New Left, whose members were largely writers, teachers and students, he came to believe that it was impossible to alter the quality of life if the economic system was left unchanged, and in his later works adopted a largely Marxist position. This move to the left in the seventies was shared by many social and cultural reformers of the period, and along with it went a reassessment of those in the Arnold–Leavis tradition as 'yesterday's men', out of touch with social and political reality.

In the 1950s, however, Leavis and other cultural critics voiced the widespread concern of many when they focused attention on the media of communication.

Radio, television, and the press

During the war, news had literally been of life and death importance, but newspapers were severely limited in size. Hence radio became the prime source of news and morale building. Winston Churchill's addresses to the nation (and the world) were food for the nation's soul and so, in a rather different way, were J.B. Priestley's broadcasts. As a result the BBC came out of the war with a formidable reputation for reliability and quality, enhanced by the establishment in 1946 of the Third Programme (now Radio 3) largely devoted to serious music and serious talk – 'dons talking to dons' some said, but to many more it was the apogee of broadcasting. Light entertainment was not neglected, for it had received a great boost during the war and the traditional sobriety of 'the Reith Sunday' (no comedy shows allowed), so called after the BBC's great but puritanical first Director General, was replaced by the Light Programme.

Starting almost from scratch after the war, television gradually began to spread and to eclipse radio as the main source of evening entertainment at home. Early in the 1950s a few voices began to be raised in the Conservative party in favour of breaking the BBC's television monopoly by introducing competition from commercial television, financed solely by advertising. How they got their way was chronicled by an American scholar, H.H. Wilson, in *Pressure Group* (1961). Leading figures in the churches, vice-chancellors of universities, and the Labour party condemned what they saw as the introduction of American-type television into Britain. Lord Reith, long retired from the BBC, warned his fellow peers against the spread of such a cultural plague to our country, and many shared his horror. Even Lord Hailsham, pillar of the Tory party, condemned the submission of a bill to introduce commercial television as 'a shoddy and squalid constitutional error'. Wilson judges that Britain was given commercial television in 1958 'against the advice of the leaders of society in education, religion and culture as well as significant sections of the business community'. The public, he averred, 'played no part in the decision'. Four years later opinion polls still showed a majority against commercial television and a great dislike of interruptive 'commercials'. For its part the commercial television lobby dismissed its opponents as 'prigs, prudes and purists'.

The advertising industry, anxious to see a powerful new advertising medium developed, lent its considerable skills to a campaign to reassure doubters. A spokesman for the cleverly named Popular Television Association (he was an Anglican canon) assured a meeting there would be no interruption of television programmes by advertising. The Home Secretary assured the House of Commons that advertisements would be inserted only at 'natural breaks', say between the acts of a play, 'especially if the first act had lasted for an hour and a half'. Such assurances were soon forgotten and rang ironically hollow within a few years. By 1970, the first Director of the Independent Television Authority, Sir Robert Fraser, felt able to say, in a retirement speech, that few people now raised the question of 'natural breaks' and the expression had become 'an academic one'.

If some saw commercial television as a threat to a healthy democratic culture, many, not least Sir Robert, believed the old system had been overturned by 'a wave of democratic thought and feeling'. The historian A.J.P. Taylor welcomed the ending of the BBC monopoly as 'the biggest knock respectability has taken in my time'. The new system was tactfully called, not commercial television, but independent television, on the grounds that the BBC was allegedly unhealthily subject to government influence. In fact, the new service was put under the control of a public body, the Independent Television Authority (later called the Independent Broadcasting Authority), very similar to the BBC's Board of Governors, and it had additionally to consider the wishes of its paymasters, the advertisers. By 1968, a commercial programme contractor was to complain in *Advertisers' Weekly* that 'it is impossible to satisfy the ITA on the one hand and the general public and the advertisers on the other'.

Sir Robert argued vigorously that ITV was 'People's TV' and that 'those of superior mental constitution' who were angrily dissatisfied with it after the first five years 'were really dissatisfied with people'. There was much talk of 'giving the public what it wants', but Norman Collins, one of the prime movers in getting commercial television established, rather gave the game away when he confessed: 'If one gave the public exactly what it wanted, it would be a perfectly appalling service.' The fifties and sixties debate about broadcasting exemplified a central aspect of the debate about democracy and culture which ran through the whole post-war period. A Select Committee (1972), discussed an 'inevitable conflict between the need to maximise the audience and the obligation to produce good quality programmes'. Lord Bernstein, the most civilised of the early television tycoons, was later to admit that you don't make more money by making better programmes; and Jeremy Isaacs, then an ITV producer, said that 'the fundamental fact about ITV is it's supposed to make money'.

Early ITV programmes were populist in the worst sense, and the young Bernard Levin resigned from being a television critic on the *Manchester Guardian* because he could no longer bear to watch such poor stuff. In 1960 Kingsley Amis described commercial television as the 'greatest single vulgarizing influence in our national life'. The Labour party committed itself to abolishing ITV when it returned to power, but the programmes were popular with working-class voters and the Labour party quickly forgot its threat.

The most devastating criticism of ITV came in the report of the Pilkington Committee (1962) set up by the government. It affirmed the need for radical reform, since 'It is no use tinkering with a machine that can only turn out the wrong product.' Its main proposal was to transfer from the programme companies to the ITA the planning of programme schedules and the selling of advertising. The programme companies would be simply that – makers of programmes which they would offer to the ITA. The proposals were not accepted, but the critique of the programming had its effect.

By the 1980s, competition had led not (as the champions of competition had prophesied) to much greater variety in programming, but to greater similarities. BBC1 and ITV became more alike, and ITV sometimes had the edge on BBC1 in programme quality. BBC2 had arrived and for a time was television's closest approach to radio's Third Programme – but not very close. Ironically, something like the Pilkington proposals were adopted when (in 1983) ITV got *its* second channel, dubbed Channel 4. Channel 4's revenue was taken from the ITV companies who in return had the franchise to sell advertising space in the channel's programmes in their areas. Further, the channel commissioned a substantial proportion of its programmes from independent producers. This distancing of the selling of advertising from the making of programmes led to the improvement in programming which Pilkington predicted, and Channel 4 successfully challenged the long-established belief (for which there was much evidence) that BBC programming would always be better and justified the claim of the channel's first head, Jeremy Isaacs, that the aim was to extend viewers' choice.

Television became the prime source of entertainment for people of all social levels. Television drama, often of very high quality, became Britain's real national theatre. Playwrights like Dennis Potter, author of *Pennies from Heaven*, wrote almost exclusively for television. But the heaviest viewing (three to five hours a day) was among the less well educated, and the most viewed programmes were usually soap operas and other light entertainment. This made applicable to Britain the views of an American writer, Neil Postman, in a book pointedly titled *Amusing Ourselves to Death* (1986). Postman argued that of the two main visions of the future in this century, Orwell's *Nineteen Eighty-Four* and Huxley's *Brave New World*, Huxley's prophecy had much more nearly come to pass than Orwell's. Orwell portrayed political oppression, Huxley portrayed a society in which people had come (in Postman's words) to 'adore the technologies that undo their capacities to think'. Orwell feared a captive culture, Huxley a trivial one. Orwell warned of people being controlled by inflicting pain, Huxley warned of people being controlled by inflicting pleasure.

As we shall see, most of the press as well as broadcasting became primarily a source of entertainment, but both forms of broadcasting in Britain were, unlike the press, required to inform and educate as well as to entertain, and radio and television gradually replaced the press as people's prime source of news. Independent Television News frequently surpassed the BBC's television news, but the BBC remained pre-eminent in radio news. Both broadcasting organisations provided excellent documentary programmes to give background depth to the inevitably brief coverage given by the news bulletins.

The news and documentaries had, in general, a non-partisan approach to political questions, which the press did not. This did not save the BBC from accusations by Tory MPs of left-wing bias and at the same time accusations of anti trade union bias which came from left-wing academics as well as the unions themselves. The term 'mass media' was unknown in 1945, but forty years later it had become commonplace for aggrieved people in the public eye, especially those on the left, to complain of the lies of 'the meeja'.

The BBC incurred the displeasure of both the Wilson and the Thatcher governments for attempting to be impartial in its treatment of government actions, and in 1985 Mrs Thatcher's Home Secretary made a blatant attempt to stop the screening of *Real Lives*, a balanced documentary about terrorism by both the IRA and their opponents in Northern Ireland. The BBC governors, charged with protecting the public interest, appeared willing to accede to the government's request, but BBC journalists, with the backing of those on the rival ITV Companies, went on strike to preserve the independence of broadcasting, and the programme was shown after some delay with only slight editing. About the same time it was revealed that MI5 vetted senior appointments to the BBC. These events were a reminder that the freedom of broadcasting can be preserved only by eternal vigilance. On this occasion, the lack of vigilance was shown by a board of governors headed (for the first time in the BBC's history) by Tory nominees as both chairman and vice-chairman; but years earlier the left-wing Tony Benn had made a notorious declaration that broadcasting was too important to be left to the broadcasters.

From the sixties onwards, the most popular television programmes were quiz programmes, ranging (in 1986) from the engagingly inane *Blankety Blank* to the absurdly portentous *Mastermind*, both on BBC. The latter programme was staged in universities throughout the land where the academic hosts seemed so dazzled by the television lights that they did not notice that the programme glorified a Gradgrind approach to knowledge as 'facts', or that it confused skill in memorising with wisdom.

For better and for worse, television was clearly the most important cultural influence in the post-war period. Its offerings spread from evening to daytime and to breakfast time and, in the mid-eighties, to experimental all-night pop music programmes. So it seems that at least some people were amusing themselves to bleary exhaustion, if not to death.

Amusement, which has been cruelly defined as the happiness of those who cannot think, increasingly became in the post-war period that main 'product' not only of television, but also of the newspaper industry, making it harder to take seriously the traditional claim that the press was the Fourth Estate of the realm and the bulwark of democracy. In 1957, Francis Williams, an experienced journalist, called his 'anatomy of the press' *Dangerous Estate*; while Tom Baistow, also an experienced journalist, called his more perceptive study of the press *The Fourth Rate Estate* (1985). Baistow chronicled the growth of 'junk journalism' whose main ingredients were 'sexual sensationalism, trivialisation of news values and political bias'. The phenomenon had been perceived by the first Royal Commission on the press reporting in 1949, which noted that the press, with few exceptions, 'failed to provide the electorate with adequate materials for sound political judgement' and its trivial concept of news values meant that the picture it gave to its readers was always out of focus. The Commission advocated a Press Council to supervise newspapers' performance and to receive complaints. A Council was established in 1953, but with sufficient members involved in newspapers to ensure that it would not be a serious critic. Its adverse judgements had little effect and it was unsuccessful in a well-meant attempt to persuade the press to distinguish between the news that was 'in the public interest' and that which was 'of interest to the public'.

The two explicitly socialist newspapers, the *Daily Herald* and the (Sunday) *Reynold's News* had long disappeared by the eighties, when eleven out of seventeen national daily papers were committed to the Tory cause, including the largest one, *The Sun*, which had a mainly working-class readership. The fact that Labour governments sometimes were elected suggests that addicts of 'tit and bum' journalism either did not take any interest in politics or turned to radio and television for 'real' news. As early as 1955, Cecil King told *Mirror* group shareholders that the advent of radio and television had altered the character of newspapers from being purveyors of news to being daily magazines. His magazines nevertheless had no regular features on books, plays, music or art. A decade later, King was to rebuke an American journalist who asked him how he could run such a wretched rag, by telling him he was applying the wrong criteria, saying 'We're in the entertainment business.' Twenty years later, Rupert Murdoch, head of the *Sun*'s publishers, gave precisely the same justification for his (even worse) product. Back in 1948, the left-wing Labour leader Aneurin Bevan had denounced 'the capitalist press' as 'the most prostituted press in the world, most of it owned by a gang of millionaires'. He exaggerated (though not much) but had he lived to see the emergence of the Australian tycoon Rupert Murdoch, he might have thought slightly better of the old-style 'press lords' and their popular papers.

The trend towards this form of journalism had started before the war. The man who edited the very successful *Daily Express* from 1933 to 1957 wrote in his memoirs that his aim had been to 'make the news exciting, even when it was dull'. In 1953, Hugh Cudlipp, then editor of the *Mirror*, proclaimed the same formula which had made his paper the largest in Britain: 'The pages were to be as stimulating and aggressive, as crammed with excitement and surprises as . . . Blackpool pleasure gardens.' Thirty years later, *The Sun* had outdone the *Mirror* in the search for the lowest common denominator of public taste and the highest level of circulation. It had started in 1965 with the claim to be 'the new paper born of the age we live in'. Newspapers have been described as the 'barometers of their age', and if *The Sun* was really the barometer of the post-war era it indicated a depressing intellectual, cultural and political climate. The paper degraded the public mind, but it supported the Tories and its editor was duly ennobled by the government which came to power in 1979.

A more encouraging aspect of the press was that the total sales of the popular press declined between 1961 and 1985 – the dailies by 10 per cent and the Sundays by 32 per cent, while those of quality dailies rose by 21 per cent and quality Sundays by an impressive 41 per cent. However, the total sales of the qualities were still only one fifth that of the populars. Moreover, the qualities themselves had to 'go down market' (a euphemism for reducing their quality) to maintain circulations. In particular, *The Times* was no longer the sober 'journal of record' on which its pre-eminent reputation was built, and *The Sunday Times'* attention to the sex lifes of politicians and film stars reminded one more and more of its stable-mate, the *News of the World*. By the eighties *The Guardian*, despite a move to capture a younger readership, often by undergraduate writing and humour, was probably the best written and most politically independent daily paper in Britain, and *The Observer* on Sunday embodied similar qualities. These virtues were rewarded by a trebling of the *Guardian*'s circulation since 1949, surpassing the *Times*, but still less than half that of the staunchly Tory *Daily Telegraph*. In 1986, the majority of newspaper readers read none of these, but fed on a daily diet of junk journalism.

One of the best of the popular papers, the *News Chronicle* was closed in 1960 for reasons which are significant. It still had over a million readers, but they were of an economic and social class which lacked the purchasing power to attract sufficient advertising, and advertising, since 1953 a powerful influence on television, also had the power to decide which newspapers would survive. Popular papers derived 25 to 35 per cent of their income from advertising, and the quality papers looked to it for 70 per cent of theirs. Hence the introduction by the 'posh Sundays' in the early sixties of colour supplements in an attempt to counter the drift of advertising from the press to television. They offered scope for lavish colour adverts, mainly for luxury goods, interspersed with articles which reflected the life style of their prosperous readership ('top people'), but often incongruously alternating with strikingly illustrated articles on the poverty of the third world or the poorer parts of Britain. Britain had travelled a long way from *Picture Post*'s black and white photo-journalism-with-a-social-conscience to the colourful glamour of these guides to the good life in the acquisitive society.

At the time of writing, there are signs that the shape and economics, but perhaps not the quality, of the press may be changed by new technology, including computerised typesetting which greatly reduces the cost of production by reducing the number of printers required. In 1986, Rupert Murdoch opened a new plant in the face of fierce opposition from sacked printers. The year also saw the birth of two new papers: *Today*, a newspaper produced by the new technology offering colour pictures but no improvement in quality; and *The Independent*, which broke new ground in quality journalism. Other new ventures are in the pipeline and it is possible that papers could be viable with much smaller circulations than in the past.

It seems improbable that newspapers will ever regain their central role in distributing what used to be called 'intelligence' to a democratic society. In 1957, an American journalist wrote a book arguing, after a detailed study of *The Guardian* and the *Mirror*, that even quality papers had become for Britishers not so much their intellectual daily bread as their daily sugar pill. In the same year, Francis Williams could boast that 'No other people on earth are such avid readers of newspapers as the British.' By 1986, the total 'consumption' of newspapers had fallen by 30 per cent. It is unlikely that the quality of British life had thereby been diminished.

The consumer society

The coming of advertising on television and its growing importance in the press were symptoms of the growth, from about the mid-fifties, of the consumer society. By the time Harold Macmillan coined his famous slogan 'You've never had it so good' for the 1959 election, consumerism had arrived. The emphasis of the post-war consensus governments had been on social need in the provision of schools and hospitals and other services which, it was thought, could best be provided communally. Now the emphasis was shifted to the needs of the individual, a shift which gained its own momentum with the proliferation of consumer goods in the sixties and which in the eighties reached its apogee with the Conservative governments' encouragement of the 'privatisation' of many hitherto sacrosanct public services and industries, and the growing private purchase of education and health services.

In the consumer society advertising became supremely important, for goods were mass produced for which mass consumption then had to be stimulated, rather than to meet an already-demonstrated need. The advertising industry became perhaps the biggest economic success story of the post-war years, with its ramifications of market research and public relations companies. In the eighties its expansion entered a new phase with the amalgamation of many already large and powerful companies. From the mid-fifties 'image' became a prime concern. Not only the image of products, but the image of people and of corporate concerns, even churches, became fitting subjects for the services of the marketing experts. In the political sphere, the process began at the end of the fifties, but reached its most controversial phase in the late seventies when the Tory party engaged one of the largest agencies, Saatchi and Saatchi, to project its image, and the whole public style and personality of its leader, Margaret Thatcher, were adjusted to accommodate the preferences of the electorate which market research and opinion polls revealed. In the mid-eighties the snowball effect of these tactics led to the marketing of the Kinnock product, associating the Labour leader with pop music and youth culture in a bid to capture the young vote. The crudeness of this approach was admitted by the Labour party publicity manager: 'Television communicates in *Daily Mirror* language, not in *Guardian* language. We aim to tell people what Labour stands for in images they can understand, not to lecture them about policy.' The previous Labour leader, Michael Foot, though well-qualified in many ways, failed primarily because he did not have the necessary televisual quality. For a democracy such developments had ominous implications.

The concentration on image affected all aspects of life. For the consumer it raised expectations of a life-style which for most could never be realised, through the depiction in advertisements of ideal families, kitchens, gardens or holidays. The hyping in advance of a book, film or pop group was used to create a best-selling image in the public mind even before the 'product' was on the market, so that 'best-selling' became a self-fulfilling prophecy. On television the daily opening title sequence of the news programmes, the fanfare of music and the tone of voice of the news announcers, created a constant expectation of dramatic events. In documentary programmes the mere presence of a television camera could alter the course of events and present a distorted image. Moreover, television could turn people of minor talent into major 'personalities' through a process of promotion which the popular press was happy to back up. In this situation credibility becomes more important than truth, presentation more noticed than content. In America, by the eighties, it had become common to call an academic lecture a 'presentation' and this significant development spread to Britain. Marshall McLuhan, the Canadian scholar, coined the phrase 'the medium is the message' to exemplify the effect of the modern medium of television on communications. With the manipulation of image, the message was too often a distorted one.

One consequence of the cultivation of image was the growth of a counterbalancing scepticism (not without its own dangers) which manifested itself in a national taste for satire. With the full encouragement of a new Director General of the BBC, Hugh Carlton Greene, a vibrant youthful weekly satirical show *That Was The Week That Was* appeared on television in 1962 and almost the whole nation united in joyful relief at the weekly dose of iconoclasm and taboo-breaking. Questions were asked about the programme in the House of Commons every week, and it undoubtedly played a part in the setting up, by Mrs Mary Whitehouse in 1964, of the 'clean-up TV' campaign. In the same year, 1962, the weekly and often scurrilous (but sometimes usefully revealing) paper *Private Eye* first appeared, and survived despite some damaging libel actions. The success of *That Was The Week* spawned, in the ensuing decades, innumerable satirical shows on television and radio, outstanding among them the anarchic and surrealist *Monty Python* of the seventies, targeting social manners, and *Spitting Image* in the eighties, with its remarkable rubber-faced puppet grotesques. These so offended some members of the establishment, particularly through its caricatures of the Royal Family, that the National Portrait Gallery banned an exhibition of the work of Fluck and Law, the puppet's creators.

Television and radio satire, however, like many other serious and popular art-forms, became inward-looking in the late seventies and eighties, increasingly satirising the personalities and products of radio and television themselves, which presented all too easy a target. Almost alone in going against this trend was the finely tuned series of political satire, *Yes Minister*, which brilliantly and hilariously exposed the power struggle between ministers of the crown and their civil servants. The minister's vulnerability in this struggle turned most of all on his concern for his public image. However, in no popular art-form was the inward-turning tendency of the eighties more apparent than in the musical. In the spring of 1986 musicals about John Lennon, Elvis Presley and Judy Garland and musical plays about Puccini and Verdi, were all simultaneously being performed on the London stage.

Satire was one spirited response to a changing British society. A more dispirited one came from a number of writers in the 1950s and early 60s. The novelists Kingsley Amis and John Braine, the playwright John Osborne and the poet Philip Larkin among others, reflected in their work a sense of the dislocation of the individual (usually working-class or lower-middle-class) in a changing society. Arnold Wesker's dramatic *Trilogy* reflected this too, but concluded on a positive note in *Roots* with the working-class heroine Beattie, a novel character for the British stage, about to embrace her cultural heritage despite the blandishments of the pop industry and the apathy of her family. Wesker's real-life disillusion followed, nevertheless, when his attempts to involve the trade union movement in setting up an arts organisation 'Centre 42' to encourage the Beatties of the world were frustrated, primarily by trade union apathy.

The alienated individual was to become a major theme of writing in the period. In popular entertainment the character projected by the radio and television actor Tony Hancock between 1954 and 1961 was the archetypal example of this theme: an outsider conscious that other people in other places were enjoying a rich life denied to him, he had the kind of pretentiousness and snobbishness and ambition which arose from trying to assume a role for which he was neither educationally nor socially qualified. Sadly, Hancock's personal life also typified an aspect of sixties alienation: the pressured isolation of the 'personality', the 'star', whose inability to live up all the time to the expectations created by the media in his audience and himself led in Hancock's case to an early death by suicide.

The plays of Osborne and Wesker and others performed at the Royal Court Theatre from 1956 marked the beginning of a renaissance in writing for British theatre and the theme of the alienated individual was to dominate the period in the work of many very different playwrights: Harold Pinter,

David Mercer, David Storey, John Arden, John Mortimer, Joe Orton, Edward Bond, Howard Brenton, Trevor Griffiths, and David Hare.

But not all artists greeted the changes in society and particularly the coming of the consumer society with dismay. A group of visual artists in 1954 who called themselves the Independence Group embraced the mass-produced urban culture of movies, advertising and science fiction with enthusiasm, and out of their enthusiasm for the new icons of the age grew pop art, which rejected any distinction between good and bad taste. 'We felt none of the dislike of commercial culture standard among most intellectuals,' said one of the group, the critic Lawrence Alloway. The question of whether there could be objective standards in art was to figure largely in the debate between artists and the Arts Council in the ensuing years.

Many of the working class also welcomed the consumer society, with its greater rewards to compensate for work which for the majority continued to be long, hard and dull; and none welcomed it more than working-class youth, who found themselves for the first time with spare cash to spend.

The youth culture phenomenon

Before the economic growth of the mid-fifties there was no such thing as a youth culture. The working-class young who were the great majority were pitched into work at the age of fifteen and expected to learn to become adults whilst handing most of their money over to their mother each week. Most of the middle-class young were kept in school uniform till eighteen (the boys in short trousers till twelve or thirteen!), and were protected from temptation by the succession of academic and professional hurdles placed in front of them and by severely restricted pocket money and a lack of leisure opportunities.

However, it would be wrong to attribute the coming of a separate youth culture simply to greater affluence. Hoggart describes a group of young men in a northern milk bar,

aged between fifteen and twenty, with drape-suits, picture ties and an American slouch. Most of them cannot afford a succession of milk-shakes, and make cups of tea serve for an hour or two, whilst – and this is their main reason for coming – they put copper after copper into the mechanical record player.

Here are features of the youth culture to come – the importance of style and music – but without affluence. The need for unskilled working-class youth to establish an identity of their own in a society in which they felt little valued no doubt contributed to the phenomenon of working-class youth culture.

It was ironic that British youth should have to look to America in order to establish a sense of their own identity. With the coming of rock'n'roll, through the records and films of first Bill Haley, and then Elvis Presley, the energising element of dance was added to music, creating such excitement that there were minor riots in cinemas and dance halls. Ballroom dancing, although popular as a means for boys and girls to meet, had had its drawbacks – the steps had to be learnt, they were restricting and formal, and might make a young working-class male look 'soft'. Rock'n'roll, by contrast, was physical, creative and uninhibited. It may not be going too far to suggest that the dance 'explosion' of the late seventies and eighties, when many new dance companies were created to respond to the great increase in audience interest, had its origins in the fifties, for rock'n'roll was followed, in the dance halls and discos (and with eighties' break-dancing, on the streets) by many different styles of creative free dancing, and ballroom dancing became one more style of 'old-time dance', even for the middle-aged and middle-class.

If American influence was important in helping to create a 'teenage' culture, as it was called in the fifties, it was the subtleties of the British class system with its rough and respectable working class impinging on the lower middle class which determined how it developed. A succession of youth cults emerged from the sixties onwards, which were largely short-lived neighbourhood allegiances, and lost their hold when the responsibilities of marriage came along. Each cult had its own obsessive style, its own music, and its own loyalties. The 'Teddy Boys' (so-called because they adopted an American version of Edwardian dress) gave way in the early sixties to 'Mods' (mainly lower white collar workers with a neat image) and their enemies, the Rockers (tough and aggressively working-class, with leather jackets and motor bikes), with whom they fought pitched battles at holiday resorts on Bank Holidays. These were succeeded by the Skinheads with their close-cropped heads and 'bovver' boots, who cultivated violence on the football terraces, were hostile to homosexuals and hippies, and inclined towards National Front politics, espousing racism. By the seventies the situation was further complicated by the raised consciousness of black youth, and a development of black subcultural groups such as the Rastafarians and Rudies, also with their own music. In the late seventies came the Punks, with their deliberately shocking but also highly creative image of mask-like face, brilliantly dyed hair in cockatoo plumes, and safety-pin jewellery (an image to be seized on by the often parasitic fashion industry). When the Skinheads re-emerged in the eighties a new enmity sprang up between Punks and Skinheads, the former reacting against the racist neo-Nazism of the latter. At a time of rising unemployment, the often violent hostility of white youths towards the blacks became more marked, and was reciprocated. But the situation had its ironies, for the music which was at the core of all the youth sub-cultures owed more to black music than to any other influence, and skinhead music was primarily reggae.

Undoubtedly, belonging to an in-group and indulging in tribal violence brought excitement into lives which seemed to have little point or goal. In the sixties Edward Bond in his play *Saved* and Anthony Burgess in his novel *A Clockwork Orange* (later filmed) caused shocked reactions by their exploration of mindless violence by the young. The subject attracted banner headlines in the press, but not enough official attention was paid to the underlying causes until serious inner city riots in the eighties forced the issue.

Colin McInnes, in his novel *Absolute Beginners* (1959, and filmed in 1986) has a character exulting that 'no one cares what your class is, or if you're boy, or girl, or bent, or versatile . . . so long as you dig the scene and can behave yourself. The result of all this is that . . . you meet all kinds of cats, on absolutely equal terms'. Although working-class and middle-class youth shared the common ground of some of the pop and rock music, this sense of classlessness proved to be an illusion, despite the rejection by middle-class youth in the sixties of the standard English of the BBC and the deliberate cultivation of rough regional accents. Whilst working-class youth countered feelings of alienation through tribal allegiances, middle-class youth culture at its best was associated with a desire to change society reflected in many of the rock lyrics of the time, although this often degenerated into an automatic all-inclusive rebellious stance. Largely campus-based, it flourished among the rapidly expanding student population which post-war education policies and the 'baby boom' of the immediate post-war years had produced. It was vociferous, and the demands it voiced amounted to a request for the removal of all constraints, whether on sexual behaviour, social behaviour, or in the choice of what to study and how to study it. Stunned parents, teachers and other authority-figures had little time in which to reconcile themselves to their young whose rejection of 'bourgeois values' was signalled by the wearing of ragged jeans, ancient, tramp-like overcoats and long, unkempt hair, who expected to sleep with whom they chose, to get up at mid-day and keep whatever hours suited them, to play deafening music non-stop, to hitch all over the country to outdoor festivals of music which local residents deplored and, most worrying, to experiment with drugs.

The presence in university departments, particularly departments of sociology (the 'in' subject of the sixties) of staff who were members of the New Left, helped in the politicisation of student youth culture. The sixties was a period of world-wide student concern over human rights issues. American campus unrest in the mid-sixties associated with the Civil Rights Movement and the protest against the Vietnam war, reflected in the protest songs of Bob Dylan and Joan Baez, had a powerful influence in Britain, where sit-ins and demonstrations focused on the question of Rhodesian independence, the South African apartheid laws, and the war in Vietnam. The often unsympathetic handling of these demonstrations by the university authorities, and the revelation that students' political activities were being recorded, in some universities, on secret files, led to further protests and a period of serious disturbance at many universities in 1968. But in Britain the demands of the students in 1968 had more to do with domestic matters such as the quality of teaching and the lack of student involvement in university decisions than in most other countries, where wider political concerns predominated.

In the late sixties the somewhat enervating influence of Californian hippy culture began to enter the British campuses, and was adopted by a minority of students. Meanwhile the majority, perceiving the early signs of economic difficulties to come, adopted a low profile and got on with their studies, and the era of student protest had passed. So, too, in the main, had the extreme generation gap of the sixties, for when sixties' youth became parents in the seventies and eighties, there was little that their children could do to shock them; and these children, wise before their time through an education of sorts in the problems of adult life which television had given them, were more like companions than children used to be.

The rejection by the middle-class youth culture of bourgeois affluence had not extended to a rejection of long-playing records and record-players. Youth culture had indeed been grounded in such paradoxes, most of all in respect of its music. A contemporary critique described the 'contradictory mixture of the authentic and manufactured – an area of self-expression for the young and lush grazing ground for the commercial providers'. Hundreds of backstreet music groups had emerged from the late fifties onwards, using their own rather than commercially produced songs. The groups contained an exceptionally large number of art school students, for in the sixties this was the one area of higher education into which admission could be gained without academic qualifications, and thus provided a haven for some of the more rebellious school drop-outs. The two most outstanding groups, the Beatles and the Rolling Stones, both included former art school students. The music, then, had originated with the groups. But behind the groups came the vast record industry, cashing in on their creativity and encouraging obsolescence, through such promotions as 'the Top Twenty', to keep people buying, whilst reaching down yearly to a younger and younger audience. In time, music critics in the press started to give rock music serious consideration, and although there was no final agreement about its musical worth, it seems unlikely that any young composer of the eighties who was an adolescent in the sixties or early seventies could fail to have been influenced by it.

Alchohol, drugs and music were the stimuli which had kept the youth cultures fizzing. For the working class the drugs were mainly purple hearts (amphetamines) bought on the black market. Middle-class youth experimented with the mind-expanding drugs of cannabis and later, the hippy drug, LSD. It was all a far cry from the milk bars of the thirties and forties and the coffee bars of the mid-fifties. In the late seventies and eighties a new, more worrying drug situation arose, when heroin became more cheaply available and was used increasingly as an escape route by unemployed youth and even school children, especially on estates in depressed areas of the country. Alchohol addiction too, became an increasing problem. In the sixties, though, the use of drugs was one means by which experience could be pushed to its extreme limits. The desire to do this was one impulse behind the extraordinary cultural upheaval of the sixties – extraordinary not least because it was happening to the notoriously reticent, inhibited and prudish British.

The permissive society

Ideologically, the permissive society of the sixties stemmed from the coming together of two separate traditions, humanism and a late romanticism. The post-war consensus on the need for a caring society had its roots in the Christian humanist tradition. But Christianity was in decline in Britain throughout the period, particularly in the Church of England and the other Protestant churches but also among Roman Catholics. Logical positivism, the predominant school of philosophy in post-war Britain, dismissed metaphysics and religion and declared moral and aesthetic propositions to be literally meaningless. This was deplored by some philosophers, Mary Warnock, in 1966, declaring that the study of ethics had been trivialised by the fashionable linguistic analysis. But its principal exponent, Professor 'Freddie' Ayer, having an easy and attractive manner, was seen on television frequently, and this may have helped the diffusion by 'drip effect' of the logical positivist stance, with its refusal to accept the existence of moral absolutes. As Christianity declined and became less confident in its moral certainties it was left to humanists to take the lead in promoting important and widely-welcomed reforms of the moral code. Capital punishment was abolished in 1965. The laws relating to abortion, family planning, homosexuality and divorce were all reformed in the late sixties. Some religious leaders sought to update their message, notably Bishop Robinson, whose *Honest to God* (1963) caused a sensation by espousing the 'new morality'. Robinson wrote that 'nothing can of itself always be labelled as wrong', giving extramarital sex as an example. The ground had been prepared for the acceptance of such opinions by the very influential *Lady Chatterley* trial of 1959, when Penguin Books were unsuccessfully put on trial for obscenity for the publication of D.H. Lawrence's *Lady Chatterley's Lover*. (The prosecution asked the jury rhetorically whether they would wish their 'wives and servants' to read such a book.) The trial's conclusion made possible the publication of many books dealing with explicitly sexual material, and was the precursor of the abolition of theatre censorship (1968), the relaxation of cinema censorship, and a much greater tolerance of sexual material on television. Lawrence, the 'priest of love', was to enjoy great popularity in the sixties, his work soon being used as an A-level text for sixth-formers, whilst Ken Russell's erotic film version of *Women in Love* had a wide appeal.

It is probable that most people welcomed what was seen as a freer and less hypocritical attitude to sex. In particular, the legalising of homosexual acts between consenting males righted a long-standing injustice which affected a much larger proportion of the population than had been realised. However, liberalisation had its opponents. In 1968, the Catholic community was shaken and divided by a papal encyclical, *Humanae Vitae*, which, against the hopes and expectations of many liberal Catholics, reaffirmed the old condemnation of contraception, including the new contraceptive pill. Most Catholics, in the mood of the times, chose to ignore the encyclical. David Lodge, himself a Catholic, accurately and amusingly chronicled the impact of Catholic moral teaching on the lives of the faithful in his novels *The British Museum's Falling Down* (1965) and *How Far Can You Go?* (1980).

If the 'permissive society' began in the sixties, the 'moral majority' also began to counter it and continued to do so through the succeeding decades. The leading figure in this movement was an unknown school mistress and follower of the moral rearmament movement, Mrs Mary Whitehouse. Co-founder of a movement to 'clean up television', she concentrated her fire largely on the BBC, which she denounced as 'sex mad', left-wing and the centre of 'a conspiracy to remove the myth of God from the mind of men'. Not surprisingly, the Roman Catholic Director General of the BBC declined to take Mrs Whitehouse seriously; but the press did and featured her regular denunciation of programmes so that after a decade or so she became a 'celebrity' – and duly appeared regularly on BBC TV as well as ITV. She inspired more than one Conservative MP to try to get more control of programme content, but despite the sympathetic interest in the eighties of Prime Minister Mrs Thatcher herself, made little headway. Her attempt in the late seventies to prosecute for obscenity a National Theatre play *The Romans in Britain* (which she had not seen) also failed, to the great relief of the theatre profession.

Real pornography flourished in cheap book and magazine form, and films with titles like *Erotic Exploits of a Sexy Seducer* (sic) reached new depths of sexual explicitness. Oddly, Mrs Whitehouse seemed neither to read nor to go to the cinema; she did not even notice the topless 'page 3 girls' which titillated millions of newspaper readers everyday. Compared with them, television was still sober and respectable in the eighties, though its humour had become much more scatalogical than it had been in the early post-war years. Most of it, however, was what in the old-time music hall used to be called 'honest vulgarity'.

If the influence of humanism was one strand of the permissive society, the other was a late romantic desire to banish controls, break down barriers and give everyone unfettered freedom to 'do his own thing' and push experience to its limits. The most obvious symbol of this desire for freedom was the miniskirt, which retreated further and further up the thighs as the decade progressed. The sixties girl depicted in the films of the period swings confidently through the streets, alone and self-contained, long hair streaming behind her, in every way a symbol of an emancipation which existed only in the minds of film-makers and fashion photographers. The actual sixties' girl was more likely to be found in a screaming hysterical mob at a pop concert, or worshipping her pop star pin-up with her friends. Hysteria was one way of pushing experience to its limits, and some pop groups incorporated it into their acts by a climactic smashing of guitars and equipment. Drugs might perform a similar function of release; so too might the mysticism of eastern religions, particularly Zen Buddhism, which gained large followings from the late sixties, being given the rebel's seal of approval when taken up by the Beatles. Meditation became so popular that Christian churches set up groups to practise it, whilst among the Christian churches it was the charismatic churches with their highly emotional appeal which went against the general trend by increasing their membership.

Hysteria, drugs, mysticism, meditation: these offered very different qualities of release. So, too, with the literary gurus of the period. J.R.R. Tolkien's fantasy *The Lord of the Rings* had a large cult following. *The Proverbs of Hell* of William Blake taken out of the context of his whole work provided popular rebellious slogans: 'Damn braces: Bless relaxes', 'The tygers of wrath are wiser than the horses of instruction' and 'Sooner murder an infant in its cradle than nurse unacted desires'. The decadent writings of de Sade provided cruel and violent images which some artists found appropriate to a violent age. The dangers inherent in the use of such images became horrifyingly real when two people under the influence of de

Sade committed the 'Moors Murders' of small children (1965). No wonder the fashionable R.D. Laing told his fellow psychotherapists: 'We, the sane ones, are out of our minds.'

Nowhere was the desire to transcend barriers and push experience to its limits more obvious than among the newer practitioners of the arts. In music, visual art and literature, form became more and more volatile, sometimes, as in minimal art, disappearing almost entirely, and taking content with it – although it could be argued that minimal content was an expression of the spiritual condition of the age. The disappearance of form was hastened by the premium placed on spontaneity of expression, which led to unrehearsed 'happenings'. These achieved particular notoriety in the theatre, with its public taboo-breaking possibilities, especially after the ending of theatre censorship. Artists explored the possibilities of sounds, materials, language and locations which had not hitherto been considered appropriate to art. The boundaries between art forms were broken down by multi-media creations such as performance art. This could take extreme forms. In 1965 two artists even discussed the possibility of publicly disembowelling a human corpse and hurling the guts at the audience! The distinction between popular art and high art became increasingly blurred – indeed, it became unfashionable to acknowledge any distinction – and the sixties saw a resurgence of Dadaesque anti-art creativity. On the plus side, these challenges to tradition promoted a zest and adventurousness in the arts which were highly stimulating. Exploding images, colours and sounds at first startled the public, but soon became absorbed into mainstream culture. But the emphasis on novelty placed a high premium on the transient at the expense of profundity. There was a trendiness, a constant expectation of the new, and a cultivation of the shocking, which created in the public a bemused tolerance, and in the critics, confusion and loss of nerve.

This confusion was inevitably reflected in the deliberations of the body responsible for the public funding of the arts, the Arts Council. Through its Contemporary Music Network, through its support for the London-based Institute of Contemporary Arts (whose activities alternated between the stimulatingly avant-garde and the mindlessly trendy, or outrageous), through its exhibitions of work by young contemporary artists at the Serpentine Gallery, and through its support of experimental theatre groups, it could hardly avoid provoking public controversy.

The Arts Council

Before the war, there had been no public subsidy of the performing arts and in 1936 Lord Keynes judged that the position of artists of all sorts was 'disastrous'. During the war, as we have seen, the arts were not just maintained, but significantly developed; so it was not surprising that at the end of it there was general agreement among politicians of all parties that public subsidy should be continued. In 1946, the Arts Council of Great Britain was established to build on the work of CEMA, with the same guiding principle, 'the Best for the Most'.

Lord Keynes, who had not only been the architect of wartime economic policies but also the chairman of CEMA, was set to be chairman of the new Arts Council, but died months before it began to operate. He fully shared the expectations of a better world after the war and made a stirring broadcast about the future of the arts. The first annual report of the Arts Council reprinted his confident forecast that:

The day is not far off when the Economic Problem will take the back seat where it belongs, and the arena of the heart and head will be occupied – or re-occupied – by our real problems – the problems of life and of human relations, of creation and behaviour and religion.

Forty years later, the economic problem was more firmly than ever in the front seat; but Keynes' statement remained an indication of what *ought* to happen.

The infant Arts Council quickly began to make its contribution to fostering the growth of the arts in Britain. Very soon, almost every theatre outside London depended heavily on its subsidies, and many new ones were built in the fifties and sixties. In London, the subsidised National Theatre flourished, and in 1976 moved into its own home on the South Bank (ending over a century of delay), and in the eighties the Royal Shakespeare Company increased its auditoria in Stratford to three and in London moved into a new theatre in the Barbican.

The commercial theatre increasingly benefited from the artistic vision and risk-taking of the subsidised theatre by transferring proven successes. In the early eighties almost half the West End theatres were occupied by such transfers. The Royal Opera in Covent Garden, the most expensive artistic organisation in the country, derived almost half its income from the Arts Council's grant, and the Welsh National Opera and Scottish Opera and the small but enterprising Kent Opera were also heavily subsidised. In the late seventies the Council took the initiative in establishing and funding an opera company based in Leeds (Opera North) which soon established an excellent reputation. Only Glyndebourne remained independent of Arts Council money at its superb home base in Sussex, but its regional touring was funded by the Council. An early venture called *Opera for all*, in which a group of singers and a pianist took a poor man's version of opera to small venues was replaced in 1980 by *Opera 80* with more singers and a small orchestra. Its touring contributed to the increasing popularity of opera in the seventies and eighties and to the social broadening of its audience.

Ballet (the Royal Ballet, Sadler's Wells Royal Ballet and London Festival Ballet) flourished with the Council's help and by the seventies modern dance found increasing favour, particularly with the young. London Contemporary Dance toured widely and so did Ballet Rambert which transformed itself from a traditional ballet company into a modern dance company. The four London orchestras were also subsidised, but to a lesser extent than regional orchestras like Manchester's Hallé, the Liverpool Philharmonic and the Birmingham Symphony Orchestra. The Council ran two art galleries in London, the Hayward and the Serpentine, and funded exhibitions which toured to regional galleries which were sometimes run by municipalities.

Except in the field of literature, where much smaller amounts were spent on grants to authors, the National Book League and the Poetry Society, the public and politicians generally agreed, until the mid-eighties at least, that the Arts Council was doing a good job. Norman St John-Stevas, on becoming arts minister in 1979, hailed it as 'one of the happiest constitutional inventions of the century'. The main feature of this constitutional invention was that it enabled the arts to receive government money without suffering government control. The money was given by government to an independent body which was interposed between politicians and artists, and so grant-making decisions were made at 'arm's length' from government. Nor were they made by bureaucrats, but mainly by volunteers experienced in the different art forms.

However, by the mid-eighties, after six years under a Tory government which had said it would 'roll back the frontiers of the state', the Arts Council under the chairmanship of Sir William Rees-Mogg was felt by many to have become 'a creature of government' and the much vaunted 'arm's length principle' was proclaimed a fraud. From our inside knowledge of the Council for over a decade until 1983, we can say that, in truth, the independence of the Council was slightly diminished but by no means abolished. The worst thing that happened was the dropping of Richard Hoggart as Vice-Chairman. He was a very effective one, but did not satisfy the question which Mrs Thatcher was said to ask about people in public life: 'Is he one of us?'. Moreover, the arts world felt that Sir William Rees-Mogg, a more executive chairman than the Council had ever had, was insufficiently committed to pressing the needs of the arts world on a government which had rejected Keynesian economic policies in favour of monetarism, which involved keeping down the level of government spending.

Not that the government's funding of the arts had ever been really adequate. Even CEMA's wartime achievements were hampered by inadequate funding, and in 1949, three years after the Arts Council began, the actors' association Equity told a select committee of the House of Commons that they had only one criticism of the way the Council had been established: 'The Government grant is too small.' In the fifties the prevailing austerity was reflected in the titles of the Council's annual reports: *Art in the Red* and *The Struggle for Survival*. Near the end of the decade a former Permanent Secretary to the Treasury acknowledged that many felt the arts had been 'stingily treated'. In the sixties, especially after the appointment in 1965 of Jennie Lee as Britain's first arts minister, the arts fared better, but by the early seventies the world oil crisis had hit the economy and arts spending was adversely affected. Nevertheless, the Labour government which was turned out in 1979 had voted a sum for the Arts Council which the incoming Tory government reduced by over £1 million.

The new government announced an important change in arts funding. The balance was to shift from public funding to business sponsorship, which was not the same as charitable giving, but a hard-nosed business deal for which the sponsor got a good return in publicity and advertising. It was, in fact, a fairly cheap way of advertising to a predominantly well-off sector of the population. The larger, popular audience was reached by sports sponsorship, especially football, cricket, motor racing and snooker, which in the eighties became a most popular sport on television. Sponsorship was generally aimed at sports and arts which would get the sponsors' name (or better still, their products' names) onto the television screen. Not only was this attractively cheap compared with the cost of television commercials, but for cigarette manufacturers it also offered a way round the government ban on television advertising of their product, which had been imposed in response to the overwhelming medical evidence of the dangers of cigarette smoking. So advertising was increasingly linked to sports and arts events. It was more blatant in sports and in 1985 an arts minister took satisfaction from the fact that we had not yet had to watch opera sung in Texaco T-shirts; but sponsors' advertising was becoming more conspicuous and at a sponsors' conference a member asked irritatedly (and ominously): 'What's so sacrosanct about the arts?'

In the fifties, the Arts Council pronounced a significant modification of the policy of 'the Best for the Most' that it had inherited from CEMA. Too widespread diffusion could, it had decided, lead to the growth of mediocrity, so henceforth the maximum was to be 'Few but roses.' This inevitably led to charges of elitism, charges which were still very fashionable thirty years later. Elitism, properly understood as the belief that the best should be for the few (a belief expounded by T.S. Eliot in *Notes towards a Definition of Culture* in 1948), should have been anathema to an Arts Council required by its Royal Charter to make the arts more widely accessible, but it nevertheless infected Arts Council attitudes and, to a lesser extent, continued to do so into the eighties. But the term elitism was often misused to attack the defence of the 'high' arts and even the attempt to discriminate between good, bad and indifferent arts products or activities, and any organisation distributing public money to the arts had to discriminate. Discrimination means, of course, that some are given grants and some are not, and the Council has always received many more applications for grants than it could possibly meet.

Particularly after the politico-cultural revolts of the late sixties, some unsuccessful arts organisations and individuals claimed that the high arts catered for two or three per cent of the population and they catered for the rest and therefore should have proportionate funding. In fact, they catered only for a different two or three per cent, but this did not prevent, for example, spokesmen for 'community theatre' groups claiming that traditional aesthetic standards did not apply to their work, where the test should be that of audience response. Those who made this claim were usually on the political left and did not realise that they were using the same arguments as the television and press tycoons. 'Never mind the quality, feel the width', a cynical maxim of some northern cloth manufacturers, had become the tacit principle of many producers of cultural 'products' in the post-war period. Another tacit principle was that all value judgements in the arts (and in morals) were purely subjective, with the corollary that, as the logical positivist philosophers had taught, such judgements were literally meaningless, being expressions of emotions rather than objective fact. Hence one sympathetic chronicler of the growing populist arts scene in the seventies observed a 'phobiac caution' about ever suggesting that one work of art was better than another.

Throughout Europe in the seventies many in the arts world began to believe that traditional arts policies, which had been devoted to 'making excellence accessible', which the Council of Europe characterised as 'the democratisation of culture', should be replaced by 'cultural democracy', which worked from the grass roots upwards, often by developing people's capacity to make their own art rather than learning to appreciate someone else's art. 'Making excellence accessible' was now seen by many on the left as 'bourgeois cultural imperialism'. The traditional culture was bourgeois culture, and therefore irrelevant to the mass of working people – who form just over half the population. The pretence that this bourgeois culture was even potentially accessible to all was, according to a widely read and approved book (Su Braden, *Artists and People*, 1978), 'the great artistic deception of the twentieth century'. The Arts Council, it proclaimed, was based on this deception; but of course, Ms Braden might have said, so was the whole of education in the arts and the remarkable influence of the BBC, before and since the war, in popularising classical music. Ms Braden was a community artist, a kind of grass roots *animateur* who activated ordinary people, often working people in areas of urban decay or rural deprivation, to make their own art. This thoroughly worthwhile activity was often a form of basic adult education in the arts. The mistake of some community artists was to assume that the cultural heritage was not for ordinary people – which was exactly what their opponents, the elitists, had more consistently argued.

After nearly half a century of wartime and post-war attempts to ensure 'the best for the most', in the eighties Britain was still a long way from achieving that goal. The gibe about 'bourgeois art' derives superficial plausibility from the fact that many post-war studies have shown that the audience for the arts continued to be still largely middle-class, though many bourgeois (to use the pejorative term) were quite philistine and shared the tastes of the proletariat. Audience research also showed repeatedly that the prime predictor of likely appreciation of the arts was not social class or income (though both these played their part), but educational level. So the main way to spread the arts was to develop the audience by education appreciation in arts.

This was, of course, mainly the responsibility of the whole educational system, from primary to adult education, but the Arts Council's two chartered duties were 'to develop and improve the knowledge, understanding and practice of the arts' and *thereby* 'to increase the accessibility of the arts'. In 1976, Lord Redcliffe-Maud in a Gulbenkian report on 'Support for the arts' affirmed that arts providers and education providers were 'natural allies' and their efforts should be more closely co-ordinated. The recently arrived Secretary General of the Arts Council had a background in adult education, and despite opposition from elitists within the Council and populists outside it, he succeeded in establishing an education unit in the Council and a policy of linking arts provision with educational back-up services. The policy 'took off' and within a few years most arts organisations had developed educational programmes linked to their work and large ones had their own education officers. Thus the concept of education, which many arts people had previously looked on with suspicion (forgetting their own educational backgrounds), was now generally accepted.

Another improvement in the seventies and eighties was the greater attention to the arts needs of the regions. Keynes had warned immediately after the war that 'Nothing can be more damaging than the excessive prestige of metropolitan standards and fashions.' The crucial word was 'excessive', for it is inevitable in a small island where all communication links lead to the metropolis, that the metropolis should be *the* centre of excellence; but it was undesirable that it should have a monopoly of excellence. Scotland and Wales had always had independent arts councils, though these were funded by the Arts Council of Great Britain which at first also had English regional offices, but (unwisely?) closed them in the fifties. The arts in Northern Ireland are separately funded. Soon afterwards Regional Arts Associations began to develop in a dozen areas. These derived three-quarters of their income from the Arts Council but in policy-making were independent of it, often fiercely so. Much of the remaining quarter of their income came from local government which was heavily represented on their governing bodies. Local authorities had failed miserably to take advantage of the opportunity given to them by Aneurin Bevan in 1948 to spend up to a sixpenny rate on the arts, most of them spending less than a fraction of one (old) penny. But through participation in regional associations, many of them learned the gentle art of patronage, only to have their growing generosity curbed in the eighties by central government rate-capping. The government's own funding of the Arts Council was in 1982 found by an all-party parliamentary select committee to be not just gravely inadequate, but *irresponsibly* inadequate. On the arts, as on health care, Britain was spending less per head of population than most of its European neighbours. Even evidence that the arts were a multimillion pound industry which more than earned its keep in taxes and as a magnet for tourists, failed to persuade the Tory government that money spent on them was a sound investment even in economic terms; though the most important return on the 'investment' was something economists could not measure.

Class, the New Left, and education

The difficulties experienced by the Arts Council, and even by those arts providers, such as the 7:84 touring theatre company or Peter Cheeseman's Victoria Theatre in Stoke-on-Trent, dedicated to drawing members of the working class into the audience for the arts, highlighted the failure in the post-war years to break down the barriers of class. By 1960 it was clear that the 1944 Education Act, which provided for secondary education for all to the age of fifteen, had perpetuated the provision of education along class lines. The public school system, providing privileged access to Oxbridge and the power-bases of society, had been left untouched, and the divisions of the state system into secondary schools, for those who failed the 11+ selection examination, and grammar schools for those who passed it, excluded most working-class children from the best schools, since success in the examination was determined not only by basic intelligence but by the cultural background of the home. The move towards the abolition of selection and the provision of comprehensive schools, which made slow progress in the post-war years, but accelerated under Labour governments and local authorities in the sixties and seventies, came up against a similar problem: schools in middle-class areas, with the children of parents who had themselves enjoyed higher education, and of whom a high proportion were in the professions, had better facilities and teaching than inner-city schools in poor areas. People who could afford it bought houses in the catchment areas of the good schools and the cycle of educational inequality became self-perpetuating. Although the school-leaving age was raised to sixteen in 1972, in the eighties nearly half the country's children left school without even one O-level and were barely literate or numerate. Moreover, under the Tory government of the eighties the state educational system was gravely underfunded and teachers underpaid, demoralised and involved in serious industrial action, while the public schools and private fee-paying schools in consequence had rising rolls, further aggravating the inequalities. Part of the so-called 'embourgeoisement' of the more affluent working class in the eighties was the readiness of some to use private education and private health care.

Those members of the working class who, against the odds, went into higher education and the arts often suffered traumas of displacement and guilt at their separation from their kin. Arthur Marwick, in his *British Society since 1945* (1982), speaking of the painter Robert Colquhoun, who became an alcoholic, offers the intuition that 'Somehow, even in the world of the arts, workers' sons (and Celts) seemed to be more vulnerable than sons of the middle or upper classes.' This vulnerability was certainly noticeable in those working-class youths who in the sixties became folk heroes on the football field. Media superstar treatment, coupled with unprecedented financial rewards after the abolition in 1960 of a ceiling to wages, created huge pressures. The highly gifted George Best was the most notable victim of this situation, succumbing to nervous strain, alcohol and high living. The next generation in the seventies learnt from his downfall and were able to handle the situation better. The glamorous life of the superstar had its echoes in working-class life. Some working men's clubs in Yorkshire (notably one at Batley) became so prosperous that they were able to engage top British and American entertainers, and working-class night clubs sprang up throughout the country where factory workers, in 1975, might pay £20 a head (as much as for a night at the opera) to watch such cabaret stars as the singer, Petula Clark, the television comedian Eric Morecambe, or the American boxer, Muhammed Ali. And although music-hall was in decline, top comedians like Ken Dodd and later Billy Connolly could fill theatres with predominantly working-class people. The contrast between Dodd's impish innuendo style of humour, and Connolly's joyous but outrageous taboo-breaking, is one measure of the more open attitudes among working-class people brought about by the 'permissive society'.

Certainly most of the working class by the sixties were enjoying a higher standard of living. Ownership of cars and washing machines became more widespread, and for the first time ever (apart from in the forces) working-class people were experiencing 'abroad' though admittedly anglicised by the agency of the package holiday. But they still had little part in decision-making in any of the important spheres of their lives: schools, workplace or housing. This lack of consultation precipitated, in the sixties, a spate of unofficial strikes. Worse, it contributed to the building of a vast amount of unsuitable housing, following the lifting, in the late fifties, of the ban on commercial building. The replacement of whole areas of old housing by high-rise flats, the takeover of the high street by multiple stores, the eclipse of the corner shop by the supermarket, and the gutting of city centres to make urban motorways all led, at first, to the loss of a sense of locality. The growing dependence on tranquillisers and alcohol by working-class women was a symptom of the malaise. The pleasure of the flats' new occupants at such amenities as bathrooms soon gave way to dismay and fear as the public areas of the buildings became vandalised and haunted by gangs of youths. A growing conviction that architecture could actually generate anti-social behaviour was given confirmation by the 1985 riot at Broadwater Farm in Tottenham, when the raised walkways on high-density but low-rise housing became a no-go area for the police from which angry youths could launch petrol bomb attacks: architectural layout, social indignation, racial feeling and criminality came together to produce, for a time, a desperate situation in which one man died. Meanwhile, the high popularity of the ITV series *Coronation Street* from the sixties to the eighties, reflected a nostalgia for a cosy working-class life which had largely vanished. The BBC's response to 'the Street', called *EastEnders*, more closely reflected life in the eighties and soon attracted a huge following.

On the left the Russian military suppression, in 1956, of an uprising in Hungary, had caused great disillusion, out of which, together with a perception that official Labour party policy was losing its radical edge, arose a new grouping, the New Left, with its journal *The Universities and New Left Review*, edited by Stuart Hall. In the early years the New Left espoused a humanistic Marxism, and was greatly concerned with problems of working-class alienation. Among those who had left the communist party after 1956 was the adult education tutor and historian E.P. Thompson, and he and Raymond Williams (to whom Thompson himself acknowledged a debt) were significant influences in the New Left. Thompson insisted that class was 'defined by men as they live their own history'. In the introduction to his seminal *The Making of the English Working Class* (1963) he expressed an angry desire to rescue workers of the past from 'the enormous condescension of posterity' – a posterity which denied their free relationships and their influence on history, by postulating deterministic theories. The book rediscovered the radical tradition in British working-class life by a detailed investigation covering three centuries, and led to many academic studies of the actual lives of working-class people. A popular book in the tradition was Ronald Blythe's moving *Akenfield: Portrait of an English Village* (1969), a study of an East Anglian village based on the tape-recorded recollections of its inhabitants. The same concern that the common people should speak for themselves was to be found among theatre groups producing documentary drama. Joan Littlewood's Theatre Workshop produced in 1963 a documentary musical *Oh What a Lovely War!* based on soldiers' songs of the First World War. Under the influence of Littlewood and of Charles Parker's 'Radio Ballads' celebrating common life, the actors at the Victoria Theatre, Stoke-on-Trent, interviewed and tape-recorded local people for a number of documentaries in the sixties, and produced, at the time of the threatened closure of Shelton steel works in the seventies, a blow-by-blow documentary on the reactions of the workers and their families. In the seventies and eighties community artists ran writers' workshops to encourage working people to set down their experiences and thoughts.

Important new ground was broken in 1964 with the establishment by (the now Professor) Richard Hoggart at Birmingham University of a Centre for Contemporary Cultural Studies, and in the same year Stuart Hall, with Paddy Whannel of the Education Department of the British Film Institute, published *The Popular Arts*, a much needed critique designed for use by teachers in schools and colleges. Hall was later to succeed Hoggart as Director of the Centre for Cultural Studies, and moved its focus to the left, concentrating on the investigation of structures in society rather than moral issues. Within a decade, young men and women nourished on French marxism were repudiating Hoggart's liberal literary approach. Many of the New Left were to move on to staff the media studies course which burgeoned in universities and polytechnics.

The continental marxists who influenced the New Left were one of a number of external stimuli in the sixties, in contrast to the rather parochial fifties. Existentialism became fashionable: Kierkegaard's version for Christians, Sartre's for secular humanists. North American scholars such as J.K. Galbraith and Marshall McLuhan, with their critiques of the new acquisitive, technological society were stimulatingly one jump ahead of British academics, largely because America was one jump ahead in affluence and technology. The structuralist ideas of the American Noam Chomsky had a widespread influence in the social sciences, and their application to literature became a source of sharp, even bitter, academic conflict.

The sixties was the decade of university expansion partly as a result of the Robbins Report of 1963. Eight new universities had been created in the years since the war, with some, like Sussex, rivalling 'Oxbridge' in their attractiveness to the best students; some colleges of advanced technology were transformed into universities. The main beneficiaries of this expansion and of the 1944 Education Act came from the lower middle class and the term 'meritocracy' coined by Michael Young in 1958 described their significant new influence. This was particularly evident in the growing communications industry of television and advertising, in fashion and photography, in the arts, and in the field of education itself. There had been a long-standing English snobbery towards the lower middle class, which was regarded as small-minded and unadventurous, but socially and culturally pretentious. In the sixties, however, some of its members were to be found in the forefront of cultural change. 'Scratch the rebel, art student, beatnik, CND supporter, jazz musician and you'll usually find a lower middle class background' wrote George Melly, jazz musician and connoisseur of popular culture, in 1963. Interviewed in 1986, the satirists John Cleese and Michael Frayn, both salesmen's sons, accounted for the large number of good writers who came from the lower middle class: 'People are much better at observing some class they're not a natural member of but which they have aspiration towards', said Frayn, and went on to describe the creative tension in 'being attracted to something and trying to resist that attraction'. It was a tension which had produced, since the fifties, a vigorous literature of the upwardly mobile in novels, plays and TV situation comedy such as *The Likely Lads*. However, not all of the lower middle class wanted cultural change. Some feared it and were forerunners of those on the right wing, led by Mrs Thatcher, who called in the eighties for a return to 'Victorian values'.

Moreover, the expansion of educational opportunity provoked a backlash from right-wing figures in the university world, notably in the publication of a series of so-called Black Papers from 1959 onwards. These attacked the Robbins' assumptions, and recalled Leavis' fears in declaring that 'more means worse' – a phrase coined by the former university lecturer turned novelist, Kingsley Amis. His hugely successful comic novel, *Lucky Jim*, an early novel of the upwardly mobile, had already in 1954 suggested a disenchantment with academic life – a sort of inversion of Hardy's *Jude the Obscure*. A character in Alan Bennett's play *Forty Years On* (1969), a headmaster in a public school, gave lyrical expression to the fears: 'The crowd has found the door into the secret garden. Now they will tear up the flowers by the roots, strip the borders and strew them with paper and broken bottles.'

The desire, in the sixties, to break down barriers went beyond a desire to make education as widely accessible as possible to a criticism of the whole ideal of institutionalised education, expressed in the influential *Deschooling Society* of the American Ivan Illich. But a less extreme development which took place in English language teaching was perhaps ultimately more influential. Creativity in art and writing had been encouraged in primary schools even in the fifties. In secondary education in the sixties there was a move to replace the teaching of English grammar by lessons in creative writing to encourage self-expression. Well-meant as this was, it too often resulted in less able children leaving school with a command of written English inadequate for the demands of adult life.

In the mid-seventies a Labour prime minister emphasised the need for education to prepare people for working life and this theme was emphasised more under the succeeding Tory government. Critics of the new emphasis called it the 'new vocationalism' but defenders of it quipped that Britain's battle for industrial survival had been lost on the playing fields of Eton through an emphasis on a classical education. The theme was elaborated in a very influential book by an American scholar, Martin J. Weiner, published in 1981, called *English Culture and the Decline of the Industrial Spirit, 1850–1980*. He found a great deal of evidence of what an American observer saw as 'a sense of doubt concerning the social utility of industry' – even among industrialists, many of whom seemed almost ashamed of their vocation. Back in the thirties, the Labour leader Ramsay Macdonald had warned that the quality of life might be sacrificed in the pursuit of material prosperity, but by 1973, Edward Heath, as Tory prime minister, gave the counter warning that the alternative to economic expansion was not an idyllic England of quiet market towns but 'slums, dangerous roads, old factories, cramped schools, stunted lives'. Weiner concluded that English history in the eighties might turn less on traditional political struggles than on a cultural contest between these two conflicting attitudes in the outlook of the English middle class.

The last aspect of education that calls for attention illustrates the foregoing clash of views very clearly. Adult education flourished after the war, although one of the key organisations promoting it, the Workers' Educational Association, lost ground to 'university extension' and to local authority provision. Since the beginning of the century, the emphasis in adult education had been on liberal or humanistic studies, one of the key figures in its development being R.H. Tawney, the economic historian who at the beginning of the century was for some years a tutor working for the University of Oxford extra-mural delegacy, teaching three-year evening courses organised jointly with the WEA. He had warned in his famous book *Equality* (1931) that the obsession with economic problems was a passing spiritual disease and told adult students that the aim of education was not to get on in life but 'to enable the life to get on in you'. By the seventies, however, the WEA began to provide more and more 'bread and butter' courses for training trade unionists, and the university extra-mural departments turned increasingly to providing lucrative training courses for managers and administrators. Some attention was still paid to the old 'liberal' tradition, but the emphasis had shifted towards the 'new vocationalism'.

What remained of liberal adult education sometimes became more superficial and entertaining. Three-year 'university tutorial courses', which had been the glory of the university–WEA partnership, were fewer and where they remained, the demands made on students were greatly reduced. They used to include regular reading and written work, but from the beginning of the post-war period, less and less of this was done and often little more was required than attendance at lectures. Many people wanted adult education, as Tawney had already ruefully observed in the fifties, but they wanted less of it.

However, in 1971 a new institution was launched which offered degree courses by part-time study, largely by 'distance learning'. This was the Open University, conceived by the Labour prime minister, Harold Wilson. By the eighties its students formed a substantial part of the country's total student body. Heavy demands were made on students' time and intellectual effort over a period of five or more years. One might say that the great tutorial class tradition had been reborn under new auspices. Radio, television and part-time tutors were used to supplement the basic teaching instrument, the carefully prepared course 'units'. The Open University's considerable success was marred by only one failure: it had not attracted the large proportion of working-class students originally envisaged; but then, since the war, neither had the Workers' Educational Association. However, because it was genuinely open, in the sense of requiring no entrance qualifications whatsoever, it was able to offer a second chance to those from all classes and of all ages who had missed out on higher education the first time round. Not least among the beneficiaries were house-bound wives and mothers.

Pressure groups in the seventies

Women had, on the whole, benefited little from the liberalising trends of the sixties. By 1970 a movement among women on the left to change society's attitude to women, and their perception of themselves, was slowly gaining ground. Simone de Beauvoir's pioneering *The Second Sex* had been available in translation since 1960, Germaine Greer's *The Female Eunuch* followed ten years later. An article by Juliet Mitchell in the *New Left Review* in 1966 stimulated the movement; its title *Women: The Longest Revolution* echoing Raymond Williams. The women's liberation campaign at first provoked hostile reactions and ridicule in the popular press, not least for turning its (necessary) attention to the male-dominated language of politics and everyday life: Ms was to replace Mrs and Miss, chair or chairperson to replace chairman. Women's classes in assertiveness-training multiplied, women's theatre groups dramatised feminist issues, women's presses (notably Virago) published new women writers of whom there were many writing from a feminist viewpoint and reissued impressive works from the past. Women academics in such diverse fields as literature, anthropology, history and art history asked new questions about women's past roles. Exhibitions of specifically women's art were mounted. Women's magazines from the glossy *Cosmopolitan* to the left-wing *Spare Rib* kept feminist issues on the boil, particularly relating to sexual issues such as rape, contraception and abortion. In educational circles the role-enforcing nature of children's literature came under scrutiny, and a new generation of writers for children took note of the problem.

Hostility in male-dominated institutions such as the trade unions inevitably produced an aggressive style symbolised by the wearing of boiler-suits (which eventually became high fashion) among early liberationists, but gradually opposition was worn down. By the 1980s W.H. Smith, who had originally refused to handle *Spare Rib*, were prominent participants in a Feminist Book Fortnight and Brenda Dean had become General Secretary of the Printworkers Union SOGAT 82. At this stage, when some feminists felt the main battles were being won, though much still remained to be achieved, the persistent and often shrill anti-male attitudes of others led to division.

Despite the passing, in the mid-seventies, of a Sex Discrimination Act and an Equal Pay Act, and the setting up of the Equal Opportunities Commission, women's pay in the eighties was still substantially below that of men, and schoolgirls who had outclassed the boys at school were still taking inferior jobs. Only three per cent of MPs were women, and the position of the working wife and mother was little improved. Nevertheless, attitudes in society had changed; a glance back to the fifties, to the role of Alison in Osborne's *Look Back in Anger* or of the women in John Braine's novel *Room at the Top* confirmed this. The women's movement had given to a new generation a growing confidence and independence of spirit.

The women's movement was one of the most significant of the large number of pressure groups which sought to change social attitudes on specific issues in the seventies. Parallel to women's liberation and in some ways interconnected was the movement for homosexual rights, the Gay Liberation Movement.

The rights of animals also became a growing issue as the factory farming of hens, calves and pigs became widespread, and anti-vivisectionists and vegetarians, once regarded as cranks, gained respectability and support. Environmental concerns came to dominate people's minds increasingly. The loss of hedgerows, ancient woodlands, ponds, footpaths, wetlands, moorlands and meadows, which had been taking place steadily since 1945, was greatly accelerated following Britain's entry into the European Economic Community in 1973, when it became profitable for farmers to industrialise agriculture still further by even greater mechanisation and application of chemicals on enlarged fields. Some species of animals: the otter, some frogs and reptiles, some birds of prey, became endangered. An even more important species, the farm worker, was becoming increasingly obsolete as mechanisation progressed, and alarm grew that with his disappearance there was a possibility of the loss of parts of rural England and its villages. Faced with these developments, responsibly portrayed in innumerable television programmes, the British people expressed their concern in a rapidly increasing membership of the various environmental bodies – The Friends of the Earth, the Ramblers' Association, The Royal Society for the Protection of Birds, the National Trust and Civic Societies. By the 1980s 'green' issues began to have political bite.

In the early seventies Fritz Schumacher wrote a study of economics, *Small is Beautiful*, which cast doubt on the role of mechanisation in society, and stressed the need to rediscover natural and small-scale processes. Regarded as eccentric at first, this work was to have considerable impact in the seventies and eighties, when the necessity for alternatives to the economics of the large scale became apparent. 'Alternative' was to become a key word of the decade. The growth of organic farming, the development of small craft industries, the campaign for real beer, the interest in alternative medicine, the return to natural fibres for clothing, the anxiety about chemical additives in food, even the move to do-it-yourself and the upsurge of interest in cooking, were all part of the search for alternatives. In style the movement was signalled by a vogue for ethnic clothes and the nostalgic flower-strewn fabrics of Laura Ashley, a sure indication that at this stage the alternative movement was a middle-class concern. It was acting in the face of heavy odds: the seventies and eighties saw the rapid growth, by take-over, of many already large businesses. But where these were concerned with consumer goods, alternative pressures by the mid-eighties were beginning to make an impact.

The relation of man to the natural world has always been a major theme of art, and profound changes were taking place in that relationship. The immediate best-selling popularity of two environmental novels, Richard Adams' *Watership Down* and Russell Hoban's *Turtle Diary* reflected both public concern and nostalgia. When a radio series of the late seventies, *The Hitch-Hiker's Guide to the Galaxy*, was published as a novel, it too unexpectedly became a best seller by combining environmental protest with space fantasy.

Such phenomena are the Geiger counters for public anxiety. When Sue

Townsend's *The Secret Diary of Adian Mole, Age 13¾* aroused a similar response in the eighties, it touched another sensitive chord, the concern over marriage break-up, which was heavily on the increase, and its effect on the children involved. If 'alternative' was a key word in the seventies, in the eighties the word was 'survival', and Adrian Mole was a survivor. Despite a rising standard of living for the 87 per cent who had work in the mid-eighties, many people felt threatened, and the desire for self-preservation was manifest in an increased concern over health care and diet, and great activity in keep-fit classes, swimming and jogging – somewhat negated by a rising consumption of alcohol to quell the anxiety. Many were the articles, books and programmes with titles beginning: 'How to survive . . .'.

This narcissistic obsession with self-preservation was analysed by the American Christopher Lasch in his book, *The Minimal Self* (1984) where he relates it to man's global fear: 'Now that Promethian man apparently stands on the brink of destruction, Narcissus looks like a more likely survivor.'

Nuclear anxieties

The global fear which cast a shadow over the likelihood of survival was of course that of nuclear holocaust, and the shadow lengthened in the late seventies when the accession of hard-line governments in the USA, Russia and the UK revived a cold war atmosphere; opinion polls showed, in 1985, that the British people were equally fearful of the intentions of the USA and the USSR. In the post-war years many people had been increasingly unhappy living in a situation where peace was guaranteed only by the threat to east and west of 'mutually assured destruction'. There was, moreover, a strong conviction that the vast and indiscriminate murder and long-term suffering caused by nuclear weapons were morally indefensible, and that the moral superiority of the victorious Americans and their allies at the end of the war had been dimmed by the atom bombing of Hiroshima and Nagasaki. In 1958, the Campaign for Nuclear Disarmament (CND) was launched and large numbers marched from London to the nuclear weapons establishment at Aldermaston, among them artists of all kinds. The playwrights Arnold Wesker and Robert Bolt, with others, were later to go to prison briefly for their part in the anti-nuclear movement.

In 1960, the Labour party annual conference voted for unilateral nuclear disarmament, against the anguished opposition of the leader of the party, Hugh Gaitskell. The vote was reversed the following year, but the debate continued within the Labour party, with many members of the New Left involved in the anti-nuclear lobby. Support for CND fluctuated in the ensuing years largely in time with the heightening and relaxing of international tension: Michael Tippett in a postscript to his *Moving into Aquarius* (1974) noted with disillusion that as long as the balance of deterrence was seen to work, the ethical disturbance fell away. However, in the heightened international tension of 1979, unilateral nuclear disarmament again became official Labour party policy. In the 1979 election, it seemed that the policy, cleverly called 'one-sided nuclear disarmament' by the

Tories, was a vote-loser, but the new Labour leader, Neil Kinnock, reaffirmed it after further election defeats in 1983 and 1987. Meanwhile, scientists confirmed the worst fears about nuclear war by predicting that the use of nuclear bombs would lead to a 'nuclear winter' over large parts of the globe with devastating effects on human, plant and animal life. By the mid-eighties, doubts were extended from nuclear weapons to nuclear power stations, built ostensibly for peaceful uses, but believed to be involved in the production of plutonium for nuclear bombs. In 1986 anxiety about 'leaks' of radioactivity from British nuclear installations, were exacerbated by evidence of official secrecy about past accidents; but even more by a serious accident to a nuclear establishment in the USSR, which increased radioactivity over much of Europe, including Britain. Harold Wilson's promise in 1964 to create a new Britain forged in 'the white heat of a technological revolution' seemed in retrospect less inviting when the white heat was at the centre of a nuclear reactor. In the same decade, the decade of the first conquest of space, the BBC Reith lecturer Dr Edmund Leach had begun his lectures with Promethean words which would have deeply shocked the Presbyterian Lord Reith. 'Men have become like gods. Isn't it about time that we understood our divinity? Science offers us total mastery over our environment and over our destiny, yet instead of rejoicing we feel deeply afraid. Why should this be?' Twenty years later people felt they knew the answer.

Michael Tippett had written of the tension he felt during the war between the artists affirming absolute values, and a society bent on destruction. His (pre-nuclear) wartime oratorio, *A Child of Our Time*, prophetically attempted to give collective expression to a sense of involvement in 'some uncontrollable catastrophe'. Few artists since have felt ready to tackle this theme. The novelist, Martin Amis, wrote in the eighties that the subject of nuclear weapons 'resists frontal assault. For myself, I feel it as a background . . . The present feels narrower, the present feels straitened, discrepant as the planet lives from day to day . . . it is ruining everything.' Nevertheless attempting a frontal assault, in 1965 Peter Watkins scripted and directed for the BBC *The War Game*, a dramatic portrayal of a nuclear attack. The Corporation decided not to broadcast it, bowing to those who felt it was too horrific to be shown. However, it was finally shown in 1985 – and won the Broadcasting Press Guild's drama award. Official timidity had not, in fact, precluded widespread anxiety, and in the early 1980s people had already been speaking of 'nuclear neurosis' among children and speculating that this might be one factor contributing to the increased violence among the young.

Economic crisis and a divided society

In the 1960s the young's ebullience had thrust them into the forefront of society's consciousness; in the 1970s and even more the 1980s, they were thrust there by the country's economic decline which produced unemployment at unprecedented levels, particularly in the older industrial areas of Scotland, Wales, Northern Ireland and the north of England, and especially among the young. A poignant indicator of this decline relative to

Britain's EEC partners was a popular television series *Auf Wiedersehn, Pet* in which a group of unemployed from the North-east sought work as 'cheap foreign labour' in Germany. Warning voices had, since 1945, predicted disaster ahead unless Britain modernised its industry. Repeated crises were weathered with difficulty, but by the 1970s the situation was becoming acute, with the decline of traditional industry and the coming to Britain of what the American Daniel Bell had termed in 1960 the 'post industrial society' of high technology – personal computers, microchip technology, fibre optics, and lasers. The country faced the prospect of a high-wage, high-tech future for the few, and for the rest, a low-wage future for some in service industries, and unemployment for many. Britain's industrial performance was outclassed by the new industrial giants of the Far East not only in traditional industries but also in the new high-tech industries, despite her scientists' and technologists' leading role since the war in many of the discoveries and techniques involved.

Back in 1959 the scientist and novelist C.P. Snow had delivered a lecture (which achieved notoriety when intemperately attacked by F.R. Leavis) called *The Two Cultures*, in which he regretted the lack of contact between, on the one hand, scientists and, on the other, intellectuals in the liberal–cultural tradition, to their mutual impoverishment. He felt that the latter undervalued science, and would be enriched by an understanding of the ordering of the natural world, and that scientists would have a greater appreciation of the wider implications of their work if they studied the humanities. In the 1980s the failure of society to value its scientists and technologists and of industry to make use of them was being cited as a major cause of economic decline.

The growing economic crisis of the seventies and eighties was responsible for deepening divisions in society with a widening of the gap between rich and poor, north and south. Among artists who had been politicised by the ferment of the sixties, there was a frustration at the failure of left-wing politics, particularly evident in the work of some playwrights (Trevor Griffiths' *Comedians* and *The Party*, David Hare's *Plenty*) and in the strident denunciations of so-called bourgeois art and society by some in the Community Arts movement. The frustrations arising from Britain's economic crisis led to a polarisation of political attitudes. The Labour party moved to the left and the Tory party to the right and in 1981 a group of frustrated moderates in the Labour party broke away to form the Social Democratic party, which formed an alliance with the Liberal party to strengthen the centre ground. In the 1987 general election, however, the Alliance's failure to 'break the mould' of two-party politics left its future uncertain.

One important focus of political frustration was the increased power of the Trade Unions, which was felt by many in all parties to have gone too far. Already, by the early sixties, it had been the subject of two films, a satirical comedy *I'm All Right, Jack* and a drama, *The Angry Silence*. After the failure of the Wilson government in 1967 to get agreement to the modest proposals of its document *In Place of Strife*, a Tory government in 1974 and a Labour one in 1979 were both brought down by challenges from the unions. Service unions with a large proportion of low-paid workers which had hitherto abjured strike action were increasingly involved: in the 1978/9 'winter of discontent' even sewage disposal and ambulance services were affected and some dead could not be buried owing to a strike by grave-diggers. Union members were divided as never before, and when the Tories swept to victory in 1979, Mrs Thatcher could rightly claim that many Trade Unionists were now voting Tory.

Mrs Thatcher's mentor, the American economist Milton Friedman, had declared that the British class system lay behind Britain's economic failure. She set out to tackle this problem, partly by detaching the more affluent of the working class from their traditional loyalties (a significant step was the encouragement of home ownership by a sale of Council houses to their tenants); and partly by curbing the power of the unions. Laws subsequently passed by the Tories to reduce Trade Union power were challenged by a bitter and ultimately unsuccessful year-long miners' strike in 1984/5, from which neither Coal Board, union, government, the opposition or the police, who were caught in the middle, emerged with untarnished reputations. People were shocked to see on their television screens brutal violence perpetrated by both police and miners. Although Britain had never been the cosy, secure country of nostalgic remembrance, and civil violence among protesting workers, rioters and football crowds had a long history, by the eighties there was considerable public alarm at the escalation of this type of violence, an alarm enhanced by the tendency of the media to exploit violent events. Violent crime, too, was rising, and rape was increasing and becoming more brutal. Tory governments were returned in 1979 and 1984 promising tougher law and order measures; but it was soon clear that these, particularly the 'short sharp shock' treatment for young offenders, were not having a deterrent effect, whilst there was public alarm at the perhaps inevitable use of greater force and even paramilitary tactics by the police. Those on the right saw the relaxed standards of the permissive society and the influence of violence in entertainment on television as the most likely causes of the situation; those on the left pointed to long-term unemployment, urban decay, the impoverished education system, and the frustration and alienation caused among the poor by the contrast between their situation and the affluent life-style portrayed in television soap operas and commercials. All agreed that increased use of alcohol and drugs also played a significant part.

By the mid-eighties many of the working class were sharing in a rising affluence. But for the low-paid and unemployed it was a time of great hardship, of inadequate housing and dependence on social security and a disproportionate number of people from the ethnic minorities were to be found among this group. Britain had always had a considerable number of non-white people in its population, but it was not until the post-war era, when immigrants often came in large groups and settled together, that their presence began to arouse resentment. In the immediate post-war period of full employment, West Indians and later Asians had been encouraged to settle in Britain to fill low-paid jobs spurned by the local people, in the textile and transport industries and the Health Service. Riots at Notting Hill in 1958 alerted politicians for the first time to racial hostility among the local whites. In the ensuing years successive governments legislated on the one hand to restrict immigration and on the other to outlaw discrimination. But despite this, discrimination continued in education, jobs and housing, and was to be found in the official world of the civil service, the forces, the police and local government, as much as elsewhere. By the late seventies and eighties riots in the decaying inner city areas inevitably had strong though often confused racial ingredients.

But by this time, too, a generation of young blacks and Asians who had grown up in Britain began to make their mark through the arts. Black and Asian music had been one of the earliest ethnic influences. This was followed in the late seventies and eighties by an upsurge of black dance and fringe theatre companies, and blacks were increasingly seen on television. In addition, there were acclaimed novels and film scripts by Afro-Caribbean and Asian writers. But it was still difficult for non-whites to enter the large established performing companies, despite the success of an all-black *Measure for Measure* at the National Theatre. Yet it had become clear that West Indians and Asians could, given the right conditions, greatly enrich British cultural life, as the Jewish immigrants of the first half of the century had done out of all proportion to their numbers, and despite initial hostility and prejudice.

Prejudice thrives particularly on competition for scarce jobs and amenities. A well-researched report, *Faith in the City* (1985), produced by the Church of England, incurred absurd government accusations of Marxist influence when it castigated both government and church organisations for social neglect. In the run-down inner city of Liverpool, Catholic and Anglican bishops were united in outspoken protest at the City's plight. Meanwhile, despite (or because of?) the more active social role of their leaders, both Anglican and Catholic Church congregations continued to decline.

It seemed, in the mid-eighties, that a spiritual vacuum waited to be filled. For more than three decades secular humanism had been the prevailing outlook. At its best it had produced a more tolerant and caring society, and brought about far-reaching and beneficial changes in relationships between the sexes and within the family. But by the eighties the caring society was being blamed for sapping the energies of the people and undermining the individual's will to create wealth, on which, it was held, the future well-being of society depended. American enterprise was held up as the model to be followed. The 'privatisation' of many hitherto communal enterprises took place. Some trade unions, in tune with the new attitudes, negotiated private health care for their members, and even offered them a stock exchange advice service.

For many individuals, a retreat into private life took place, which often meant, literally, a retreat into the home. The Englishman's home became, more and more, not his castle but his entertainment centre, with radio, television, video recorders, cassette and record-players, and computer games. By the mid-eighties there were more video-tape libraries than book-shops. The cinema, once the poor man's 'Picture Palace' and his only contact with luxury, had by the eighties lost nine-tenths of its 1945 audience; many people preferred to see their films in the home. Even the Bingo Halls which had replaced many cinemas were closing down. Theatres and concert-halls, too, were struggling to retain audiences, with a consequent pressure to present the popular and readily accessible. Musicals dominated the London stage, and theatrical productions of all kinds placed increasing emphasis on electronic spectacle.

To sum up: the period covered by this volume began with the wartime discovery of the social value of the arts. For the next forty years or so, when the world situation still inspired more fear than hope, all governments were committed to subsidising the arts because of their contribution to the quality of life. This was one aspect of the welfare state, whose creation was generally regarded as one of the good things to have come out of the trauma of the war. By the 1980s, however, this concensus was fading, and after the 1987 general election (which the Tories won for a remarkable third time in a row), the arts minister spoke rather more strongly than the first Tory minister had done in 1979 about the need for arts organisations to look more to the market for their funding and less to the government. Further, unlike his predecessor he added a condemnation of the 'welfare state mentality' of the arts world.

This pejorative use of the term 'welfare state' by a government minister marked a significant change, not just for the arts world, but for all who believed that something remained of the national unity of purpose and desire for a more just society that had emerged from the war.

Part II
Studies in The Individual Arts

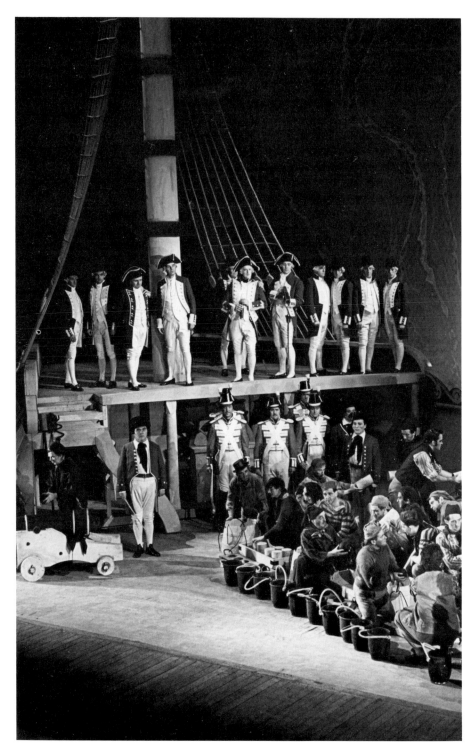

Scene from the Benjamin Britten opera Billy Budd, *staged at Covent Garden in 1953. Set design by John Piper.*

1 Music

PAUL GRIFFITHS

Introduction: a more musical Britain?

If one were to seek any single change in British music since 1945, that change would have to be the simple fact of increase. Of course, these things are difficult to quantify, but there hardly seems any room for doubt that very much more music is very much more available in the 1980s than was the case in the 1940s. Only the means have changed. The gramophone had played a role in the dissemination of music since the beginning of the century, but it was only after the introduction of the long-playing record, in 1950, that record players became almost universal household features, and that an enormous repertory of music became accessible: by 1970 people of quite average means could have their choice of music, whether Gregorian chant, or the *Ring*, or the latest pop, sounding in their own homes, under their own control. The fact has often been remarked, but its implications are so far-reaching, changing music from a social into a private art, that they have to be considered at the start of any discussion of music in modern Britain. So much else is merely contingent: the increasing demand, so it seems, for technical perfection in concert performances, so that the artificial precision of records is emulated; the invitation to rank different performances of the same work (something impossible, of course, before there were records), and so, perhaps, to give more attention to the performance than to the work; even the fossilisation of the repertory around a few readily marketable names, despite the fact that the gramophone has undoubtedly made a much wider variety of music obtainable than ever can have been the case before.

The issues here inevitably go far beyond the immediately British experience, but one effect of the gramophone has been to internationalise musical culture: a local eccentricity, like the appetite for oratorios in Victorian England, can hardly be accommodated to the laws of mass marketing. But those laws are not altogether simple. They have emphasised the classic status of a central repertory – Mozart, Beethoven, Brahms and the rest – but they have also indicated the advisability of variety, if on verifiable terms. It is, indeed, hard to avoid the observation that the prodigious growth in popularity of 'early music' (the term denotes more an attitude of mind than a period, but originally seems to have meant music from before the time of Haydn), that this growth came at a time, since the late 1960s, when the established repertory from Haydn to Stravinsky had been fully recorded, and that there was a commercial need for a new area that had some claim to public attention – a claim that could be backed up by academic expertise, which unavoidably was not forthcoming to support more recent music. Yet it would be wrong to suggest that musical taste since 1945 has been directed entirely by commercial imperatives. Much more plausible is the belief that there has also been a change of sensibility, a dissatisfaction with the romantic view of the self propounded in the music of those few golden decades around 1880: hence, perhaps, the enormous growth in the popularity of Mahler since 1960, not least in Britain, for it is in Mahler's symphonies that this dissatisfaction is most acutely expressed.

The wireless has also played a part in this change of sensibility. Serious music was an important part of BBC broadcasts from the 1920s onwards, and the BBC Symphony Orchestra had been founded in 1930, but a much more significant development came within our period with the establishment of the Third Programme on 29 September 1946 (see chapter 5, pp. 161–7). The intention seems to have been that the channel should be a medium of intellectual communication, when such a thing could still just be conceived: it provided a forum for drama, poetry, philosophical and scientific talks, etc.,

Sir Adrian Boult conducting the BBC Symphony Orchestra in the Albert Hall (1950).

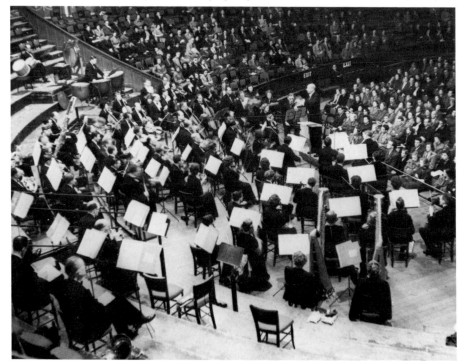

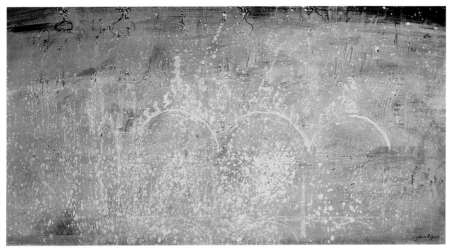

1. *Set by John Piper for Benjamin Britten's opera* Death In Venice *(1973).*
   (See p. 58)

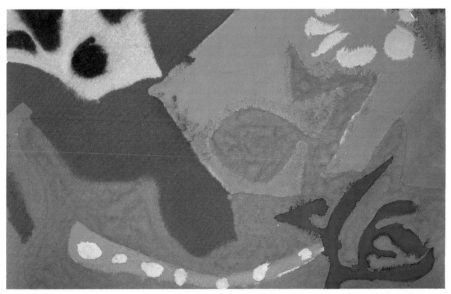

2. *Patrick Heron,* April 27 *(Gouache, 1985; Newlyn Art Gallery)*. *(See p. 106)*

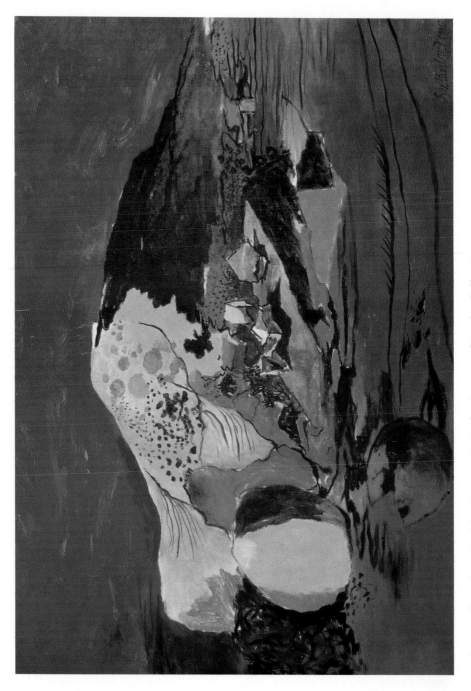

3. Graham Sutherland, Red Landscape (1942; Southampton City Art Gallery).
(See p. 120)

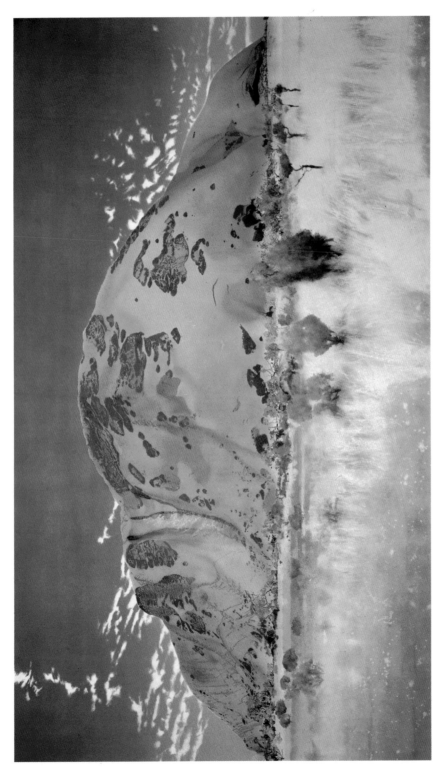

4. *Michael Andrews*, The Cathedral, North-East Face, Uluru (Ayers Rock) 1985
(*Saatchi Collection, London*). (*See p. 116*)

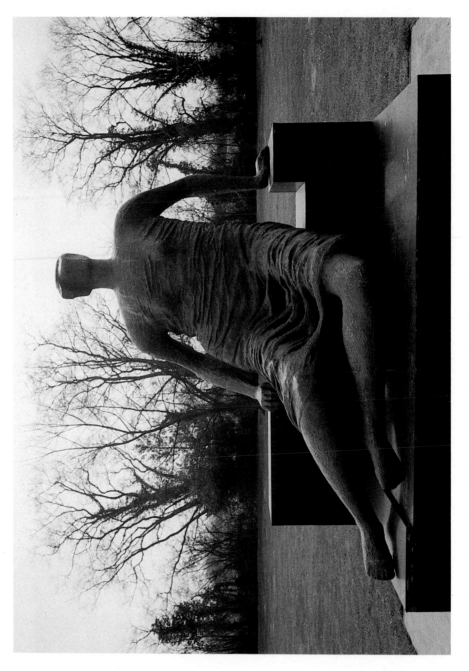

5. *Henry Moore, Draped Seated Woman (1957; Henry Moore Foundation).*
(See p. 135)

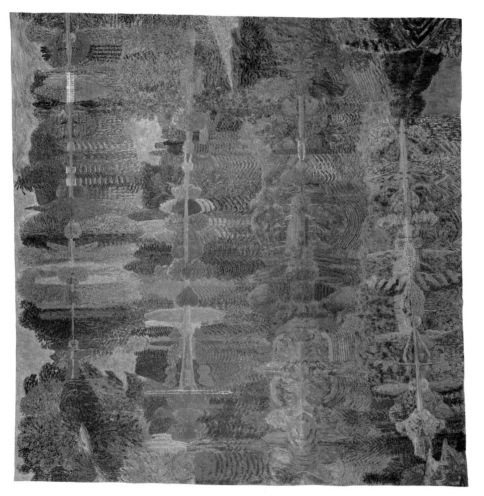

6. *Adrian Berg, Sheffield Park, Autumn (1986; private collection). (See p. 119)*

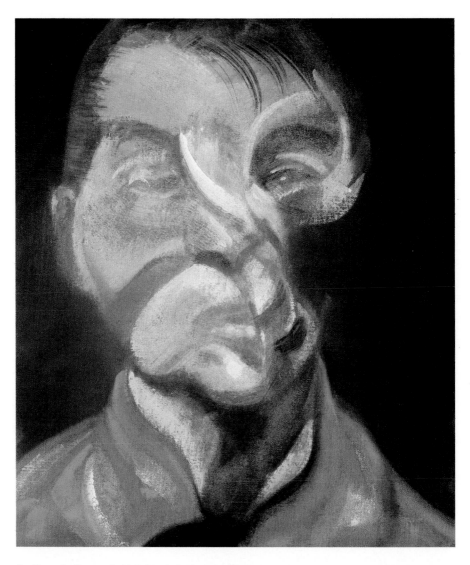

7. *Francis Bacon,* Self-Portrait *(1972; Collection Gilbert de Botton, Switzerland).* *(See p. 128)*

8. *Bernard Leach, Plate (1975). (See p. 183)*

9. *Michael Cardew, Bowl (1975). (See p. 183)*

10. *Lucie Rie, Bowl (1982). (See p. 189)*

11. *Jacqui Poncelet, Shoe (1984). (See p. 188)*

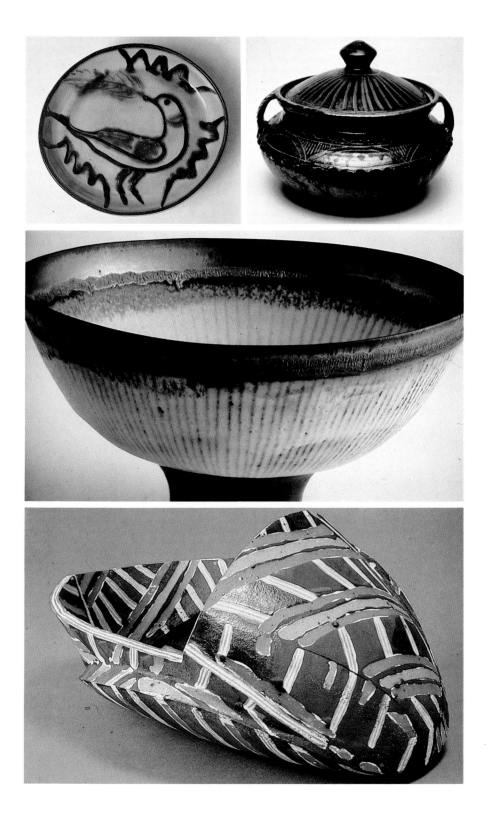

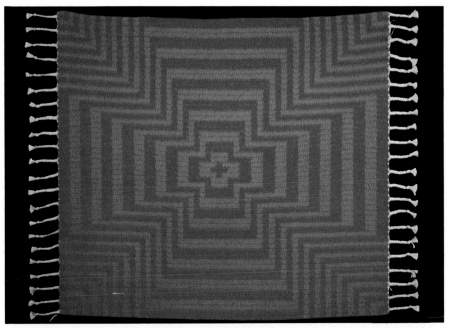

12. Peter Collingwood, Rug (1979). (See p. 177)

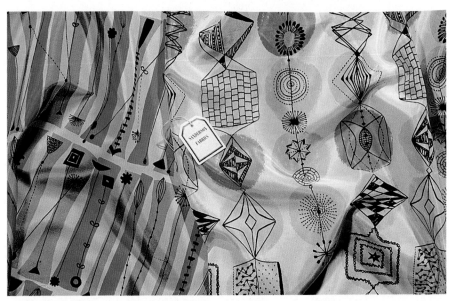

13. Lucienne Day, textile design for Sanderson (1953). (See p. 298)

besides music. However, in 1964 the evening Third Programme was joined by a daytime Music Programme, and in 1970 the two were subsumed into Radio 3. Whereas it was possible for the Third Programme to be addressed notionally to an alert listener of wide interests, Radio 3 became the provider of a service: classical music for sixteen hours or so per day. Again, the change need not be construed as one-sidedly malevolent. The BBC ceased to cater for a particular audience because it ceased to be obvious that there was an audience with the leisure and inclination to look to the radio for new developments in the arts and sciences. The certainty that existed in 1946 – that there was a certain corpus of intellectual material to be seriously presented – was no longer a certainty for the following generation, and to some extent the BBC itself, by assiduously promoting the new music that threatened cultural coherence, had carried the seeds of its own demise as an active agent in artistic culture: the boundaries had been stretched too far for the assured guidance the Third Programme had offered to continue to be credible. On the musical front, its greatness coincided with the period when William Glock was its controller of music (1959–72), a period when windows were flung open into the deep medieval past and into the contemporaneity of such composers as Pierre Boulez and Karlheinz Stockhausen.

But there may be still larger forces at work here. Historical analyses are always transitory, and none more transitory than those concerned with the recent history of an art form. Even so, there seems to have been a general awakening at the end of the 1950s to the fact that the musical world no longer ran according to the rules of diatonic harmony and sonata form: hence the otherwise seemingly contradictory vogues for Mahler and for medieval and Renaissance music; hence too the appearance, not only in Great Britain but throughout the world, of composers who rejected a very great deal in the musical status quo. In England the main exemplars of this trend were Harrison Birtwistle, Peter Maxwell Davies and Alexander Goehr, but they had their like-minded contemporaries throughout Europe and the United States. Even those composers who had already been active in the same direction, like such radical explorers of twelve-note serial music as Boulez and Stockhausen, only gained widespread acknowledgement at the end of the 1950s (serial music is structured to keep all the notes of the chromatic scale in play). And it may not be irrelevant that this was also the period when popular music took on its modern form through the unprecedented world-wide enthusiasm for recordings made by such artists as Elvis Presley, Bill Haley and the Everley Brothers. In an important sense, the years 1954–5 – the years of *Le Marteau sans Maître*, Presley's first recordings and Davies's first published compositions – mark a more important break than does the end of the Second World War. And perhaps this is particularly true of Britain, where the first decade after the war has in retrospect some curious features of a deliberately conservative musical culture.

It is as if the effort to rebuild and radically to reform, exemplified in France in the figure of Boulez, had been diverted in Britain into a re-establishment of traditional norms, celebrated almost outspokenly in the Festival of Britain in 1951. Physically the most permanent monument of that event was the Festival Hall on the south bank of the Thames in London: an auditorium designed for orchestral concerts of the kind that had developed during the early part of the century, and still inevitably used as such near the century's end. As for the Festival's musical commissions, the most important were for operas, among which Britten's *Billy Budd* has proved most durable. Little seems to have been heard of electronic music, which was already a field of active endeavour in Paris, New York and Cologne, but which was almost ignored by British composers until twenty years later. And little was yet heard of twelve-note music, which again had taken hold of young composers' imaginations in France, Germany and the United States. Those composers who emerged in Britain during the first decade after the War – Peter Racine Fricker, Iain Hamilton, Alun Hoddinott and others – looked rather to the more conservative modernism of Bartók, Hindemith and Berg, all of whom had found ways to keep alive the force of major–minor tonality. And although Britain gained as immigrants composers of a more radical outlook, including the Schoenberg pupils Egon Wellesz and Roberto Gerhard, they were not much celebrated until the 1960s.

Perhaps the delay had something to do with what is always described as a characteristically English conservatism; or there may have been some connection with the fact that British musicians, unlike their colleagues in countries that had been subject to Nazi dominion, had not been officially deprived of modernism, and so reacted with a less enthusiastic acceptance of it at the coming of peace. Curiously, the pattern of events had much in common with that in those countries, like Poland and Hungary, where a state antagonism to musical modernism continued into the 1950s. Of course, in Britain there was no Stalinist cultural policy, but the fact of the concurrent thaw in Britain and eastern Europe in the late 1950s may suggest that none was needed. Conservatism may have been fuelled on both sides of the iron curtain just as effectively by the wish to forge a national identity in established genres, and by a backing-off from the uncertainties of atonality and other radical innovations.

Two prominent features of British musical life since 1945 might support that view: the growth of opera, and the development of music composed for schoolchildren, the one implying an ambition of traditional character, the other suggesting a wish to belong in that earlier stage of culture which children occupy by right. The first performance of Britten's *Peter Grimes*, at Sadler's Wells Theatre on 7 June 1945, is the most notable landmark in the history of recent British music: an emblem not only of the arrival of a great composer but also of the long-awaited flowering of British opera. That same year performances recommenced at Covent Garden, where there was a strong emphasis during the first decade on native work, with a revival of Purcell's *Fairy Queen* to establish the founding of English opera in history, and with the premières of Britten's *Billy Budd* and *Gloriana* (1953), Bliss's *The Olympians* (1949), Vaughan Williams's *The Pilgrim's Progress* (1951), Walton's *Troilus and Cressida* (1954) and Tippett's *The Midsummer Marriage* (1955). The changed climate of the later 1950s inevitably meant a reduction in this sort of activity, and during the next fifteen years only Tippett's *King Priam* was introduced by the company.

But still the British taste for opera as performance art has grown, perhaps encouraged by radio and television broadcasts, and by the increasing repertory of opera on record. New companies were formed outside London – Welsh National Opera in Cardiff (1946), Scottish Opera in Glasgow and Edinburgh (1962), Kent Opera in Canterbury (1976), Opera North in Leeds (1978) – while Covent Garden became one of the leading houses on the international circuit, and Sadler's Wells Opera, performing in English, grew into a new, larger theatre, the Coliseum (1968), and into a new name as the English National Opera (1974). Also important, not least because of the new works they introduced by Britten, Berkeley, Walton, Birtwistle and others – were the activities of the English Opera Group (1946–76), whose touring productions were seen at the Aldeburgh Festival, in London and elsewhere. By the 1970s, with both the Royal Opera at Covent Garden and the English National Opera at the London Coliseum giving seasons through ten months of the year, and with regular appearances by the provincial companies in most large cities, British audiences for opera must have become higher than at any previous time; and even if the creative achievement may not have continued at the intensity of the period from *Peter Grimes* to *The Midsummer Marriage*, British composers have produced many of the most remarkable operas of the post-war era, including those of the five composers who will demand more detailed treatment later in this chapter.

Two of those composers, Britten and Davies, also contributed to the enlivening of school music, Britten through the cantata *St Nicolas* (1948) and several later works involving boys' choir (*Let's Make an Opera*, 1949; *Noye's Fludde*, 1958; *The Golden Vanity*, 1966), Davies through a still more considerable output of children's music that embraces choral, instrumental and operatic pieces, and that was originally stimulated by practical work as head of music at Cirencester Grammar School (1959–62). His encouragement there of improvisation and composition by pupils was regarded as revolutionary at the time, but has since become quite normal, displacing in large part the previous occupations of singing folksong arrangements and listening to records in an effort towards 'music appreciation'. Of course, to some degree the change was a response to a change in the listening habits of the young, for the explosion of pop music in the late 1950s provided for the first time a musical diet aimed principally at the adolescent, who thereby gained a ready alternative to Vaughan Williams and Beethoven. Resistance on the part of school students is tolerably avoided by making music largely a practical activity, in the same way as the teaching of visual art in schools is primarily through creative work, but there is more involved here than a supine yielding to pressure. The decay in the teaching of music as a discipline, with traditions, great composers and rules, is part of the decay in the belief that high Western culture has any prerogative: the rise of creative music in schools cannot be separated from the decline of the Third Programme, or the quickening of interest in early music, or the closer concern with styles of performance than with musical substance, or the attachment to ancient and exotic musical traditions shown by composers.

But British music since 1945 is much too complex to be seen merely in terms of dissolution and failure of confidence. Pointing in a quite different direction is the operatic development, the evolution of musical festivals and the quite startling growth in the sheer numbers of professional composers. Here, perhaps, the growth is inextricably linked with the decay: there can be more composers because the culture is more diversified, and the culture is more diversified in part because there are so many composers. Nevertheless, the change is extraordinary. Whereas in the 1930s there were perhaps a dozen composers whose works would have been thought worth, say, regular air time, now there are a hundred or more, most of them with teaching posts in schools, conservatories and universities. This is, of course, a global and not a uniquely British phenomenon, but it is all the same remarkable in a country whose traditions of composition are quite shallowly rooted in history.

Equally remarkable is the abundance of festivals, many of them making a point of commissioning new music, and the most important of them all founded in the few years after the end of the war: Cheltenham in 1945, Edinburgh in 1947, Bath and Aldeburgh in 1948. From the first, the Cheltenham Festival was particularly concerned with new British music, and it has promoted a wide variety of composers from the generation of Fricker to that of Robert Saxton, if with a leaning towards symphonic and chamber music of a conservative cast. The Edinburgh and Bath Festivals were deliberately much more international in tone, and the Edinburgh Festival under the direction of Lord Harewood (1961–6) played a part in the opening out of British music that was being fostered at the same time by William Glock at the BBC: Schoenberg was featured in 1961, Boulez in 1966. Aldeburgh's role was different. Founded by Britten and Peter Pears, it retained until after Britten's death a close association with his music: a large number of his works, including operas (*A Midsummer Night's Dream*, 1960; three church parables, 1964–8; *Death in Venice*, 1973), chamber works written for the cellist Mstislav Rostropovich and songs intended for Pears, were heard for the first time at the Aldeburgh Festival; indeed, comparatively little of Britten's music after 1960 had a première anywhere else. In this corner of British music at least, therefore, a general phenomenon is intimately linked with an individual.

Benjamin Britten

Britten was born in 1913 in Lowestoft on the East Anglian coast, not far from his eventual home at Aldeburgh. He began composing abundantly at the age of five, and in later years he published some of his schoolboy pieces, including a set of Five Waltzes (sic) for the piano, written when he was around ten years old. At the age of thirteen he began lessons with Frank Bridge, and by the time he was fifteen, when he wrote a set of Four French Songs for soprano and orchestra, he had achieved an individual tone of voice beyond the influence of his teacher and of those European composers – Stravinsky, Bartók and Berg – in whom Bridge took a then frowned-upon interest. This boyhood mastery is something he shared with relatively few composers: perhaps Mozart and Mendelssohn are the only other outstanding examples, and in all three cases a quality of innocence remained in the music of the man, as if composition continued to involve a return to a cast of mind that had been discovered in childhood. Certainly Britten seems not to have needed, nor to have gained much from, the formal studies he went on to undertake with Ireland at the Royal College of Music (1930–4). His intention then to study with Berg, whose *Wozzeck* had powerfully impressed him in a broadcast performance (already the BBC was influential), came to nothing, and the prospect of a Britten educated in twelve-note music in the mid-1930s remains a tantalising alternative history. It may be significant, though, that he was not much influenced by the scores that he could have studied at that time, or by the most adventurous music of his teacher Bridge, whose Third and Fourth Quartets are less key-centred than anything Britten produced before the 1950s.

What he learned most from the music of his contemporaries – curiously like Davies in the next generation – was how readily the new could be turned to parody the old: it was the lesson pre-eminently of Stravinsky's neoclassical music, though the satires of such a work as the *Variations on a Theme of Frank Bridge*★ for string orchestra (1937) are at once more boyish and more affectionate. There is a link here with Auden, who was Britten's colleague at the GPO Film Unit from 1935: *Night Mail* (1936) was one of the documentaries on which they collaborated, and the artistic relationship flourished in theatrical projects (*The Ascent of F6*, 1937; *On the Frontier*, 1938) and concert works (*Our Hunting Fathers*,★ an exuberantly inventive pacifist statement for soprano and orchestra, with a significantly child-voiced title, 1936; *On this Island*, the first of Britten's many song cycles, 1937). The partnership lapsed when Auden moved to the USA, but in 1939 Britten followed him there, and together they worked on the opera *Paul Bunyan* (1940–1), which the composer suppressed until the last year of his life. This brief American interlude was, however, extremely productive. Britten produced his First Quartet (1941),★ a variety of orchestral works, and the *Seven Sonnets of Michelangelo* (1940), the first of a long succession of works he wrote as repertory for himself and his henceforth lifelong companion Peter Pears. He also discovered in America the subject for a more ambitious opera than *Paul Bunyan* in the story of Peter Grimes recounted by Crabbe, who also provided a mirror for his East Anglian sensibility and a reason for returning home. He and Pears duly recrossed the Atlantic in 1942, and in 1944 he began work on the opera, which was completed and performed the next year.

Peter Grimes★ established, as the musical-style *Paul Bunyan* had not, Britten's gift for opera, which depended on word setting that is both extravagant and apt in the manner of his acknowledged model Purcell, on the creation of atmosphere through orchestral interludes (an inheritance from *Wozzeck*, where the orchestra similarly seems to be lavishing compassion on the characters it supports), on the ability to create distinct musical characters in even the tiniest roles and then create ensembles with those characters in view, and not least on a deep personal engagement with the central figure. In most of Britten's later operas, too, there is a clear community of feeling between the composer and his main character (the Governess in *The Turn of the Screw*★, Aschenbach in *Death in Venice*★), and it is this that creates a

---

★ In this and later sections I have indicated with an asterisk ★ those works, of the many I discuss, which seem to me of outstanding importance.

sense of personal, almost confessional intimacy rare in opera. But *Peter Grimes* shows such intimacy immediately at its most intense. In making the central character more sympathetic than he is in the Crabbe, Britten also made his exclusion from society the less plausible. To some extent his separateness can be understood as that of the gifted individual: unlike the rest of the Borough, Grimes has imagination, and thereby he is the archetypical artist. But it seems clear that Britten felt himself to be isolated not so much by his artistic activity as by his sexual nature, and that Grimes the outcast, acutely sensitive but profoundly misunderstood, was a projection of his own feelings as a homosexual in a society where homosexual expression was strongly repressed, or perhaps, more profoundly, of his feelings as a personality which censured a vital part of itself.

If so, then his divided self would have found an echo in the divided nature of the tonal language in his time. No composer after Schoenberg's break into atonality could use major–minor harmony in entire security that this was the natural, inevitable language of music; there had to be a degree of irony. In early Britten, in works like the Bridge Variations, this had been expressed as parody, but in *Peter Grimes* and most later works it becomes rather an awareness of a fall from a musical state of grace. The yearning sevenths of Grimes's part are emblems of a yearning for the pure harmony of an earlier stage in musical history (Britten's reverence for Mozart and Schubert above Beethoven, and his distaste for Brahms, can be understood in the same light).

Another division in Britten's psyche was that between his extreme privacy and his flair for the theatre, and it was a division he sought to overcome in his pursuit after *Peter Grimes* of opera as a chamber medium. The two works he wrote for Covent Garden were both commissions that could hardly be turned down: for the Festival of Britain and for the Coronation (*Gloriana*). But otherwise his operas were all for relatively small casts and small instrumental ensembles: *The Rape of Lucretia* (1946), for soloists and an orchestra of a dozen, provided the impetus for the formation of the English Opera Group, for whom Britten wrote all his subsequent operas with the exception of the two Covent Garden pieces. Among those works, *Albert Herring* (1947) is one of the exceedingly few operatic comedies since Rossini and Donizetti, and not least funny because it offers a light treatment of one of Britten's perennial themes: the corruption of innocence. Albert, the straightforward simpleton in a social comedy set in an English village, accepts his corruption quite cheerfully, but such is not at all the case in Britten's next chamber opera, *The Turn of the Screw* (1954), based on the Henry James short story. Since the ghosts have to be present on stage and sing, they inevitably have a much more concrete existence than they do in the original tale of children who may or may not be in touch with spirits. The relationship between the ghosts and the children, however, becomes more ominous: the children know much more than they ought. And once again, an essential Britten theme is connected in a very direct way with the state of the musical language: innocence for him is the blithe tonal harmony of Mozart; corruption is the complicatedness of a later age, represented very directly in *The Turn of the Screw* by an underlying progression through the twelve notes of the chromatic scale. On a more local level, one of the most telling moments in the opera is that where the children's nursery rhyme, seemingly so innocuous in its harmony, is twisted into much murkier waters, audibly enacting the process of corruption.

Britten's response to some of the ideas of twelve-note serialism in *The Turn of the Screw* was of course not an individual whim but part of the general re-evaluation of modernism that has already been mentioned. In his case it led to no break with an essential key-centredness: indeed, it is hard to see how his musical personality could have existed without a highly troubled tonal harmony in which pure concord could be seen as an impossible ideal or as a land of lost innocence. Nevertheless, he found in the breakdown of genres something to which he could respond. In particular, he shared with Mahler the view that songs and symphonies were not incompatible (*Spring Symphony*, 1949), and went further in bringing songs, on poems by Wilfred Owen, into a setting of the Latin mass for the dead in his *War Requiem* (1961). He also took advantage of the new freedom of musical dramatic form. His seven operas of the crowded years from *Peter Grimes* to *Gloriana* are fairly conventional in structure, providing opportunities for songs, ensembles and set-pieces (though *Albert Heering* deals in these things with a light-hearted irony). However, *The Turn of the Screw* takes place much more in a fluid recitative, and has the feel and pacing of a film: fully formed song is now reserved, in a manner that had already been indicated in *Peter Grimes*, for suggestions of another world beyond the opera, whether it be a malevolent, corruptly enticing world in the summonses addressed by the ghost Quint to the boy Miles, or a world of already corrupted innocence in the children's songs. Lyrical expression is associated with a loosening of control, and enters the opera with a Dionysiac allure.

It is here as it is with Britten's understanding of tonality: there is a yearning after the clarity and smoothness of Schubertian song, but also a fear that the simple melody has lost its innocence, and a knowledge of inevitable estrangement from that springtime of musical culture. Similar feelings would seem to underlie Britten's sympathy for the music of the Far East, which he encountered during a recital tour with Pears in 1955; for here was an art that appeared to have kept its innocence. The rich metallophone resonances of the Balinese gamelan then entered his own orchestration, most notably in the full-length ballet *The Prince of the Pagodas* – though this particular kind of rapture had already been suggested by the use of the celeste to accompany Quint's most seductive appeals in *The Turn of the Screw*. Then in his last opera, *Death in Venice*, the gamelan sounds appear again, and the association with youthful energy becomes quite explicit as they underscore the boys' beach games.

Japan also made its contribution. Impressed by performances of a Noh play, Britten and his librettist William Plomer transposed it into an English, Christian, medieval setting to create *Curlew River** (1964), the first of a triptych of 'parables for church performance'. The transposition was facilitated by Britten's realisation that he could achieve a Noh-style formality within his own culture by looking back to the church dramas of the Middle Ages, and he has *Curlew River* performed as if by a community of monks and boy acolytes: the work begins with a plainsong processional, which then swerves into original music, while the oriental influence is maintained in the dominance of textures that are heterophonic rather than contrapuntal (i.e. the instrumental lines tend to be staggered versions of the same melody). Thus where other works, like *Peter Grimes* and *The Turn of the Screw*, had contained windows into a region of lost or unattainable content, *Curlew River* takes place entirely in such a world. And in such a world it can present a quite unproblematic view of the operation of the divine: a woman, mad with grief at the disappearance of her son, is ferried across the river to his grave, where his spirit appears to her as 'a sign of God's grace'. Inevitably the sign is given in the voice of a child: an important part of Britten's musical personality springs into focus if one tries to imagine it having been done in any other way, for the pervasive melancholy of *Curlew River* is an expression of the composer's knowledge of his distance from the world he is creating, his exile both from personal childhood and from that childhood of time when belief was secure.

His version of *A Midsummer Night's Dream* (1960) has similarly the unreality of a fantasy world, similarly conveyed by the use of boys' voices, here for the chorus of fairies. But its lift from the everyday is achieved too by the very deliberate use of orchestral effects evocative of woodlands and night-time, and by the casting of Oberon as a counter-tenor. His becomes the principal role. In the compression of the play made by Britten and Pears, the quartet of lovers are reduced to excuses for fairy magic, and the opera is much more concerned with the dream *per se* than with the dream as a means of sorting out the tangle of feelings. But the hempen homespuns provide an occasion for the return of parody, which had been rather set aside since *Albert Herring*. In particular, the play of Pyramus and Thisbe is enforced with all the potentially ludicrous means of nineteenth-century operatic rhetoric.

Britten's last two operas, *Owen Wingrave* (1970) and *Death in Venice* (1973), were both collaborations with Myfanwy Piper, who had been the librettist for *The Turn of the Screw*, and they return to a similar interweaving of short scenes in the manner of a film: *Owen Wingrave* was indeed conceived for television, though *Death in Venice* is still more fluid in its dramatic structure. One important effect of this is to make it quite impossible for a production to use realistic sets, so that the work has to be seen as a projection of Aschenbach's own narratives. This infiltration of narrative into drama had occurred before, notably in *Billy Budd* and *The Turn of the Screw*, and it seems to have given Britten a way into his operas, a voice through which the music could be imagined. What is new in *Death in Venice* is the fact that the narrator is an artist, and that what he shows is Britten's own anguish at the difficulty of giving expression to beauty in a mistrustful age (colour plate 1).

All of Britten's operas after *Billy Budd* were written for the English Opera Group, and in most cases the roles were designed for particular singers, not least Peter Pears. His quite distinctive voice, itself suggesting a lyricism compromised by intellectual doubt, was the intended vehicle for a major role in every opera – Grimes, Captain Vere, Quint, the Madwoman in *Curlew River*, Aschenbach – to the extent that an important part of Britten's operatic world was his creation: it has proved difficult for later singers to avoid his particular vocal qualities. But Britten needed that stimulus. Those songs which were not designed for Pears (as most of them were) he composed for other specific singers, and most of his instrumental music was also addressed quite directly to the intended performers. The result was an output that includes very few works that do not contain the image of some musical personality other than the composer's own, which may be another expression of his insecurity. However, right at the end of his life, after *Death in Venice*, he produced a work which is partly a musical revisiting of the opera and the city, but which is also an essay in abstract form: his *Third String Quartet*★ (1975). In its five-movement form, and in some robust, ostinato-based treatment of the medium, this has connections with Bartók's quartets, but perhaps more important is its linking of hands with the very beginnings of the quartet tradition in early Haydn. For once, though, the past is seen not with regret but with a confidence in the possibility of continuation; it suggests an assurance that most of Britten's music had, very essentially, felt itself in need of.

Michael Tippett

Britten's self-doubt one must construe as more personally than professionally motivated, simply because during at least the first decade after the Second World War his supremacy in British music was complete. Nor is this just the view of hindsight. The fact that it was he who was chosen to compose an opera for the Coronation testifies to the esteem in which he was held even before he was forty; also noteworthy is the fact that few younger composers in that period were able to escape his influence. Even his elders were placed in the shade: the high reputation of Michael Tippett, for instance, is a phenomenon of the late 1960s, by which time he had been active as a composer for more than three decades.

Tippett's late arrival, however, was also innate. Born in London in 1905, he studied at the Royal College of Music between 1923 and 1928, but then went back to R.O. Morris for further instruction in 1930–2 and produced nothing he considered worthy of publication until the end of the decade: his Concerto for double string orchestra (1938–9) is his first work to have been published without revision, and nothing before his First String Quartet (1934–5) has appeared in print. Thus while Britten, nearly nine years younger, was making a name for himself through such works as his Sinfonietta (1932) and Christmas cantata *A Boy was Born* (1933), Tippett was living obscurely in the Surrey town of Oxted, teaching at a preparatory school and conducting the local choral society.

The choral work was important, for it encouraged, or perhaps only confirmed, a feeling for the sprung rhythms of English madrigals, and it also brought him into an active engagement with socialism, for from 1934 he conducted two choirs run by the Royal Arsenal Cooperative Society in south London. The madrigalian rhythms, involving syncopations and different kinds of propulsive movement in different simultaneous voices, became a distinguishing feature of his music of the late 1930s, allied with the influence of the neoclassical Stravinsky and Bartók. At the same time, his work for a broader musical society continued, and in 1940 he became director of music at Morley College, an institute for adult education in London. Also in that year he joined a pacifist organisation, the Peace Pledge Union, and in 1943 he spent two months in prison for refusing to undertake military service. By that time he had, too, come to public notice as a composer through performances of his oratorio *A Child of Our Time*★ (1939–41).

Despite the marked difference in their rates of musical development – Britten writing distinctive music in his middle teens, Tippett not until his mid-thirties – the two composers shared many musical assumptions: the central importance of Stravinsky, the continuing usefulness of the standard forms (oratorio, quartet, concerto), the vitality of the more distant English past (madrigals and Purcell, who was a model for both of them), which was much more important to them than the recent achievements of Elgar, Holst, Vaughan Williams and Delius. The essential difference in creative personality is that Tippett was always conscious of his role as an artist in society – as conscience, prophet, even therapist – whereas Britten's awareness was always most deeply of his separation. Hence Tippett's concern to work on his public through the public acts of oratorio and full-scale opera, in contrast with Britten's preference for the more intimate genres of chamber opera and song.

A Child of Our Time was the first of these public acts, very deliberately based on the public acts that Bach had provided for Leipzig in his Passions, but overlaying the implied original narrative with a modern story. The 'child of our time' is a Jewish boy who shot a Nazi diplomat in Paris, and thereby unwittingly unleashed a new outburst of persecution, though the work is concerned less with the events than with a commentary upon them. Tippett asked Eliot to write the text for the piece, but the poet advised him to undertake the task himself, and he followed that advice not only here but also in his subsequent operas. It was a problematic decision. Tippett's prose is awkward and unclear, and increasingly littered with undigested quotations and vernacular expressions; it is, in a word, incoherent. But the incoherence is functional, for the essential message of his works (and he is an artist very much concerned with messages) is that clear-cut answers can be of no value. One might have expected, for instance, that *A Child of Our Time*, composed at the height of the war by a composer of socialist sympathies, would be a diatribe against Nazism, but it is not: it reaches its culmination in the statement that the human individual must recognise the good and the evil within his or her own personality, and thereby move towards integration (Jung was an important influence on Tippett's thinking). Thus where Britten expresses a sense of alienation from past completeness, Tippett looks for a completeness to come, in entirely secular terms.

His solution to the problem of finding a secular replacement for Bach's chorales was startling, but also startlingly successful: negro spirituals serve the purpose, providing a warm musical grounding at regular intervals in the sequence of recitatives and arias. The choice was musically apt because of the connections through English folksong between the harmony of the spirituals and that of Tippett's own music. And it was psychologically right because spirituals too are concerned with a journey from present alienation to future integration. On yet another plane, it demonstrated that supposed cultural divisions – between high art and a popular tradition, Europe and American, white and black, contemporary and established, individual and communal – can be reconciled within a single work.

Before embarking on another grand statement of controlled heterogeneity, Tippett concentrated on developing the style of his works of the late 1930s, though with an increased lyricism that the oratorio seems to have released: there were two more string quartets (1941–2, 1945–6), a First Symphony (1944–5), choral pieces and a 'cantata' *Boyhood's End* (1943) for Britten and Pears, who at this time were beginning their distinguished career as recitalists, Britten as accompanist matching Pears in his fine musical sensitivity. Then in 1946 he began the process of stylistic expansion involved in the composition of *The Midsummer Marriage*,★ which took him until 1952 to complete. By then this restatement of Shakespearian (*A Midsummer Night's Dream*) and Mozartian (*The Magic Flute*) themes had acquired a range of reference that embraced the dream plays of Yeats and Shaw, the later poetry of Eliot, a vision of the human psyche taken from Jung, the previously acquired musical synthesis of seventeenth-century English and contemporary European styles, blues, and a new bounding movement that could keep its propulsive energy even through musical textures alive with decoration. This, and the luminous orchestration making such a feature of high woodwind and violins in their upper register, continued to course through the works that followed the opera, and that seem like satellites of it: the *Fantasia concertante on a Theme of Corelli*★ for string orchestra (1953), the Piano Concerto (1953–5) and the Second Symphony (1956–7).

A set by Barbara Hepworth for Michael Tippett's opera The Midsummer Marriage *(1955).*

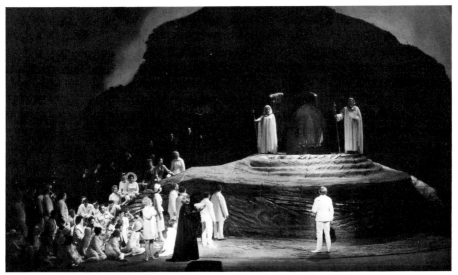

The Midsummer Marriage was presented for the first time in 1955, in a production designed by Barbara Hepworth, but its stylistic incongruities and its half-baked philosophising made more impression than its exuberant invention, and it was only after a BBC broadcast a decade later, followed by a commercial recording in 1970, that the opera began to be valued: this was, as has already been mentioned, the time when Tippett's music generally started to rise in general esteem. To some degree this must be because *The Midsummer Marriage* belongs more to the late 1960s than to the period of the Festival of Britain: its generosity, its optimism, its confidence in a community of spirit between male and female, European and Asian, above all its espousal of youth in opposition to age, these are all things that speak of the high summer of belief on the part of the post-war generation that they had inherited the earth and universal goodwill was about to break out. The opera is not, of course, without its conflicts: it is essentially a trial in which a young man and a young woman have to learn wholeness within themselves before they can achieve wholeness together. He, of the earth earthy, has to be awakened to the realm of mind; she, originally eschewing the bodily, has to reach a balance between the intellectual and the carnal. But conflict is less central to the piece than celebration, and the spiritual education of the young couple is carried out not in operatic argument so much as in balletic ceremony. Much of the second act is occupied by a sequence of 'ritual dances' in which the progress of the absent central pair is represented in metaphor. In that respect these dances are a metaphor within the metaphor, for the opera is placed not in any believable world but rather in a land of symbol developed from the many literary and musical influences on Tippett at this time.

After the great wave of *The Midsummer Marriage* had spent itself, in the late 1950s, Tippett found a much more hard-edged manner for his second opera, *King Priam* (1958–60). The change might be explained in terms of the new subject matter, for an opera dealing with the Trojan War plausibly demanded a starker style than had been fruitful for a mythical-pastoral fantasy set in the landscape of southern England. But it would be no less a simplification to suggest that the subject was prompted by the change in musical language: Tippett has even acknowledged that he was impressed at the time by the non-developing structures of the avant-garde, and his own practice has much in common with that of Messiaen in shuffling different blocks of musical material, each of the images clearly and sharply featured. Less easy to explain is the dramatic substance of the work. Tippett has said that it is about the nature of free will, but it is perhaps more deeply about the possibility of a modern musical style reinvoking the myths from the furthest recorded past of our civilisation. It is as if Tippett had realised that the nature of his musical style, at the stage it had now reached, was to connect more readily with myth than with the psychological drama that had still remained a part of *The Midsummer Marriage*.

Once again, a change of style heralded in an opera was continued in instrumental works, in this case the Second Piano Sonata (1962) and the Concerto for Orchestra (1962–3), and then taken to an ultimate in the complex cantata *The Vision of St Augustine* (1963–5), which suggests the compaction and ellipsis of a little-regarded artist talking to himself. But by the time he started work on his next opera, *The Knot Garden* (1966–9), Tippett's music was beginning to gain recognition, which may account for the greater openness and confidence of this work, and for its integration of the rapid cross-cutting of *King Priam* with the exuberant flow of *The Midsummer Marriage*, with which it may be compared as a modern morality. Again there are connections with Mozart (*Così fan tutte*) and Shakespeare (*The Tempest*), though the setting is more realistic than in *The Midsummer Marriage*: the opera takes place in a country house and garden, and it concerns the sorting out of amorous and sexual difficulties through play-acting. As in *A Child of Our Time*, black American music – now jazz and blues, associated particularly with the homosexual couple Dov and Mel – suggests an immediacy and groundedness of feeling which is the goal of the whole enterprise. And there is similarly a movement towards the blues as fulfilment in Tippett's Third Symphony (1970–2: here a soprano blues in the finale answers the disruptive fanfare taken over from Beethoven's Ninth Symphony) and in his fourth opera *The Ice Break* (1973–6), which is a global counterpart to the domestic *Knot Garden*, intent on exposing and resolving, within three very short acts, conflicts not only between individuals but also between races, generations and political groupings.

The ability to write *The Ice Break* could perhaps only come from Tippett's awareness of his social mission and from the recent demonstration, through the great upsurge of enthusiasm for his music around 1970, that his voice was being heard. His subsequent music has gone on in that assurance. The Third and Fourth Piano Sonatas (1972–3, 1984) and the Fourth String Quartet (1977–9) are quite consciously placed within the genres that Beethoven pursued in his last years, but Tippett has also continued to exert himself as a composer more publicly. His Fourth Symphony⋆ (1976–7) draws on the orchestral method of the two preceding operas, developing a continuity that can accommodate extreme change of motif and texture, while the Concerto for string trio and orchestra (1979) reintroduces whole the lyricism of *The Midsummer Marriage*, preparing for the oratorio *The Mask of Time* (1977–82), which in its multifarious literary and musical borrowings, and in its conviction, is Tippett's summa.

Around Britten and Tippett

From the perspective of the 1980s, the pre-eminence of Britten and Tippett among British composers of their generation seems absolute, but the relatively late acceptance of Tippett as a major master must be a warning that valuations may change; and in any event, at least a brief survey of other composers is necessary in order to give some impression of the rich texture of British music in the 1950s and 1960s. To accept an easy division, those composers may be grouped as conservatives and radicals: the success of Britten and Tippett may not be unrelated to the ability they showed to overcome that division, and to draw radical tendencies into an essentially conservative language, the language of major-minor tonality voiced in the established genres of opera, song, symphony and string quartet.

Among those who were more fixedly traditionalist in their outlook, Edmund Rubbra stands out as the major continuer of the symphonic ideal represented in the previous generation by Bax and Vaughan Williams. He followed the latter in his closeness to the music of the English sixteenth century, but not in any reverence for folksong: the modal character of his music seems to have come rather from plainsong, perhaps particularly after his conversion to Roman Catholicism in 1948. His works include masses and motets, and the ninth of his eleven symphonies is a *Sinfonia sacra* on the Resurrection, with soloists and chorus (1972–3). Polyphony is also an important feature, and sharply distinguishes his style from that of Vaughan Williams. His symphonies are pervasively polyphonic – the term 'orchestral motet' has been applied, not at all inappropriately – and his feeling for intensive counterpoint in ample harmony also informs his cycle of four string quartets.

Rubbra's Catholicism is a link with Lennox Berkeley, though Berkeley's background was from the first more international: unlike Rubbra, who studied with Holst, he was a pupil of Nadia Boulanger in Paris (1927–32), and gained from her the usual veneration for the neoclassical Stravinsky and Fauré. Following that direction, his association with Britten in the 1930s was perhaps inevitable, and the two composers were even able to collaborate on an orchestral suite, *Mont Juic* (1937). Berkeley was also close to Britten in his operas, which include the full-length *Nelson* (1953) and three smaller works written for the English Opera Group. But he retained a francophone insouciance (Poulenc is the obvious comparable figure, in terms both of polished irony and religious devotion), so that there was no connection with the more deeply troubled areas in Britten's musical personality. His output includes symphonies and much chamber music, though the more frequently performed works are religious: masses, other liturgical pieces and a set of *Four Poems of St Teresa of Avila* for contralto and string orchestra (1947).

Within this sphere of unproblematic tonal composition, Alan Rawsthorne may represent a midpoint between Berkeley's wit and Walton's opulence. In 1930–2 he studied in Europe with Egon Petri, which brought him into contact with the music of Busoni, and more decisively that of Hindemith (his contemporary Arnold Cooke, born in 1906, was the only English composer actually to study with Hindemith). Like Tippett, he made a late and hesitant start as a composer, and most of his output, which consists principally of orchestral works and chamber music, dates from after 1945, from a period when, briefly as it turned out, there seemed the real possibility of a fluent, abstract, neoclassical style of English composition in a Hindemithian mould. Tippett might have been the leader of that school if he had not been distrained by the very non-abstract aims of *The Midsummer Marriage*. Peter Racine Fricker, his successor at Morley College, for a while took the Hindemithian style to its most dissonant extreme, accepting the influences of Berg and Schoenberg in his works of the late 1940s and early 1950s, when one of his leading colleagues in this direction was Iain Hamilton. But in the early 1960s both Fricker and Hamilton left for the United States, as part of the then much-debated 'brain drain', Hamilton going to Duke University in

North Carolina in 1961 and Fricker to the University of California at Santa Barbara in 1964. Even before then, both had become more conservative figures, and certainly that has been Hamilton's role in his major works presented in the 1970s and 1980s, many of which have been full-scale operas (*The Catiline Conspiracy*, staged by Scottish Opera in 1974; *The Royal Hunt of the Sun*, staged by the English National Opera in 1977, with *Anna Karenina* following from the same company in 1981).

The loss of emigrants was countered by the influx of musicians who had fled from Nazism in the 1930s, or who arrived as students and remained. Among the former group, mention has already been made of Wellesz and Gerhard; others included the Hungarian composer Mátyás Seiber, who was a pupil of Kodály, but whose wide-ranging interests also included Schoenbergian serialism and jazz. Along with Tippett and later Fricker, he was one of the composers who made Morley College a spearhead of radicalism in the late 1940s and 1950s: he had arrived in England in 1935, and joined the college seven years later. He was highly influential there as a teacher, his pupils including Hugh Wood and Anthony Milner, but he made no strenuous efforts to promote his compositions, which include three string quartets and two cantatas on passages from novels by Joyce (*Ulysses*, 1946–7; *Three Fragments from 'Portrait of the Artist as a Young Man'*, 1956–7). His main value, perhaps, was that he awakened a Schoenbergian conscience in British music: a respect for the high Austro-German tradition, a rigorous self-criticism in the pursuit of musical truth. In that respect his work was shared and continued by a man who was not a composer, but who probably had more influence on British composers than any other single person: Hans Keller. Born in Vienna, he too arrived in England as a refugee from Nazism, in 1938, and from 1949 to 1979 he worked for the BBC, while also exerting a strong influence through his essays, his coaching of string quartets and his personal contacts with composers, from Britten (whose Third Quartet, partly stimulated by discussions with him, was dedicated to him) to those of the youngest generation.

Egon Wellesz came from the same Viennese background, but was much less publicly active, working in Oxford as a student of Byzantine chant and a composer of symphonies, string quartets and other works which suggest Bruckner as much as his teacher Schoenberg: he felt no compunction about returning to tonal harmony, though Schoenberg's insistence on active polyphony remained with him. Curiously, Roberto Gerhard, the other Schoenberg pupil resident in England, though at Cambridge, moved in precisely the opposite direction. Around the time of his studies with Schoenberg, in the 1920s, he had written twelve-note pieces, but after his arrival in England, in 1940, he wrote in a widely varied but fundamentally tonal, neoclassical and decidedly Spanish style, his major work of this period being an operatic setting of Sheridan's *The Duenna*, broadcast by the BBC in 1949. Then during the next decade, principally in his first two symphonies (1952–3 and 1959) and his First String Quartet (1955–6), he returned more intensively to the twelve-note serial method and to traditional large-scale instrumental movements, though with the direction conveyed less by thematic development than by rhythmic vigour, brilliant variety of colour and perpetual evolution of the serial note groupings.

Gerhard's flair for colour led him to take an interest in electronic music long before most serious composers in Great Britain. In 1954 he began using his own equipment in the composition of incidental music for the theatre, radio and films, and he was one of the first to work at the Radiophonic Workshop set up by the BBC in 1956. Rather oddly, the Workshop did not attract the many younger composers who were then emerging – quite in contrast to what was happening in France, Germany and Italy, where avant-garde musicians found a natural home in electronic music studios established by broadcasting authorities. Instead the Radiophonic Workshop was almost exclusively devoted to the production of signature tunes and incidental music for radio and television programmes, and Gerhard's electronic pieces – including tape compositions like *Audiomobile 2 DNA* (1963) and also his Third Symphony (1960), which brings orchestra and tape together – remained isolated in English music until younger composers, notably Harrison Birtwistle and Jonathan Harvey, began to work with electronic means a decade later. Gerhard himself, too, preferred more normal resources in the energetic music of his last decade, which includes a Concerto for Orchestra (1965) and a Fourth Symphony (1967), as well as the beginnings of a cycle of chamber pieces based on signs of the zodiac: *Gemini* for violin and piano (1966), *Libra* for sextet (1968) and *Leo* for decet (1969). Like Tippett and Britten during this period, Gerhard was influenced by younger composers (his Second String Quartet of 1960–2 rivals Penderecki in its range of playing techniques) and encouraged to play a prominent part in the most optimistically avant-garde phase that British music has known.

Among those who came to England as students rather than as established musicians, the Natal-born Priaulx Rainier arrived in 1920 as a violinist and only began to concentrate on composition after a period of study with Boulanger just before the war. Unlike Berkeley, however, she was led to admire more the rhythmically dynamic than the classical aspects of Stravinsky, and she also developed a denser harmonic style, more in the region of Hindemith and Bartók: her *Barbaric Dance Suite* for piano (1949) and other works of that period placed her with Fricker and Hamilton in the forefront of what seemed a new beginning in British music.

That new beginning was not, however, entirely a post-1945 phenomenon, nor was it entirely dependent on immigrant impetus, for there was a home-grown radicalism that had its origins in the 1930s. At that deeply conservative moment in established British culture, it was enough for Britten to emulate Stravinsky in order to be shocking, and yet the BBC was making it possible for Schoenberg and Webern to visit London and conduct their works. Inevitably something of the experience rubbed off, not least on Elisabeth Lutyens, daughter of the architect and wife of Edward Clark, who was responsible for inviting Schoenberg and his more radical pupil Webern to the BBC. She was almost certainly the first British composer to write twelve-note serial music, which she did in her Chamber Concerto no. 1 for nonet (1939), a work of mollified Webernian style. Out of this came, particularly in the 1960s and 1970s, a vast output, embracing several operas, orchestral works, chamber pieces and much vocal music, particularly in the form of cycles or cantatas for one or more voices with instrumental ensemble. Her influence during that period, through example and through teaching (her pupils included Robert Saxton), was immense: like Gerhard, she suddenly, after a period of struggle, neglect and indecision, found the musical current moving with her, and responded productively.

Humphrey Searle was the only other native-born English composer of this generation to embrace serialism as a strong item of musical belief. He had studied with Webern in Vienna in 1937–8, but only after the war did he start using the serial technique, at first in a distinctly Webernian manner. He soon came, however, much closer to Schoenberg and Berg in his works of the 1950s and 1960s, which include five symphonies, a piano sonata and three operas: *The Diary of a Madman* (1958), *The Photo of the Colonel* (1964) and *Hamlet* (1965–8). His choice of this last, almost excessively well-known play testifies to something quixotic in his musical personality, and it is noteworthy that he did not share Lutyens's and Gerhard's enthusiasm for the musical tide of the 1960s but was at his most creative under the much less propitious circumstances of the 1950s.

Though he was never quite a serial composer, Alan Bush (b.1900) claims a place among the radicals of this generation by virtue of such pieces as his *Dialectic* for string quartet (1929). But as the title of that work may imply, his vision of musical radicalism was as a corollary of political radicalism, as indeed it was for other composers at the time, not only abroad (Kurt Weill was an exact contemporary) but also in England: Tippett's connections with left-wing institutions (among which Morley College must be counted in a William Morris kind of way) have already been mentioned, and the pacifism expressed by both Tippett and Britten in the 1930s may be seen as the political component in an anti-establishment stance that went deep into their music. Bush's political engagement, however, was more actively partisan and unshakeable. His admiration for Soviet-style communism was not diminished by the revelations about Stalin's rule, nor by the events of 1956 and 1968, and he has followed in his music a brand of socialist realism, writing symphonies and operas with a social message in a supposedly widely communicable tonal language. All of his operas – *Wat Tyler* (1948–50), *Men of Blackmoor* (1954–5), *The Sugar Reapers* (1961–4) and *Joe Hill* (1965–8) – had their first performances in the German Democratic Republic.

A commitment to tonality, however, may not be motivated by political considerations, as in Bush, or encouraged by religious belief, as in Rubbra and Berkeley: it may be stirred quite simply by a conviction that tonality is essential to musical coherence and expression. That, in essence, is the view of Robert Simpson, who has been remarkably uninfluenced by any music later than Nielsen. His command of a language of long-range harmonic progression and conflict is compelling, and not unworthy of the tradition in which he sets himself: that of Beethoven, Bruckner and Nielsen most especially (he has written with close insight on all three composers). For most of his life, until around 1980, his music was neglected, though he had a vigorous career at the BBC, where he was largely responsible for the revaluation of another tonal symphonist, Havergal Brian. However, in the light of his pursuit, in the symphonies and string quartets that are his almost exclusive works, of tonal ideals at odds with the prevailing climate, it may be that his music represents the period's real avant-garde.

The generation of the thirties

The arrival of an avant-garde of the more usual sort, however, has generally been placed in Manchester in the mid-1950s, among a group of students which included three composers who were to dominate British music in the generation after Britten and Tippett: Harrison Birtwistle, Peter Maxwell Davies and Alexander Goehr. The direction they took was facilitated by their teacher at the Royal Manchester College of Music, Richard Hall, who was a retiring figure as a composer, though radical in the kind of music he produced, suggesting what Bax might have done had he followed his intention of studying with Schoenberg: his symphonies, piano concerto and string quartet combine some elements of twelve-note serialism with an Englishly modal style. But just as important was Goehr's personal background. His father Walter Goehr was another of the musicians who arrived in England after the rise of Hitler: he was a pupil of Schoenberg who emigrated in 1933 (Alexander had been born in Berlin) and worked as a conductor and composer, also being associated with Morley College, so that his son grew up in an atmosphere where both Tippett and (spiritually) Schoenberg were familiar presences; and it was this combination of English tradition with Continental revolution that was to prove decisive for the 'Manchester group'.

The three composers were together in Manchester during the years 1952–5, and together they studied the few European avant-garde scores that were then available: the first book of Pierre Boulez' *Structures* for two pianos, notable for applying rules of serial construction to aspects of rhythm, loudness and attack as well as pitch, Karlheinz Stockhausen's *Kontra-Punkte*, a few works by Luigi Nono. They also studied Indian music, and medieval music, particularly English medieval music, which appeared to connect with the newest music from Europe in suggesting calculated principles of composition being used independently of 'logical' harmonic progression in the post-Renaissance sense. Goehr's orchestral *Fantasia* (1954), which used modern methods of construction along with a medieval polyphonic technique (that of the 'cantus firmus', where a basic melody proceeds through the piece in long note values), influenced the development of the whole group, and opened the door to Davies's continuing absorption in syntheses and dichotomies of medieval and modern.

From Manchester Goehr went to Paris to study with Messiaen (1955–6), as both Boulez and Stockhausen had done, while Davies went to Rome for lessons with Petrassi (1957–9) and Birtwistle, in many ways the most English composer of the three, remained at home. He was also slower than the others to make a mark. His first published composition, *Refrains and Choruses* for wind quintet, dates from 1957, and it was only with the decet *Tragoedia* (1965) that he emerged in full force, by which time both Goehr and Davies had achieved a degree of prominence, even notoriety. Goehr accepted the equation between artistic and political radicalism, and wielded a language of Schoenbergian expressive ferocity in his early cantatas *The Deluge* (1957–8) and *Sutter's Gold* (1959–60). Davies's art was from the first more private (a comparison with the Tippett–Britten antinomy suggests itself), but similar artistic premises, and most notably a similar feeling for Schoenberg, brought him to a style interleaving unquiet contemplations with rages of the most extreme harmonic tension, the style of such works as his Trumpet Sonata (1955), Five Piano Pieces (1955–6), *Alma redemptoris mater* for wind sextet (1957) and *St Michael* for orchestral woodwind and brass (1957). Both composers were rapidly given platforms at the major festivals, and promoted by the BBC, especially after Glock's providential assumption of musical authority there in 1959. The premières of *St Michael* at Cheltenham in 1959 and of *Sutter's Gold* at Leeds in 1961 provoked outrage, one of the inevitable qualifications of an avant-garde, and so distinguished the two composers' arrival.

From this point their paths were a little too different to be followed together. Goehr took a post as producer at the BBC (1960–8) and then began a career as a University teacher, culminating in his appointment as Professor of Music at Cambridge in 1976. The move into academic life might appear the retreat of one who had in his music since the early 1960s been exploring the possibilities of re-engagement with sonata form, but his output of symphonies, quartets, fugues and chaconnes is done with a degree of irony, motivated not only by a profound, very Schoenbergian feeling that the achievements of the main Austro-Germany tradition offer a measure of musical value, but also by a pleasure in the exercise of craft. And even though Schoenberg has remained very much his musical godfather, some of his most seemingly conventional works, like the Little Symphony (1963), or the Symphony in One Movement★ (1969–70), or the Third String Quartet (1975–6), do not sound at all like re-tellings of familiar stories but rather impress with their individuality, which may be granted in part by an understanding of serialism that allows some notes to be more equal than others conveying some sense of a new consonance, rather in the manner of George Perle's twelve-tone modality. Also, Goehr has continued to produce works which, like *Pastorals* (1965) and the *Deux Etudes★* (1981), both for orchestra, are more freely formed.

The tension between the spontaneous act and the conventional response is one that underlies all his music, and that comes to the surface dramatically in the confrontation between individual and society in his operatic works. The full-length opera *Arden Must Die*, first produced by the Hamburg Staatsoper in 1967, is an adaptation of the anonymous Elizabethan tragedy *Arden of Faversham*, which becomes a Brechtian morality in the rhyming couplets of the librettist Erich Fried (these also bring Goehr's music into the region of Weill and Eisler, especially where musical distortion and stylistic parody are used to suggest the dishonesty of the characters). *Naboth's Vineyard* (1968) is a biblical allegory along the same lines, though taking note also of *Curlew River* in its allusion to the Noh drama, for which Goehr discovers a Western equivalent not in medieval ecclesiastical practice but rather in Monteverdi's *Il combattimento di Tancredi a Clorinda* (his interest in that work also gave rise to a 'paraphrase' on it for solo clarinet in 1969). Like Britten, Goehr followed one innovatory work with two more to make a triptych, these successors being *Shadowplay* (1970), on the distinction of imagination from reality, and *Sonata about Jerusalem* (1970), which treats a Jewish story of people deluded by the promises of a false messiah. This leads directly on to his second large-scale opera, *Behold the Sun*, which again was written for a German house, having its première at Duisburg in 1985. The plot concerns the Anabaptists and their dream of creating a heaven on earth, but the allegory widens to embrace both earlier and later dreams of revolution: much of the choral music comes straight from the cantata *Babylon the Great is Fallen* (1979), which concerns the vision of Jewish nationhood, and there are implicit connections not only with the contemporary Near East but also with the continuing dialectic between revolution and progressivism in left-wing European politics. If Goehr's varied output has any single thrust, it is to claim that both are vital, the new dream and the reverence for the old.

Davies's music suggests compromises of a much more uneasy sort. On his return from Italy he took his post as director of music at Cirencester Grammar School, and he has admitted to learning much there, not only about the provision of music to children but also about more fundamental questions of practicability and communication. Yet though his music became less complicated in its surface detail and more obviously expressive, it hardly became more comfortable. *O Magnum Mysterium*⋆ (1960) indicates one reason why. Skilfully devised as a school Christmas entertainment that will not embarrass the thoughtful adult, it offers musical experiences at four levels: a carol tune sung by a solo voice, the same tune and others in harmonised settings, instrumental meditations for a modest school orchestra, and finally an organ fantasia requiring considerable expertise. But all the music is by Davies, and all of it is audibly based on the substance of the opening carol tune, in a tritone-laden modal style relating at once to medieval English music and to the more recent past of Stravinsky's sacred choruses. The implication is of a steadily more intense contemplation of the same 'great mystery' of the Nativity, which of necessity moves from the ready acceptance of childhood to the doubt, turmoil of questioning and negation of a modern adult mind.

Much of Davies's later music is religious, including most definitely the cycle of works on the Henrician composer John Taverner, whose setting of the 'In Nomine' section from the Benedictus in his *Gloria Tibi Trinitas* mass became the subject and stimulus for polyphonic inventions by composers up to and including Purcell. Davies's contributions to this same genre include the seven *In Nomine* for ten instruments (1963–4), mixing original movements with arrangements of the Taverner and later sixteenth-century pieces, two orchestral fantasias on the Taverner *In Nomine* (1962 and 1964) and the opera *Taverner*⋆ (1962–8). Of course, Davies was attracted to the subject by the historical precedents for composing *In Nomine*, but no less important was what was then believed (it has since been set in doubt) of Taverner's life. The story was that he had been a great servant of the church in his activity as a composer of masses and antiphons – the greatest English composer in the period immediately before Tallis – but that he had then been converted to the Reformed faith, renounced music and become a systematic persecutor of the old religion. Davies's opera is, on one level, a study in the perception of religious truth, the differentiation between truth and fantasy, the role of music in presenting and perhaps inevitably distorting accepted statements of belief. But it is most essentially concerned with the personality of its central character, with his conversion as a delusion and shockingly destructive distraction of himself from what he was most positively: a composer.

The agent of that delusion and distraction is Death, who is quite clearly a projection within Taverner's mind (where most of the action takes place) of its most urgently self-destructive components; and the means by which Death operates are those of parody, with parody piled on parody until the composer-hero cannot distinguish truth from falsehood. He accepts what seems the firmest certainty he is offered, the sword of the persecutor, and willingly abjures the comparative complications of musical compositions. As much as *Behold the Sun*, or indeed Schoenberg's *Moses und Aron*, the work is a terrible warning against the easy answer in a time of doubt, but it is also a personal testament from a composer whose very facility – in particular, his ability to imitate and to devise transformations of shape and style – must have led him to doubt what was real in his own creativity. And, on a yet broader plane of morality, it asks how anyone in the late twentieth century, when no absolute remains, can discern a correct or authentic course of action.

It is inevitable that parody should run deep through the substance of the opera, and that the second act, after Taverner's abysmal conversion, should be a barbaric parody of the Schoenbergian first. It is a much blacker parody than Britten's, as black and as bleak as Mahler's, and it gave Davies entry to a world of expressionist violence that might have seemed to belong exclusively to the Vienna of Mahler's later symphonies and Schoenberg's *Pierrot lunaire*. To risk a nearer approach to that world might have been dangerous for what remained of Davies's certainty of himself as a composer, but apparently it was Harrison Birtwistle's idea that the two of them should collaborate in setting up and directing a new ensemble, the Pierrot Players, to consist of the personnel required for the Schoenberg work with the addition of a percussionist. Both men had by this time gone to Princeton for further periods of study, Davies in 1962–4 and Birtwistle in 1966; both, too, had used the opportunity to get on with their operas, Davies writing much of *Taverner* there and Birtwistle working on *Punch and Judy*. From the first, the Pierrot Players were intended to have a repertory of smaller theatrical pieces that could be played in concert halls and toured (twenty years before this had been the same intention for the English Opera Group). On 30 May 1967, in the Queen Elizabeth Hall in London, the group appeared for the first time, when Davies provided the overture (*Antechrist*) and Birtwistle the dramatic work (*Monodrama*). That piece, however, was soon withdrawn, and within three years the Pierrot Players' repertory had become thoroughly dominated by Davies's works of music-theatre, including most notably the mad scene *Eight Songs for a Mad King* (1969) and the exploration of the Stations of the Cross for nude dancer, solo cellist and ensemble, *Vesalii Icones*★ (1969). In 1970 Birtwistle accordingly left the organisation and the group was immediately re-formed as the Fires of London under Davies's sole direction.

Davies's works of this period, which include also a George Trakl setting for screaming nun and weird orchestra (*Revelation and Fall*, 1966) and a rejigging of chamber pieces by Purcell for strident ensemble in foxtrot style (*Fantasia* and *Two Pavans*, 1968), are plainly intended to shock, though what is most shocking about them is their evidence of creative hysteria. He has described his immense orchestral adagio *Worldes Blis** (1966–9) as an attempt to collect the fragments of his creative personality, though the work makes an impression much more of expectation than of achievement, and the later settling of his musical style remains controversial. At the beginning of the 1970s he took up residence on the island of Hoy in Orkney, and almost at once his music became on the surface more calm. The best of his later dramatic works for the Fires of London is a benign comedy, *Le Jongleur de Notre Dame* (1978), whereas those that attempt a return to expressionism cannot match the intensity and savage daring of *Eight Songs for a Mad King* and *Vesalii Icones*. And on the instrumental plane, he turned from foxtrot parodies (*St Thomas Wake* of 1969 is the most frenetic and developed piece in that style, subjecting a keyboard piece by John Bull to the attentions of a thirties band and a symphony orchestra) to symphonies and sonatas. With the image of Sibelius replacing that of Mahler in the background, his three symphonies (1973–6, 1980, 1984) are progressively more stable and secure in form and even in tonality, achieving, as a logical consequence of his earliest music, a modal understanding of major and minor keys that can produce a near consonance that is still utterly fresh: the scherzo of the Second Symphony is the most striking case. But while Davies's success in making new contributions within the canons of convention has been praised, and even while his wild excursions from the canons (most amusingly in the *Sinfonietta Accademica* for chamber orchestra of 1983) have been noted, it is still his music of the *Taverner* and immediate post-*Taverner* period that arouses most attention.

This may be partly because the very size of his subsequent output has blunted its impact: apart from the symphonies and the trilogy of chamber symphonies to which the *Sinfonietta accademica* belongs, his works since the move to Orkney include a church opera (*The Martyrdom of Saint Magnus*, 1976), a chamber opera (*The Lighthouse*, 1979) and three music-theatre pieces, a full-length symphonic ballet (*Salome*, 1978), a song-symphony (*Black Pentecost*, 1979), a violin concerto (1985), two works of string-quartet-like density for the instrumentalists of the Fires (*Ave Maris Stella*, 1975; *Image-Reflection-Shadow*, 1982), a brass quintet (1981), a substantial piano sonata (1980–81) and much else. In addition, he has vigorously exerted himself as a composer in the community, directing an annual arts festival in Orkney from 1977 to 1986 (the St Magnus Festival) and composing operas and other works for local school and amateur forces.

Birtwistle's activities, by contrast, have been modest, and his whole reputation rests on no more than a dozen major works: two operas (*Punch and Judy**, 1966–7; *The Mask of Orpheus**, 1973–83), two music-theatre pieces (*Down by the Greenwood Side*, 1969, *Bow Down*, 1977), two works for large orchestra (*The Triumph of Time**, 1972, *Earth Dances**, 1985), a composition for voices and instruments on fragments of Sappho

(. . . *agm* . . ., 1978–9) and a sequence of pieces for the London Sinfonietta (*Verses for Ensembles**, 1969; *Meridian*, 1970–1; *Silbury Air*, 1977; *Carmen Arcadiae Mechanicae Perpetuum*, 1977; *Secret Theatre*, 1984), the work of which organisation merits a parenthesis. Founded in 1968 by the conductor David Atherton and administrator Nicholas Snowman, its programme was similar to that of Boulez' Domaine Musical in Paris: to provide an alternative chamber orchestral repertory, playing neglected music of the past (this was soon dropped, in both cases), classics of the twentieth century and new works by native and foreign composers, often with the composers themselves directing. The Sinfonietta, maintaining performance standards that brought it international acclaim, has presented music by Stockhausen and Carter, Boulez and Tippett, Kagel and Berio, Ligeti and Henze, besides providing an important impetus to British composers of the Goehr-Davies-Birtwistle and subsequent generations. And where the Fires of London became inextricably linked with the music of just one composer (though they have performed new works by many others), the Sinfonietta, being larger and more adaptable, has provided a broader platform.

Otherwise it could not have gone on attracting the attention of a composer as unwilling as Birtwistle to address the same issues in the same way twice, despite the fact that his musical personality has an integration that again compels contrast with Davies. The sources of that personality are not hard to discover: they lie in the more austere, ceremonial and fractured music of Stravinsky, whose Symphonies of Wind Instruments is a work of proto-Birtwistle; in similar indications in Varèse and Messiaen; and in a feeling for the theatre of the musical act and the myth of its constant reproduction (the score as playscript, the score as notation of a legend to be heard again and again). But the meaning of Birtwistle's personality is extraordinarily elusive. In a time when nearly all composers have felt it necessary to offer their compositions along with an implicit or even explicit ideological programme, offer them as instances of some more general type (serial compositions, tonal compositions, sonata forms, political cantatas or whatever), Birtwistle's music exemplifies nothing but itself and retains an essential mystery. And it may be that mystery which leaves it capable both of a theatrical boldness (felt directly because it is unexplained) and of an entrance into the world of myth.

The theatre of his orchestral works may be a suggested theatre of sounding gesture: the repeated calls of the soprano saxophone along the length of *The Triumph of Time*, for instance, or the ticking clocks of percussion and the lumbering fanfares that recur from work to work (this presence of the same idea, sometimes quite precisely the same idea, in different works is one feature of his artistic wholeness: it may even appear that each work is a different view of the same landscape). Or it may be theatre indeed. *Verses for Ensembles* makes the concert platform into a stage for a play without words, with different levels for the different ensembles of wind and percussion, and separate stations to be taken up by a pair of trumpeters and by woodwind soloists at special moments. *Secret Theatre*, a little less ambitiously, distinguishes between a solo line and an accompanying texture by having the players of the former (who may number up to five) stand at one side, so that the structure is graphically displayed.

The converse of this is that in Birtwistle's stage works the action is just as musical as what happens in the pit. Both *Punch and Judy* and *The Mask of Orpheus* are dramas of repetition, where events take place over and over again but never twice in the same way, just as Birtwistle's music is often based on different levels, some simultaneous and some successive, of varied ostinato. In the first opera the fundamental story is adapted from traditional puppet shows in a characteristic return to cultural material known before the age of understanding: the original shows are intended for young children, and they appear to date back to the medieval childhood of western culture. The repeated events in the opera are Punch's frustrated quest for Pretty Polly and his murder of a father figure. A psychological explanation might suggest that Punch is a dramatisation of infant mentality in Freud's view of it as actively sexual and murderous and there is a plausible element of that in the violence of some of the instrument writing. But such an explanation does not get near the cyclical character of the opera, which makes it as much a ritual of the seasons (which the much simpler *Down by the Greenwood Side* quite clearly is) and a projection of the working of memory.

The Mask of Orpheus is more outspokenly about the memory of its own subject matter, for it is a tangle of tellings of the most venerable operatic myth, not quoting from Monteverdi, Gluck and the rest, but contributing a late twentieth-century view, in which different accounts of events are sung, mimed and acted in a complex of simultaneous alternatives, successive changings and interleaved allusions. Each of the central characters has three incarnations on stage, and sometimes all three are present; there are also mimed enactments of other, related myths, taking place to the electronic music that is one of the most inventive features of an abundantly rich score that otherwise emphasises wind and percussion. It is the increasing knottedness and complexity of the skein of stories that provides the opera's dynamic, not any particular narrative, and so the work discovers a means of providing a coherent theatrical experience without the equation between narrative and harmonic progression through which the birth of opera had been possible, and to which it has almost always seemed indissolubly linked.

The achievements of Birtwistle, Davies and Goehr have kept them at the apex of British music throughout a period of three decades, overshadowing others of their generation. But it was not always so. Richard Rodney Bennett made his name as a modernist prodigy while he was in his teens, before anyone had heard of the Manchester composers, and he went to Paris to study not with Messiaen but, more radically with Boulez, in 1957–8. Not surprisingly, he caught something of Boulez' avant-garde fervour at the time, but the history of his subsequent output is almost emblematically the history of the response of British culture to foreign innovation: it is a history of compromise. Berg (and indeed Cole Porter in his lighter music) soon became more important to him than Boulez, and his most important works are concertos, a wide variety of vocal pieces, and expressionist operas, among which *The Mines of Sulphur* (1963) was written for Sadler's Wells Opera and *Victory* (1968–9) for Covent Garden.

If foreign study marked Bennett's music only ephemerally, it was much more important for his contemporaries David Blake and Cornelius

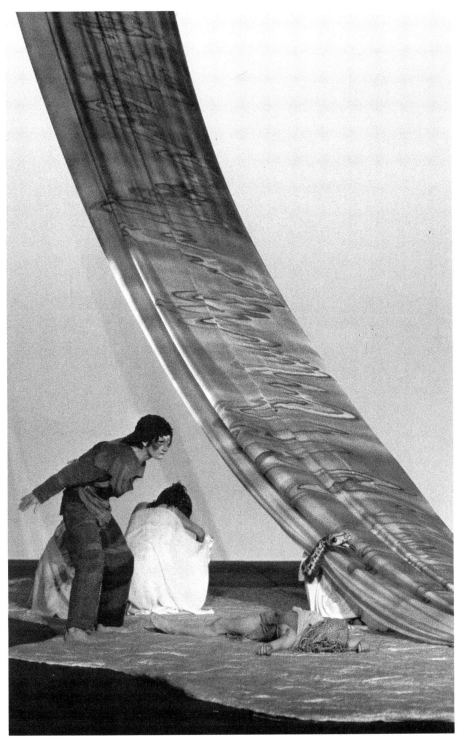

The world premiere of Harrison Birtwistle's opera The Mask of Orpheus, *staged by English National Opera in May, 1986.*

Cardew, both of whom went to Germany, though to very different composers: Hanns Eisler and Karlheinz Stockhausen respectively. Blake accepted from Eisler both a Schoenbergian inheritance and a political conscience, expressed in his opera *Toussaint* (1977) and in his more numerous chamber works. He has also been himself a respected teacher, following Wilfrid Mellers as professor at York University in 1979 – and here one may note the importance of university music departments in British music since the 1960s. Before that time, university music meant essentially performance and musicology: none of the important composers of the Britten–Tippett generation, for instance, was a university graduate. But Mellers established the York department in 1964 after the pattern of music faculties at American universities, with an emphasis on composition, and he attracted composers to the staff: David Blake (from 1964), the Messiaen pupil Robert Sherlaw Johnson (1965–71) and the Berio pupil Bernard Rands (from 1974). The Cambridge department under Goehr also took a turn towards encouraging composition, and by the late 1970s most university music faculties had a prominent composer on the staff, which had not at all been the case before Mellers' pioneering work at York: a decade later Fricker and Hamilton would hardly have needed to emigrate in order to secure academic posts.

Cardew was not a composer of that kind. While Goehr, Davies and Birtwistle were at the Royal Manchester College, he and Bennett were studying at the Royal Academy of Music in London and following similar enthusiasms: hence their departure to study with Stockhausen and Boulez respectively. But where Bennett became a more conservative artist, Cardew grew more radical than his teacher. He remained in Cologne from 1958 to 1961, and during that period he was Stockhausen's assistant in the composition of *Carré* for four vocal-instrumental groups (1959–60) as well as his pupil; but his musical aims, partly incorporated within the substance of *Carré*, were moving towards the intentionlessness and spareness of Cage. Alone among British composers, he took part in the European avant-garde movement around 1960 towards the introduction of large degrees of choice and chance into musical performance (*Two Books of Study for Pianists*, 1958; *Autumn '60* and *Octet '61* for any instruments). Back in London he produced two enormous works in which conventional notation is replaced by graphic designs and verbal instructions (*Treatise*, 1963–7; *The Great Learning*, 1968–70); he also, in the second half of the 1960s, played improvised music with the ensemble AMM, and was a highly effective spokesman on behalf of 'experimental' music, i.e. music which broke away from the professionalism and insistence on tradition implicit in the avant-garde. The distinction between iconoclasts and progressives, anarchists and reformers, is an old one, and for a time around 1970 it seemed that British music had separated into such camps, the one occupied by Cardew and younger composers like Gavin Bryars, the other held most prominently by the 'Manchester group'.

In 1969 – that extraordinary year of *Verses for Ensembles, Eight Songs for a Mad King, Vesalii Icones* and *Worldes Blis* – English experimentalism too reached its apogee with the foundation of the Scratch Orchestra, a loose assembly of composers and performers for whom musical talent in traditional terms was not a criterion. The Scratch Orchestra was set up as an anarchist collective, in which, nominally, all members were free to present compositions and improvisations, but the organisational vacuum was soon filled by a swing towards Maoism: in 1971 the association took on an overtly political character, and Cardew took to emulating Chinese composers in seeking a political correctness within his music. That meant a return to tonality, often of folksong style, and the setting of exhortatory texts; it also meant a repudiation of all his earlier music, and of that of Stockhausen and Cage on which his previous positions had been based. His works of this period include protest songs and sets of piano variations on political themes, but also an extraordinary book, *Stockhausen Serves Imperialism* (1974).

But Cardew's lonely path of abnegation and revolt was not the only English reaction to Stockhausen. Jonathan Harvey found rather enrichment in discovering both Stockhausen and Davies from the point of view of a Britten-influenced insularity, and the result in his music of the 1960s was a switchback of styles, sometimes within the same work. But in 1969–70 he went to Princeton to study with Babbitt, and was much more impressed by what he found there than Davies and Birtwistle had been just a few years before. Babbitt-style serialism gave him the means to integrate the widely spread elements of his musical personality, and much of his subsequent music has been precisely modelled on a journey towards integration, which is often explicitly a metaphor for a spiritual journey, and which is often assisted in musical terms by the intervention of electronic music on tape as an infinitely malleable integrating matrix. Examples of Harvey's work in this medium, little exploited by British composers even into the 1980s, include *Inner Light 3* for large orchestra and tape (1975), the purely electronic *Mortuos plango, vivos voco* (1980) and *Bhakti* for small orchestra and tape (1982). The last two of these were created at the Institut de Recherche et de Coordination Acoustique/Musique, a computer music laboratory directed by Boulez in Paris, and it was there too that the tapes for Birtwistle's *The Mask of Orpheus* were composed.

This same gifted and influential generation includes, however, composers who have felt themselves much less abruptly displaced from the past, most notably Nicholas Maw, who, like Bennett and Cardew, studied at the Royal Academy of Music, but who came more slowly to public attention. He too studied abroad, in Paris with Boulanger and the Schoenberg pupil Max Deutsch (1958–9), and his early works show a wide range of enthusiasm unusual for the period, extending from Webern to Richard Strauss by way of Britten and Bartók. Out of that breadth of musical experience he has created a style which shows the possibility of development within a twentieth-century diatonic tradition, and the continuing possibility too of the rapturous romantic statement, such as he first achieved in *Scenes and Arias* for three women singers and orchestra (1962). The appearance of such a work at such a time, just when the direction of British music seemed to have been set by Davies and Goehr, caused a stir, and perhaps brought about the characterisation of Maw as retrogressive. His use of a fundamentally tonal language is, however, quite fresh, authentic and prodigally inventive, and it may seem – particularly in view of the conventionalising tendencies in Goehr's music of the 1960s and Davies's of the 1970s – that new interpretations of past materials are as validly a part of contemporary musical culture as are extreme ruptures with tradition. There is also the inevitable tendency, as time passes, that the shockwaves of the new diminish in force, while the originality of such music as Maw's becomes more striking and surprising. His works include an opera written for Glyndebourne, *The Rising of the Moon* (1970), two string quartets (1965, 1982), a set of *Life Studies* for string orchestra (1973–6) and another set of *Personae* for solo piano (1973–86).

The generation of the forties and fifties

One further effect of passing time, as this history nears the present, is that the number of composers vastly increases, and with it the difficulty of isolating the more interesting or more representative figures. Only partly is this due to the confusion inherent in looking at the present from the point of view of the present. On a more objective level, there really are more composers working actively in the 1980s than there were in the 1930s or even in the 1960s, as far as that may be judged by the number being published and professionally performed. To some extent that may be due to the optimism of the 1960s. Composers who were born in the decade after the war, or thereabouts, came to maturity during a period when contemporary music was being energetically and intelligently promoted by the BBC under Glock, and when Goehr, Davies and Birtwistle were providing role models.

Moreover, composition was being encouraged at universities to an unprecedented degree. As has already been noted, the major composers born in the 1930s were all educated at music colleges, whether in Manchester or in London, whereas their juniors have tended to be graduates: from Oxford (Bill Hopkins, Nigel Osborne, Stephen Oliver, Gordon Crosse), Cambridge (Robin Holloway, George Benjamin, Robert Saxton), Nottingham (David Matthew, Colin Matthews), Birmingham (John Casken) and elsewhere. Universities have also provided several of these and other composers with teaching positions, though composition has not become quite so exclusively a campus activity as it is in the United States: perhaps it has been prevented from becoming so by the work of the BBC, implicitly insisting that music in the late twentieth century remains a public art, and secondarily by the patronage of the Arts Council, which again has worked on the assumption that there is a public function for new music, and which has funded appearances of the London Sinfonietta, the Fires of London and other groups in London and beyond.

Yet that assumption of a public value in new composition becomes ever less obvious. It seems to be in the nature of musical languages that they convey a hypothesis about what human beings are: most notably the diatonic language of around 1600 to around 1900 conveys a view of separable, individual, whole personalities growing in a measured fashion through time from birth to death, and related to one another, despite their individuality and separability, by a few unchangeable constants. The problem for music in the present age is that this view of humanity is no longer plausible, and therefore cannot be musically communicated; and yet it is the view in which our sense of our selves has been formed, and therefore its denial cannot easily be accepted. The fact that Beethoven, Brahms and Tchaikovsky remain more popular than Schoenberg, Boulez and Birtwistle is not due to a natural conservatism in the species, nor of course to a conspiracy of ugliness among the twentieth century's composers; the reason is perhaps more likely to be the inevitable resistance of the human mind to the acknowledgement of meaninglessness. It is not easy to see how so profound a psychic gap may be bridged, but the lesson of the most recent music, not least in Britain, is perhaps that creative ways are beginning to emerge for the restoration of the old certainties (coherent harmonic progression, rhythmic stability, even major-minor tonality) but with the recognition of their fictiveness. Superficially, therefore, the generation of the 1940s and 1950s may appear to be withdrawing from the avant-garde territory conquered by their elders, but the process may be more valuably seen as one of steady progress towards a kind of music that may yet be more widely and deeply accepted and enjoyed.

There are, however, two hindrances to that progress which were unknown in previous eras: the massive availability of the music of the past, and the still more massive availability of music designed to appeal as widely as possible, both supported by strong commercial interests. Those interests can affect only the marketing of Beethoven, not the sounding substance, but in the case of popular music the pressure to sell as many copies as possible is intense, and hardly conducive to musical subtlety. Only at one point in recent history did commerce find itself backing questing, resourceful musical spirits, and that was in the 1960s, the era of the Beatles, who made their first international recordings in 1962 and their last in 1970. There were many reasons for this turn of events. One must be quite simply the musical creativity of the four musicians themselves, and in particular of John Lennon and Paul McCartney. Another may be the comparative innocence of the record business at that time: having helped create a group of stars, the commercial impetus continued to back them through their quite extraordinary musical development, with no-one realising that they could have been dropped for something else. Then again, the Beatles' period of creative growth coincided with the maturing of the immediate post-war generation, the generation which had passed through the childhood of rock and roll, and which was ready for a development in popular music to coincide with its passage into adulthood. But the possibility of such a development proved chimerical, and since then popular music has remained the preserve of those most deeply in need of its comforting of the ego, most hungry for its provision of variety, and most needful of it as a means of social intercourse: adolescents.

The later music of the Beatles therefore occupies a rare and privileged position, in that it was exceedingly popular and yet free to be as imaginative as its creators knew how. For a while that brought it interest from those one has to call in this context 'classical' composers: the McCartney song 'Yesterday' was arranged as a guitar solo by Davies, and Roger Smalley and Tim Souster both wrote works seeking some rapprochement between the world of Stockhausen and that of rock. The communication also went the

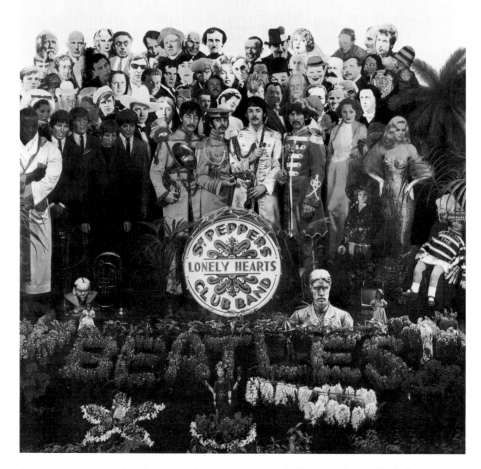

Record sleeve design for the Beatles' Sergeant Pepper's Lonely Hearts Club Band
(1967).

other way, for Stockhausen featured among the heroes grouped in
photographic montage on the sleeve of the Beatles' *Sergeant Pepper's Lonely
Hearts Club Band* (1967), which was the climax of their achievement. No
longer simply a chain of songs, *Sergeant Pepper* is a dramatic cycle, linked by
the conceit that the songs are sung by the band named in the title, and
arranged with a carefulness for connection and contrast unusual in anthology
records of any kind. The use of studio techniques normally associated with
electronic music had begun in *Revolver* (1966), as had the extension of
subject matter far beyond the usual range of love songs, and the parallel
extension of musical means: McCartney's 'Eleanor Rigby', one of the tracks
from *Revolver*, is concerned with loneliness, and occupies the Dorian
modality of a folksong, with accompaniment for string quartet. But *Sergeant
Pepper* goes much further, drawing in a full symphony orchestra as well as
influences from Indian music, and concerning itself with the expansion of
self-awareness that the Beatles had discovered through drugs, through Indian
mysticism, and perhaps not least through their freedom to undertake musical

experiment. For the moment experiment feeds on integrated conception, but in their next release, an untitled double album (1968), their diverging personalities explode in a sequence of parodies, Lennon moving, under the influence of Yoko Ono, towards Cageian experimentalism, McCartney holding uncertainly to his home ground of lyrical balladry, and the other members of the group exerting themselves more decisively: George Harrison in his feeling for Indian culture, and Ringo Starr in his unselfconscious naivety. Two more LPs remained, *Abbey Road* (1969) and *Let it Be* (1970), but the disbandment of the Beatles seems in retrospect to have become inevitable when their freedom had provided the opportunity for them to flourish as creating individuals. All of them, most especially McCartney and Lennon, continued to make records, but an era of productive innocence had ended.

The brief period of the Beatles' greatest creativity coincided very strikingly with an outburst of energy in their contemporaries, as represented by the first operas of Birtwistle and Davies, the founding of the Pierrot Players, the London Sinfonietta and the Scratch Orchestra, or Maw's opera for Glyndebourne. But while all this was, as has been suggested, an enormous stimulus to younger composers, it has also seemed in retrospect the glory of a golden age, contributing to a certain feeling of post-coital depression in British music since 1970. This may be reflected in the relative slowness of younger composers to make a mark; though at the same time that slowness must be attributed to the fact that the categories had been filled. When Goehr, Davies and Birtwistle were writing their first works, in the second half of the 1950s, they were tilling virgin territory, but that could not be the case for those who came after. Those three, with very few compositions to their names, were all receiving prestigious commissions and the attention of publishers while they were still in their mid-twenties, which has not been the experience of most of their successors. And it is those commissions and those publications that seem to be necessary for a young composer to establish credibility. The role of publishers is particularly crucial, for acceptance onto the list of a reputable publisher is a guarantee of seriousness, or so it seems. In the 1950s the key house was that of Schott, the publishers of Tippett, Fricker, Rainier, Goehr and, to begin with, Davies. Then in the 1960s Boosey & Hawkes became more active, securing Davies and Maw, though they lost Britten to Faber in 1964. Universal Edition, the publishers of Boulez, Stockhausen and Berio, also began to fish the seas of British music at this time, and landed Birtwistle and Cardew. Chester Music and Oxford University Press, too, began around this time to establish lists of young composers. From the point of view of publishers, contemporary music is unlikely to be profitable in the short term, though it certainly occasions publicity and establishes professional worthiness; from the point of view of composers, however, a publisher is almost essential, not only for them to establish their own professional worthiness but also to take care of the negotiation of commissions, copying of parts, and so on.

However, the British composer of the 1940s generation most esteemed in Continental Europe grew up quite apart from this cosy symbiosis, and is published by a house, Peters Edition, with few British representatives: Brian

Ferneyhough. Like most English composers of the century, he went across the Channel to complete his studies, with Ton de Leeuw in Amsterdam (1968–9) and with Klaus Huber in Basle (1969–71), but unlike most of them he stayed, teaching at the Musikhochschule in Freiburg from 1973 and also at the avant-garde stronghold of Darmstadt, where Davies and Goehr had gone in the 1950s to hear Stockhausen and Boulez lecture. He also made his reputation as a composer in Germany and France before his music was much known in England (the turning point came with the performance and recording by the London Sinfonietta of his *Transit* for voices and chamber orchestra in 1977), and his music grows very directly out of the European avant-garde achievement of the late 1940s and 1950s with nothing of the Englishness to be found in the comparably based early music of Davies and Goehr. His works are notated with immense exactitude and complication, and prefer the margins of performability and indeed perceptibility: the effort to play, and the effort to hear, register and comprehend, are essential to the meaning of his music, which nobly strikes out against the restriction of vision and the conservatism in so much music since 1970.

Paradoxically, however, it is the conservatism in British music that has seemed most vital during that period: the change is marked at the most exalted level by the comparative calmness of Britten's and Tippett's works after their accommodations to the avant-garde in the 1960s. Among younger composers, the resurgence of romanticism can be seen, for example, in the works of David Matthews or that of Michael Berkeley, son of Lennox. It can be seen too, in a more self-questioning manner, in the music of Robin Holloway, who is a central figure of this period in his ability to write in a wide variety of styles, romantic, neoclassical and modernist, sometimes within the same work, and in his seeming insistence on music as a language of feeling whatever the style. He is also one of the most prolific composers of the period, with an output embracing a full-scale opera (*Clarissa*, 1968–76), orchestral works, a wide variety of chamber pieces and an abundance of songs.

By contrast with his broad church there is the narrow endeavour of Bill Hopkins, who studied in Paris with Messiaen and also with Barraqué (1964–5), of whom the latter was a deep influence on his artistic beliefs. Fiercely self-critical, as his teacher was, he left only a small number of works, whose complexity and whose stylistic region may suggest a comparison with Ferneyhough, though there is also in his music a rich if fractured lyricism that testifies to an underlying humanist thrust, an urge to speak, Beckett fashion, against the impossibility of speech. And the invocation of Beckett here is not idle. His *Sensation* for soprano and quartet (1965) sets French poems by Beckett after more rapturous expressions from Rimbaud, and his *Etudes en série* for piano (1965–72) are intensive meditations on Beckett's later prose works.

Not surprisingly, most British composers of this generation have found some compromise between Holloway's carrying of capacious musical baggage and Hopkins's rigorous self-reliance. Among those who have established their own musical worlds, Nigel Osborne, Oliver Knussen and Robert Saxton may be mentioned. For all of them, as for the great majority of their contemporaries, the European avant-garde of the 1950s remains decisive: Osborne has worked at Boulez' studio in Paris; Saxton was a pupil of Berio; and though Knussen's leanings are more towards the American stream of international modernism that has its chief representative in Carter, his music too belongs in the clear, new realm of Boulez, Berio and also Ligeti. Quite what distinguishes the works of these composers as British or English is not easy to discover, unless it is only Osborne's eagerness in working with contemporary English poets, notably Craig Raine, the librettist of his opera *The Electrification of the Soviet Union* (1986–7). But then there is the example of another composer of this generation, John Tavener, nearly all of whose music is religious, with a large part of it placed formly within the Greek Orthodox tradition. It may be, as it was with Britten in the 1930s, that an exuberant internationalism masks a new contribution to the British musical character; or it may be that nationalism has become as elusive a concept in music as self-expression.

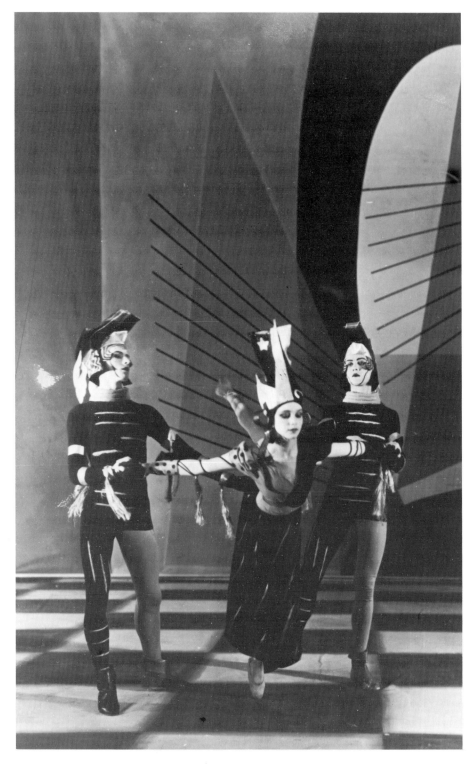

June Brae as the Red Queen in Ninette de Valois' ballet Checkmate *(1937)*.

2 Ballet

FERNAU HALL

Introduction: historical overview

Though London played a crucial role in the development of the modern art of ballet (something very different from the danced interludes performed as part of Renaissance and Baroque opera), there was no continuity of balletic tradition in London, because the theatres had no subsidy from a monarch, and thus ballets fell into oblivion when fashion changed. Permanent subsidised companies could resist changes in fashion, and retain ballets in their repertoire, so that they survived – even though ballets could not be written down in a satisfactory way before the second half of the twentieth century. This did not matter during periods when ballet flourished: then London became a major creative centre of ballet. But during periods of decadence traditions were almost totally lost.

The first serious ballet in the modern sense of the word – i.e. a self-sufficient theatrical work quite independent of opera, and taking the form of expressive dancing (also of mime) – was created in London in 1717 by the English dancing-master John Weaver: '*The Loves of MARS AND VENUS*; A Dramatick Entertainment of DANCING, Attempted in Imitation of the PANTOMIMES of the Ancient Greeks and Romans.' But for a long time Weaver had no British successors: there were later periods when major works were created in London, but not by British choreographers.

From 1911 onwards, with the beginning of regular visits by the Russian company directed by Sergei Diaghilev, the revived art of ballet – at a very high level – became once again familiar to London audiences. The death of Diaghilev in 1929, and the vacuum created by the dissolution of his company, made it possible for two remarkable women to establish major ballet companies in London. Thanks to the work of these two women and their associates, London became once again the creative centre of the ballet world.

Marie Rambert (1888–1982) was something very rare: a supremely gifted artistic director, determined to create conditions conducive to the creation of masterly new ballets, with dancers able to do justice to them, and the collaboration of highly imaginative stage designers. This Polish-born artist has shown her extraordinary musicality when Diaghilev asked her – aged only twenty-five, and studying with Dalcroze – to work as Nijinsky's musical guide when, creating his intensely original choreography for *The Rites of Spring*, he had to cope with a Stravinsky score far more complex than any previously commissioned for a ballet.

Rambert thus became deeply involved with the creative work of the Diaghilev Ballet in its golden age. Having learned much about ballet teaching while taking the classes of Enrico Cechetti – the company's great teacher – she set up her own ballet school in London in 1920, and formed a number of fine dancers, thus making it possible for her to organise performances from 1926 onwards and to establish a permanent company in 1930, giving two seasons at the Lyric Theatre, Hammersmith.

From 1931 to 1939 this company performed on Sundays at the Mercury Theatre (and was therefore called the Ballet Club – for ticket-purchasers had to be club members, because of the Sunday-observance laws). Though the stage was tiny (18 feet wide and 18 feet deep), the standard maintained by Rambert was superb, in every aspect of ballet: choreography, dancing, music, stage design, stage lighting and much else. She would allow nothing to go on stage unless it had originality and quality; indeed, the quality she achieved was such that almost every new ballet was put into the constantly growing repertoire. Two choreographers of outstanding ability emerged under her aegis – Frederick Ashton and Antony Tudor – and she also fostered a number of other talented choreographers as well as a remarkable number of fine dancers. What is more, she arranged for the staging of wonderful productions of nineteenth-century ballets and Diaghilev ballets.

Box-office receipts were inevitably low – the theatre had only 144 seats – and so Rambert was unable to pay wages to her dancers, who thus tended to drift away. In due course, Ashton and Tudor also departed; yet Rambert managed to maintain standards. The Ballet Rambert continued to do fine work during and after the war, even though Rambert never succeeded in equalling the extraordinary achievements of the pre-war golden age. Eventually the task of running a ballet company of fine quality, without a home theatre in London and with an inadequate subsidy, became impossible. Rambert – always ready to move ahead – happily agreed to the suggestion by Norman Morrice that her company should be transformed into a company strongly orientated towards modern dance, even though the dancers continued to have ballet training. (In her youth, she had been deeply influenced by the great pioneer of modern dance, Isadora Duncan; and she had taught a form of modern dance, for Dalcroze.)

Like Rambert, the Irish-born Ninette de Valois (b.1898) acquired invaluable experience while working for Diaghilev (who employed her as a dancer). Though de Valois lacked Rambert's extraordinary flair for creating conditions in which numerous outstanding choreographers and dancers could emerge, she had many fine qualities – notably a gift for organisation, far-sightedness, a realisation of the supreme importance of putting the nineteenth-century 'classics' permanently at the centre of the repertoire, the ability to see Margot Fonteyn's potential for developing into a great dancer, and a firm determination to put all musical matters into the hands of Constant Lambert (whom she called 'the British Diaghilev'). She took good advantage of the fact that at the Sadler's Wells Theatre (where the Vic-Wells Ballet settled after a preliminary period when Lilian Baylis had it alternate between the Old Vic and the Wells) she was able to present ballets on a fair-sized stage, in a theatre with 1,500 seats, with an orchestra in an orchestra pit, and where the Vic-Wells organisation was able to pay her dancers wages enough to live on. (The Vic-Wells Ballet was formed as an addition to an organisation which ran both a splendid drama company and a worthy opera company, performing at cheap prices outside the West End.)

A number of the leading dancers of the Vic-Wells Ballet came from the Ballet Club. They included Anton Dolin and Alicia Markova, who had danced for Diaghilev; Margot Fonteyn (b.1919), trained by Russian teachers in Shanghai and London; and Robert Helpmann (b.1909) from Australia. Though Ninette de Valois created numerous ballets herself for a time, she brought in Frederick Ashton from the Ballet Club and made him her chief choreographer in 1935, and commissioned authentic productions, at full length, of major ballets surviving from the nineteenth century: *Swan Lake, Giselle, Casse-Noisette* (*The Nutcracker*), *Coppélia, The Sleeping Beauty.* And she brought in, as musical director, conductor, composer and arranger, Constant Lambert – a man of high culture and extraordinary gifts, one who had matured so rapidly that Diaghilev had commissioned a score from him when he was still a student at the Royal College of Music.

There was a big gap between the leading soloists of the Vic-Wells Ballet and the *corps de ballet* dancers, and a number of the ballets it staged proved ephemeral. But at its best it was very good indeed; and, like the Ballet Club, it had no need to fear comparison with the Ballet-Russe company giving a long season in the West End every summer. During the War, performing every night – on tour or at the New Theatre in London – the Sadler's Wells Ballet went from strength to strength, much helped by the development of Margot Fonteyn into a ballerina of the highest quality. After the War it became the resident company at Covent Garden, firmly established as one of the world's great ballet companies, and in due course changed its name to the Royal Ballet.

Constant Lambert had played a very important role in the development of the company, and his untimely death in 1951, when he was only forty-six, represented a serious loss to the company. Thanks to him, the company performed ballets using existing or commissioned music by leading British composers: Vaughan Williams, William Walton, Arthur Bliss, Lambert himself. Just before his death he arranged for a splendid score to be commissioned from a young composer Denis ApIvor, *a Mirror for Witches*; and ApIvor later composed for the touring company the score of *Blood Wedding*, so well suited to ballet and the theme of the Lorca play that the ballet held the stage for years in spite of mediocre choreography by Alfred Rodriguez.

After the War the popularity of ballet continued to expand in Britain, and a number of other companies were formed. By far the most important of them, the Festival Ballet (later called London Festival Ballet) was founded by

Anton Dolin and Alicia Markova in 1950. Under a succession of artistic directors, this company had an erratic artistic policy; but after Beryl Grey (previously a ballerina with the Royal Ballet) took over as artistic director, in 1968, its quality steadily improved until it rivalled the Royal Ballet.

With regular tours by London Festival Ballet and the touring company of the Royal Ballet, performances of ballet became common in cities all over Britain. Moreover two important regional companies were established: the Scottish Ballet centred on Glasgow, and Northern Ballet Theatre centred on Manchester.

A pioneering modern dance company, the Dance-Drama Group, had been established in Britain in 1930 (at Dartington Hall, near Totnes in Devon) by Margaret Barr, who had had some training with Martha Graham in America before coming to Britain and establishing her own technique and her own style of choreography – strongly dramatic, and using much mime. Faced with the unattractive prospect of becoming submerged in the German modern dance company the Ballets Jooss, also based at Dartington, the Dance-Drama Group left, and eventually disbanded in 1938.

It was not until 1966, when the Ballet Rambert was reorganised, that another major modern dance company came into existence in Britain. Soon afterwards it was joined by another: London Contemporary Dance Theatre. Its director was Robert Cohan, for years one of Martha Graham's leading dancers, and at first its leading dancers were Graham-trained Americans. Other dancers were British, and had their Graham-style training at the London School of Contemporary Dance. (By now, Martha Graham preferred the term 'contemporary' to 'modern'.) British dancers gradually replaced the Americans even in leading roles, but Robert Cohan remained director, and the dancing and choreography remained deeply influenced by Graham.

Many young dancers now devoted themselves to modern/contemporary dance, and trained at London Contemporary Dance School and elsewhere. Only very few could hope to join the two major established companies, and this led to the formation of many small groups, varying widely in quality.

One of the most important creative achievements affecting British ballet was made in London in the fifties by Rudolf Benesh, who invented Benesh Movement Notation and perfected it with the help of his wife Joan Benesh, then dancing in the Sadler's Wells Ballet. The task which Rudolf Benesh faced was one of immense difficulty: the satisfactory recording of bodily movements requires a notation coping with something like two hundred times as much information as the notation of music, and a dance notation must be readable, economic and basically very simple as well as precise, complete and totally integrated with music notation. Rudolf Benesh succeeded so well that choreologists trained in Benesh Movement notation were taken on the staff of all the leading ballet companies in Britain, thus making it possible for ballets to be accurately preserved and revived; and the use of the notation spread around the world. Now, like plays and operas, ballets can be studied and analysed 'in the study' as well as in performance, on the stage.

Frederick Ashton

Frederick Ashton, one of Marie Rambert's students whom she encouraged as early as 1926 to try his hand in choreography (*A Tragedy of Fashion*, staged for a revue), had been greatly excited by the sophisticated, cosmopolitan ballets staged by Diaghilev in the twenties, when his ties with Russia had been broken. Rambert, anxious to widen the horizons of her students, had a habit of taking them to see the performances in London of the Diaghilev Ballet, and Ashton was deeply influenced by these ballets – above all by Bronislava Nijinska's ballet *Les Biches*. When he danced in the Ida Rubinstein company of which Nijinska was the choreographer, this influence was reinforced.

His own flair for light-hearted, witty, frivolously satirical comedy flowered in his first major ballet *Façade* (1931), based on an orchestral suite which William Walton had adapted from the instrumental music he wrote as an accompaniment to the recitation of poems in dance rhythms by Edith Sitwell. One of the best items in the suite of dances, the Polka, was created for Alicia Markova. This began with an episode which seemed daringly provocative at the time: the dancer calmly removed her skirt and began to dance in her panties. As choreographed by Ashton, this solo satirised simultaneously ballet, tap-dancing and ballroom dancing: the arm movements are those of tap-dancing, but the dancer used her pointes and kept in the rhythm of a polka. (When Margot Fonteyn, near the beginning of her career, took over this dance, she made it marvellously witty.) In Popular Song two men moved through musical-comedy routines, looking bored to death. The Tango was created for the great Diaghilev soubrette ballerina Lydia Lopokhova (guest artist for the Ballet Club): she revelled in the chance of dancing so impudently (as later did Margot Fonteyn). *Façade* became one of the most popular ballets in the Ballet Club repertoire, and from 1935 became no less popular when performed by the Vic-Wells / Sadler's Wells / Royal Ballet.

For many years Ashton created romantic ballets with Margot Fonteyn as the central figure. These all used lyrical patterns of steps which made good use of Fonteyn's exquisite line and her musicality, with much the same patterns of steps (slightly modified so that they fitted the music) appearing in ballet after ballet. Fonteyn danced beautifully in all of them; but they fell into obscurity after a certain time, being replaced by other romantic ballets with similar patterns.

It was different with *Symphonic Variations* (1945). Ashton approached this ballet in a new way, after a break enforced by his wartime service in the armed forces. He began by working out a complex symbolic theme (involving Woman, Winter, the Moon, and so on) which he felt he could adapt to César Franck's *Symphonic Variations*. But then he had the excellent idea of abandoning this theme almost completely, leaving only the ghost of it behind. As a result he created an abstract ballet in which he was able to use all his favourite patterns of steps with freshness and refined musicality. He used only six solo dancers, and kept all of them on stage the whole time: apart from putting together fresh and elegant variations of his favourite patterns, he invented lovely new dance-images, with the dancers' arms curving over

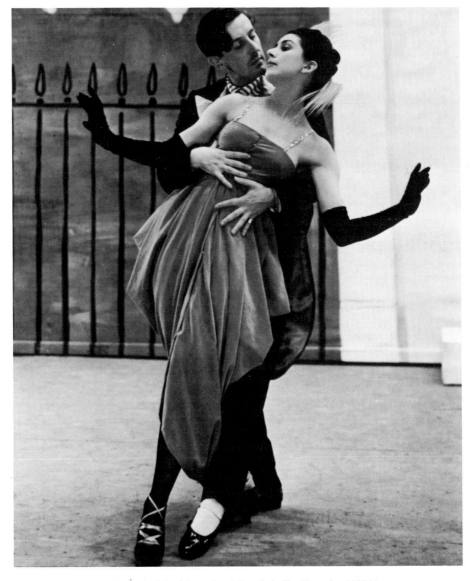

Margot Fonteyn and Frederick Ashton in Ashton's ballet Façade *(1931)*

their heads. Sophie Fedorovitch – who had been Ashton's mentor for years – designed very simple, elegant costumes, and adapted a type of graph (showing complex equations) so that it made a fine background, avoiding all suggestion of a definite period or place. Margot Fonteyn looked magical in this ballet. Regrettably, it is not often performed, for it demands a good deal of rehearsal time; but it never loses its appeal, when performed by fine artists.

New versions of old ballets are usually unsuccessful, for choreographers who have grown up in an era very different from that in which the ballet was created cannot create freely in the period style. Nonetheless, Ashton's new version of *La Fille mal gardée* (1960) showed him to be a master of time-travelling; indeed, he seemed quite at home in the late eighteenth century. Nonchalantly he introduced elements from other periods – his Widow Simone, for example, was adapted from the English pantomime dame as perfected by comedians in the nineteenth century, and in her clog dance he combined tap-dance steps with authentic clog-dance steps; but he got away with these stylistic intrusions. Greatly respecting the great Diaghilev ballerina Tamara Karsavina (with whom he had danced in the early years of the Ballet Club) he invited her to revive for him a mime scene from the traditional Franco-Russian version, showing the heroine Lise dreaming of marriage and bringing up children: this fitted amazingly well into Ashton's ballet.

Among Ashton's more notable subsequent works were *The Dream* (1964), *Monotones* (1966), *Enigma Variations* (1968) and *A Month in the Country* (1976).

Ninette de Valois

Nearly all the ballets created by Ninette de Valois for the Vic-Wells Ballet soon fell into oblivion, for they gave her little chance to show her flair for expressionism. The fact that *Job* continued to survive, after its creation in 1931, was due to its music by Vaughan Williams, its fine settings inspired by etchings by Blake, and some strong expressionist dancing assigned to Satan (a role created by Anton Dolin), Job's Comforters, and the War, Pestilence and Famine trio.

De Valois showed her true quality in 1935, when she brought to life a series of prints by Hogarth: *The Rake's Progress*. As the ballet went on, it became more and more ferociously expressionist, culminating in a scene in Bedlam when the Rake (superbly danced by Walter Gore and then by Robert Helpmann) performed a dance of madness and died. In smaller roles, dancers who had looked somewhat dim in other ballets performed with splendid dramatic intensity. The only serious flaw derived from the fact that Markova, cast as the heroine, insisted on dancing on pointes – thus breaking the period flavour of the rest of the ballet. When the ballet was transferred to the Royal Opera House, it never looked right, for its scenery was ill-suited to a large stage; but it still looked splendid when performed at Sadler's Wells.

Another expressionist ballet by de Valois, *Checkmate* (1937), also proved to have enduring quality. Here the influence of two expressionist choreographers, greatly admired by her – Léonide Massine and Kurt Jooss – was very clear, but well assimilated. In this ballet de Valois skilfully adapted the patterns of movement of chess pieces – the Knight, for example, often used a *pas de basque*, moving around two sides of a triangle – and her choreography made fine use of the skill of Harold Turner (one of the dancers who moved to the Vic-Wells Ballet from the Ballet Club). June Brae, trained in the Russian school, showed a splendid combination of eroticism and cruel heartless power as the Black Queen. Of all the fine dancers who later took over this role, Maina Gielgud, bringing to it all the dramatic intensity of the Gielgud family, was best able to rival June Brae's superb quality. Robert

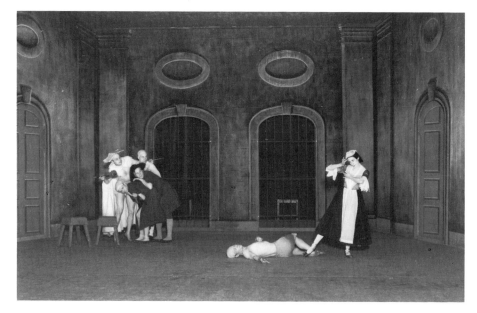

The Mad Scene in Bedlam from Ninette de Valois' ballet Checkmate *(1937).*

Helpmann was splendid in the mime role of the Red King. The ballet gained much from the colourful, poster-like decor designed by the fine poster artist McKnight Kauffer, and from the strongly theatrical music of Arthur Bliss – though he went astray in composing a tango for the triumphant solo of the Black Queen.

Though *The Rake's Progress* and *Checkmate* have taken their place as a permanent addition to the repertoire, the supreme achievement of de Valois was the creation of the company now called the Royal Ballet.

Antony Tudor

It would be hard to overestimate the significance of Antony Tudor in the history of world ballet. Though he and Ashton worked side by side at the Ballet Club, their temperaments and their approaches to ballet were very different. Tudor, though familiar with the type of sophisticated, somewhat frivolous ballet staged by Diaghilev in the later twenties, broke clean away from this style in his very first ballet: *Cross-Garter'd* (1931), a skilfully crafted balletic version of the garden scene in *Twelfth Night*. From then on he developed at an extraordinary rate, absorbing a very wide range of influences: Spanish dance, Kabuki dance, Indian dance, Javanese dance, the American modern dance of Martha Graham, the German modern dance of Kurt Jooss, and much else.

The choreographer whom he admired most was Fokine, and he was strongly influenced by the ballets of this great Russian choreographer. By the time he created his first masterpiece, *Jardin aux lilas* (1936), he had developed a highly original approach to choreography, and achieved a new level of poetic complexity: in characterisation, evocation of mood, the use of subtle musicality and expressive dance-imagery. Though the influence of Proust was profound, he made no direct use of Proust's great novel, *A la recherche du temps perdu*, and – quite unlike Proust – achieved an extraordinary level of concentration with one scene following another smoothly but rapidly. Fokine had established in *Les Sylphides* – even before Diaghilev formed his company – that dance-images could achieve such intensity and richness of poetic expression that a ballet which, in the nineteenth century, would have needed two or even three acts, could find totally satisfying embodiment on stage in something like half an hour. Now Tudor went even further: he used a piece of music by Chausson, *Poème*, with such musicality and imagination that in $16\frac{1}{2}$ minutes – the length of the music – he created a tightly structured and fully satisfying ballet that communicated so powerfully, at so many levels, that it seemed to last much longer. Tudor even controlled the flow of time within the ballet: at one point, for example, Caroline – forced to marry a man she does not love, and given no chance to say farewell to her lover, though they meet briefly at times in the presence of others – takes a long, sad farewell from all her friends, in her imagination, while time stands still for everyone else on stage. Notwithstanding its great originality – indeed, this ballet could be said to establish a new era in ballet – *Jardin aux lilas* appealed deeply to audiences all over the world, and has been taken into the repertoire of many ballet companies.

Ever since Tudor had reached artistic maturity, he had made each new ballet a foray into the unknown, treating a new type of theme in a new way. Only one year after *Jardin aux lilas*, in 1937, he created a ballet of supremely austere and tragic power, with dance-images of such mysterious originality and expressiveness that they almost defy analysis: they communicate feelings and moods far beyond the reach of words. Using Mahler's great song-cycle *Kindertotenlieder* (Songs for the Death of Children), he created a ritualistic ballet in which the dancers portrayed people, living in a remote northern seaside village, whose children have all been drowned. Though the dancers needed a strong classical technique, they rarely performed movements which could be described in the technical terms of ballet; and though each soloist performed highly individual images, the ballet as a whole had a mysterious unity of style which set it apart from all other ballets. The first soloist was a stoic: though the terrible blow of fate she had experienced crushed her limbs inward, she also performed out-turned movements which suggested that she would come through. The second female soloist, in contrast, was quite crushed, and dependent on the support of her husband. In the final, highly ritualistic scene, the villagers all achieved tragic resignation, and moved off-stage with austere and very moving formality. The designer, Nadia Benois, reinforced the austere mood of the ballet with her simple costumes and stark decor: the singer, dressed like the dancers, sat on stage and took his own place in the action of the ballet.

In 1939 Tudor went to America. Working for Ballet Theatre, he staged his existing ballets and created new masterpieces, establishing Ballet Theatre/American Ballet Theatre as one of the world's great companies. But the company declined in quality after 1950, and Tudor was forced to

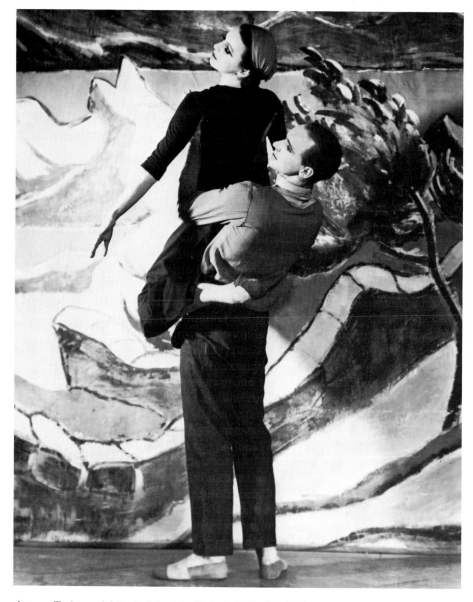

Antony Tudor and Maude Lloyd in Tudor's ballet Dark Elegies, *to music by Mahler (1937).*

abandon the creation of major ballets. Indeed, it looked as if he would have to concentrate on teaching for the rest of his life. In 1966, however, Frederick Ashton (then director of the Royal Ballet) persuaded him to return to London and create a new ballet for the Royal Ballet. This turned out to be *Shadowplay*, a mysterious and fascinating ballet with a Buddhist theme: the hero, the Boy with Matted Hair, could be considered as the son of Buddha, faced with much the same temptations as the Buddha himself as he searched through meditation for enlightenment. By now Tudor was a Zen master, and he treated his Buddhist theme with profound understanding, calling on the dance styles of Thailand, Java, China and Japan as well as classical ballet traditions as he created his dance-images. With characteristic insight, he saw great possibilities in young Anthony Dowell, and induced him to give a performance of marvellous innocence, understatement and power in the central role. In the same way he gave mysterious and powerful roles to Merle Park (first seductive, then destructive) and Derek Rencher (the all-powerful king of the jungle). With this ballet Tudor found his way back to creativity at the highest level. Returning to American Ballet Theatre in 1974 as associate artistic director, he created a magical work a year later, *The Leaves are Fading* – building this ballet around the magical talents of Gelsey Kirkland.

Kenneth MacMillan

Of all the choreographers who emerged within the two companies associated with the Royal Opera House and the Sadler's Wells Theatre after the war, Kenneth MacMillan (b.1929) stood out because of his skill and inventiveness in creating *pas de deux*. As a choreographer, he had certain weaknesses – notably a lack of flair in structuring ballets, and a tendency to pad his ballets out to inordinate length. But he found an ideal basis for a ballet in the best of the Soviet full-length ballets, *Romeo and Juliet* – devised by Leonid Lavrovsky, following closely the action of the Shakespeare play, and using music commissioned from Prokofiev.

In the MacMillan version, the big scenes involving masses of dancers were weak; but the choreographer was seen at his best in the succession of *pas de deux* for the two leading characters. A number of remarkable ballerinas – including Lynn Seymour, Antoinette Sibley, Margot Fonteyn, Merle Park, Gelsey Kirkland and Alessandra Ferri – did wonders with the role of Juliet, and the ballet achieved a permanent place in the repertoire.

La Sylphide

Beryl Grey's supreme achievement as artistic director of London Festival Ballet, just before she left, was to commission the Danish dancer Peter Schaufuss (b.1949) to stage a production of a ballet which survives, alongside *Giselle*, as one of the most inspired achievements of the Romantic Ballet: Bournonville's Danish version of *La Sylphide* (1836). Some sections had got lost in the production surviving in the repertoire of the Royal Danish Ballet, and in 1983 Schaufuss imaginatively replaced the missing parts with his adaptation of surviving fragments of other Bournonville ballets. The result reached a kind of perfection very rare in ballet. Eva Evdokimova (b.1948), one of the supreme ballerinas of the second half of the twentieth century, trained in the Russian school in London by the great teacher Maria Fay and in the Bournonville school in Copenhagen, was unforgettable in the title role: exquisite, mysterious, intensely musical, and deeply moving. Schaufuss, inheriting the Bournonville tradition from both his father and his mother, was ideally cast as James.

Christopher Bruce

Trained in ballet, Christopher Bruce (b.1945) joined the Ballet Rambert as a young dancer in 1963 – before its transformation into a modern-dance company – and he stayed with it after the transformation, showing remarkable flexibility and sensitivity.

As a dancer, he did wonders with two challenging roles. One was the very strange role which Nijinsky created for himself in *L'Après-midi d'un faune*, saved from oblivion because Rambert had arranged for Leon Woizikowsky to stage this extremely original ballet for her company in 1931, and it was recorded on film. The other was the title role in *Pierrot lunaire*, the highly imaginative work which the American choreographer Glen Tetley – trained in the ballet technique by two outstanding English teachers (Antony Tudor and Margaret Craske) and two pioneers of American modern dance (Martha Graham and the German-American Hanya Holm) – had created in 1962 in New York. As Pierrot, Bruce danced with even more power and subtlety than Tetley himself had done, and his performance – together with the work as a whole – did much to establish the Ballet Rambert as a company drawing strength from ballet traditions as well as those of modern dance.

In 1969 Bruce established himself as an original, highly talented and very promising choreographer in *Living Space*, a ballet using as accompaniment the words of a narrative dialogue poem and showing the experiences of two people who meet, fall in love, marry, quarrel and so on – the two roles being admirably danced by Bruce and Sandra Craig, matching their dancing to the words. But Bruce dropped this remarkable ballet after Sandra Craig left the company, feeling that only she could do justice to the female role.

With *Ghost Dances* (1981) Bruce – by then a freelance choreographer, though still retaining his association with the Ballet Rambert – showed mastery in the way he tackled a very different theme. This work came to grips with the tragic fate of those murdered in Latin America by oppressive rulers, and tackling this theme symbolically, drawing on the attitudes to death of Latin American Indians, some of whom seek to keep alive the spirits of dead people by drinking a soup made from their bones.

At the end of each dance by ordinary people (including very poor ones) Bruce had three ghost-dancers, wearing strange skull-masks derived from Indian ghost-masks, come on stage and take away the dead bodies of people who before had been dancing in a joyful way – though their music suggested a certain melancholy, and this, too, appeared in their dancing. The dancing of the masked figures was very mysterious, in dim lighting that made them look ghostly, and caused the bare slopes of the Andes as shown on the backcloth (designed by Bruce himself) to look ominous. As it happened, the only flaw in this superb ballet was caused by the use Bruce made of bright tones reaching high up on the backcloth, thus distracting attention from the brightly-lit joyful scenes. One magnificent artist, Frances Carty, danced with great power in solos and *pas de deux*.

The influence of Tudor's ballet *Dark Elegies* could be seen throughout *Ghost Dances*, above all in the ritualistic and austere quality of the group dances; but Bruce, knowing this ballet so well, was able to use its influence in a highly personal way.

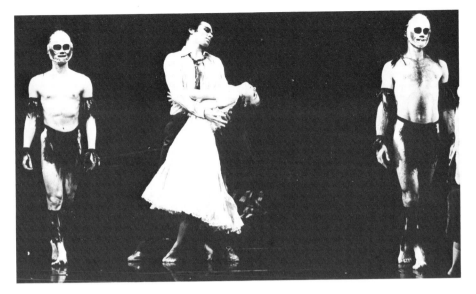

Christopher Bruce's Ghost Dances, *performed by the Ballet Rambert (1981).*

After *Ghost Dances* Bruce's work continued to vary considerably in quality; but in 1986 he created a remarkable work, *The World Again,* for the London Festival Ballet. This was inspired by an orchestral piece with the same title by Geoffrey Burgon, who had shown in his work a remarkable flair for the use of orchestral colour and the evocation of changing moods. As the central figure in this ballet Bruce used Janette Mulligan, causing her to express mysterious moods and feelings which before had seemed outside her scope. Most of the time she seemed oppressed by fate; but in one passage she moved about the stage with freshness and confidence, radiating a mood rather like that of Miranda in *The Tempest,* enthralled by what she calls a brave new world.

Walter Noble excelled himself in his design for the backcloth, with its huge globe which the stage lighting caused to change in harmony with the changes in the mood of the ballet. This globe could well be another planet, seen from space. But when the central figure, after passing through anguish, weakness and death, moved towards the globe, she was met by strange figures coming from beneath it, as if welcoming her into another world.

Though Bruce's choreography showed clear influences from two choreographers he admires greatly – Tudor and Jiri Kylian (notably his *Return to the Strange Land*) – it retained its own mysterious identity; and the ballet-trained dancers of London Festival Ballet, wearing flat shoes, responded well to his demand for a fusion of ballet and modern dance. Especially interesting was Bruce's use of ambiguity: the exact nature of the theme was by no means as clear as in his previous works, but the dance-images were so compelling that this ambiguity was an asset.

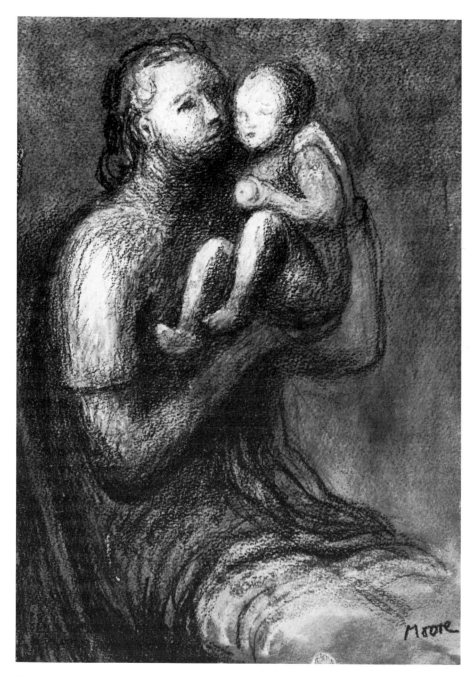

Henry Moore, Mother with Child Holding Apple II *(1981; The Henry Moore Foundation)*.

3   The Visual Arts

PETER FULLER

Introduction

Contemporary critical taste tends to depict the 1930s as a period of 'progress'
for art in Britain, which was rudely interrupted by war, and the onset of
what Alan Bowness (Director of the Tate Gallery) once called, 'a dark decade
in British art'. The 'forgotten fifties' are sometimes portrayed as a confused
extension of this dark era; and brighter days are assumed to have returned in
the early sixties with expanding American influence, the emergence of 'pop
art', and the breaking of wave upon wave of new art world styles,
culminating in the 'new expressionism' of the 1980s.

The perspective presented here, however, is rather different. As the clouds
of war gathered, 'progressive' artists increasingly found themselves severed
from any public, and ranged in narrow, entrenched and tendentious
positions. Paradoxically, the war had an invigorating, and restorative, effect
on artistic activity. The late 1940s were a period of exceptional cultural
optimism. In a review of the exhibition 'Art in 1946 and After', M.H.
Middleton predicted that although Britain might be shedding 'the political
commitments of a great world power' she seemed destined 'to hold a position
of leadership we have never previously known as the artistic centre of the
world'. Such views were not only received wisdom; they appeared to be fully
justified by the achievements of our finest artists. But after only a few years
of peace, these high hopes soon dwindled; the confidence that new forms of
patronage would lead to a 'Golden Age' for the arts was replaced by a
bewildered recognition of the reality of a decadence, characterised by
subservience to empty American fashions, and an understandable dwindling
of the public for the newest art.

By the late 1930s, Ben Nicholson and his 'Circle' believed in the
internationalism of an avant-garde, which stood out for purist abstraction.
They were vehemently opposed by the surrealists who believed in
imaginative expression, originating from the unconscious. The modernist
critic, Herbert Read, found himself 'in the position of a circus rider with his
feet planted astride two horses'. The Artists International Association tried to

maintain a broader 'Unity of Artists for Peace, Democracy and Cultural Development', but, in practice, many of the most active AIA members were committed to social, socialist, or some other kind of 'realism'. Several were also associated with the Euston Road School, founded in 1938, which endeavoured, not unsuccessfully, to oppose the excesses of modernity by tempering the traditions of Sickert with a touch of Cézanne. The wider public tended to be simply dismayed by what it perceived as the antics of the avant-garde, a situation which was only aggravated when, for example, Salvador Dali delivered a public lecture in a diving suit.

The arts of war

John Ruskin once argued that 'war is the foundation of all the arts'; it is a sobering thought that the truth of this improbable and uncongenial argument has been demonstrated in Britain twice this century. The First World War introduced a new and terrible dimension into English pastoralism. After his experiences on the Western Front, Paul Nash wrote, 'Evil and the incarnate fiend alone can be master of this war and no glimmer of God's hand is seen anywhere.' He carried this vision of an injured and godless landscape over into the Second World War, where it found expression in *Totes Meer* (1941), in which a dump of wrecked German planes is associated with the Dead Sea.

Kenneth Clark, Chairman of the War Artists' Advisory Committee, felt it was his principal duty to ensure that as many artists of talent survived as possible. And so, often to their own annoyance, artists found themselves deployed in chauffeur-driven cars on the peripheries of the conflict. Many of the best Second World War works are scenes in the bomb shelters, among the ruins, down the mines, in steel mills, or in underground armament stores. The war emerges not so much as a theatre of action as a metaphor, or symbol, of an injured landscape which has a significance that reaches beyond the simple chronicling of hostilities. The finest paintings of the period belong to a long tradition of 'Higher Landscape', or landscape as means not just of depiction, but for conveying moral and spiritual truths.

Even before 1939, some of the best younger British artists – John Piper and Graham Sutherland among them – had already begun to look back into Britain's past, and out across her landscape, for influence and inspiration. Ivon Hitchens, too, had tried to absorb the lessons of cubism, abstraction, and surrealism, and to apply them to his own vision of the English countryside. As the lights went out all over Europe, the most creative artists of the day began to realise that the roots of a truly modern British painting lay here. A feeling of inferiority *vis-à-vis* an overseas avant-garde, which had dominated the 1930s, disappeared, together with the members of that avant-garde themselves.

A national sensibility, which Robin Ironside retrospectively identified as 'neo-romanticism', flowered. The finest products of this movement include Sutherland's Pembroke landscapes; John Piper's studies of the Welsh mountains; Henry Moore's famous 'shelter drawings'; and Paul Nash's last series of visionary landscapes. A younger generation – Michael Ayrton, Prunella Clough, John Craxton, John Minton and Keith Vaughan among them – developed these 'neo-romantic' concerns. Traditional in its preoccupation with landscape and natural form, the work of all these artists was modern not only in its pictorial forms, but also in its structure of feeling – invoking a rocky, and thorn-ridden world of nature gone awry. Such painting was not characterised by blinkered insularity; for example, the Glasgow artists, Robert Colquhoun and Robert MacBryde, who came to London in wartime, combined neo-romanticism with an acute awareness of continental modernism. Nor was it exclusively linked to landscape: Francis Bacon and Lucian Freud were among those who shared some of the central neo-romantic concerns, but were more involved with the figure than with the ground. The new sensibility extended even beyond those who could be described as 'belonging' to neo-romanticism. During the war, purist abstractionists, like Ben Nicholson and Barbara Hepworth, withdrew to the fishing village of St Ives, where they, too, rediscovered the redemptive power of landscape. Commenting later on her stringed sculptures of the war years, Hepworth wrote, 'The strings were the tension I felt between myself and the sea, the wind or the hills.'

Nor was the public for this new work lacking. John Rothenstein, who was appointed Director of the Tate Gallery in 1938, has recorded how, during the war, 'there was an unprecedented demand for opportunities of seeing works of art, which there was, at first, no adequate means of satisfying'. This demand he attributed to 'the enhanced seriousness of the national temper'. The Tate was crippled by bomb damage; and the National's collections had been evacuated to Wales; but when the Tate organised an exhibition of works by younger British artists at the National, the crowds were so large that the police had to be called in to marshal them.

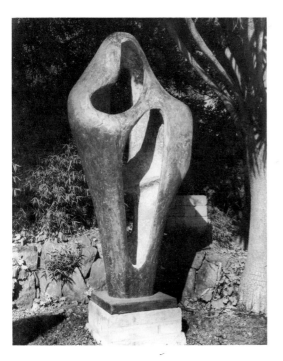

Barbara Hepworth, Figures for Landscape *(1960; Barbara Hepworth Museum, Tate Gallery)*.

Such responses strengthened the position of CEMA, the wartime Committee for the Encouragement of Music and the Arts, and laid the foundations for a new system of public patronage which, for better or for worse, was to come to dominance in the post-war years. The war seemed to have healed the rift that had opened between the artist and the public. As Grey Gowrie has written of Nash's and Moore's contributions, in particular, 'In an age when patriotic art has been, with a few exceptions, synonymous with bad art, [their] war work . . . celebrated England by making her travail universal.'

The golden age of state patronage

After hostilities had ended, CEMA was transformed into a permanent Arts Council; according to its architect and first Chairman, John Maynard Keynes, state patronage of the arts had crept in, but it had done so 'in a very English, informal, unostentatious way – half-baked if you like'. But Keynes' conception of the potential of the Council was almost grandiose. He said it was 'to create an environment to breed a spirit, to cultivate an opinion, to offer a stimulus to such purpose that the artist and the public can each sustain and live on the other in that union which has occasionally existed in the past at the great ages of communal civilized life'. This was to be achieved *not* by any direct coercion or instruction of artists, but rather by following wherever they might lead. In this way, the West was supposed to shine as a torch illuminating for the Eastern bloc countries the aesthetic glories that might be expected to emerge from a system based on artistic freedom rather than the dominance of an *art officiel*. The Arts Council was but the cherry on the top of the rising cake of 'half-baked' state patronage. The activities of the British Council, in promoting British artists overseas, were successfully extended. Government grants to the national museums increased, and the art education system was greatly expanded.

At first, there was every indication that the new Golden Age of which Keynes had dreamed was coming into being. Those who had supported the best new art of the 1920s and 30s – Kenneth Clark and John Rothenstein among them – found themselves in positions of increasing cultural influence. The public interest in modern art, stimulated by the war, was sustained and deepened. In the early decades of the twentieth century, cheap books on contemporary artists had been virtually unobtainable; but publication of the influential Penguin Modern Painters series, under the general editorship of Kenneth Clark, marked the beginning of a boom in popular art books, which has continued to this day. A major exhibition of Picasso and Matisse, at the Victoria and Albert Museum in 1945, initiated an era of lavish exhibitions of the best overseas art. These attracted vast crowds, and influenced the work of contemporary British artists who were themselves well represented in the 1951 'Festival of Britain'. Inevitably, particular works aroused indignation, and even outrage; the award of a £500 prize in the Festival's '60 Paintings for '51' exhibition to the abstract painter, William Gear, even provoked questions in Parliament. Nonetheless, it seemed to be accepted that modern art had a major part to play in the reconstruction and forging of a new Britain.

Indeed, that same year the architect, Basil Spence, received a commission to rebuild Coventry Cathedral, which had been reduced to ruins. He immediately commissioned Graham Sutherland to produce a tapestry which would dominate the new building. When it was unveiled in 1962, Sutherland's version of *Christ in Glory in the Tetramorph* (i.e. with panels representing the emblems of the four evangelists), like the Cathedral itself, aroused intense public feelings and passions; but its scale, glory, and originality cannot be denied. Such courageous patronage could only have been bestowed on a contemporary artist in these heady and hopeful days.

Simultaneously, British art, cleverly nurtured by the British Council, began to achieve a wider recognition than ever before overseas. In 1946, an exhibition of 'Modern British Pictures from the Tate Gallery' was sent abroad for the benefit of 'friends and allies'. Moore, Nicholson, Piper, and Sutherland were all well represented, and well received. Moore's international reputation was further advanced when he was awarded the international prize for sculpture at the 1948 Venice Biennale, where his works were exhibited alongside Turner's landscapes. The following year, Moore had a major exhibition in the Musée d'Art Moderne in Paris; in 1950 Barbara Hepworth's sculptures were exhibited, in Venice, beside Constable's paintings; and, in 1952 and 1954, Graham Sutherland's and Ben Nicholson's international reputations were confirmed by their respective one-man shows there.

It would be wrong, however, to imply that all this was achieved without opposition. Although these artists were now warmly supported by the Arts Council, the British Council, and the Tate, they were bitterly opposed by an older, and yet continuing, cultural establishment. For example, in 1948, Sir Winston Churchill attended the Royal Academy Dinner, and Sir Alfred Munnings, the President, knew his speech would achieve the maximum publicity. He announced that he found himself President of a body of men who were 'what I call shilly-shallying. They feel that there is something in this so-called modern art.' Munnings proceeded to disabuse them. He said, 'there has been a foolish interruption to all efforts in Art, helped by foolish men writing in the Press, encouraging all this damned nonsense, putting all these young men out of their stride'. But, Munnings assured his listeners, 'I am right – I have the Lord Mayor on my side and *all* the Aldermen and *all* the City Companies.' Munnings asserted that the 'newly-erected, extraordinary member of the Academy – Winston Churchill' was on his side, too. And he launched into an attack on the 'highbrows' and 'experts' who 'think they know more about Art than the men who paint the pictures'.

Munnings was certainly belligerent and bigoted; he was also speaking at a time when a genuine efflorescence of British art seemed to be taking place. But, with hindsight, it can be said that his argument was not entirely without reason. For all the high hopes and early achievements, the new 'Keynesian' institutional patronage was ultimately to prove no more adept at fostering a healthy artistic tradition than the crusty world of the Academy, with its clients in the City, the Livery Companies, and the shires. After the electoral defeat of 1951, the new public patrons lost their nerve – and never regained it. After some years of confusion in the 1950s, the values affirmed through emergent neo-romanticism were replaced by the vitiating imperatives of a commercialised and institutionalised American-inspired 'avant-garde'.

The importance of the anti-vanguardist opposition to the emerging new consensus in the art institutions is highlighted by the fact that, by 1948, the fires of neo-romanticism were largely extinguished. The leading protagonists – Moore, Piper, and Sutherland – could no longer, even loosely, be considered a group; each was now a major *individual* talent. Some of the younger neo-romantics, like Minton, died prematurely; others, like Ayrton, Craxton and Vaughan, were destined to work in isolation from all fashionable trends. British art was to become progressively prised apart from its roots in natural form and common tradition; indeed it began to slip and slide into a period of decadence. 'Progressive' artists found themselves isolated, once again, and prevented from playing any significant part in the nation's cultural life. During the 1950s, there was a curious resurgence of the tendentious preoccupations of the 1930s.

For example, after the 'conversion' of Victor Pasmore in 1948 – heralded by Herbert Read as the most 'revolutionary' event in British art since the war – the issue of abstraction versus realism again became a matter of contention. Pasmore had a background in the Euston Road School, which in the immediate post-war years offered an 'objective' alternative to neo-romanticism. He went on to paint romantically feathery, pointilistic studies of *The Hanging Gardens of Hammersmith* and other London parks. And then, in 1948, Pasmore surprised everyone by producing pictures which, in his words, had 'no descriptive qualities at all'. Instead, he wanted to imitate the structural processes of nature; but the key to its underlying forms eluded him. In 1950, after a visit to St Ives, he flirted with abstracted appearances again. But he continued to yearn for a man-made system of harmonious proportions and associated with a group of urban constructivists – including Kenneth and Mary Martin, Adrian Heath, and Anthony Hill – who mounted London's first post-war abstract exhibition at the AIA galleries in 1951. (The AIA had revised its constitution to exclude support for a specific political position.) Later in the decade, however, less systematic forms of abstraction became more prevalent. These paralleled *art brut*, *art informel*, and *tachisme* in Paris, which, until 1956, was again regarded by British artists as the centre of all that was good and great in contemporary art – although, in truth, the heady days of the Parisian modernist renaissance were long since over. The Scottish abstractionist, Alan Davie, was perhaps the first British painter to be influenced by Jackson Pollock and New York abstract expressionism, which he encountered in Peggy Guggenheim's collection in Venice, in 1948, although Davie's painting always owed more to, say, Celtic mysticism than New York style.

The tendentious fifties

The return of a Conservative government in 1951 heralded a change in the status of the visual arts. Although the pattern of subsidy established by the post-war Labour government was maintained, and indeed greatly expanded, during the Macmillan era, the Keynesian hopes for a state within which contemporary art occupied a place at the very centre of national life began to recede. A symbol of this change of climate occurred when an All-Party Committee commissioned Graham Sutherland to paint a portrait of Sir Winston Churchill for his eightieth birthday in 1954. Churchill detested the result which he described as 'an old man on his stool, pressing and pressing'. According to Lady Churchill, he was wounded that Sutherland had depicted him as 'a gross and cruel monster'. In public, Churchill seemed to be echoing Sir Alfred Munnings when he sneeringly referred to the portrait as 'a striking example of *modern* art'. Conservatives tended to dislike the painting, Labour supporters to like it, confirming Churchill's suspicion that it was part of a conspiracy to ridicule him and prise him from power. The picture vanished from public view; in 1978 it was learned that Lady Churchill had ordered it to be destroyed. But modern art had long since ceased to play a significant part in national, cultural life.

Graham Sutherland, Portrait of Sir Winston Churchill (1874–1965) *(1955; destroyed)*.

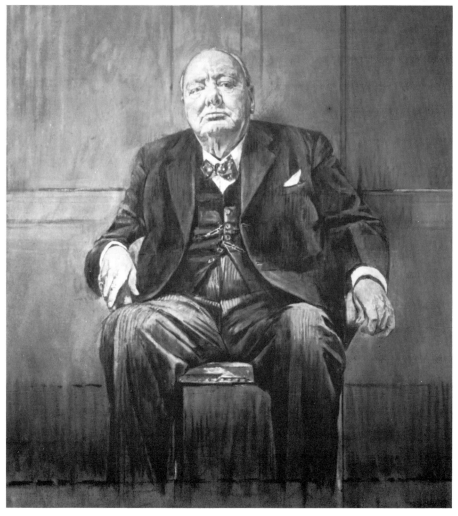

Although neo-romanticism had little influence over a rising generation of sculptors, painters, and critics, something of its spiky angst can be detected in the sculpture of Kenneth Armitage, Reg Butler, Lynn Chadwick, Bernard Meadows, and Eduardo Paolozzi, which was shown alongside Moore's at the Venice Biennale of 1952. The following year, Butler won the first prize in an international sculpture competition held for a monument to 'The Unknown Political Prisoner'; but his design was never built. In the late 1950s, Elizabeth Frink, the youngest of the new sculptors, produced some remarkable studies of injured bird-men, and fallen warriors. Over the ensuing decades, she resolutely pursued her own path, unaffected by prevailing fashions. Despite a formal awkwardness, her running and mounted men, and the massive heads of her goggled power-mongerers, established her as easily the most accomplished British sculptor of the male figure in the post-war years. By and large, the fragmented, 'existential' and urban imagery of this generation lacked the consoling strength and the relationship to landscape which had characterised the best of Moore and Hepworth.

At first, this could not be said of a new generation of St Ives painters, some of whom acknowledged their debt to the older neo-romantics. For example, Bryan Wynter, who worked in the Cornish fishing village, knew and was influenced by Colquhoun, MacBryde, and Minton. Similarly, Ivon Hitchens had some effect on the work of Patrick Heron; but Heron was defiantly antagonistic towards what he took to be the literary associations and 'writhing lines' of Piper and Sutherland. Heron's own painting, influenced by Braque and Matisse, was moving towards colour abstraction; but he also established himself as the critical advocate of a group of artists many of whom – including Paul Feiler, Terry Frost, Roger Hilton, Peter Lanyon, William Scott and John Wells – had some connection with St Ives.

Heron's polemical purpose, spelled out in exhibitions like 'Space in Colour', held at the Hanover Gallery in 1953, was to emphasise that painting was, first and foremost, an art of illusion, and that colour was 'the utterly indispensable means for realising the various species of pictorial space'. (colour pl. 2). Heron wanted to provide an answer to John Berger, the critic who had displaced him at *The New Statesman*, and who was vociferously arguing for 'realism'. Berger, a Marxist, explained that the final criterion by which he judged a work of art was expressed through the question, 'Does this work help or encourage men to know and claim their social rights?' In the catalogue of 'Looking Forward', an exhibition of 120 paintings he organised for the Whitechapel Gallery in 1952, Berger declared that he wanted to show the work of painters who were more concerned with the reality of the subject than with the 'reality' of their subjective feelings about it.

By applying such criteria, Berger convinced himself that minor sculptors like George Fullard and Peter Peri were better than Moore, whose work he dismissed as a 'Piltdown sculpture' or Hepworth, whom he accused of 'basic emptiness'. In painting, Berger staked a great deal on the 'kitchen sink school', especially John Bratby, Derrick Greaves, Edward Middleditch, and Jack Smith, all of whom, at that time, could more properly have been described as *expressionists* rather than as *realists*. None of them possessed the pictorial strength of Josef Herman, whose archetypal paintings of the miners and fishermen of Wales were enthused with a symbolic monumentality, which owed something to his collection of African sculpture. But Berger criticised Herman for 'subjectivism', and or aspiring to 'a kind of universal consoling recognition', i.e. for seeking spiritual rather than merely social truths. Berger, however, was nothing if not an eloquent advocate; in 1956, the kitchen sink painters were treated to the accolade of a showing at the Venice Biennale, under the auspices of the British Council. Subsequently, Bratby's colours grew brighter; his expressionist 'handwriting' ever more conspicuous; Smith, never easy with his 'social realist' tag, turned entirely abstract. Berger roundly denounced his erstwhile protégés and gave up as a regular critic of British art.

In the absence of a shared symbolic order of the kind that neo-romanticism had begun to provide, art seemed destined to thrash around once again in the shallows of verisimilitude, political tendentiousness, or 'pure' abstraction. David Sylvester was one of the few critics who perceived that a 'symbolic realism', rooted in natural and anatomical form, but extending beyond it into a domain of value, could provide a way beyond this impasse. But, by the end of the 1950s, institutional taste began to change in ways which neither Heron, Berger, nor Sylvester had foreseen. The museums and fashionable galleries began to favour art forms which reproduced the cellophane values and anti-aesthetic techniques of modern advertising; alternatively, they elevated the extreme subjectivity of American-inspired abstraction.

For 1952 was also the year when the Independent Group – including the painter, Richard Hamilton, the sculptor, Eduardo Paolozzi, and the critics Lawrence Alloway and Reyner Banham – began meeting at the Institute of Contemporary Arts. The emphasis, at first, was on the relation between art, technology, and science. Alloway, for example, was at first an advocate for the constructivists. But the group 'graduated' towards an obsession with mechanical products, rather than natural forms, and eventually a preference for 'admass' and the urban environment, rather than landscape. Hamilton, at one time himself an abstract artist, once explained that his own 'return to nature' in the mid-fifties 'came at second hand through the use of magazines rather than as a response to real landscape'. Independent Group artists were behind the exhibition, 'This is Tomorrow', which opened at the Whitechapel in 1956, the year that the Kitchen Sink painters left for Venice, and included Hamilton's notorious collage, *Just what is it that Makes Today's Homes so Different, so Appealing?*

In 1957, Hamilton defined his position in a letter, much-quoted ever since, in which he said that pop art was:

Popular (designed for a mass audience), Transient (short-term solution), Expendable (easily forgotten), Low cost, Mass produced, Young (aimed at youth), Witty, Sexy, Gimmicky, Glamorous, Big Business.

Alloway was the first to use the term 'pop art', though initially he applied it only to the products of the mass media, rather than to what artists made. Later 'pop art' became the generic term for all fine art which looked to advertising and commercial spectacle for 'inspiration'. Alloway explained that the development of these media was dissolving traditional conceptions of culture. The media were themselves coming 'to act as a guide to life defined in terms of possessions and relationships'. Artists should take note – as Hamilton did in pictures like *She* (1958–61), which identified modern woman as synonymous with the 'cool' image of the female projected in advertisements for kitchen appliances: and old fashioned 'humanists' should leave the stage.

While all this was going on, one such 'humanist' painter – incidentally one of the greatest British artists of this century – was dying in obscurity. After attending the Slade, between 1911 and 1913, David Bomberg had become a Vorticist; but he was an early 'post-modernist', and quickly dissociated himself from the arid, mechanical aesthetic. Bomberg spent the remainder of his life searching for a way of painting through which he could express higher sentiments in a secular way. Though his late paintings were often regarded almost as an aberration, or a throwback, it was only in them that he felt he had found himself. Bomberg advocated rigorous attention to appearances; but he maintained that, in and of itself, the eye was 'a stupid organ'. He came to believe that the artist should search for what he called 'the spirit in the mass'. Bomberg's work after the Second World War received little official attention; before his death, he had become disillusioned and embittered. But his drawing class at the Borough Polytechnic, between 1945 and 1953, attracted talented pupils – including Frank Auerbach, Dennis Creffield, Leon Kossoff and Roy Oxlade, all of whom developed, rather than imitated, his methods, and remained faithful to his increasingly unfashionable ethic of high seriousness, and unswerving commitment. The achievement of Auerbach and Kossoff in the 1970s, and 1980s, was second to none.

David Bomberg, Ronda Bridge, the Tajo *(c.1956; private collection)*.

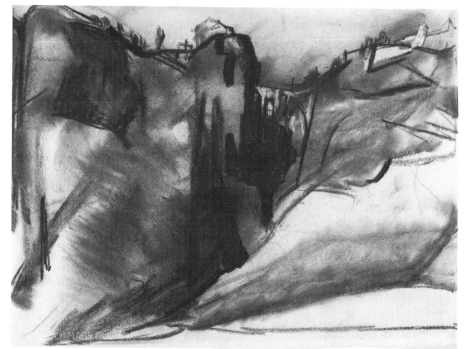

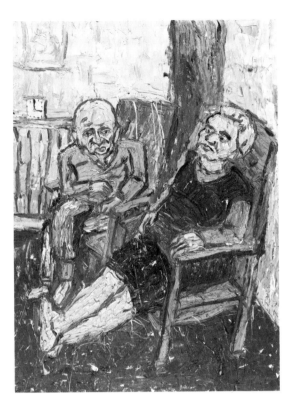

Leon Kossoff, Two Seated
Figures *(1980; Tate
Gallery, London)*.

To the fashionable art world in that artful year of 1956, the only serious
rival to pop, however, seemed to be abstract expressionism – an American
movement, whose members attempted to express emotions through paintings
from which almost all illusionistic imagery had been removed. This new work
was seen extensively in London for the first time in the last room of a Tate
Gallery exhibition, 'Modern Art in the United States'. Its impact was
confirmed through the show, 'The New American Painting' in 1959.
American cultural agencies were determined to promote this style because
they hoped that, in the Cold War, it would be seen as a symbol of the
existential 'freedom' of artists in the West. In the late 1950s, American
abstraction swept through the studios in this country. Heron was one of the
first to defend it. But, to his alarm, he was soon to discover that the
achievement of the so-called 'Middle Generation' painters of St Ives, which
had, in fact, had a considerable influence on developments in American
abstraction in the 1950s, was simply brushed aside in favour of the inflated
second-hand work of a younger group of abstract painters. This new
generation boorishly proclaimed their central values as 'professionalism' (i.e.
commercialism) rather than amateurism; predictably, they looked to
American style, rather than English landscape, as a source. Bernard and
Harold Cohen, Robyn Denny, John Hoyland, and Richard Smith first
attracted attention through an exhibition called 'Situation', at the Royal
Society of British Artists, in 1960, where canvases had to be both abstract
and at least thirty square feet in size. Of this group, only Hoyland was

subsequently to produce work of enduring merit, and that, intriguingly, at a time when he moved from the city to the countryside. A more significant abstract artist was John Walker, an excellent draughtsman who retained some conception of depicted space.

An antipodean aesthetic?

The irony of all this was that by 1958, the abstract expressionist movement had degenerated into 'Tenth Street', or rate, abstraction in New York. Only Mark Rothko was to produce new work which endeavoured to express significant human feelings. A far more important exhibition from the perspective of the British tradition was, or rather ought to have been, the Whitechapel Show of 1961, 'New Australian Painting'. As Kenneth Clark, who wrote the forward, perceived, Australian painters like Sidney Nolan, had created a new kind of Higher Landscape painting which did not just depict appearances, but endeavoured to express and convey values and morals. Although what these Australians were doing could be related to the war-inspired imagery of Paul Nash, Graham Sutherland, and even Henry Moore, they took as their starting point not an injured European landscape, but the great 'natural' wasteland of the Australian outback. Nolan and Arthur Boyd both spent most of their lives in Britain in the 1960s. Boyd, in particular, deserves to be regarded as one of the foremost artists working here after the Second World War. His Nebuchadnezzar series of the 1960s, Suffolk landscapes of the early 1970s, and great Shoalhaven paintings of the 1980s – all of which deal with man's struggle to come to terms with an alien environment, and a 'godless' universe – transformed a tradition of landscape painting in this country the roots of which can be traced back to the seventeenth century.

But this profoundly original Australian work created only a passing whirl

Arthur Boyd, Bathers and Pulpit Rock *1984–5; Collection Fischer Fine Art Ltd, London).*

of dust within the British art world. Inevitably, perhaps, America was to exert an ever greater influence. Across the Atlantic, the market in modern art was expanding as never before, introducing a new note of rabid commercialism; and the explosive arrival of pop art on the American scene seemed an appropriate response to these developments. In Britain, the public for the visual arts was, by this time, considerably smaller; the taste of those who ran the institutions of art was more important than the imperatives of the market place. Unfortunately, however, these institutions were now falling into the hands of a generation of career-conscious art-bureaucrats, who were more concerned with the promotion of that which was new, than with art as an expression of beauty, significant form, or aesthetic values of any kind. Pop art thrived.

The triumph of pop

At this time, tragic changes were also instigated in the art education system. In the mid-1950s, Richard Hamilton, Victor Pasmore, Harry Thubron, and Tom Watson began to advocate a new system of art education, known as 'Basic Design'. As Dick Field has written, the watchword of Basic Design was 'a New Art for a New Age'. 'Basic Design' shifted the emphasis away from the idea of painting and sculpture as 'Liberal Arts' which embodied aesthetic values; and displaced drawing as the centre and focus of an education in art. Students were encouraged either to immerse themselves in 'Mixed Media', photography, and the techniques and values of contemporary advertising and mechanical production (pop art); or, alternatively, to regress to a pristine infantilism (abstract expressionism). Awareness of the *traditions* of painting and sculpture as 'Liberal Arts' deteriorated. Most art schools were eventually assimilated into the Polytechnics – a move which was later to have disastrous consequences in the tight economic climate of the 1980s. The Coldstream Report embodied the destructive and ultimately 'deskilling' view that art education should not be too closely related to painting and sculpture, because the fine arts 'derive from an attitude which may be expressed in many ways'.

In 1961, a second wave of British pop artists erupted at the 'Young Contemporaries' exhibition. These included Peter Blake, who mingled nostalgia, banality, and commercialism into an image of England as eternal Lymeswold; Allen Jones, who mistook art for pornography; and Peter Phillips, who is now justly forgotten. Many of these artists were associated with the Royal College of Art; the most talented, David Hockney and Ron Kitaj, were eventually to emerge as defenders of the traditional aesthetic and ethical bases for the fine arts. But, for a time, their work was associated with the trivial concerns of pop. Closely related were the geometric patterns of 'Op' typified in the work of Bridget Riley, who at least succeeded in contributing to the design of the Woolmark, for the woollen industry. Little wonder that when Keith Vaughan saw 'The New Generation' exhibition at the Whitechapel Gallery in 1964, he complained in his journal, 'After all one's thought and search and effort to make some sort of image which would embody the life of our time, it turns out that all that was really significant

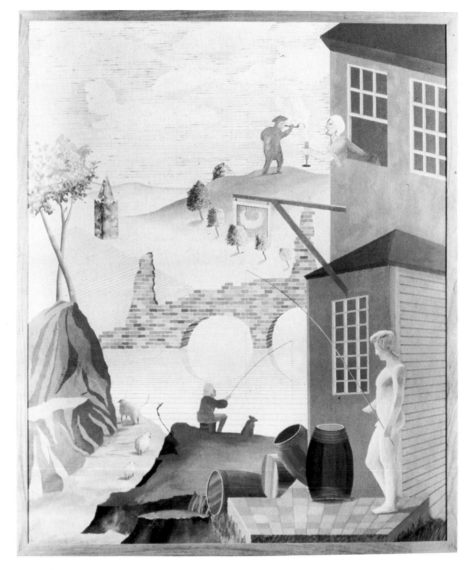

David Hockney, Kerby (After Hogarth) Useful Knowledge 1975 *(Knoedler Kasmin Fine, Arts, London)*.

were toffee wrappers, liquorice allsorts and ton-up motor bikes.' Vaughan understood how the stranded dinosaurs felt when the hard terrain, which for centuries had demanded from them greater weight and effort, suddenly started to get swampy beneath their feet. 'Over-armoured and slow-witted they could only subside in frightened bewilderment.' For over a decade, the dinosaurs indeed disappeared from view.

Although Henry Moore's work was entering a new and fascinating 'Late Phase', very few young sculptors were even aware of the fact. Anthony Caro, and the 'New Generation' sculptors, like Phillip King, Tim Scott, and William Tucker, were grabbing all the critical attention with their fashionable

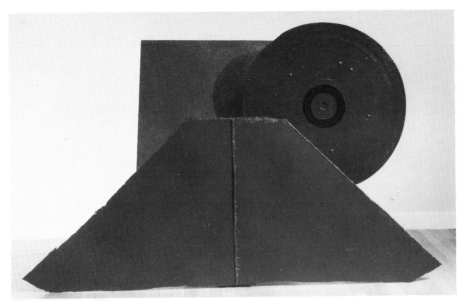

Anthony Caro, Twenty-four Hours *(1960; Tate Gallery, London)*.

but vapid 'radically abstract' constructions in welded steel, or fibre glass. The 1960s are often depicted as an 'exciting time' for the visual arts in general, and sculpture in particular: in fact, this was a period of decline, even decadence. Some of Caro's pupils, like Barry Flanagan and Nicholas Pope, began to reduce sculpture to the mere placement of virtually unworked materials in stacks, heaps, piles or bundles. Richard Long collapsed the subtle sense of landscape which had characterised an earlier generation of British sculptors into the presentation of documentary 'evidence' (i.e. maps and photographs) or the barren arrangement of gathered stones. Practitioners like Gilbert and George declared that their own bodies were 'Living Sculptures', and made videos of themselves getting drunk. The 'conceptualists' came into vogue with an exhibition called, 'When Attitudes Become Form', and sub-titled, 'Live in your head!', at the Institute of Contemporary Arts in 1969. Victor Burgin, who characteristically exhibited 'Some Instructions for an Interior Location', denounced painting and sculpture as 'the anachronistic daubing of woven fabrics with coloured mud', and the 'chipping apart of rocks and the sticking together of pipes', respectively. Conceptualists preferred words – though they had no sense of poetry – photographs, maps, twigs, stones, and bits of string. As Anne Seymour put it in her introduction to 'The New Art', an exhibition of *dernier cri* conceptualism held at the Hayward Gallery in 1972, the artist need no longer be 'tied to a host of aesthetic discomforts which he personally does not appreciate'.

A new dark age?

In these dark days, Kenneth Clark made an exemplary series of television programmes, *Civilization*, which reminded a large and enthusiastic television audience of the achievements of the European tradition. This was answered by Berger in a polemical riposte, *Ways of Seeing*, also a television series and book. Berger argued that there was an intrinsic relationship between oil-painting and private property; that the Western pictorial tradition was 'sexist'; and that modern advertising was simply the extension, and fulfilment, of this unsavoury Western tradition. In the book, though not the television series, Berger exonerated 'masterpieces' from these criticisms, without explaining how they had managed to escape. Such criticisms were presented as a radical assault on 'bourgeois values'; but they also reflected the anti-aesthetic orthodoxies of the day. The institutional art of the 1970s saw the triumph of every kind of anti-art, political tractarianism, and 'feminist' polemic. As such art showed no concern for the good, the true or the beautiful, it produced no masterpieces.

Douglas Cooper was not alone in believing that the stewardship of the Tate had fallen into the wrong hands; in 1976, the historian of cubism, and authority on Sutherland, instigated a national debate concerning the acquisition, by the Tate Gallery some years previously, of *Equivalent VIII*. This 'sculpture' consisted of a stack of fire-bricks by the American 'minimal' and 'conceptual' artist, Carl Andre. The Gallery only made itself even more foolish when one of its curators defended the 'limpid clarity' of the said bricks in *The Burlington* magazine and argued that they were really no different from any other major sculpture. Meanwhile, another Tate curator candidly admitted that he regarded contemporary art as a hermetic 'sub-culture'. 'The Government', he stated, 'is backing my game, my passionate interest, and as long as I can continue to persuade it to do so, I will. I'm on to a good thing and I would not dream of questioning it.' Nor was it just the Tate; rows understandably ensued concerning the exhibition of soiled nappy liners and, on another occasion, used tampons at the publicly funded Institute of Contemporary Arts. One of the 'artists' involved had received extensive backing for foreign tours from the British Council. And this is what had become of John Maynard Keynes' great dream of a new Golden Age of the arts flourishing within a modern Welfare State!

By the mid seventies, there were overdue signs of a reaction. The old formalist positions began to reassert themselves, in exhibitions like William Tucker's 'The Condition of Sculpture', or *Artscribe* magazine's 'Style of the Seventies'. But these only set the argument back one step. More radical was the argument advanced by Ron Kitaj, and supported by David Hockney, in favour of a return to drawing. Kitaj also underlined the corroding effects of vanguardist 'internationalism' in the arts, and celebrated the achievements of an alternative English tradition. 'The bottom line', wrote Kitaj in the catalogue to 'The Human Clay', an exhibition he organised for the Arts Council in 1976, 'is that there are artistic personalities in this small island more unique and strong and I think numerous than anywhere in the world outside America's jolting artistic vigour.'

Andrew Brighton and Lynda Morris extended Kitaj's argument for a revised understanding of the recent past with their exhibition, 'Towards another Picture'. This included, alongside avant-gardists, the work of academic and populist painters, like Terence Cuneo, who depicted Lord

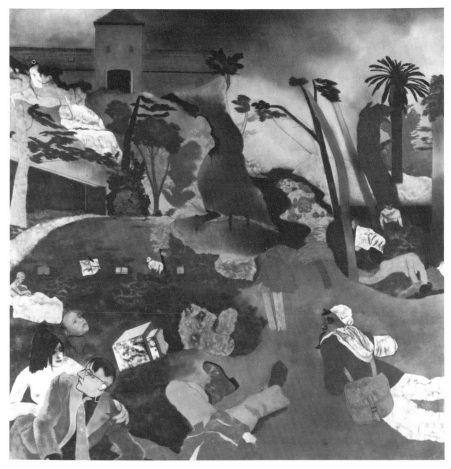

Ron Kitaj, If Not, Not *(1975–6; Scottish National Gallery of Modern Art)*.

Mayors and steam trains, and David Shepherd, who specialised in African wildlife – particularly elephants. The 'bottom line' implied by this exhibition was that the modernist art establishment was promoting a particular 'line' in contemporary art. Who was to say that David Wynne's black marble study, *Guy the Gorilla*, (1962), was of less aesthetic and sculptural value than Andre's *Equivalent VIII*?

This sort of work also had broader implications. As Lawrence Gowing, a sensitive ex-Euston Road painter who became Slade Professor of Fine Art in 1976, once wrote, the received history of British art in the twentieth century, 'in which there is no place for anyone who cannot be labelled', will have to be rewritten. The standard accounts of British art since 1945 characteristically ignore the contribution made by those painters whose principal affiliation has been to the Royal Academy. They rarely say much about the work of Bernard Dunstan, who has long painted delicate, impressionistic studies in the tradition of the Camden Town School; or about Richard Eurich, Peter Greenham, Thomas Monnington, PRA, Ruskin Spear, John Ward, and Carel Weight, all of whom have produced vivid and highly personal work in our period. The Academy has also served the useful function of providing a geriatric space 'upstairs' for ageing Vorticists, angry young men, pop artists, and even abstractionists as they have passed out of fashion. Predictably, with the questioning of modernist premises in the 1980s, the Academy has become something of a force in the world once again.

More vital still have been those aesthetically conservationist traditions of British art which were neither modernist nor academic. No account of post-war British art would be replete without mention of such great 'independents' as L.S. Lowry who began to exhibit his pictures of 'stick-men' in Manchester and Salford industrial settings in 1939, and became almost a folk hero after the war; Edward Burra, who pursued a blacker, more exotic, and yet no less idiosyncratic vision; or Cedric Morris, whose pedagogy and brilliantly-coloured paintings owed little to passing fashions.

These artists were all individuals, re-inventing tradition for themselves. Others, however, were affected by the continuing influence of the Euston Road School, which, after the Second World War, was felt most strongly at the Slade School of Art, under the professorship of William Coldstream, who developed a system of drawing based on relentless measurement. The work of some of Coldstream's pupils and disciples, like Patrick George and Euan Uglow, is mannerist and without merit; but, after a long struggle, Michael Andrews, an existential 'realist' painter, flowered into one of the finest British painters of the 1980s, with a great series of landscapes based on Ayers Rock (colour pl. 4). Gowing himself, and Rodrigo Moynihan, are among the versatile and 'unclassifiable' artists associated with the Slade who have received less critical attention than they deserve. Gowing, in particular, entered a tortured 'late phase' of courageous, if unbecoming, self-exposure. Gowing's nude studies of his tormented and ageing self can be compared with Robert Medley's unheroic paintings of a standing, naked male figure. Medley also stubbornly defended a humanist tradition of painting when he taught at Camberwell School of Art, and subsequently at the British school at Rome. Even harder to pin down are certain imaginative painters, like David Jones, Cecil Collins and Norman Adams, who, though sometimes spoken of as 'surrealists', seem rather to belong to a visionary and spiritual tradition which can be traced back to William Blake.

In the 1980s, however, the late modernist tradition itself seemed to undergo a 'return' if not to painting, then at least to paint. The exhibition, 'A New Spirit in Painting' was opportunistically organised by a group of young art bureaucrats to fill a gap in the Royal Academy's 1981 exhibition programme. Sir Alfred Munnings would not have approved, but Hugh Casson, then PRA, gave his imprimatur, even comparing the show with Roger Fry's pioneering exhibition of post-impressionism at the Grafton Galleries in 1910. But 'A New Spirit' introduced a new expressionistic mode of painting, the ugliness of which knew no bounds. Nor did the cynicism with which it was taken up and promoted by commercial interests. Many conceptualists, who had previously renounced paint, now started to splatter everything with it.

True to form, the Tate succumbed to the new vogue. Widespread apprehension was voiced concerning the influence exerted over this national modern and British collection by Charles and Doris Saatchi, who had made a considerable fortune in the world of advertising, and who were thus in a position to spend considerable sums in the world of art. This very substantial patronage was not always well advised or well bestowed. These fears were not allayed when the Tate Gallery mounted an exhibition of works by the young American 'new expressionist' Julian Schnabel, which was heavily criticized; nor when in 1984 the first Turner Prize – which was organized under the Gallery's auspices and was intended to honour the individual who, in the opinion of the jury, had made the greatest contribution to art in Britain in the previous twelve months – was awarded to Malcolm Morley, who had not in fact lived in Britain for a quarter of a century and who, during that time, had held only one one-man show here. The Saatchis acquired fourteen of Morley's works for their collection, which in 1985 was put on view to the public in St John's Wood in London.

The situation in sculpture was equally bad. The conceptualism of the 1970s was displaced by the tacky 'new sculpture' of the 1980s – a funky and formless constructivism, making use of discarded consumer durables and urban detritus, whose leading practitioners included Bill Woodrow and Tony Cragg. The Arts Council and the British Council lost no opportunity to promote this aesthetically worthless fashion. The decadence of the art institutions in the 1980s ran even deeper than it had done in the 1880s, when Whistler, Sickert, and Steer pioneered a revolution in taste.

Signs of hope

It would, however, be wrong to suggest that the situation appeared without hope. As the 1980s wore on, there were signs that the institutional art world was out of step with the new and more 'conservationist' cultural mood of the time. Doubts about the value of ever-increasing production and ecological concern were rendering obsolete the enthusiasm of the art establishment for the shabbier aspects of modernity. Simultaneously, it began to be recognised that many older painters, whose roots stretched back to before the American influx of the late 1950s, were producing some of their best work in the otherwise bleak years of the 1970s and 1980s.

Sutherland returned to Pembrokeshire in 1968, and, during the 1970s, he produced his finest paintings since the war years there. In Suffolk, Arthur Boyd, too, began to paint the English landscape; he also returned' intermittently to his native Australia, and produced haunting pictures informed by his perception of two antithetical 'natures'. These artists went unnoticed by the critics, but the vogue for expressionism at least led to a revaluation of the late works of David Bomberg. His most talented pupils, Frank Auerbach and Leon Kossoff, received the recognition that had so long been denied them; as if spurred by this belated attention, their work achieved a new strength and maturity. Auerbach represented Britain in the 1986 Biennale, and revealed that through imagination, combined with relentless dedication to drawing and tradition, he had become a painter of unrivalled stature. The change in fashion also focused attention on the vividly-coloured

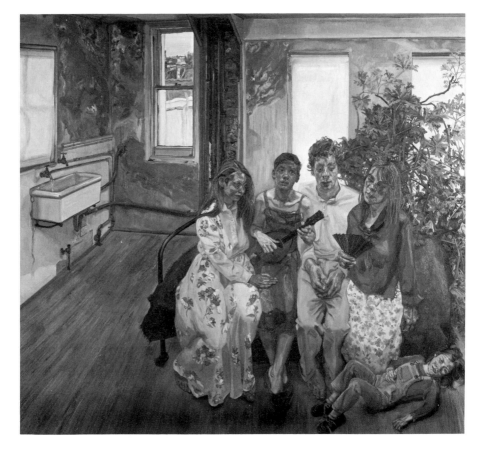

Lucian Freud, Large Interior, W.11 (after Watteau) *1981–3; private collection)*.

imaginings of Ken Kiff, who drew heavily on imagery derived from his own psychoanalysis. Lucian Freud's painting, too, manifested a new-found painterliness, and a searing vigour. *Large Interior W.11 (after Watteau)* must be reckoned among the masterpieces of the 1980s. Alan Davie, forgotten by the critics, but not by discriminating collectors, had long since abandoned abstract expressionism; his work, too, seemed to enter a late phase of unprecedented visionary landscapes.

In 1985, the second Turner Prize was awarded to Howard Hodgkin, an independent colourist of a rare sensibility, who produced glowing, jewel-like pictures, reminiscent of Rouault. Kitaj's visionary landscapes of the seventies, and his Jewish 'Holocaust' pictures of the 1980s, were of higher quality than anything he painted in his fashionable pop art phase; and Hockney, too, pressed his restless yet magnificently decorative questioning of modernist conventions.

In this period, the antics of the landscape conceptualists, with their gathered twigs and stones, and their framed maps and photographs, sadly overshadowed the original contribution of certain landscape painters. Mary Potter developed the delicate manner, with its pastel shades, and mergence of

Wilson Steer and Ben Nicholson, which she had begun in the 1920s.
Winifred Nicholson painted some of her finest pictures in the seventies.
Sheila Fell died in 1979 before her achievement in landscape painting was
acknowledged. But, by the mid-1980s, Adrian Berg's acute vision of the great
English parks (colour pl. 7) and John Hubbard's embracing fusion of abstract
expressionism and English landscape had begun to receive some recognition.
Interestingly, Therese Oulton, one of the few British painters of any promise
to emerge from the muddy waters of the new expressionism, also showed that
she had stronger roots in the tradition of British, imaginative landscape
painting.

Nature and raw flesh: Sutherland and Bacon

'Graham Sutherland is the most distinguished and the most original English
artist of the mid-twentieth century.' With these words, Douglas Cooper
opened his monograph on Graham Sutherland, published in 1961; Cooper
concluded that Sutherland was recognised in European artistic circles as the
only significant English painter since Constable and Turner. Cooper certainly
intended to imply Sutherland's superiority to Francis Bacon. But
Sutherland's critical reputation was already on the wane, and Bacon's was
still rising. At the time of Bacon's second retrospective at the Tate Gallery in
1985, Alan Bowness, the Director, wrote, 'His own work sets the standard for
our time, for he is surely the greatest living painter; no artist in our century
has presented the human predicament with such insight and feeling.' But
how just is the contemporary evaluation of the relative achievements of
Britain's two major post-Second World War painters?

   For a time, Sutherland and Bacon were friends, and, in the 1950s, they
shared more than a taste for roulette. They had a direct influence on each
other, and their work has much in common. Both artists constantly refer to a
vanished tradition of European painting, for which religious symbolism and
belief were of central importance. The work of both men is eccentric to
modernist concerns; their subjects are landscapes, animals, portraits, and
crucifixions. Although their imaginations constantly seem to touch upon each
other's, they also diverged widely. It isn't just that Sutherland was a 'nature'
painter, whose principal subject was landscape whereas Bacon is, first and
foremost, a painter of the human figure. Sutherland's paintings are haunted
by a yearning for spiritual redemption; he is the last serious artist who has
practised an aesthetic rooted in natural theology. As John Hayes has written,
'For Sutherland, landscape, and all its elements, bears the impress of the
divine creation, of which he seeks to catch a reflection.' Indeed, no painter,
this century, seems closer to the sensibility of Ruskin, who once wrote 'the
Great Spirit of nature is as deep and unapproachable in the lowest as in the
noblest objects'. In Pembrokeshire in the 1930s (and again in the 1970s),
Sutherland studied 'sea-eroded rocks', and noted how precisely they
reproduced in miniature 'forms of the inland hills'. For Sutherland, as for
Ruskin, 'the Divine mind is as visible in its full energy of operation on every
lowly bank and mouldering stone, as in the lifting of the pillars of heaven,

and settling the foundation of the earth'. But Bacon acknowledges only sense and sensation, and can affirm no more than a mundane sense of damnation.

Graham Sutherland was born in 1903; after a false start as an engineer, he trained as an etcher at Goldsmiths College. He converted to Catholicism in 1927. Throughout the 1920s, he was greatly influenced by Samuel Palmer. 'It seemed to me wonderful', he wrote later, 'that a strong *emotion*, such as was Palmer's, could change and transform the appearance of things.' Sutherland's earliest etchings were idyllic images of rural England – unfashionably 'overbitten' in technique. In *Pastoral*, of 1930, Sutherland's imagery began to change. A note of menace became apparent in his twisted root and branch forms; but he gave up etching a few years later. He made a living as a designer and commercial artist, and then in 1934, visited Pembrokeshire, where, in his words, he began to learn painting. He responded immediately to 'the exultant strangeness' of the place, which, despite its 'magical and transforming' light possessed 'an element of disquiet'. It was, he wrote, 'no uncommon sight to see a horse's skull or horns of cattle lying bleached on the sand'. He noted, too, 'the twisted gorse on the cliff edge . . . twigs, like snakes, lying on the path, the bare rock, worn, and showing through the path, heath fires, gorse burnt and blackened after fire' and 'mantling clouds against a black sky'.

In one sense Sutherland remained faithful to what he had seen in Palmer: he continued to transform appearances with powerful emotions; but Pembrokeshire encouraged him to develop the twisted imagery hinted at in his last etchings. In pictures like the ominous *Gorse on Sea Wall* of 1939, Sutherland revealed a rocky, spiky, and even hostile Nature, a fallen world, rather than a garden created by God, for man. This feeling was only heightened by the onset of war. Sutherland became an official War Artist in 1940. He drew first in the East End of London and around St Paul's; he made compelling images of damage and devastation, for example of burnt-out paper rolls, in a warehouse. Later, he produced infernal drawings of men at work in a steel furnace, and in the womb-like caverns of the Cornish tin-mines. In France he drew caves with, as he put it, 'a terrible sweet smell of death in them'. The war enabled Sutherland to incorporate images of mechanical destruction into his ominous vision. But paintings like Southampton Art Gallery's fiery *Red Landscape*, of 1942, underline the imaginative continuity between his response to an injured and injurious nature, and his war work (colour pl. 3).

In 1944, Canon Walter Hussey perceptively invited Sutherland to undertake an 'Agony in the Garden' for his church, St Matthew's in Northampton. But Sutherland had set his mind on another religious subject. Although he had never seen the concentration camps, he had received a black-covered American Central Office of Information book containing photographs of Belsen, Auschwitz and Buchenwald. As a result, the idea of the depiction of Christ crucified became more real to him: and, as he put it, 'it seemed possible to do this subject again'. In 1945, while brooding on his crucifixion, Sutherland started to draw thorn bushes, attending intently to their structure as they pierced the air. As he did this, 'The thorns rearranged

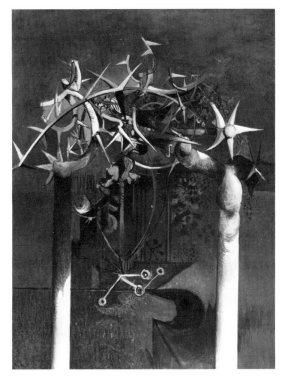

Graham Sutherland, Thorn Tree
(1945–6; British Council).

themselves, they became, whilst still retaining their own pricking, space-encompassing life, something else – a kind of "stand-in" for a Crucifixion and a crucified head.' Sutherland's fine paintings, like *Thorn Tree* of 1945/6, were, in effect, preparations for a crucifixion. In 1946, he strung himself up with ropes on a makeshift, packing-case cross, and sketched himself in a mirror. After months of experiment, he returned to his original conception of a tortured, symmetrical rendering of a Christ distanced from us by a small tubular railing round his feet – to emphasise the dreadful otherness of the event depicted. The crucifixion, Sutherland wrote later, interested him because 'It is the most tragic of all themes yet inherent in it is the promise of salvation.'

In the spring of 1945, Graham Sutherland contributed to an exhibition at the Lefevre Gallery which included Francis Bacon's *Three Studies for Figures at the Base of a Crucifixion*. Bacon, the son of a Dublin race-horse trainer, was six years younger than Sutherland; he had left home early after an incident in which he was discovered wearing his mother's clothes. He had no formal training in art, but began painting in the 1920s – without success. He worked as an interior designer: hints of tubular, Bauhaus furniture recur, often as a sort of space-frame, in much of his later work. Although Herbert Read reproduced a Bacon *Crucifixion* in his book, *Art Now*, Bacon destroyed almost all his early painting. *Three Studies* was his first mature painting, and it revealed many of the characteristics that were to recur in his later work.

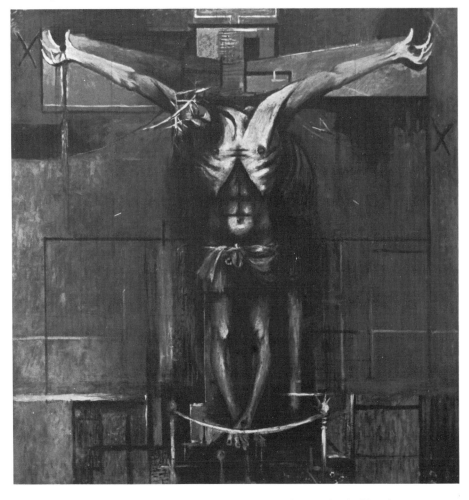

Graham Sutherland, Northampton Crucifixion *(1946: St Matthew's Church, Northampton)*.

These included the use of extreme anatomical and physiognomic distortion as the principal means of expression; a general tenor of violence and relentless physicality; and iconographic and formal allusions – e.g. through reference to the crucifixion, and the triptych format – to an abandoned tradition of Christian religious painting.

The *Three Studies* was followed by a *Figure in a Landscape*, 1945; but Bacon soon moved his mutilated creatures indoors where they have tended to remain. In the late 1940s came a series of macabre, isolated heads which reflected an obsession with the mouth and teeth. These merged with a series of screaming popes, based on Velasquez's portrait of Innocent X. Further studies of caged animals, enclosed figures, and grinning popes in front of carcasses of beef followed. Many of these contain indications of Bacon's preoccupation with the incidents and accidents of photography. *Two Figures*, 1953, depicted a violent act of buggery, and declared Bacon's preoccupation with sadistic, homosexual imagery. Towards the end of the 1950s, his palette

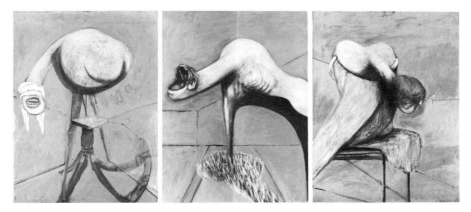

Francis Bacon, Three Studies for Figures at the Base of a Crucifixion
(c.1944; Tate Gallery, London).

briefly lightened: the studies he made for a portrait of Van Gogh even
contain suggestions of borrowed sun-light. But the 1960s saw his return to
more characteristic themes and moods.

Three Studies for a Crucifixion, 1962, is a massive triptych in virulent reds,
oranges, purples and blacks, the centre panel of which characteristically
displays a naked and bleeding figure splayed upon a bed. The right-hand
panel is an illustration of Bacon's view that Cimabue's great *Crucifixion* is no
more than an image of 'a worm crawling down the cross'. Bacon insists,
however, that his interest in the subject has nothing to do with its symbolic
resonances – least of all with any hint of salvation. The explanations he gives
for his involvement with the crucifixion have always been formal: 'The
central figure of Christ is raised into a very pronounced and isolated position,
which gives it, from a formal point of view, greater possibilities than having
all the different figures placed on the same level.'

After the Second World War, it seemed, briefly, that Sutherland's painting
was about to assume a central role in the nation's cultural life. In 1950,
Sutherland was commissioned to paint a massive mural for the 'Land of
Britain' pavilion at the Festival of Britain; he conceived of *The Origins of the
Land* on the scale of a cliff-face, suggesting geological strata, and
incorporating a pterodactyl. Sutherland represented Britain at the Venice
Biennale in 1952; and he and Gainsborough were the artists selected for
retrospectives at the Tate Gallery during the Coronation summer, the
following year. Philip James explained that they were both 'incontestably
English in their style and vision'.

But, that same year, Sutherland painted one of the most pessimistic of all
his paintings, *Christ Carrying the Cross*. Sutherland depicts Jesus at his
moment of collapse. He is shown falling to the ground amid strange
architectural ruins. An odious thug, with grinning teeth – explicitly recalling
similar figures by Francis Bacon – boots him mercilessly. In this picture, at
least, we are offered no hint of a resurrection. It is tempting to read the work
as an allegory which expresses Sutherland's growing doubts about the
Baconian culture which was emerging in post-war Britain.

If so, it was prophetic. In 1951, Sutherland had also been invited to design a vast tapestry of the Risen Christ to form the centre piece of Basil Spence's new Coventry Cathedral. This absorbed much of his time over the decade. Working within tight theological constraints, Sutherland conceived a bold, frontal image of the Christ, whose face fuses the power of Egyptian sculpture, the hieratic stillness of the Byzantine Pantocrator, and elements drawn from Sutherland's own physiognomy. But both the design and the weaving of the tapestry were subject to delays and prevarications; there were misunderstandings between the artist, the architect and the Cathedral authorities. By the time it was unveiled, in 1962, both British culture, and Sutherland's position within it, had changed.

The ethics of hope and 'reconstruction' had been replaced by the callous banalities of consumerism; the shallow concerns of the pop art movement were booming. Despite – and, to some degree, because of – Cooper's impassioned advocacy, Sutherland's reputation had collapsed among artists, critics, and the cultural *cognoscenti*. Sutherland lived for much of the year in France, where the tapestry had been woven; but he was becoming an exile in something more than a physical sense. His *Risen Christ* seemed like some strange iconic survival from a forgotten age of faith.

Churchill's rejection of Sutherland's portrait of him (see p. 105) seems to have brought home to the artist his displacement from the mainstream of British cultural life. The following year, he bought a house at Menton, in France; soon afterwards, he became embroiled in a bitter struggle with the Tate Gallery – which he rightly perceived was falling away from its former high ideals. But cut off from its roots in the landscape and tradition of Britain, Sutherland's art did not prosper. His palette had been lightening and brightening before he moved to France – partially as a result of his study of Picasso and Matisse. But something repetitive, and stereotyped, entered into Sutherland's handling in the 1960s; at its worst, his painting seemed to have lost its way, to have made too many concessions to accepted modernist styles. His virtuosity as a graphic designer seemed sometimes to inhibit his development as a painter. At times, he was in danger of producing pastiches of Picasso or Matisse. Two groups of works must be exempted from these general criticisms; in the 1960s, Sutherland painted a number of animal pictures, and a series of related prints known as *A Bestiary*. Like his landscapes, these works involved intense imaginative transformation – or 'paraphrase', as he called it. In some of them, he imbued an established genre with new layers of symbolism, and imaginative resonance. But the other and more significant exception is Sutherland's work in portraiture.

In 1949, Somerset Maugham suddenly and unexpectedly invited Sutherland to paint his portrait. Eventually, Sutherland agreed to do so, and the startling result opened an entirely new chapter in his art. He has often been criticised for painting the rich and famous, even for accepting portrait commissions – as if these were things that the 'serious' modern artist did not do. But Sutherland was drawn towards those who were creative, powerful, influential, or successful – in life, and in art. He liked sitters whose faces were, in effect, social masks, etched with the lines of history and experience, which revealed as much as they hid. Lord Beaverbrook, Kenneth Clark, and the neurotically hyper-sensitive Edward Sackville-West, he knew well. But his portraits of Helena Rubinstein, Konrad Adenauer, and Lord Goodman are also compelling.

Although, as John Hayes has put it, 'likeness has always been the essential ingredient in Sutherland's portraiture', he has treated 'likeness' as a means to an end, rather than an end in itself. The point has often been made that if Sutherland's landscapes suggest human, and divine, presences, his portraits similarly recall landscape and reveal the depths of the *human* spirit. Nowhere is this more evident than in the creased and craggy features of Sutherland's Somerset Maugham. Sutherland argued that if you falsified physical truth, you were in danger of falsifying psychological truth. And so he did not caricature, flatter, or idealise. Portraiture, Sutherland insisted, 'is a matter of accepting rather than imposing'. He once explained that it was 'an art of letting the subject gradually reveal himself unconsciously so that by his voice and gaze as well as by his solid flesh your memory and emotions are stirred and assaulted, as with other forms of nature'. Or, as Douglas Cooper put it, Sutherland waited while the sitter 'composes his own portrait'. This, we feel, the ageing Churchill did for him. Churchill responded by complaining that he had been depicted as 'a gross and cruel monster'. But what, one wonders, would he have thought if the 'greatest living painter', whose work (according to the present Director of the Tate Gallery) 'sets the standard for our time' had attempted his likeness?

In the early 1960s, Bacon's work began to change, too. It became of a more personal, one hesitates to say 'intimate' character. He made increasing use of those in his personal circle as models – though he usually worked from photographs rather than life. He preferred 'low-life' characters, who accompanied him on his drinking and gambling bouts. The distorted faces and figures of Muriel Belcher – the owner of a Soho drinking club Bacon frequented – Isabel Rawsthorne, Lucian Freud, and George Dyer – Bacon's lover – recur and recur.

Andrew Forge, the distinguished British critic, has argued that the 'scandal' of Bacon's painting resides in the fact that he has rejected the conventions that have dominated the art of his lifetime. Not only does Bacon dismiss abstract painting as fashionable pattern-making, but he also makes a claim for a traditional art of the human figure which takes its stand on *likeness*: 'The gap between Sargent and Cézanne, between Sir William Orpen and Matisse was unbridgeable. Dimples, moist eyes, half smiles were taboo. Bacon affronts this taboo.'

It is certainly true that Bacon appeals exclusively to a system of 'expression', dependent upon the anatomy, gesture, and physiognomy of the depicted subject. But so, in his portraiture, did Sutherland, and so, of course, do many lesser artists whose work holds no 'scandal' for us. The scandal of Bacon's work must lie elsewhere – in his particular way of handling likeness. I used to argue that Bacon caricatured his subjects. Caricature is a tendentious portrayal of character based on the distortion of specific features. Caricature is, in effect, an intentionally biased rendering of the 'social mask' through which all men and woman – especially those with a public persona –

present themselves to the world. But caricature depends on *difference*; it accentuates specifics. And Andrew Forge is surely right when he says that Bacon has no interest in 'social masks'; unlike the traditional portrait painter, he would never paint an individual 'as' an admiral, faithful wife, scholar, statesman, or whatever. Indeed, Bacon seems barely aware that such people exist. Whether he is depicting Isabel Rawsthorne, Muriel Belcher, George Dyer, or indeed himself, the brutal 'revelation' is always the same.

Bacon himself has often suggested that his distortions clear away veils and screens, and reveal his subjects, 'as they really are'. But before we assent to this, we must first go along with Bacon's judgement on his fellow human beings. In this sense, his approach is the opposite of Sutherland's; Bacon would *never* let the sitter 'compose his own portrait'. There is only one aspect of human being which he attends to. Indeed, we have to go back a long time to find something similar; Reynolds, too, rejected the psychologically

Francis Bacon, Two Figures *(1953; private collection)*.

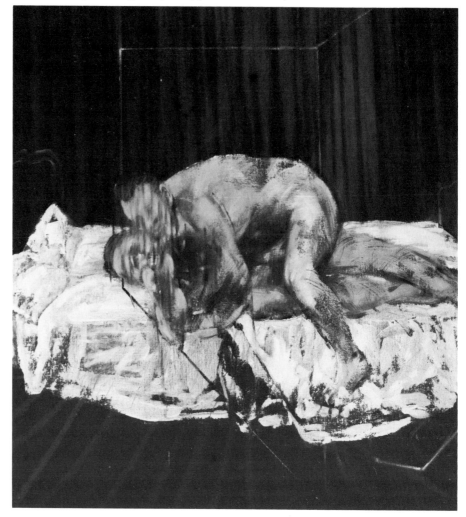

revealing portrait, and caricature, alike. For example, he was commissioned to paint William, Duke of Cumberland, 'The Butcher', infamous for his massacre of the Jacobites after the Battle of Culloden. The Duke was grossly overweight, prodigiously ugly, and blind in one eye. But he emerges from Reynolds painting as a splendid, almost majestic fellow, set off against an imaginary landscape. For Reynolds, this was not flattery, but edifying idealisation; he believed that by painting even 'The Butcher' in this way, he was revealing the universal good. Manifestly, Bacon does not idealise: but, in a similarly universal way, he denigrates. It really does not matter whose likeness he exploits: their face will emerge as that of 'a gross and cruel monster' – *and nothing else*. For Bacon, an individual's face is no more than an injured cypher for his own sense of the irredeemable baseness of man.

In 1967, Sutherland went to Pembrokeshire for the first time since the war, to take part in a television film. He believed he had exhausted the imaginative possibilities this landscape offered him. But once there, the country drew him again. He returned for a longer visit the following year, and then again, frequently, until his death in 1980. The remarkable paintings Sutherland produced throughout the 1970s are more than an old man's spiritual home-coming; he finally fused his English nature romanticism with what he had learned from the best twentieth-century French painting, to produce some of the most original and elegiac British paintings of recent years. *Conglomerate I*, 1970, bears witness to Sutherland's Ruskinian capacity to see in a pebble the grandeur and scale of a mountain range; the troubled root forms of *Picton*, 1971/2, are heavy with presentiments of a return to the earth, of impending death; whereas *Forest with Chains II*, 1973, suggests the eventual triumph of the organic over the mechanical – though Sutherland characteristically denied conscious symbolic intent. *Bird over Sand*, 1975, based on a bird flying over Sandy Haven at low-tide, brings to mind the desolate and historic imagery of *The Origins of the Land* – made for the Festival of Britain; it also reveals the relationship between Sutherland's vision of an alien nature and that put forward by the Australian-born painters, Arthur Boyd and Sidney Nolan.

In 1978, Sutherland painted *Thicket: with Self-Portrait*, a picture which has been justly described as his 'testament'; it shows the artist, aged, and almost wizened, drawing intently, while above him soars a mass of vegetable and organic forms, which, like the monsters in Goya's *Sleep of Reason*, seems about to absorb him into itself – except that in *Thicket* there is no terror. Only one more major work followed: *Path through Wood*, 1979. The figure of the artist has disappeared; but the vegetable forms are now frozen into a monumental stasis. The silence of eternity replaces the rushing urgencies of growth. Ruskin seems almost to have had Sutherland's last paintings in mind when he praises the 'infinite wonderfulness there is in this vegetation', which, he says,

becomes the companion of man, [ministering to him] through a veil of strange intermediate being; which breathes, but has no voice; moves, but cannot leave its appointed place; passes through life without consciousness, to death without bitterness; wears the beauty of youth, without its passion; and declines to the weakness of age without its regret.

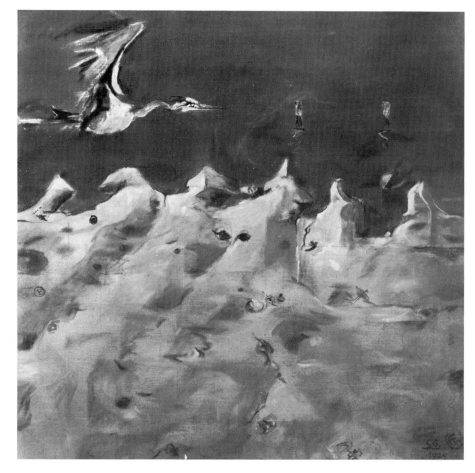

Graham Sutherland, Bird Over Sand *(1975; private collection)*.

Within a matter of months of painting *Path through Wood* Sutherland was
dead.

For Bacon, by contrast, the 1970s were marked only by the restatement of
his by now well-established themes; figures seated in front of crucified
carcasses; scenes of animal buggery; disintegrative portraits of self and others
(colour pl. 7); and images of lonely and naked men seated on lavatories,
beneath bare light bulbs, or vomiting into sinks. Bacon's handling of his
forms – though not of the paint materials themselves – became looser;
stereotyping, mannerism and repetition held sway. His chronic inability (at
once formal and psychological) to unite figure and ground became more
pronounced. The only development was a movement away from reliance on
the photographic image towards a new element of mythic symbolism – but it
often seemed arbitrary, even absurd. It was as if the Eumenides, in forms
resembling pink elephants, had returned to haunt the sordid events in hotel
rooms, or the sphinx had materialised amidst the used dressings of a casualty
ward. Bacon drew less upon his day-do-day life in the 'sexual gymnasium' of
the modern city; the references to the recognisable circle of friends

diminished; those to Aeschylus and Ingres greatly increased. But, although Bacon's painting was greeted with increasing acclaim, nothing reduced his relentless sense of surgical, but increasingly meaningless, despair, of paint thinned not so much with turpentine, as formaldehyde.

How then ought we to assess the achievements of these two painters? It was often said of Sutherland that, in the 1930s, he owed much to the surrealist

Francis Bacon, Lying Figure *(1969; private collection).*

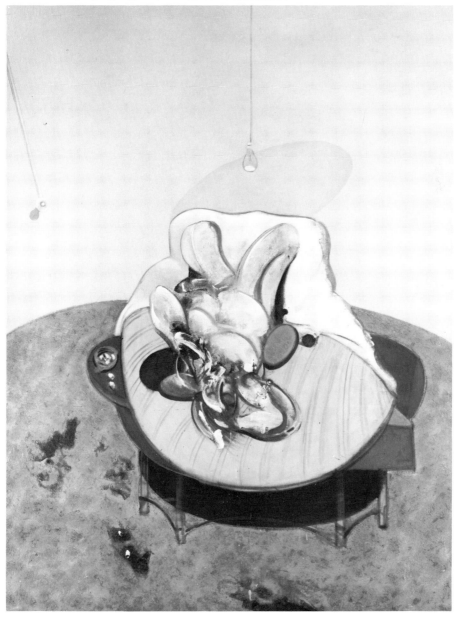

movement. But his roots lay in an older, English tradition of imaginative transformation of the appearances of nature. (Sutherland's weakness, perhaps, lay in the fact that a certain fatal facility, or a sense of graphic design, rather than deeply felt expression, occasionally entered into his work.) The personal and cultural events of the 1950s and 1960s alienated him from that common tradition – with debilitating effects on his art. But he returned to it, triumphantly, in the 1970s, fortified by what he had learned from the European modernist tradition. Though sadly neglected by the *cognoscenti* of the world of art, Sutherland's late pictures confirmed that his vision was not nostalgic; rather he was prophetic. After his death, there was much talk of a new 'post-industrial', 'post-modern' world, in which the restoration of a lost ecological harmony between man and nature had become essential for human survival. Sutherland's painting does not seem to demand that we share his belief in the risen Christ. Rather he realistically acknowledges that we live in a world in which there is, to quote the historian, Leo Marx, a 'machine in the garden', or a rusting industrial chain-saw in the forest. He seems to affirm the intractable, unmalleable 'otherness' of the world of natural objects. And yet he insists, like Ruskin before him, upon the *necessity* of an imaginative, spiritual, and aesthetic response to nature, *regardless*.

Bacon's numerous critical supporters have repeatedly insisted that he is a great 'realist' who paints the world as it is. Michel Leiris has recently argued that Bacon 'cleanses' art 'both of its religious halo and its moral dimension'. Bacon himself has said that his paintings can offend, because they deal with 'facts, or what used to be called truth'. Yet Bacon is indifferent to particular truths concerning the appearance, and character, of his subjects. No one could accuse him of being a respecter of persons: in his view, men and women are raw and naked bags of muscle and gut, capable only of momentary spasmodic activity.

'Realism' in art inevitably involves the selective affirmation of values. Whether one accepts Bacon as a 'realist' or not will depend upon whether one shares his particular view of humanity. Bacon is an artist of persuasive power and undeniable ability; but he has used his expressive skills to denigrate and to degrade. He presents one aspect of the human condition as necessary and universal truth. Bacon's work may currently be more highly esteemed than that of Sutherland; but this merely tells us something about the values of those who make such a choice. Bacon's skills may justly command our admiration; but his tendentious vision demands a moral response, and I believe, a refusal.

The very existence of a talent like Sutherland's indicates just how partial Bacon's 'realism' is. But one might also ask, is his conception of human being more 'realistic' than, say, Henry Moore's? Moore finds no difficulty in affirming the possibilities of consoling relationships between mother and child, and even between adult individuals of the opposite sex. Like Sutherland's paintings, Moore's greatest sculptures also celebrate the potentialities of a human relationship with the natural world beyond the walls of the water-closet. It is tempting to quote St Paul: 'whatsoever things are lovely, whatsoever things are of good report; if there be any virtue, and if there be any praise, think on these things.'

Moore and after

'Complete sculptural expression', Henry Moore once wrote, 'is form in its full spatial reality.' No sculptor this century had a greater grasp of such 'spatial reality'. Moore also believed that a good work of art, is 'an expression of the significance of life, a stimulation to greater effort in living'. Although resolutely secular, the robust grandeur of Moore's vision constitutes one of the most commanding spiritual affirmations of our time.

Moore was born in 1898, in the Yorkshire town of Castleford. Much, he believed too much, has been made of the fact that he was the son of a mine-worker. The first sculptures he saw were in Methley Church; but the majestic local landscape was probably a stronger formative influence on him. Moore's talents did not go unrecognised, at home or at school. After active military service, he went on to study art at Leeds, where he discovered Roger Fry's *Vision and Design*, with its illustrations of negro sculpture. While he was a student at the Royal College of Art, in London, he spent much of his spare time in the archaeological sections of the great museums. He soon began to question what he was being taught; and, encouraged by Jacob Epstein, he started to make a close study of African and ancient Mexican sculpture. In 'primitive' art, Moore found an 'intense vitality' and a 'virility and power'; he felt such sculpture was 'made by people with a direct and immediate response to life', and was not just an activity 'of calculation or academicism'. At this time, he developed the view (which he was later to revise) that Greek sculpture, and the Western tradition which had sprung from it, was only a 'digression' which need no longer 'blot our eyes' to 'the main world tradition of sculpture'; he wrote enthusiastically of the achievements of 'Palaeolithic and Neolithic sculpture, Sumerian, Babylonian and Egyptian, Early Greek, Chinese, Etruscan, Indian, Mayan, Mexican and Peruvian, Romanesque, Byzantine and Gothic, Negro, South Sea Island and North American Indian.'

Moore's own work of the 1920s reflects these influences. He reacted strongly against the vapid classicism, and the 'pointing-up' techniques favoured by his teachers, and he became an advocate of the doctrine of 'truth to materials', first suggested by the French sculptor Gaudier-Brzeska, who had died in the trenches. He was also affected by what Eric Gill had to say about the importance of direct carving in stone. Both his sculpture and his teaching at the Royal College were heavily criticised. Moore's early exhibitions were dominated by works on two of the themes which were to remain of central importance throughout his life: the mother and child, and the reclining woman. He was accused of encouraging 'the cult of ugliness' and of showing 'utter contempt for the natural beauty of women and children' in a way which 'deprived even stone of its value as a means of aesthetic and emotional expression'. In fact, Moore's technical and formal innovations were attempts to widen the emotional range of his sculpture. Instead of treating the infant–mother relationship as a sight, or object of sentimental feeling, he tried to give expression to what the relationship felt like *from the inside*. Similarly, although he rejected glib, classical canons of beauty, his insistence on 'truth to materials' served to accentuate the association he wished to make between his great reclining women, and the earth itself. A writer in *The Yorkshire Post* perceptively commented of one such figure that it was like 'a Grampian landscape', and referred to its refusal to be separated from the terrestrial rock from which it was hewn. Moore underlined these associations in later works by peaking the breasts and bunching the knees of the figures so that they appeared almost as mountain ranges. His first phase really came to an end with the carving, in 1932, of the great *Mother and Child* in Green Horton Stone which is now in the Sainsbury Centre, near Norwich.

In the 1930s, Moore was associated with 'Unit One', a group, founded by Paul Nash, and including Barbara Hepworth and Ben Nicholson. These artists felt they stood 'for the expression of a truly contemporary spirit, for that thing which is recognised as peculiarly of today'. But this was an odd position for Moore, given that there had hitherto been nothing conspicuously 'of today' about his work. Indeed, he rather seemed to be intent upon affirming certain dimensions of sculpture, and of lived experience, which modernity was determined to exclude. But, in the 1930s, the focus of Moore's work shifted. He was influenced by European surrealism, and the British abstract movement. For a time, he appeared to become interested in formal experimentation, for its own sake. As he himself came to recognise, there was something repetitive about his numerous stringed sculptures. Nonetheless, he evolved many of the new sculptural conventions and devices – such as joining the front and back of a figure with a hole – which were to play such an important part in his later work. They also allowed him immediately to

Henry Moore, Recumbent Figure *(1938; Tate Gallery, London).*

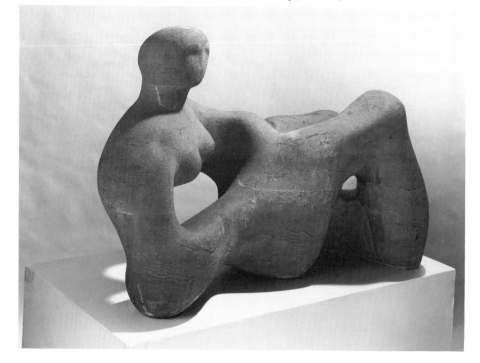

transform his great reclining figures. 'My sculpture is becoming less representational,' he explained in 1937, 'less an outward visual copy, and so what some people would call more abstract.' But, he added, this was 'only because I believe that in this way I can present the human psychological content of my work with the greatest directness and intensity.' In the marvellous *Recumbent Figure* of 1938 (now in the Tate Gallery) the device of the hole allows Moore to join the inside and the outside of the figure in such a way that it is, at once, both an object and an environment.

Moore's second phase ended with the outbreak of war. In 1940, his London studio was bombed, and he moved to Perry Green, near Much Hadham, in Hertfordshire. For three years, he made no sculptures; but drew instead. Moore is a draughtsman of genius, combining acute observation with symbolic transformation. The War Artists' Advisory Committee acquired many of his 'shelter drawings' of Londoners sleeping under blankets on the platforms of the tube and commissioned another lesser, but, I believe, underestimated group depicting miners at work on the coal face, near his home town of Castleford.

The shelter drawings confirmed that Moore's sensibility thrived in a neo-romantic climate, rather than among the tendentious modernist groupings. The drawings are not just reportage; rather they have a mysterious, even mythological, quality. Moore's statuesque nursing mothers, and all the imagery of mergence in the draped blankets, and swaddling bands, seem to indicate that the roots of this mystery are to be found not so much in religious experience as in the infant–mother relationship. Moore seems to suggest that the ambiguities of this first relationship are repeated in the adult's relationship to the sustaining environment. Such themes, of course, had long characterised his greatest sculptures. As John Read once put it, 'This blending of human and natural form, this ability to see figures in the landscape, and a landscape in the figures, is Moore's greatest contribution to sculpture.' Although this preoccupation had never previously manifested itself in *sculpture*, it has a long history in the British romantic tradition. Ruskin (whose drawings Moore greatly admired) had also scrutinised the anatomy of hills and mountains. Like Moore, he found in the lowlands 'a spirit of repose', but saw 'the fiery peaks' as 'heaving bosoms and exulting limbs, with the clouds drifting like hair from their bright foreheads'.

The return to sculpture came in 1943 when Canon Walter Hussey commissioned Moore to carve a Madonna and Child for St Matthew's in Northampton. Completed in 1944, this work makes nonsense of the claim that Moore's imagination was essentially primitive, or indelibly anti-classical. The Madonna has lost none of the freshness, and vitality, which springs from the direct carving of the stone, but possesses a repose, authority, and equilibrium – in Moore's phrase, an 'aloof mystery' – which is rare in twentieth-century art. The work has sometimes been seen as 'reactionary' because it involves none of the 'punctured' formal ingenuity, fusing inner and outer, of earlier figures. But Moore had conceived the piece to be enclosed by the space of the neo-Gothic transept of St Matthew's. The Madonna can be contrasted with the first painting of Francis Bacon's maturity, *Three Studies for Figures at the Base of a Crucifixion*, made at the same time. Bacon's forms

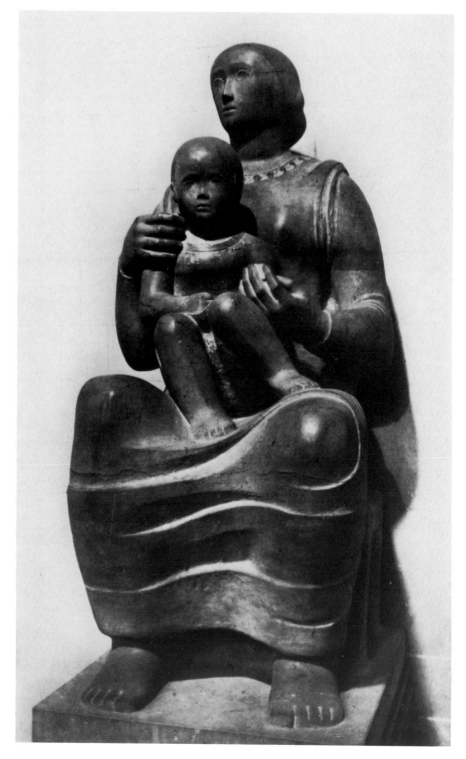

Henry Moore, Madonna and Child *(1943–4; St Matthew's Church, Northampton).*

express a brutal degradation of the Western religious impulse, an incapacity in the wake of the war, to perceive anything in man except evil, and bandaged corruption. Moore's Madonna is also resolutely secular – a human mother with a human child. But these two works demand a choice: we must decide whether, in a world apparently deserted by God, we prefer to see our fellow human beings as sacks of mutilated, spasm-ridden muscle; or as creatures still capable of composure, dignity, and spiritual strength.

Through the war drawings, the Northampton Madonna, and the intelligent patronage of the British Council, Moore's reputation grew not only in Britain, but throughout the Western world. During the 1940s and 1950s, Moore created some of his best-known pieces: the great carved stone *Memorial Figure*, of a reclining woman, situated in Dartington Hall, Devon – of which Moore himself said, the figure's 'raised knee repeats or echoes the gentle roll of the landscape'; the bronze *Family Group*, now in front of the Barclay School in Stevenage; the *Draped Reclining Figure*, of 1952/3; the famous *King and Queen* of the same time; the *Harlow Family Group* of 1954/5; and the vast UNESCO *Reclining Figure* in travertine stone of 1957/8. Moore emerged in the 1950s from the rarefied enclave of those interested in abstract and avant-garde art to find sculptural forms which expressed the bravest ethical aspirations of the post-war world. As Grey Gowrie puts it, 'until the 1960s, when a new, urban aesthetic took hold, [Moore] was almost everywhere regarded as the most powerful British artist since the death of Turner'. This period of his work was drawn to a close through the elmwood *Reclining Figure* upon which he worked intermittently between 1959 and 1964. This sculpture is a consummate expression of all that he had learned up to this date about the image of the reclining female figure as a symbol of consolation and reconciliation: its strange undulating forms mingle inner and outer into a new kind of unity. This magnificent *Reclining Figure* embraces us with the sort of experience we gain from the Northampton Madonna *and* the church which encloses and envelops her.

But by the time it was completed, the *Reclining Figure* was already an anachronism in terms of Moore's own development. Alan Bowness was the first to argue that 1958 marked the end of Moore's third phase as a sculptor primarily conscious of his social role, and the beginning of a new and more personal 'late period'. In recent years, it has been fashionable (especially among artists and critics) to praise the first two phases of Henry Moore's development – the 'direct carving' of the 1920s, and the experiments of the 1930s – at the expense of the public sculpture of the 1940s, and the 'late phase' which began in 1958. This is a short-sighted view. Moore achieved his full stature as a sculptor only in 1943. In the late 1950s, the monumental grandeur of the finest public pieces gave way to an expressive vision, the complexity, originality and scale of which no other sculptor in the post-war era has begun to approach (colour pl. 5).

Nothing demonstrates this more vividly than what happened to Moore's reclining women. In the 1960s, this familiar theme underwent cataclysmic changes. The epic figures began to fragment and to cleave into their several parts. The great rocks and cliff faces of breasts, torso and mountainously raised knees severed, and floated apart, as if some geological convulsion was trembling upwards from the lower strata of Moore's imagination itself.

Moore describes this process in a characteristically matter-of-fact way. 'I realised', he once said, 'what an advantage a separated two-piece composition could have in relating figures to landscape. Knees and breasts are mountains. Once these two parts become separated you don't expect it to be a naturalistic figure; therefore you can justifiably make it like a landscape or a rock.' But the fact remains that these changes led to some of the strangest sculptures ever made of the female figure, sculptures which seem menaced by a constant threat of disintegration, even disappearance. The illusion seems about to fade into the materials and it is redeemed – only at the last moment – by the cohesive and unifying power of Moore's formal arrangements.

It is improbable that it was just the accident of a commission from the Nuclear Energy Centre in Chicago which led to the terrifying helmeted, immensity of *Nuclear Energy*, of 1964. For the work of Moore's maturity offers more than a new aesthetic experience. His shattering earth mothers seem to express his vision of what was happening to the sustaining environment of nature – and indeed of human culture, itself. If we look back over Moore's work we cannot help but notice how small a part mechanical and technological imagery plays within it. One of the many meanings of Moore's work may be the implication that when we lose sight of our sense of unity with nature, then there is a danger of destroying both ourselves – and indeed, perhaps nature itself. For all its variety, changes of emphasis, and imagery, Moore's mature work exhibited a remarkable unity of vision and purpose. His sense of nature was not something to be set apart from human culture. As he himself once said, 'Culture . . . is an organic process. There is no such thing as a synthetic culture, or if there is it is a false and impermanent culture.' Moore's great reclining figures resist – although they acknowledge – the threat of disintegration, and present us with an aesthetic of ecological harmony, which can justly be described as equivalent to that of the great medieval cathedrals, in our own time.

Henry Moore, Three-Piece Reclining Figure No. I *(1961–2; Henry Moore Foundation)*.

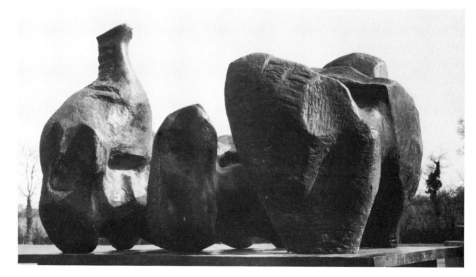

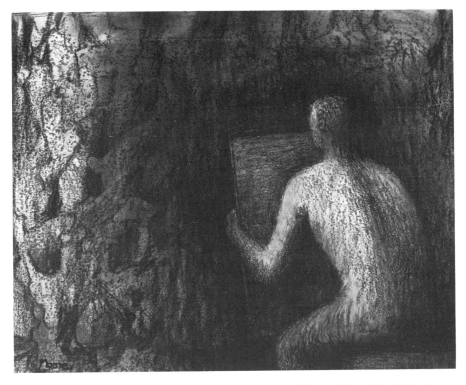

Henry Moore, Man Drawing Rock Formation *(1982); Henry Moore Foundation).*

Today, Moore's reputation stands in an ambiguous position. Before his death, he had achieved unprecedented recognition for a sculptor. No city in the West seems complete without at least one Henry Moore in a park, on a plaza, or outside a modern building. But younger sculptors, and 'informed' critical opinion, were looking to other things. Much has been made of Moore's 'inflation of scale', and his 'monumental' ambition. Not all such criticisms are without foundation: those aware of Henry Moore's failing physical powers in his last years could only regard with a certain cynicism the continuous production of 'original' full-scale casts and carvings issuing from his studio. Practices for which Moore – not always justifiably – condemned the Victorians were, apparently, legitimised by his own advancing years. Lesser sculptors no doubt manifested less monumental faults.

The real tragedy was that when Moore died in 1986, his achievement, and the originality of his 'late phase', were but little regarded by younger sculptors. Most prefer to trace descent from Anthony Caro, a former engineer, who learned the rudiments of sculpture under Charles Wheeler, PRA. Between 1951 and 1953, Caro was an assistant to Moore. He emerged as an expressionist sculptor of moderate ability; but in 1959 he met Clement Greenberg, an influential critic of American abstract painting who recommended a change of direction. In 1960, Caro made *Twenty Four Hours*, an abstract work in painted sheet metal, consciously echoing the flatness of

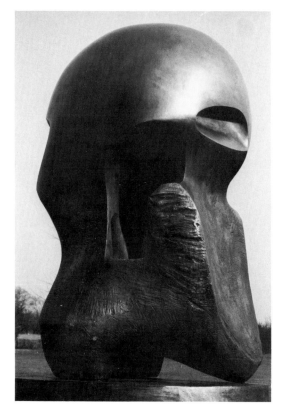

Henry Moore, Atom Piece *(1964; Henry Moore Foundation).*

the American 'post-painterly' painting Greenberg was doing so much to promote.

Caro declared himself opposed to all anthropomorphic or 'natural' form. He dispensed with traditional sculptural techniques, like carving and modelling, in favour of the placement of preconstituted, industrial elements (like I-beams, tank-tops, and sheet steel) joined together by welds. He abandoned plinth and pedestal, and showed no concern with mass, volume, the illusion of internal structure, or the qualities of his materials. His wife frequently covered the steel elements with coats of brilliant household paint so the metal appeared weightless as plastic or fibreglass.

Such work had little in common with anything that had previously been regarded as sculpture. Caro first came to public attention in Britain with his Whitechapel exhibition of 1963, which *The Times* greeted with the headline, 'Out-and-out originality in our contemporary sculpture'. It was a year in which it seemed that some radical, cultural transformation was about to take place in Britain. With the Profumo affair, the old men of British politics were swept off their plinths; Harold Wilson, the Labour leader, spoke of the 'white heat of the industrial revolution'; and there was much talk of the nationalisation of steel. On all sides one could feel a cult of newness. The nation was shaken by the *Honest to God* affair: the Bishop of Woolwich caused a scandal with a popular book about 'Death of God' theology in which he argued against the anthropomorphic conception of deity, and recommended bringing God off his pedestal to reconstitute him as the 'ground of our being'. Caro's work was nothing if not of its time: it reflected the superficial, synthetic, urban, commercial, American values which dominated the 1960s.

Caro had declared that sculpture could be anything; but his rebellious pupils took him more literally than he intended. Barry Flanagan and Nicholas Pope reduced the art to the placement of barely worked materials. Others started digging holes, taking photographs, and even walks, and calling that sculpture too. Gilbert and George became fashionable by declaring their own persons as 'Living Sculptures' – and the Tate bought a video-tape of them getting drunk. The 1980s saw a return to 'objects', rather than events, or performance, as sculpture; but the so-called 'New Sculpture' relied on flippant collaging of improbable materials – car doors, broken refrigerators, used tyres, etc. 'Sculptors' like Tony Cragg and Bill Woodrow consciously refused aesthetic form; their work involved no identifiable skills, and offered no vision of man, woman, or beast. Although 'The New Sculptors' received seemingly limitless institutional promotion, they intended a continuing insult to tradition – upon which originality depends.

Back in 1962, Moore himself had said, 'We're getting to a state in which everything is allowed and everybody is about as good as everybody else.' He warned that both artists and public were going to get bored, 'You've got to be ready to break the rules but not to throw them all over unthinkingly.' He added, 'Someone will have to take up the challenge of what has been done before.' In 1986, somewhat late in the day, Caro appears to have recognised this; he sheepishly returned to figurative sculpture.

There were others, however, who have more seriously engaged with the challenge of what has been done before. Glynn Williams was an accomplished carver before he became caught up in the silliness of the 1960s, when he worked in fibre-glass, and with mixed-media 'environments'. All that he now regards as a dark night of his sculptural soul. In the 1970s, he returned first to traditional materials like wood, and later stone; and then abandoned construction in favour of carving. Finally, towards the end of the decade, he re-immersed himself in tradition, embraced illusion, and produced an exceptional series of formally original sculptures, the subjects of which were mothers and children, human hands, acrobats, nude male figures, and even a modern *pietà*. Williams' vision has all the freshness, originality, and *joie de vivre* of a blind man who has recovered his sight. Unlike 'the new sculpture', which excites only cynicism and contempt beyond the confines of the art world, Williams' work has been greatly in demand for shopping precincts, theatre foyers, hospitals, and housing estates throughout the country. Nor was Williams alone; in the mid 1980s, Lee Grandjean, a colleague of Williams' at the Wimbledon School of Art, produced sinuous wood carvings, like *Willow*, 1985, which exhibited a more poetic, yet nonetheless thoroughly sculptural, sensibility. Sadly, however, both Williams and Grandjean have been ignored by the Tate Gallery and the British Council – who appear to have abandoned the sculptural ideals which they did so much to popularise and promote after the Second World War.

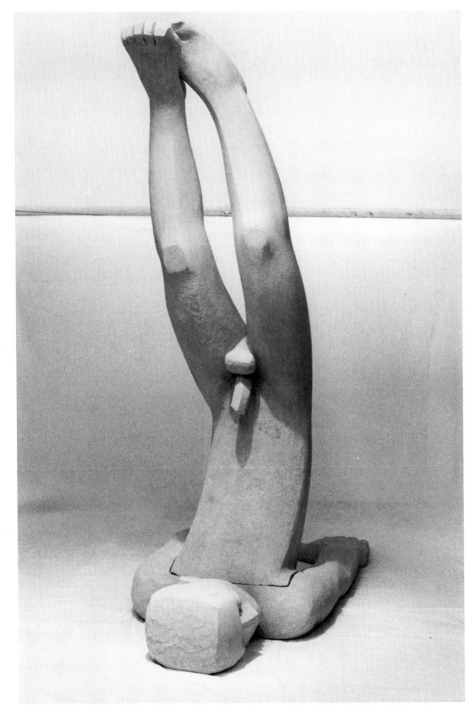

Glynn Williams, Stone Rise East *(1985; Bernard Jacobson Ltd, London)*.

Conclusion: decadence and hope

No one could deny that during the thirty years after the close of the Second World War, the visual arts, in Britain, sunk to a level of decadence unprecedented in our national history. The condition of painting and sculpture was infinitely more parlous than in, say, the late Victorian era, though this scarcely inhibited the derision with which modernist critics viewed the past. It could not reasonably be argued that this sad decline came about through any 'genetic' lack of talent: indeed, in the years immediately before the Second World War an unusually gifted generation of artists – including Moore, Sutherland, Hepworth, Nicholson and Piper – arrived at their full aesthetic maturity at about the same time. Nor could it be said that the state was neglecting the arts, in any material sense, since the scale of its involvement and patronage throughout our period was greater than at any time in the past.

Those inclined to look further for the origins of this malaise have most frequently blamed the activities of the dealers in art; but this hypothesis, too, is inherently improbable. A free market in art may not inevitably enhance the level of aesthetic production, but there is no evidence that, in and of itself, it is necessarily destructive of aesthetic life. Historically, the mercantilism and commercialism of the Dutch and Venetian Republics were associated with an efflorescence of painting. Similarly, although in our own time intense market activity sometimes accompanies extreme aesthetic degradation – e.g. in the case of Julian Schnabel – such activity is often also associated with work of exceptional quality: no painter has been more 'commercialised' than Graham Sutherland; and even the most 'successful' of the 'new sculptors' cannot approach the sums which Henry Moore's feeblest works command in the market-place. By and large, dealers prefer to handle works of enduring quality; they are an easier sell, and their 'investment value' can more safely be guaranteed. But the market is ultimately indifferent. Wherever a demand exists, or can be fabricated, there will always be some dealers prepared to pander to it, or to inflate it. They will do so whether that demand is for Montagu Dawson's paintings of tea-clippers on the foamy surf or such 'avant-garde' foibles as canned excrement, folded blankets, broken fridges or the legendary pile of bricks. But the taste for such things is not ultimately 'caused' by the market; if anything, it reflects the preferences of the art bureaucrats who now run the institutions of art. The market may have exacerbated the decadence; but if, under other circumstances, excellence had prevailed it would have elevated it.

The aesthetic confusion of our times must be seen as part of a more widespread collapse of ethical, cultural and religious response. Aesthetic life cannot thrive given the disintegration of the 'shared symbolic order' of a kind which religion provides; it becomes especially vulnerable when laudable ideas derived from political democracy are extended in such a way as to outlaw discrimination within the cultural field, and to undermine the evaluative dimension in human response. For example, in the 1960s, it became almost an article of faith among sculptors that a noxious, anaesthetic and evil substance, like fibre glass, possessed as great inherent aesthetic value as the finest Carrara marble.

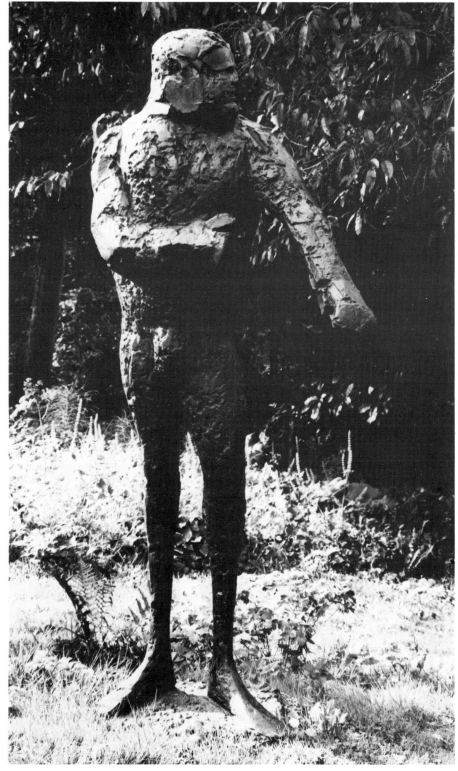

Elizabeth Frink, Judas 1963 *(Waddington Galleries, London)*.

A potent cause for the displacement of the fine arts after the Second World War was undoubtedly the expansion of a mega-visual tradition of non-fine art visual techniques and practices. Our era saw the expansion of mechanical and electronic means of visual reproduction into a belching torrent. The dominant visual representations in post-Second World War culture were not those of the painter; rather they were the television screen, film, the advertising poster, and the colour magazines, for ever supplemented by new photographic, video, holographic, and computer-generated techniques. Many artists made the fatal mistake of colluding with this outpouring of visual anaesthesia. Indeed, from the late 1950s onwards, it was repeatedly argued by 'progressive' artists that art could only 'advance' through acceptance of these mechanical and electronic means. A handful of exceptionally talented artists occasionally made use of the new technology in interesting ways: David Hockney, in particular, exposed the limitations of the photographic image, and even succeeded in wringing an aesthetic effect from xerox machines. Far more frequently, however, artists were seduced by these new means in ways which eliminated any possibility of imaginative expression.

In general, it can be said that the greatest art of our time has inevitably involved an element of *refusal* of modernity, and an affirmation of precisely those aesthetic and spiritual values which the modern world, by its very nature, has come to exclude. The situation is complicated by the fact that those who have adopted such a conservationist position have sometimes felt it necessary to defend what they have done with the *rhetoric* of modernity. Thus Moore's revival of direct carving, in the 1920s, was often described as being aesthetically 'progressive'; in fact, of course, it was a re-affirmation of the aesthetic potentialities of one of the oldest human arts in the face of its mechanisation and reduction. This had commenced in the nineteenth century, but, Moore notwithstanding, these processes were taken to new lengths in the twentieth. In general, it seems that insufficient emphasis has been paid by critics to the conservationist element in the greatest art of our era: it is certainly original, but endeavours to be so on the basis of tradition. The most significant artists of our time have consistently adopted the position, described by the conservative historian, Maurice Cowling: 'modernity is the practice we have and the life we lead, and . . . we have all to accept it and live as it commands us, even when we despise it'.

Nowhere is this stance more vividly realised than in the work of the best pupils of the late David Bomberg, especially Frank Auerbach and Leon Kossoff. Both adopt an artistic ethic which many assume to be 'out-dated'. This involves them in a relentless, daily commitment to the pursuit and practice of drawing, a celebration of the greatest painting of the Western tradition, an affirmation of the individual imagination, and an almost complete indifference to the technical means of modernity. (Auerbach has characteristically placed on record his admiration for Constable and Rembrandt, and his contempt for television.) Neither of them appear to have been influenced by the fashionable aesthetic ideologies of our time, nor have American art and culture had the slightest influence upon them. But, today, even those of very different aesthetic tastes and persuasions are coming to recognise that, in their differing ways, Auerbach and Kossoff are two of the finest British painters of the post-war era.

The absence of American influence over their work is undoubtedly significant. The degree to which British art suffered, from the late 1950s to the late 1970s, from the corrupting influence of American fashions can hardly be over-emphasised. After initially defending the work of American abstract artists, Heron was among those who began to open our eyes to the way in which the American achievement, such as it was, was far more dependent upon prior British discoveries than had hitherto been assumed. More generally, it could be said that the undue emphasis upon American work led

Frank Auerbach, Portrait of E.O.W. *(Whitworth Art Gallery, Manchester)*.

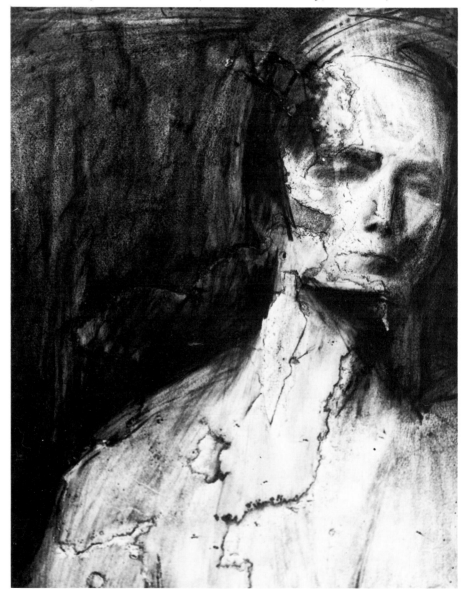

to the tragic eclipse of an indigenous sensibility whose influence is discernible from the time of Turner and Constable, to the achievements of Moore and Sutherland; this tradition was based upon an imaginative response to natural form, indeed to the whole world of nature.

Insecurity concerning the value of the British visual tradition had been exacerbated by the patronising tone of early modernist critics, like Roger Fry and Nikolaus Pevsner, towards British achievements in art. Fry was certainly perceptive concerning the art of France; but he found it necessary to bolster his position by a denigration of even the memory of Turner, and an insistence upon the 'provincialism' of the British sensibility which has persisted in 'advanced' criticism ever since.

Nonetheless, today there is a growing recognition that if the achievements of British art in the nineteenth century were greater than the early modernist commentators allowed, those of the best British artists of the twentieth century – e.g. Moore, Hepworth, Nicholson, Sutherland and Bomberg – are second to none. Certainly, there is nothing in the mid-century French, German, or American traditions which can confidently be placed above them. More generally, it might be argued that now that modernist preoccupations are greeted with somewhat less enthusiasm than they once were, that quality which was once dismissed as British 'pastoralism', or British ruralism, is acquiring a universality, the significance of which extends far beyond these shores. For if our native tradition involves something less than unqualified enthusiasm for ever-increasing production, it also affirms the necessity of developing a new, imaginative response to the natural world, what Bomberg designated as a quest for 'the spirit in the mass'. Indeed, the best British art appears to possess the capacity to speak more eloquently to the ecological and environmental concerns of a 'post-modern', 'post-industrial' age than ever it could to the mechanical utopianism of 'progressive' modernity. As ethical philosophers, naturalists, and poets alike, speak of the necessity of some kind of renewed imaginative affiliation with the natural world, if we are to survive as a species, there is likely to be a more positive assessment of the highest achievements, past and present, of the British tradition. And so, despite the cultural vandalism of those who presently control the institutions of contemporary art, some of us have begun to dare to hope that all might not be lost.

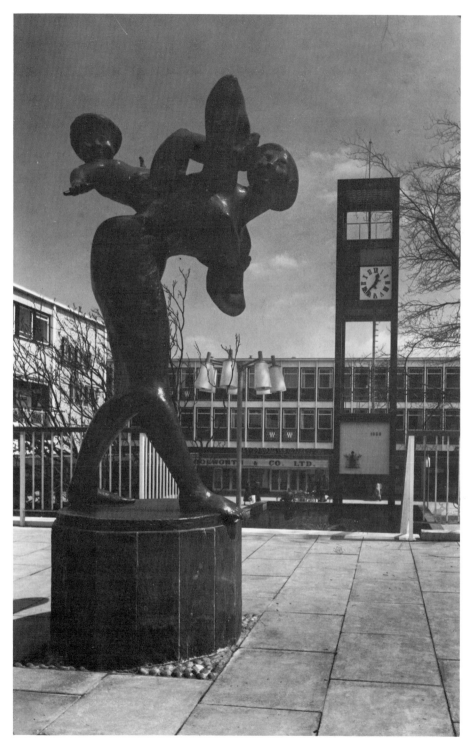

Stevenage town centre: the first major pedestrianised town scheme in Europe. In the foreground, Joyride *by Frantisek Belsky.*

4 The New Towns

ANDREW SAINT

Introduction

The British New Towns sprang from a moral imperative more than an artistic or even an economic one. The visitor who seeks from them a self-contained aesthetic experience or specially satisfying works of modern architecture is doomed to disappointment. But for the enquirer into national cultures, the New Towns have exceptional value. Conceived on a unique scale of ambition, they embody the most self-confident, collective strain in British post-war life – a strain which for a time seemed to be leading the nation towards an austere but just and classless version of social democracy. The New Towns were the last concerted achievement of British planning and architecture to command admiration abroad. But they will endure less for their impact on the theory and practice of town-building than as historical setpieces, carried out against the odds at a time of conflicting pressures and values.

The New Towns are the culmination of a peculiarly British planning tradition. They were not untouched by foreign influence; Scandinavian, and Dutch ingredients were present in their formative years, American ideas more regularly and strongly so. But their philosophy was rooted in a profound continuity in British culture, that of anti-urbanism – the belief in the superior morality of the countryside and its patterns of life. That belief was branded upon British intellectuals by the shock of industrialisation, the swelling of London's population and the proximity of the urban slum. As early as 1821, William Cobbett argued that 'the dispersion of the wen is the only real difficulty in settling the affairs of the nation and restoring it to a happy state. But dispersed it must be; and if there be half a million or more of people to suffer, the consolation is, that the suffering will be divided into half a million of parts.'

The time between Cobbett's remark and the New Towns Act in 1946 can be split into equal periods, one in which urban agglomeration continued unchecked, the other in which proposals for the 'dispersion' of the British industrial population took shape, first in literature and propaganda and then through a town-planning movement. Throughout that second phase, pity and fear were the subconscious spurs to urban reform: pity for the condition of the urban working classes, and fear for what they might do if they were to multiply further.

The movement to return the 'rootless' urban masses to the land crystallised after 1900 around Ebenezer Howard and the Garden City Association, as a means of cleansing the Victorian city and relieving the middle-class conscience. This pattern of thinking had large consequences for the character and vitality of the New Towns. The physical form of the first garden cities, Letchworth (1903) and Welwyn (1920), descended intact to the early New Towns. They were conceived as self-contained communities, separated from other settlements by a belt of agricultural land. Within the towns too there were distinct areas for living, working and 'rational recreation'. The almost invariable house-type was the 'cottage', constructed on sanitary principles, cleverly grouped and landscaped and tricked out with some rationalised, rustic detailing. But the civic and commercial centres of the two towns were laid out almost apologetically, as though urbanism was something to be contained rather than explored. Industry – that unpleasant necessity – was tucked dutifully away out of sight.

Funded by private means, Letchworth and Welwyn were agonisingly slow to build. They were not profitable enough to attract rapid investment and spawn imitators, the reformed tenure envisaged was watered down, while the numbers drawn out of London proved small and their cultural life arduous to establish. Pragmatic advocates of dispersal therefore came to confess the need for state support. It became their aim to 'sell' the idea of garden cities or 'satellite towns' (the American phrase) to those charged with national housing policy after 1918. A number of factors helped their arguments to prevail. One was the social inadequacy of the acres of public housing built on the outskirts of Britain's cities between the wars, climaxing in the vast desert of the London County Council's Becontree Estate. Then the Barlow Commission on the distribution of the industrial population, reporting in 1940, focussed upon the drift to the south-east and called for redress and the establishment of new planned communities. Finally came the impact of the Second World War and the enthusiasm which it fostered for reconstruction, particularly for the healing of wounds inflicted upon London.

The New Towns programme, though national in scope, was at first weighted towards London and the regional problems of the south-east. As a formal proposal, government-sponsored New Towns first saw the light in Patrick Abercrombie's plans for London, commissioned in 1943 by the infant Ministry of Town and Country Planning, the London County Council and surrounding authorities. Lewis Silkin, the relevant minister from 1945, had been in charge of pre-war slum clearance for the LCC. Silkin embraced New Towns wholeheartedly, secured a rapid report on their viability from a committee chaired by Lord Reith and rushed through the legislation with exceptional speed in 1946. Of the fourteen sites designated in the first five years eight, including all the first four (Stevenage, Crawley, Hemel Hempstead and Harlow), were devoted to relieving London. Three of the remaining six (Corby, Cwmbran and Newton Aycliffe) were meant to salvage communities which had multiplied to meet the needs of war production and lacked good housing and industrial diversity. Two (East Kilbride and Glenrothes) were planned near Glasgow, a city second only to London in the wretchedness of its housing.

The 'first generation' of New Towns have a strong resemblance. The garden-city lobby was still powerful, national planning had been centralised under a new and vigorous ministry, and the authority vested in the development corporations for planning the towns was almost despotic. Few trained architect-planners then existed; those that did were mostly direct or indirect disciples of Patrick Abercrombie and the pre-war Liverpool School of Architecture. This led to a model of plan indebted to Letchworth and Welwyn Garden City, with functions firmly zoned and segregated by well-landscaped open space and major roads. Industry, still expected to be heavy, dirty and noisy, was relegated to one or two areas on lines investigated in the inter-war trading estates. In the middle would be a civic and shopping centre, while the housing all around was broken into 'neighbourhoods'. Compared to the ideal towns of the Renaissance these plans look informal, even picturesque, on paper. In the event they turned out too rigid for a modern economy, too greatly governed by geography and zoning and not attentive enough to intangibles. A few of the foundations like Hemel Hempstead and the 'New Town' extension to Welwyn were grafted on to sizeable, settled communities, but in most places existing hamlets and villages became mere sideshows. Since the new centres tended to be built only after housing and industry had been well established, a hiatus often occurred during which the life of the town had no focus. Grappling with the banality of market forces and the limitations of garden-city thinking on urban centres, the development corporations and their architects found it hard to carry out these centres with conviction. This left a damaging psychological void at the heart of the first-generation New Towns, still perceptible today when the centres are complete.

Out in the 'neighbourhoods', the early New Towns did better. Here, American experience of containing traffic refined the existing body of British knowledge about the layout of low-density housing. As the towns had higher target populations than the garden cities, it seemed wise to break them down into communities with their own modest sense of identity. Clarence Perry in the inter-war Regional Plan of New York had proposed traffic-free neighbourhood units, each large enough to support a primary school, and the Reith Committee commended the idea. In view of the young population of the New Towns and the post-war jump in the birth-rate, the clustering of neighbourhoods around schools was natural. The neighbourhoods differed in size, from some 3,000 to 10,000. There were usually a few shops and a thin, ill-financed icing of social facilities. Architecturally the neighbourhood's most distinctive expression was 'Radburn planning', an American innovation whereby house-fronts faced on to common greens and paths while roadways were relegated to the back. Radburn planning did not come into its own until after 1960, when it brought a more intricate and enclosed pattern of design to many New Town neighbourhoods.

Much of the sameness in the early New Towns derives from the dominance of low-density housing for rent, built at a time when economies bore hard and continuously upon design and materials were restricted. The mechanisms of dispersal and the emphasis upon industrial employment meant that the social band attracted to the towns was narrow. So the architectural changes were rung upon very few themes. Harlow, planned by Frederick Gibberd, exemplifies the search for variety tried in some towns, whereby neighbourhoods were divided among different private architects. There are superficial variations of style, but they hardly raise the level of design above what Lewis Mumford termed the 'brightly commonplace'. Almost all architects had in the end to submit to the conventions and restrictions of low-cost, low-density housing. At Peterlee in Durham, Berthold Lubetkin planned something more adventurous – a compact centre mixing small flats and houses. But he soon ran into difficulties and delays over subsidence and resigned in 1950 before building began. A conventional pattern of development ensued.

The New Towns were painfully slow to start, because of economic restrictions and problems of infrastructure. This led to conservatism in design and to disillusionment with their ability to meet the objectives of dispersal. 'Out-county' estates of the old, monotonous type absorbed many more Londoners in the decade after the war than the New Towns did. People began to feel that the expansion of established towns was a saner way to redistribute population than the forcing of isolated new communities. Hence the Town Development Act of 1952 and the subsequent expansion of Thetford, Bletchley, Andover, Swindon, Skelmersdale, Leyland, Witham, Basingstoke, Haverhill and other towns. A few of these schemes blossomed into complete New Towns in the 1960s, but most amounted only to glorified industrial and housing estates less remote from civic and social life than the old suburban ones.

In 1953, at the height of impatience with the New Towns, the *Architectural Review* attacked them for their open, 'prairie' planning, condemned their monotony and called for increased densities in future development. Even defenders of low densities joined in the complaints. 'A space-hungry generation has, I fear, developed eyes that are bigger than its stomach', apologised Lewis Mumford. 'Because the new planners are mainly in revolt against congestion and squalor, rather than in love with urban order and co-operation, the New Towns do not yet adequately reveal what the modern city should be.' It was argued too that the neighbourhood idea did not correspond to observed social patterns and detracted from the vitality of the centres. Existing New Towns had to fill out before the Government would designate more, and the switch to town development precluded further grand gestures. The exception was Cumbernauld outside Glasgow, the one New Town designated during the 1950s. Here Hugh Wilson, the chief architect, staked his plan upon a monumental multi-level centre, with shopping, leisure and civic activities and offices gathered up in a single half-mile of construction. Cumbernauld also broke with the neighbourhood and responded to the car with a frankness that earlier towns, premised on walking, cycling and public transport as enough for their modestly circumstanced populations, had never done. Cumbernauld was briefly influential, providing the model for the

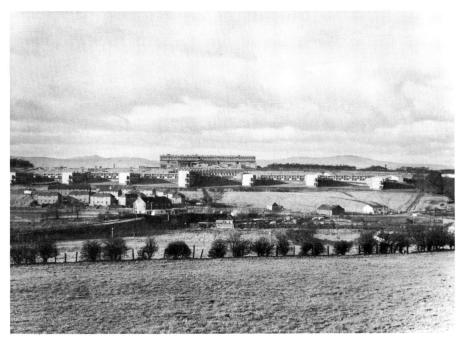

Cumbernauld New Town, Glasgow: a distant view, c.1963, showing the raised town centre in the background.

'second generation' of New Towns, amongst them two dramatic but abortive projects promoted by local authorities, the LCC's plan for Hook (1961) and Buckinghamshire's for a butterfly-shaped city designed around a monorail (1962–4). The New Towns sanctioned in the 1960s, Telford, Runcorn and Washington in England and Livingston in Scotland, were less full-hearted. The costly road network at Cumbernauld had not paid off, while the centre proved as arid as its predecessors and more inflexible. The moment of monumentality in British New Towns passed with little to show for it.

As city-planning became more intricate and economic in bent during the 1960s, British planners began to withdraw from imposing pre-conceived architectural form upon new communities, on the grounds that a town ought to offer opportunities within a loose set of guidelines rather than create patterns which could not be completed and rigidities which would be regretted. Much of this philosophy derived from the vision of prosperity, mobility, leisure and change emerging from the United States, particularly from California. Milton Keynes, the largest New Town of the 1970s, is the place where this looseness, this resolve not to impose, is most palpable. But on examination it is remarkably like the early New Towns on a maturer and larger scale. For all the talk of indeterminacy, planners, architects and developers have still to determine. While the basic economic structure and the prejudices of the housing market remain, new towns will come out in a similar way.

It is too early still to judge the New Towns as complete communities and cities. But they can be assessed in terms of the tasks they were built to fulfil. As a tool for redistributing the British urban population they did much, but symbolised more. We need not concur in the *dirigisme* implicit in 'decanting' populations or the autocracy with which the development corporations went about their tasks. Nor do we have to acquiesce in what has happened to the working-class areas of British cities. Nevertheless the environments to which those 'decanted' moved were, in the main, healthier and their economic opportunities were enhanced. Building the New Towns proved arduous enough; regenerating the inner cities has proved more so, and would probably have been no easier if the New Towns had not been built.

The accusations of dullness cast in the teeth of the New Towns could be directed at many provincial places. Any artificially stimulated settlement will have limitations for its first half-century; the test is what happens after that. If the towns lack the social diversity needful for a balanced life, that is because class-considerations were implicit from the start in the dispersal policy. The mechanisms for attracting the middle classes were always deficient; even at Milton Keynes there is still the whiff of a massive, dispersed ghetto.

The New Towns are an extraordinary testimony to the continuities in British culture. They represent the recasting of Edwardian attitudes about planning, class, industrial life, social reform, individual freedom and personal morality to fit the changes and opportunites furnished by post-war government policies. If they do not look more exciting, that is partly because they perpetuate an old puritan attitude in British culture, that style and show are distractions from the task of improving lives. This task the British New Towns may fairly be said to have done.

Stevenage and Milton Keynes

Stevenage was the first British New Town, designated in November 1946, a week after the New Towns Act received royal assent. In its early years it came close to disaster. Lewis Silkin, the Minister responsible for the Act, chose Stevenage from several sites for satellite towns suggested in the Greater London Plan of 1944, and proceeded to charge at local interests with the blunt battering ram of pre-war planning legislation. The result was confrontation and minor civil resistance. When Silkin visited, his tyres were let down and sand was dropped in his petrol tank; in a celebrated gesture, the name of the station was changed to Silkingrad. After protracted battle, the courts confirmed Stevenage's designation; but by then time had been lost, sympathies dissipated and economic cuts were at hand. This, on top of a rash of changes in the membership of Stevenage Development Corporation (culminating in the McCarthyite sacking of its third chairman, Monica Felton, by Hugh Dalton), meant that Stevenage was desperately slow to get started, falling behind later and less contentious foundations.

The first plan for Stevenage has been in broad intent adhered to throughout, despite major recasting in 1949 and an enlargement in 1966, when the projected population was increased from 60,000 to 105,000. It originated with Gordon Stephenson and Peter Shepheard, two Liverpool-trained architect-planners who had helped their former teacher Abercrombie

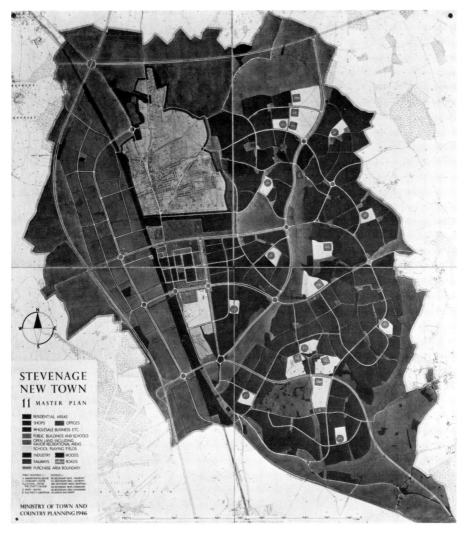

STEVENAGE
NEW TOWN

11 MASTER PLAN

RESIDENTIAL AREAS
SHOPS   OFFICES
WHOLESALE BUSINESS ETC
PUBLIC BUILDINGS AND SCHOOLS
OPEN LAND INCLUDING
MAJOR RECREATIONAL AREAS
SCHOOL PLAYING FIELDS
INDUSTRY   WOODS
RAILWAYS   ROADS
PURCHASE AREA BOUNDARY

MINISTRY OF TOWN AND
COUNTRY PLANNING 1946

Master plan for Stevenage, devised by Gordon Stephenson and Peter Shepheard of the Ministry of Town and Country Planning (1946). The earliest and most influential of New Town plans.

with the Greater London Plan, including a preliminary layout for a satellite town at Ongar. Stephenson and Shepheard were working within the Ministry of Town and Country Planning when they made the plan for Stevenage. They were intended to carry it through, but in the event the Ministry refused to release them and the Development Corporation appointed the veteran Clifford Holliday in their stead. Later chief architects, notably Leonard Vincent (1954–62), were more effective than Holliday. The position of chief architect was consistently important at Stevenage, which 'farmed out' less of its development than Harlow and some other towns. In retrospect its neighbourhoods are no less various for that, and the town centre has gained in consistency.

Stevenage lies between Letchworth and Welwyn Garden City, and their influence is palpable on its plan. An industrial area, sited around an existing factory built as part of Stevenage's pre-war expansion, occupies one side of the railway, and the town centre the other. Neighbourhoods radiate around the centre, separated by roads and open space, while to the north is the old town. 'Men must live near their work' was one principle of the Reith Committee. At Stevenage the early neighbourhoods are within bicycling distance of the factories, but the segregation afforded by the railway is complete. Later neighbourhoods, added after planners had woken up to the motor car, are some way from the workplace and town centre and have bigger shopping areas in compensation.

The neighbourhoods at Stevenage show improvement over the years. Stony Hall and Bedwell, the first, lack privacy or subtlety. At Stony Hall, tall flats were even built at the start, handsome (by Yorke, Rosenberg and Mardall) but incongruous and unpopular, as the Development Corporation soon realised. The spaces in and between these developments are still somewhat barren and the 'garden commons' often failed to materialise. In districts of the 1960s like Pin Green and Chells, by contrast, a full and confident version of Radburn planning was deployed. Here the memory of stranded, suburban council housing dissolves in favour of closely clustered warm brick houses, intricate pathways, imaginative planting and a safe and sensible *rapprochement* with the car's importance in modern life. As in other New Towns, the neighbourhood centres are neither large nor strong enough. But

Early housing at Whomerley Wood, Stevenage, c.1953. The appearance is not far removed from the old 'byelaw street'.

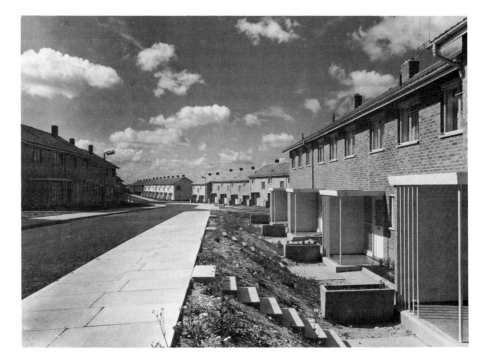

like the neighbourhoods of Hertfordshire's other New Towns, Stevenage's enjoy the bonus of fresh-looking schools, the county having since 1945 been a pioneer in standards of school-building. The Stevenage schools show the tradition of flat-roofed, prefabricated building at its best. Sited usually on the edge of open space, they offer a needed contrast to the acre of repetitive brick housing.

The town centre is Stevenage's particular pride. The first large-scale fully pedestrianised town centre in Europe, it was conceived in Stephenson and Shepheard's original plan. In 1950 Stephenson resumed work on it, in association with Clifford Holliday and the American planner Clarence Stein. Endless difficulties, not least the continuing popularity of the old town centre to the north, delayed it. Holliday's successor Leonard Vincent finally convinced a dubious Development Corporation by taking them to visit the Lijnbaan pedestrian precinct in Rotterdam, and his simplified, tightened-up version, planned in 1954, was built in 1957–8. It has the virtues and vices of its good-mannered modesty. It is low, unified, practical and almost wholly unmemorable, like the conventional chain stores which it contains. The only gesture is a clocktower in Town Square, which sports a glowering relief of Lewis Silkin, friend and enemy to Stevenage, on its side. The spaces around the centre are not for lingering in or savouring. It is possible to admire and learn from the artificial, contained centre of the new town, hard not to prefer the easy-going, still-thriving centre of the old one to its north.

Milton Keynes grew out of the mundane expansion of Bletchley in north Buckinghamshire. Bletchley was the first place to take up the Town Development Act of 1952. In partnership with the London County Council, it proceeded to spawn a suburb of average environmental quality to take 'overspill' industry and population from London. When in the early 1960s the impetus of the New Towns movement was renewed, among those to respond was Fred Pooley, Buckinghamshire County Council's chief architect and planner. Goaded by expanding population forecasts, Pooley and his team in 1962–4 devised a plan for a North Buckinghamshire New City of 250,000, larger than any existing New Town, to pick up from Bletchley in taking Londoners and to help relieve pressure on the prospering towns in the south of the county. 'Pooleyville', as it was facetiously called, consisted of a figure of eight planned around a free monorail, with high-density housing areas clustered close to the monorail stations and a multi-level centre of Cumbernauld-Hook parentage at the centre of the system. This imaginative but rigid conception was scotched by the Ministry of Housing and Local Government's unwillingness to allow Buckinghamshire to do anything so daring on its own.

But the Ministry took over the idea, sticking to the approximate size and site already suggested. This meant engulfing three towns (Bletchley, Wolverton and Stony Stratford) and many villages in the new city. After public enquiry, a development corporation was established and the planning consultants Llewelyn-Davies, Weeks Forestier-Walker and Bor were picked in 1967. Llewelyn-Davies's firm had just completed a plan for Washington New Town, County Durham, based on a hierarchy of roads arranged in a grid

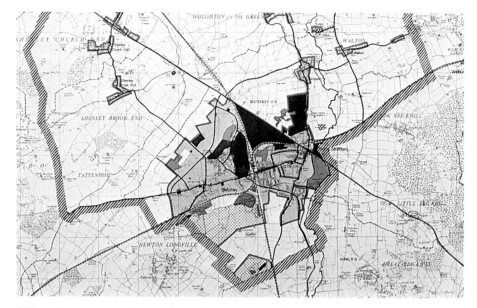

Milton Keynes, town plan; designated area as of April 1969.

with limited interconnections. The importance of road-planning in the New Towns had by then been appreciated, but its potential for rigidity was only just dawning. Llewelyn-Davies and his new partner Walter Bor (who had worked on the LCC's Hook scheme) were looking for fresh ideas. These came particularly from California, where city-planners were advancing the view that spatially discrete units were a misguided and constraining way of organising communities. Christopher Alexander put this case in mathematical and architectural terms in his essay of 1965, 'A City is not a Tree'; and in 1967–8 Melvin Webber, a Berkeley academic visiting London, gave some guest lectures which stated a similar position in economic and libertarian language. Webber was taken up by Llewelyn-Davies and made consultant to the Milton Keynes team for issues of 'urban society'. So the superficially Californian appearance of the city goes deeper than might be imagined.

The plan evolved in 1968–70 attempted therefore to bring to the British New Town tradition greater 'opportunity and freedom of choice' – the highest of six goals enunciated in the final plan of 1970. Physically, this meant a revised version of the Washington grid, with a mixture of land uses and a low-key transport system attuned to the car but without multi-level interchanges. The consultants avoided architectural prescription. Under Derek Walker (1970–6) and later chief architects, this exercise in practical, pluralistic planning has been carried through with consistency, vitality and patience. Milton Keynes is one of very few places in present-day Britain where architectural and planning ideas have been carried out on the grand scale. There are sceptics and haters of the city, but there has been no major dissension or disaster.

At heart, Milton Keynes remains an English New Town writ large. It has dismantled the pieces from a first-generation town, compacted them and reassembled them on a vast chess board with more open space between. The neighbourhoods remain, reinforced rather than blurred by their individuality and by the encompassing grid roads. The original plan advocated points of focus at midway places along the perimeter of each grid, corresponding with bus stops and pedestrian subways linking the neighbourhoods, but these have not materialised. So shielded are the perimeter roads by lavish landscaping and planting that a sense of division is almost complete. The shopping centre, sited atop the district's best ridge and executed with conscious monumentality and American sleekness by the Development Corporation's architects, is a magnet for miles around. But there is still not enough to do there. The station plaza, all mirror glass and empty acreage, is a lonely slog from the shops for the pedestrian along one of Milton Keynes's myriad of underused paths. The centre is yet unfinished, so the verdict may be premature. But the rhetoric of opportunity is often belied by an experience of limitation.

To set against this, Milton Keynes offers greater choice of housing tenure, type, layout and style than previous New Towns. From afar, the impression is of an endless blur of Buckinghamshire pink brick against a rolling landscape; near to, one finds radical post-Radburn layouts, prefabricated terraces, timber-framed houses, historicist detailing and even a scatter of solar-heated houses. A whole range of post-war housing ideas is there to choose from, from the minimal to the eccentric. The old villages have been absorbed and reinvigorated without losing their identity. The sheds of modern industry raise their soulless bulks without embarrassment or

Central Milton Keynes in 1978. Milton Keynes Development Corporation architects. In the middle of the picture, the vast shopping centre.

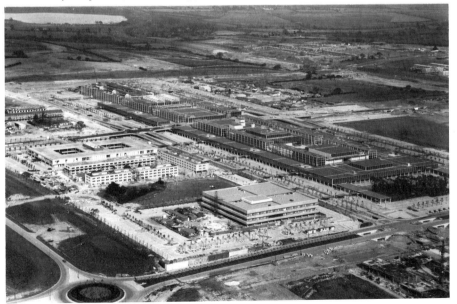

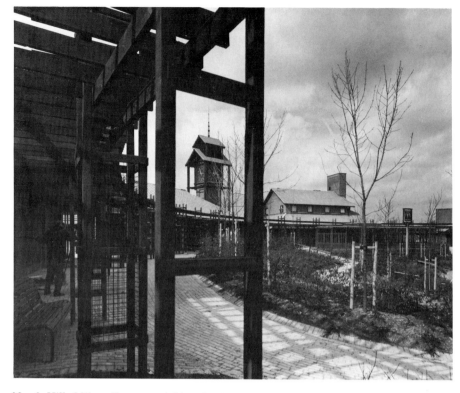

Neath Hill, Milton Keynes: neighbourhood shopping centre. Milton Keynes Development Corporation (1977–9). Warm brick, thick planting, and vernacular vocabulary.

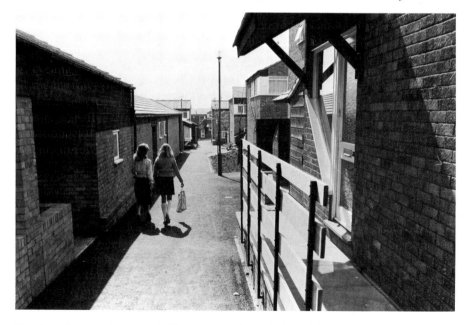

Housing scheme at Eagleton, Milton Keynes, in the informal English-village tradition of town planning, designed by Ralph Erskine for Bovis Ltd (1973–5).

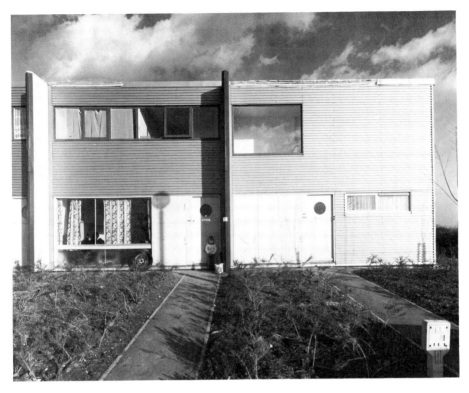

Netherfield, Milton Keynes: housing in a high-tech version of the terrace tradition. Milton Keynes Development Corporation architects (1973–5).

concealment; the Development Corporation's architects perfected a system of industrial building which offered some variety of appearance, while the managers succeeded spectacularly in luring companies to the city. Leisure at Milton Keynes has lost its old-style austerity. Boating, fishing, cycling, jogging and press-up areas on a woodland 'trail' have replaced the narrow culture of the allotment and the Sunday walk. 'Wouldn't it be nice if all cities were like Milton Keynes?', the advertisements of the early 1980s repeatedly simpered. Undoubtedly not: but Milton Keynes remains the most hopeful as well, probably, as the last of the great post-war British experiments in town-building.

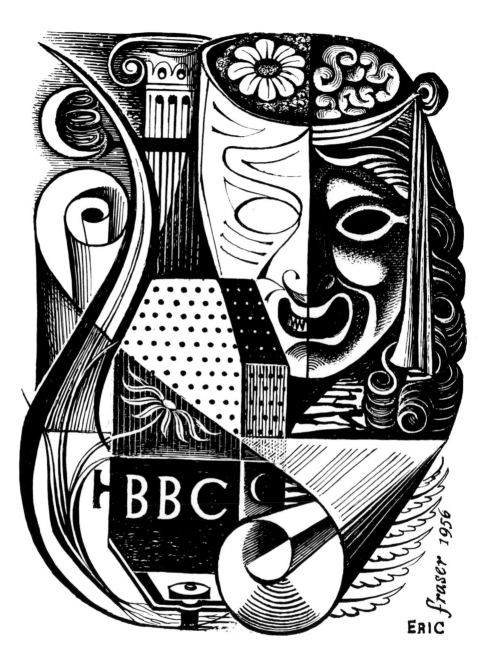

Eric Fraser's design which appeared in the Radio Times *for 21 September, 1956, celebrating the tenth anniversary of the BBC's Third Programme.*

5   The Third Programme

BORIS FORD

The third programme? What's that? I suppose you mean Programme 3.
(Member of the BBC Information Office)

For a younger generation, the Third Programme lies apparently unknown
and ill-documented in that limbo between the present and the not-yet-
historic past, though it is there on the shelf, taped for eternity. But on 29
September 1946, its inauguration by Joyce Grenfell in a programme entitled
How To Listen (and How Not To, How They Used To, and How You Must)
was one of the most improbable and positive happenings of the immediate
post-war years. Joyce Grenfell was followed by Bach's *Goldberg Variations*,
and Bach by Field-Marshall the Rt Hon. J.C. Smuts reflecting on world
affairs. And then there followed a full-scale concert of appropriately
celebratory English music, beginning with a newly commissioned Festival
Overture by Britten.

That first week was, understandably, a glittering shop-window for the new
Programme. Having been given *Comus* and Szigeti and the whole of *Man and
Superman* earlier in the week, astonished listeners were offered, on the Friday
evening, a Spanish concert, E.H. Carr appraising foreign policy, Donizetti's
Don Pasquale, Sartre's *Huis Clos* (with the original cast of Peter Brook's
production), and, to round it off, Schnabel playing Beethoven's *Hammer-
klavier* Sonata.

The character and aims of the Third Programme had been announced in
the *Radio Times* for that week by Sir William Haley, the Director-General of
the BBC. He stated the BBC's responsibilities to what might be termed 'high
culture' in uncompromising terms:

a public service such as the BBC has to feel . . . that it is providing for all classes of
its listeners, and that it is, among its other functions, presenting the great classical
repertoire in music and drama and – so far as they are broadcastable – in literature,
and the other arts . . .

The Third Programme will have no fixed points. It will devote to the great works
the time they require. It will seek every evening to do something that is culturally
satisfying and significant. It will devote occasional series of evenings to some related

masterpieces, a Shakespeare historical cycle, all the Beethoven quartets, or a series of Mozart operas . . . Its talks will include contributions from the great European thinkers. Its whole content will be directed to an audience that is not of one class but that is perceptive and intelligent.

If the Director-General seemed to be basing his announcement somewhat unadventuresomely on the safe classics of culture, it was still a forthright and notable statement of new policy. And it was received at the time with considerable and quite widespread enthusiasm, including listeners who admitted that they personally were unlikely to listen to this new programme; especially when they learned from George Barnes, the first Head of the Third Programme, that it 'is for the alert and receptive listener' who is prepared to 'meet the performer half-way by giving [the programme] his whole attention'. He explained that music would occupy a third of the programme, and that he hoped to broadcast an opera every week and a full-length play once a month – a bold decision for an audience that had yet to be converted to opera. By contrast there was to be only a meagre half-hour a week for the visual arts.

Looking at the programmes over the following years, it is striking how well the standard was maintained. To pick out the major programmes is to give a picture that unfairly overlooks the excellence and variety of the everyday concerts, recitals, talks, features, and plays. But they are a reminder of the degree to which Sir William Haley's words were taken seriously. Thus, to mention only the highlights for the corresponding week of September in the following two years:

1947   Aristophanes' *Lysistrata*
       On *Finnegan's Wake*
       Two Brahms, Schubert, Mendelssohn anniversary concerts
       Cosi Fan Tutte, Fidelio, The Marriage of Figaro, Don Giovanni (Vienna State
       Opera, with Krips and Kraus)
       Talks on Blake, Thomas Carlyle, Turner and Constable
       Berkeley's *Stabat Mater*
1948   Bach's B Minor Mass
       Eliot reading *Four Quartets*
       Stravinsky's *The Tale of the Soldier*
       Peggy Ashcroft reading Shakespeare's *The Rape of Lucrece*
       Shaw's *St Joan*
       Two Beethoven concerts (Vienna Philharmonic)
       Eliot's *Family Reunion*

During this week of 1948 alone the following 'stars' were heard: Eliot (records), Suddaby, Pears, Osbert Sitwell (records), Goossens, Margaret Mead, Solomon, Ashcroft (records), Furtwangler (twice), Boulanger (twice), Curzon, Patzak, Schwartzkopf, Maria Becker, Raymond Mortimer, Landseer, Kubelik, Gielgud (records), Butterfield, Backhaus, Arrau, Edith Sitwell, and Boult.

The Programme included a fairly generous attention to contemporary works – indeed, in 1951 Edward Sackville-West wrote that 'the performance and dissemination of new music depends to a very large extent on the goodwill of the Third'. Under the direction of William Glock, the music programmes were of a consistently high and imaginative quality. But the most significant feature of the Third was that it gave considerable chunks of time to major programmes in all the arts. There was a feeling of spacious liberality about an evening spent (though surely no one could have spent a *whole* evening) with the Third and also of an easy familiarity, or at least a would-be familiarity, with the wide world of culture. The programmes were collectively planned and discussed, so that, as Alan Pryce-Jones observed in his review of the Third's first five years,

a single object can be attacked from different angles, for example, the second centenary of Goethe's birth was celebrated not only by a series of talks, but by the readings of poetry, by Louis MacNeice's vivid translation of *Faust*, and by apposite music as well.

For Pryce-Jones, one of the Third's 'signal successes' was that it took active steps to re-establish continental contacts destroyed by the War, and he instanced a single week in which the Third broadcast an opera recording from Italy, a Danish orchestra, a Viennese choir, two talks on Manzoni (one by an Italian), and a play by Pirandello. And also the Third 'was able to clutch distinguished visitors as they pass through its orbit', visitors such as Gabriel Marcel, Nicholas-Berdyaev, Julien Green, and Thomas Mann.

One of the Third's other 'signal successes' was features. Laurence Gilliam, who was head of the Features Department, said bluntly that 'Radio must initiate or die'. He recruited as writers of original features a large number of imaginative poets and novelists such as Elizabeth Bowen, George Orwell, Geoffrey Grigson, Rayner Heppenstall, Louis MacNeice, Dylan Thomas, W.R. Rodgers, Wyndham Lewis, V.S. Pritchett . . . Douglas Cleverdon, one of the most distinguished producers working in this quintessentially radio medium, said that most of the writers he worked with were poets. Certainly features seemed to offer unusual creative scope, and the best of them, like *Imaginary Conversations* (such as Pritchett's 'The Gambler', a conversation between Dostoevsky and Turgenev) or programmes created out of living material like Rodgers' 'The Bare Stones of Aran', or 'parables' like Bronowski's 'The Face of Violence' and Dylan Thomas's 'Under Milk Wood', gave the impression of being carefully-shaped, inter-disciplinary works of art.

The Third Programme's characteristics and qualities made it, inevitably, an easy butt for philistine ribaldry. As George Melly observed,

[the notion that] it is sometimes more important to engage the full attention of a small number of people, even a very small number of people, than to divert millions at a comparatively superficial level

naturally came under attack; and

when a concept is under attack, a word is found to cover it, and the word they use to put down criticism on an informed level is 'elitist'.

A rather different witness, Sir John Wolfenden, the Vice-Chancellor of Reading University, looking back on ten years of the Third Programme, insisted that Third Programme listeners 'are not intellectual snobs who refuse to have anything to do with anything but the Third'. But it is true, he added, that 'the Third Programme and tap-listening do not go together'. Quite simply, Sir John felt, if he were to be deprived of the programmes for which he found himself switching over to the Third, his life would be the poorer; 'for the Third adds a touch of taste and educated enjoyment to our lives which we can get nowhere else', or only, for many people, with great difficulty.

For it is now in danger of being forgotten how dramatic a transformation the Third Programme brought about in the lives of a great many people with a taste for artistic and cultural matters, especially those who lived outside London and a very few major cities. For instance, in the September week of 1956 when Sir John was writing, listeners were offered the following 'highlights' on the Third:

> Debussy's *Pelléas et Mélisande*
> A talk: *Art in Africa*
> A talk and discussion: *The Inexactness of Language*
> *Siegfried* by Giraudoux 'Reading a Poem':
> R.P. Blackmur on a poem by Stevens
> *The Streets of Pompeii*, a play by Henry Reed
> Byrd's 5-Part Mass
> John Ford's play, *The Broken Heart*
> A symposium on the Coventry Cathedral windows
> A discussion: *Training the Teachers*
> Beethoven's Mass in D
> A lecture by Auden

In the corresponding week of 1957 the Third broadcast Wagner's *Siegfried* and *Gotterdämmerung*, both introduced by Ernest Newman, as well as Gorky's *Yegor Bulichov* and the first of four programmes on Baudelaire's poems. Before the advent of the Third, few people could hope to encounter such a variety of music and drama and literature and talks in a year, let alone in a week.

This variety was the distinctive feature of the Third Programme. Hans Keller, in a talk entitled 'My Philosophy of Radio', spoke of the Third's principle of 'mixed cultural programming':

the principle of preventing automatic listening, promoting selective listening, and causing functional surprises, . . . forcible widenings of the mind, by successions of programmes from entirely different areas of mental life . . .

This principle was firmly adhered to. What seems to have changed, over the Third Programme's second decade, was the richness and standard of the cultural mix. The September week for 1968 offered the following quite representative highlights:

> The Story of Kaspar Hauser, by Terence Tiller
> Bach's St John Passion
> Natalia Ginzberg's play, *The Advertisement*
> 'Chaliapin Speaks' (as told to Gorky)
> Sound poems by Ernst Jandl
> A feature programme on historic organs
> *L'Idée Fixe*, by Valéry
> Various concerts

If that week can only be described as less rich by comparison with the Third's own former standards, it does none the less seem to reflect a loss of imaginative energy. It feels like a wayward assortment rather than a coherent mixture. Douglas Cleverdon believes that the Third Programme ('a gauge of English cultural life at its most unrestrained') became 'more and more metropolitan and clever: élitist in the worst sense, and self-indulgent in relation to audience-demand'. On the other hand, Melly, writing as an *aficionado* of popular entertainment, was highly critical of 'a certain caution and conservatism, and even [a] blindness and stupidity in the face of new ideas and forms' which, he felt, characterised some of the Third Programme's more 'élite' broadcasters.

'Audience-demand' and 'audience-response', at least as measured by the Audience Research Department of the BBC, had never unduly preoccupied the Third Programme team. The BBC hierarchy had accepted from the first that the size of the 'market' for the Third would be modest by the standards of the Home and the Light Programme: only 2 per cent of the over-21 population were rated as 'good' and another 8 per cent as 'fair prospects' as listeners to the Third. A study in 1956/7 found that just under a million and a half people were listening to the Third once a week or more often; and between 200,000 and 250,000 listened each evening. Trifling though such audience ratings were by current radio comparisons, they represented an astonishingly good reception for programmes of an ambitiously high and demanding standard (especially as some 20 per cent of listeners were unable to receive the Third Programme's transmissions).

But whatever its quality, or maybe because of its still comparatively high quality, the number of the Third Programme's listening public declined steadily, if not dramatically. What was dramatic was the loss of listeners and the shift of resources from sound radio as a whole to television. Towards the later sixties it became clear that there was going to be a new policy for radio, and the odds were that it would take the form of what was euphemistically called rationalisation. Supporters of the Third Programme grew increasingly apprehensive and vocal about the BBC's intentions, but not to much avail. The BBC went ahead with its policy document, *Broadcasting in the Seventies*, in spite of a barrage of criticism not only from the élite listening public (like the 40 members of the High Table of King's College, Cambridge, and the PEN Club, and a cast of distinguished actors and actresses), but more significantly from 134, or virtually all, the BBC staff working with the Third Programme.

The new plan for radio, put at its simplest, was to introduce a large degree of 'streaming' into the four channels: 'pop' on One, light music on Two, serious music with a little talk in the intervals of concerts and a small amount of drama on Three, and talk plus some popular classical music on Four. The Third Programme would disappear. It was argued by Charles Curran, the new Director-General of the BBC, that the aim was to maintain the quality of what had been done on the Third, and that the joint planning of Radios Three and Four would produce a better service for the minority audiences which listened to both of them. This was strongly challenged by the BBC staff who, contrary to regulations, wrote in their letter to *The Times*:

What we object to is the abandonment of creative, mixed planning in favour of a schematic division into categories on all four programmes; and, above all, the refusal to devote a large, well-defined area of broadcasting time to a service of the arts and sciences.

With the abolition of the Third, the plan envisaged that 'the daytime stream of music will be maintained and it will now be extended more into the evening'. In the course of a discussion, the composer Peter Maxwell Davies insisted that '"the daytime stream of music" isn't anything like the old Third Programme, which was never a stream of music'. And he described how, as a 'not particularly curious nor particularly bright boy at school', he would listen to a symphony or some other music on the Third and then, leaving the radio on, would find himself listening to a talk about plankton or a broadcast of Villiers de L'Isle Adam's *Axel*:

I would never have come across this broader culture had it not flowed on from the one thing that I was interested in, the music. I fear, now, that people are probably going to lose whole realms of experience.

There is no doubt, from correspondence at the time, that Maxwell Davies was speaking for a very great many people who had come to depend on the Third Programme, not only for the large amount of sheer enjoyment that it offered, but also for their cultural education. What they were offered instead was, for the most part, a 'stream' of excellent music, which now occupies about 75 per cent of Radio Three's evening time. Perhaps because Radio Three found itself broadcasting so much music each day, each week, each year, the number of what I have called 'highlights' seemed to fall off markedly.

That the Third Programme was richer and more varied culturally than anything offered on British radio or television today can hardly be contested. Without a full-scale evaluation, which would entail listening to the tapes of very many of its programmes, the Third can only be assessed on the evidence of one's distant recollections and of its printed programme. These were very impressive, and they confirm, I believe, that the closing-down of the Third Programme in 1970 was a consequence, as it was a sign, of a loss of cultural stamina and commitment on the part of the BBC's top management. An anonymous contributor of an article to *The Times*, himself an experienced broadcaster, was clear where the responsiblity lay:

Changes in radio are long overdue. Anybody working in radio for the last five years can only have been appalled by its stagnation and the way in which inertia at the top succeeded in drying up the flow of ideas and suggestions for change.

At the same time, for all the enlightened and creative energy of its early years, the Third contributed to its own downfall by pursuing a policy, indeed it was a philosophy, of providing the 'best' and letting the audience take it or leave it. At a time when a variety of pressures, such as the rise of television, the reduction in radio budgets, and the everpresent hostility of the troglodytes, must have made the continuance of the Third problematic, it needed to a far greater extent to seek new audiences and to help people enter its privileged world. As Hans Keller remarked, and he was himself a most distinguished member of the Third's music staff, 'there is no quality at the production end without quality at the reception end . . . if you don't hear it's good it might as well be bad'. What did the Third Programme do over the years to help its listeners 'hear it's good'? And what did it know or seek to discover about the cultural world inhabited by less sophisticated listeners?

The Third Programme was studiously uneducational when it should only have been unpedagogic and uninstructional. 'A Shakespeare historical cycle, all the Beethoven quartets, or a series of Mozart operas', let alone 'the great European thinkers', to take Sir William Haley's examples of Third Programme fare, are profound and complex works of art and philosophy for every listener, and they are no more self-explanatory than Maxwell Davies's latest symphony. To assume otherwise was to be guilty of treating the Third as a highbrow preserve, and inviting listeners to class themselves among the 'élite'. It was, I fear, this aloof urbanity that largely contributed to the demise of a Programme which had been launched with such enlightened enthusiasm and promise, and which for some twenty years was a cornucopia of cultural riches.

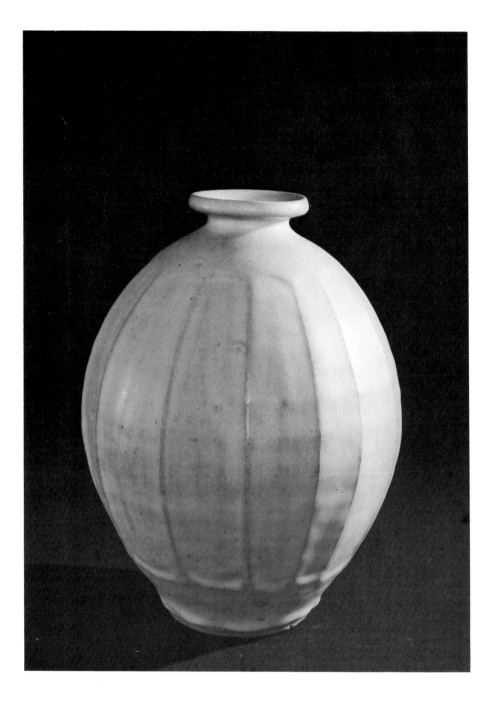

Bottle with cut sides by Katherine Pleydell-Bouverie (1970). Stoneware with matt cream glaze; height 27.6 cm.

6 The Crafts

CHRISTOPHER FRAYLING

Introduction: concepts of 'craftsmanship' since the War

A visitor to the Country Pavilion at the Festival of Britain in 1951 would have found nothing to challenge the popular definition of 'the crafts', derived distantly – and not always accurately – from the thinking of John Ruskin, William Morris and the Arts and Crafts Movement of the late nineteenth century. Wandering past an embroidered relief mural entitled 'the Country Wife', the visitor would have reached the 'rural crafts' section of the Pavilion, devoted to the work of still practising wheelwrights, thatchers and basket-makers in the countryside. In the early 1950s, through countless new books about *English Popular Art*, *The English Craftsman* or *Life in an English Village*, and in countless reprints of George Sturt's *The Wheelwrights' Shop* or the rural reminiscences of W.H. Hudson, Edward Thomas and Richard Jefferies, the popular definition of the crafts would have gone something like this:

Crafts must be made of natural materials, preferably in beige;

Crafts must be functional;

Crafts must be the work of one person, perhaps featuring visible thumb-prints or surface imperfections to prove it;

Crafts must be the embodiment of a traditional design (unless of a musical instrument);

Crafts must be in the 'artisan' rather than the 'fine art' tradition;

Crafts must be rural products;

Crafts must be untouched by fashion (which, it was automatically assumed, meant 'badly made fashion');

Crafts must be easily understood;

Crafts must last, like a brogue shoe or a fine tweed;

Crafts must be affordable (even if, like William Morris's work, affordable mainly by Oxbridge Colleges, Anglican churches and collectors);

Above all, crafts must provide a *solace*, in a rapidly changing world.

The same person, visiting 'The Craftsman's Art' exhibition at the Victoria and Albert Museum in 1973, might have deduced from the cover of the catalogue – the title, with traditional lettering carved in slate by Harry

Meadows, and a butterfly perched on the bottom right-hand corner – that the exhibition would also be devoted to craft-work derived from the thinking and practice of the Arts and Crafts Movement. But the butterfly was a suspiciously 'arty' touch, a visual clue to an exhibition celebrating the craftsman's *art* rather than the craftsman's *craft*. Inside the exhibition, John Makepeace's Chest of Drawers (1972), a free-standing sculptural pillar of plywood and acrylic drawers cantilevered on a stainless steel column, competed for the visitor's attention with Wendy Ramshaw's gold and silver Necklace (1972), which may have fallen like a meteorite from a galaxy far, far away. Both exhibits belonged to a new craft world where, instead of having straw in their hair, many of the craftspeople had recently graduated from art school; and where, as James Noel White's catalogue Introduction pointed out, 'Painting is becoming sculpture, is becoming ceramic, is becoming three-dimensional weaving, is becoming jewellery.'

In an important lecture entitled 'Craft: art or design?' the industrial designer Misha Black argued that the development of the crafts in the 1960s and 1970s had a lot to do with three graduates of the Fine Arts from Leeds Polytechnic who had walked 150 miles in East Anglia with a 10-foot yellow pole tied to their heads: conceptual, minimal and performance art had encouraged the exhibition-going public (to say nothing of collectors) to look elsewhere for the values they used to associate with fine art, and they'd found these values in the craft world.

The visitor to *this* exhibition might have wondered whether 'The Craftsman's Art' had anything at all to do with the concept of 'the crafts' as commonly understood. The 1970s definition would have gone something like this:

> Crafts can be made with machines, and maybe even *by* them, if numerically-controlled technology goes on improving;
> Crafts can be made with synthetic materials, in all colours of the rainbow;
> Crafts can be non-functional, and may even conform to the American Customs and Excise definition of 'art' – that it must be 'totally useless';
> Crafts can be made in limited production;
> Crafts can be designed by one person and made by another (as they often were, in fact, in the original Arts and Crafts period);
> Crafts can provide designed prototypes for industry;
> Crafts can be made in towns, and usually are;
> Crafts can be high fashion, and *still* be well-made, although they needn't be;
> Crafts can use ideas borrowed from the fine arts of painting and sculpture;
> Crafts can be transient;
> Crafts can be very expensive indeed (again like William Morris's work . . .)
> Above all, the role of the crafts is to provide a *challenge*, often by means of an ironic statement about traditional notions of 'the crafts'.

When asked whether he thought pottery (or rather 'ceramics') was an art or not, the potter Michael Cardew replied: '. . . all that nonsense I refuse to talk about. It really is too stupid. The question is "are you a craftsman or not. Answer yes or no."'

Of course, the polarity between the image of 'the crafts' contained in the Country Pavilion of 1951, and the equivalent image contained in 'The Craftsman's Art' exhibition of 1973 is in a sense an artificial one. For 'The

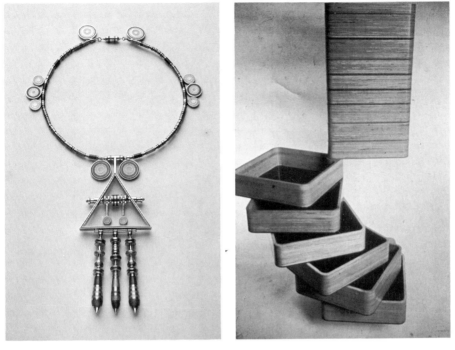

Necklace by Wendy Ramshaw 18 ct yellow gold and silver; enamelled, turned, and engraved.

Chest of drawers by John Makepeace (1972). Plywood, acrylic and stainless steel; chest formed from a pillar of drawers cantilevered on a column of stainless steel.

Craftsman's Art' exhibition included, as well, the traditional 'crafts' definition in its spectrum of 'new work by British craftsmen': it contained carved dishes in French walnut by the designer–maker David Pye, and stoneware jugs by the potter Mick Casson, which seemed to be in a direct line of descent from the Arts and Crafts tradition. As if to symbolise the fact, the exhibition was designed to look more like an overcrowded 'sale of work' than an exhibition of fine art: its design harked back to the 'craft galleries' of the 1950s, rather than looking forward to the post-modernist gallery settings of craft shows in the later 1970s and the 1980s.

The crafts certainly developed what might be called a Cinderella-complex in the years between 1951 and 1973 – an urge to transform 'the skill of old England' into an art form which would command respect in the world of the galleries – but it would be a mistake to conclude (as others have) that the complex affected all (or even most) practising craftspeople in the same period. The concept of 'the artist–craftsman' – which referred back to William Morris and the fine art workmen of the Arts and Crafts Movement, but which was to change its meaning as art changed its meaning – *was* enshrined in the stated purposes of the Crafts Advisory Committee (before it became the Crafts Council) in 1971: '. . . to advise the Minister for the Arts on the needs of artist–craftsmen'. As early as 1948, the Board of Trade had been persuaded by the artist, wood engraver and writer on the crafts, John

Farleigh, to help support the Crafts Centre of Great Britain in 'the preservation, promotion and improvement of the work of designer–craftsmen in the fine arts'. So Bernard Leach was correct in predicting, in *A Potter's Book* (1940), the gradual acceptance of the 'artist-craftsman' – by government, even – as a figure on the *artistic* landscape. But he could not have predicted the changes in the fine art world (and in the teaching of fine art) which were to alter that concept beyond all recognition by the 1970s. And he was very wide of the mark when he stated categorically that there would 'no longer' be any 'journeyman craftsmen' working in Britain during his lifetime.

In a sociological survey of an estimated 20,000 independent professional craftspeople entitled *Working in Crafts*, published, rather bravely, by the Crafts Council in 1983, it emerged that a substantial proportion of the crafts constituency *are* in fact 'journeyman craftsmen' (in Bernard Leach's sense of the term) who have very little interest, or rather very little time to be interested, in the worlds of fine art *or* design. In response to the question 'The Crafts Council is too arts-minded', 59 per cent of the full-time practitioners agreed, while 17 per cent were unsure: in response to the related question 'Carrying on a tradition is important to me', 58 per cent of the full-time practitioners agreed, while 23 per cent were unsure – a remarkable correlation. In response to both questions, the male practitioners tended to agree more than the females, while the full-timers of both genders tended to agree more than the part-timers. Clearly, the 'arts' orientation of the Council was being welcomed by those part-time artist–craftsmen who had some connection with colleges of art and design (26 per cent of the *total* number were in the category of 'teachers'), while it was being rejected by the majority of full-time practitioners who were struggling to earn a living, through batch production, in the crafts.

Working In Crafts proved conclusively that Bernard Leach's artist–craftsmen, 'working for the most part alone or with a few assistants', had become an important, and statistically significant, addition to the crafts scene – but that the scene was a great deal more varied and complex than the Crafts Council had predicted. The survey also established that, unlike in the art world or the design world, nearly 55 per cent of *all* practitioners in the crafts were female – the percentage being considerably higher in the 'part-time' and 'semi-professional' categories: this conclusion led to some considerable debate about whether the word crafts*men* was still appropriate. Even in the politically radical atmosphere of the Arts and Crafts Movement of the late nineteenth century, a firm distinction seems to have been drawn between the 'male' crafts of furniture-making, pottery, and metal-work, and the 'female' crafts which were more associated with the home environment. The *Working In Crafts* survey amply demonstrated that, by the 1970s, these strange distinctions had well and truly broken down.

The contrast between the Country Pavilion of 1951 and 'The Craftsman's Art' show of 1973, overstated though it may be, can tell us a great deal about the changing relationship between the craft world and both the art world *and* the design world in the years since the Second World War – years which have seen the most significant developments in the crafts since the days of

William Morris. Shortly before he died, Michael Cardew told me that, in his estimation, most people still believe that 'art is wonderful, craft is admirable and design is teachable'; 'I wonder', he added slyly, 'where these beliefs come from – because there really *isn't* anything particularly *admirable* about working as a craftsman.' Certainly, the central question of whether or not the crafts are or should be *admirable* has been posed and re-posed in the post-war period, with very significant effect, by the world of art, craft and design. And the three key traditions of craft-work – the designer–craftsman tradition, the Arts and Crafts tradition and the craftsman's art tradition – have all, at one time or another, had to come to terms with it.

The *Working In Crafts* survey, when distinguishing between the various crafts practised in England and Wales today, concluded that only 490 professional craftspeople are working in 'rural and minor' occupations – that is, 2.4 per cent of the total: by 'rural and minor' occupations (minor in the numerical sense), the survey meant 'traditional crafts that used to be major industries but which now survive in a limited way', such as the making of horse-drawn carriages and, perhaps, the thatching of stacks, porches and roofs; and 'cottage crafts, such as making corndollies, that are practised on a small scale'. Given this tiny number of surviving 'rural craftsmen', which surely can't be as tiny as the survey concludes, it seems extraordinary that 'rural and other' occupations still represent the most potent image of the crafts, for most of us, even today. Perhaps it's because so much of modern advertising is committed to the view that there is a corner of the English mind that is forever Ambridge. This phenomenon is so pervasive that in a recent survey of *The State of the Language*, the word 'crafted' is described as one of those words which 'beguile as well as inform'. When advertising people use 'crafted' as a substitute for 'manufactured', the survey goes on, they are attempting to 'delude the public into believing that something has been made by hand, in a carefully old-fashioned way'. The hoardings do not actually say this – they simply 'smuggle it in' (Dwight Bolinger, 'Fire in a wooden stove', from *The State of the Language*, ed. L. Michaels and C. Ricks, 1980, p. 384). Hence the 1970s and 1980s slogans for selling cars 'Handbuilt by Robots' and 'more space, more craft' – in which the reassuring connotations of 'handbuilt' and 'craft' seem calculated to offset the less reassuring connotations of 'robots' and space-age technology. Craft is trustworthy and admirable, microchips are not – at least not yet. Assembly lines may be manned by robots, the corner grocery-shop may have long since been demolished, convenience foods may seem too processed for comfort – but the advertisers can rely on the simple word 'crafted' to relieve for a moment the complex anxieties which these social and economic processes have created.

Of course, the word 'crafted' isn't confined to the billboards, and the ad-men didn't conjure this imagery out of thin air. As a result of the 1960s and early 1970s 'craft revival' (the product of a period of economic optimism, and of revival*ism*, when nearly 40 per cent of all professional 'journeyman craftsmen' first set up their businesses), the word can be seen above most of those shops, linking the main routes to tourist attractions, which used to be known as 'souvenir shops'. *Shell Book of Country Crafts* actually predicted that this would happen: 'the gift shop', it said in a hopeful way, 'is changing its image, to the advantage of everyone'. Many of these craft shops aimed to supply a market which, in the words of one commentator, 'combines an insatiable appetite for the visibly hand-made with a strong degree of price-resistance to what is more expensive than the equivalent machine-product', with the inevitable result that they were (and are) stocked with 'craft products' from countries in the Third World, which are cheaply made under conditions of sweated-labour. One of the more unpleasant ironies of the polarisation of the craft world into craft shops at one end of the spectrum and artist–craftsmen at the other, is that while craft shops in the 1960s were importing 'crafts for tourists' from Japan, Korea and Africa, some artist–craftsmen were importing their 'craft philosophies', for very different purposes, from the same sources.

In opposition to all this popular imagery of 'the crafts' – 'bringing it all back home' – stand the three main traditions of post-war work in 'the crafts'. For the Arts and Crafts tradition, 'home' is the writings and practice of William Morris and immediate disciples – which made 'the fine crafts' visible again, in bold contrast to what were seen as the dark, satanic mills of (usually northern) industrial Britain. For the designer–craftsman tradition, 'home' is the wartime dream that the traditional skills and values of British craftsmanship could be applied to the system of mass-production, either directly (as in Utility furniture) or by example. For the craftsman's art tradition, 'home' is, indirectly, the first Bauhaus manifesto of Walter Gropius, where 'architects, sculptors and painters' were all exhorted to 'turn to the crafts' – not 'return' to the crafts, as it has been consistently and disastrously mistranslated. 'Home' is also that tempting space in the art market which has been vacated by most of the significant British art movements since pop.

Whatever the conceptual and practical differences between these three traditions which have emerged in the last forty years, they have one basic thing in common: they all resent, deeply, any association with the popular image of 'the crafts'. Most craft shops, it has often been said by contemporary artists, craftsmen *and* designers, are full of very good examples of very bad craftsmanship.

The designer-craftsman

In 1947, King Penguin published *The English Tradition in Design* by John Gloag. The book attempted to trace the inter-connections between 'the English tradition' of craftsmanship and workmanship, and 'the English tradition' of design for industry. Its aggressive conclusion was that until industrial designers made a decisive break with the Arts and Crafts tradition, there was little future for British design:

. . . the real English genius for design was masked by a false 'Olde England' . . . [which] is neither old nor English but a shallow sham . . . the *real* English tradition in design is alight and alive today all about us – in the wayside shelter of glass and steel, made for Green Line coach passengers; in the cast iron telephone kiosks designed for the GPO; in our pillar boxes and telephone instruments; in the radio sets designed by R.D. Russell and Wells Coates . . . In such work, the spirit of England resides.

(pp. 35–6)

These sentiments represent one extreme in the post-war debate about the relationship between design and craftsmanship. Others (like Gordon Russell) might argue that designers needed to experience a period of handwork in order to get to know their materials; that craftsmen could be useful to industry, if they made high-quality experimental pieces which contrasted favourably with the general shoddiness of mass-produced goods; that craftsmen should continue to produce well-designed and well-made prototypes, which might or might not go into industrial production. Such ideas had been attributed to William Morris (whose own designs were being rediscovered by the post-war generation, through exhibitions such as 'Victorian and Edwardian Decorative Arts' at the Victoria and Albert Museum in 1952), and had been propagated by the Bauhaus. But a vociferous part of the design establishment rejected them in the post-war years, in their urge to promote the industrial designer as the new hero of the British design story.

   In some ways this apparent parting of the ways is surprising, since Gordon Russell was such a dominant figure in the design establishment at this time – and he brought to the new Council of Industrial Design a deep understanding of the Cotswold tradition in furniture design, as well as a passionate belief in the contribution of individual makers to machine production: in his autobiography, *Designer's Trade*, Russell tells of how the Utility range was offered to the furniture trade during the war, and how delighted he was that the range conformed to the Arts and Crafts philosophy. In the mid-1960s, when Sir Gordon Russell (as by then he was) was chairman of the Crafts Centre, he expressed the more general relationship between craftsmanship and design in this way:

For most ordinary purposes the machine, rightly directed and used, can supply our day to day needs. But the ultimate in standardisation leads to boredom. For infinite variety and unique quality hand production remains a sound method. It is bound to be slow, yet for single articles it is naturally cheaper and quicker than the machine, for neither elaborate tooling up nor even, in many cases, complete drawings are necessary. The imaginative craftsman can make experiments with ease, even altering the design while working on the job. Out of such design research, properly organised in collaboration with a firm, ideas of considerable importance may emerge . . .

('Craftsmanship in a machine age', in *Design*, July 1965)

   One reason why craft and design seemed on the face of it to be going in separate directions just after the war (despite Gordon Russell), was that there was a certain amount of faith in the ability of craftsmen to survive on their own terms – with a little help from the welfare state. Sir Stafford Cripps of the Board of Trade, shortly after master-minding the 'Britain Can Make It' show for the Council of Industrial Design, gave a very small grant to the grandly named Crafts Centre of Great Britain, for the support of 'designer–craftsmen in the fine arts': the Centre's Council was to be, in effect, a federation of five existing craft societies. In time, the original Crafts Centre argued itself almost into oblivion – with the fine arts faction and the design

function forever slugging it out with the more down-to-earth Arts and
Crafts people about exhibitions policy. But in the mid 1960s, under the
Chairmanship of Graham Hughes, art director at Goldsmiths' Hall, the
Council was given a brand new brief – to provide a showcase for art school
graduates who did not wish to become either practising fine artists *or*
industrial designers. Curriculum changes in the art schools were beginning to
result in a new generation of craft graduates from an art environment who, as
the silversmith and designer David Mellor has recalled, 'became more
interested in trying to control their own tiny bit of life, and to want actually
to make things themselves' – as distinct from the equivalent graduates in the
1950s (like himself) 'who had generally wanted to design for industry'.

In summer 1965, the Design Council mounted a major exhibition on the
theme 'Can craftsmanship help to raise the standards of industrial design?' It
approached the question from two separate, but related points of view:

that a degree of manual ability frees the designer from absolute dependence on the
productive and prototype resources of industry . . . [and] that designing by making
gives to products a distinctively valuable quality, a quality which deserves more
systematic support and encouragement.

Two of the craftsmen featured prominently in the exhibition were David
Mellor and the weaver Peter Collingwood.

The work of David Mellor, who trained as a silversmith, covered 'the
whole range of activity from completely one-off pieces of craftsmanship in
silver or other materials to designs which are produced in large quantities':
cutlery for Walker and Hall of Sheffield (the Pride range, 1954, the Symbol
range, 1961), as well as a cross for Southwell Minster; presentation pieces for
Graham Hughes at Goldsmiths' Hall; the official pattern for British
embassies, 1963; as well as designs for a cast-iron heater, traffic signs and a
litter-bin. The Design Council exhibition illustrated how, in his Sheffield
metal-working shop, the craftsman had experienced 'a constant interaction
between his handwork and his industrially produced pieces'. In 1962, David
Mellor had been made a Royal Designer for Industry (the first craftsman to
be admitted since Reynolds Stone) and he had been followed three years later
by his contemporary at the Royal College of Art, Robert Welch. Welch had
set up his workshop in Chipping Campden, in exactly the same building used
by C.R. Ashbee for *his* experiment in craftsmanship and 'the simple life' half
a century before. It was typical of the new generation of designer–craftsman
that Welch wasn't even aware of the coincidence that Ashbee had once
owned his workshop until some time after he'd moved there. Unlike Ashbee,
Robert Welch used Chipping Campden as his base for designing and
producing stainless-steel wares for J. and J. Wiggin (including a toast-rack),
the Campden range of cutlery (with David Mellor – produced at the
suggestion of the Council of Industrial Design), and a range of special silver
for Churchill College, Cambridge.

Another designer–craftsman promoted by the Design Council was Peter
Collingwood, an extremely inventive weaver. His larger commissions had
included a huge hanging for the indefatigable Sir Gordon Russell, and rugs
for the University of York and New Zealand House. The presence of
Collingwood's work in the exhibition of summer 1965 was not intended to

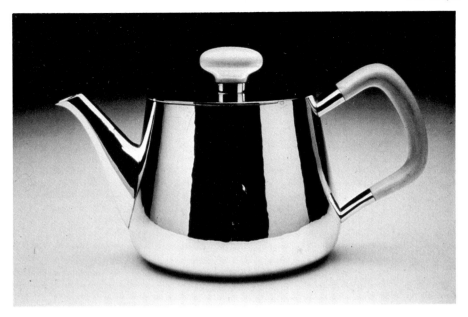

Oval teapot by Robert Welch (1972). Sterling silver with hammered finish, flush hinge, and ivory handle and knob.

show that it had industrial applications – although the pieces were capable of machine production, the 'technical ideas' from which they sprang would have required completely new ways of using the machines – but rather that 'the richness and inventiveness of his weaving places it with the very best design of any kind in Britain today' (colour pl. 12).

Three years after the Design Council's 'craftsmanship' show, David Pye, the Professor of Furniture Design at the Royal College of Art, published his seminal book *The Nature and Art of Workmanship* – a book which took a few well-aimed shots at the 'flock of duck-billed platitudes' which tended (and still tend) to surround contemporary thinking about the crafts – platitudes such as 'craftsmanship must be about function', 'truth to materials', 'hand-work is good for you', and 'free workmanship is better than regulated workmanship'. David Pye's scatter-shots were meant to clarify the relationship between the workmanship of risk (a phrase he preferred to 'craftsmanship') and design – and they amounted to a manual of 'practical philosophy' for those who designed, those who made, or both. *The Nature and Art of Workmanship* was grounded in Pye's own practice as a maker of carved dishes and bowls, and of immaculately turned wooden boxes, as well as in his experience of teaching many of the young designer-makers in wood who were to emerge in the 'Craftsman's Art' era of the 1970s. David Pye's continuing critique of the influence of John Ruskin on contemporary *practice* ('his social views might have plenty to offer the *man*, but very little to offer *his work*') helped greatly to focus the issue on the actual contribution of one-off pieces to an environment dominated by products of the workmanship of certainty:

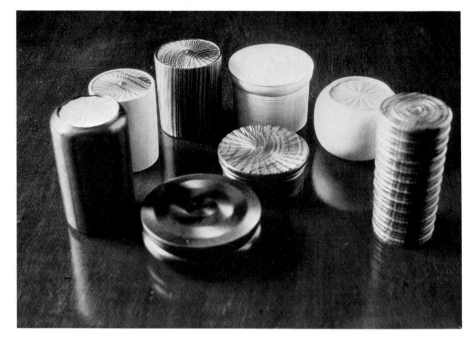

Wooden boxes by David Pye (1981). Turned kingwood, English and African blackwood, wild service tree, plum, and Rio rosewood; some with engraved lids. Diameters 3.5–7.5 cm.

a workman who will not be judged by his work is contemptible, and there is no possible criterion of workmanship except the work . . . THE TREE IS KNOWN BY ITS FRUIT

What Pye cannot have foreseen was that his book would become the Authorised Version for a new generation of makers.

In 'The Craftsman's Art' exhibition, a series of David Pye's own carved dishes and bowls – in rosewood and walnut – appeared as part of the 'woodware' section, among all the wooden sculptures and fine art puppets; while pride of place in the 'furniture' section was given to two pieces by John Makepeace (a fact which occasioned much confused comment at the time): the chest of drawers mentioned earlier, and a stool made up of pieces of yew linked by a series of complex joints. It was ironic, since of the two contributions Makepeace's work seemed to be more sculptural in its impact – perhaps because of the virtuoso skill which had gone into its construction, and of its flamboyant emphasis on originality. Four years after the exhibition, John Makepeace established his own School for Craftsmen in Wood, at Parnham House in Dorset, where he also runs his workshop for designing and making individual and group furniture. Although critics tend to react to his work as if to objects of fine art, Makepeace remains convinced that his furniture cannot be described either as 'fine art' or as 'design' – 'the thing that distinguishes the craftsman proper is the delight of the maker and hopefully the delight of the user'. The qualities of workmanship and showmanship in his furniture (for it *is* furniture) stand out on their own as examples of conspicuous production to the trade, and as alternatives for the wealthy consumer; but his virtuoso objects will never find more than a distant echo in an industry where time is, as always, money.

The arts and craftsman

'Factories have practically driven folk-art out of England', wrote Bernard Leach at the beginning of *A Potter's Book*, the book which, more than any of his pots and jugs and dishes produced at St Ives in the inter-war period, introduced 'a new type of craftsman, called individual, studio or creative' as a figure to be taken seriously by the art world and the craft world:

> . . . the artist-craftsman, since the day of William Morris, has been the chief means of defence against the materialism of industry and its insensibility to beauty.
>
> (p. 1, 1976)

In reaction against those post-Bauhaus designers for industry who, he reckoned, were engaged in 'an over-intellectual effort to discover norms of orderliness and utility', Leach worked hard to re-define and promote the concept of the 'artist–craftsman' as keeper of the flame, by writing numerous books and articles which blended Japanese and Chinese philosophy with advice on 'how to make pots', by lecturing, visiting schools and conducting courses, and by broadcasting on the wireless. Although he always insisted that his major work was called *A Potter's Book*, not *The* Potter's Book, it was to become, from the late 1940s onwards, the essential text (in Michael Cardew's words)

> for those potters who work as artists . . . also for the number of people who, although not necessarily craftsmen, are interested in pottery, whether in commerce or manufacture, as teachers, as collectors, or simply as intelligent consumers.
>
> (Preface, p. xix)

For Bernard Leach, the 'artist–craftsman' represented a complete way of life.

His basic argument – contained in the opening chapter of *A Potter's Book*, which (perhaps surprisingly) owed a great deal to Herbert Read's *Art and Industry* – was that

> The art of the craftsman, to use Read's terminology, is intuitive and humanistic (one hand, one brain); that of the designer for re-duplication, rational abstract and tectonic, the work of the engineer or constructor rather than that of the 'artist'. Each method has its own aesthetic significance. Examples of both can be good or bad . . . *No doubt the work of the intuitive craftsman would be considered by most people to be of a higher, more personal order of beauty.*
>
> (p. 2)

By fusing the social theory of William Morris (minus the socialism) with the practical philosophy of *mingei* (the Japanese tradition of 'the unknown craftsman' and 'folk hand crafts', which he personally helped to revive), Bernard Leach helped to create a heroic image for the individual craftsman who successfully combined the processes of purpose, planning and making in his or her work.

Like most of the pioneers of the inter-war years, Bernard Leach stumbled upon his craft almost by accident. For, despite the foundation of the Central School of Arts and Crafts as a school of craftsmanship in 1896 by W.R. Lethaby, most of the art schools in London were still dominated by the Fine Art tradition – and, if craftsmen-to-be attended College, it was more than likely that they worked in painting, sculpture or printmaking rather than in the craft disciplines. Leach studied painting under Henry Tonks and etching under Frank Brangwyn; Enid Marx was later to cite Paul Nash as a seminal influence on the design of her textiles; Phyllis Barron was to recall that Augustus John, Walter Sickert and Roger Fry 'encouraged' her work in hand blockprinted fabrics. So most of the pioneers who first broke with the medieval rhetoric of the Arts and Crafts people, and re-introduced the idea of the craftsman as expressive *artist*, originally approached their craft from well within the fine art world of the day. They set themselves the task of learning the crafts as artists. And part of the attraction of moving to St Ives and Newlyn in Cornwall (as did Leach, Cardew and Pleydell-Bouverie) or to Ditchling in Sussex (as did Ethel Mairet, Eric Gill, Edward Johnston, and the printer Hilary Pepler who published manifestos on the value of craftsmanship for all of them), was that these locations seemed to house thriving *artistic* communities where heroic 'artist–craftsmen' would feel very much at home. In their origins and in their practice, the pioneers of the inter-war years were a whole world away from the social revolution of William Morris – but then, so was William Morris. As Phyllis Barron succinctly put it, 'we were rich'.

Bernard Leach had been brought up in Hong Kong and Tokyo by his grandparents: when he returned to Tokyo in 1909 at the age of twenty-one after studying at the Slade School of Art and the London School of Art, it was to teach etching – with the aid of an etching-press which he'd taken with him – to Japanese students.

By the time he set up his own pottery about a mile outside St Ives, in 1920, Leach had been learning about Japanese, Chinese and Korean ethics, aesthetics and techniques for eleven years, with guidance and stimulation from, among others, the philosopher Dr Soetsu Yanagi and the young artist–potter Shoji Hamada. From the practical point of view, St Ives was in fact a very odd choice – since tin-smelting had virtually stripped the area of wood (which he needed for firing his Japanese-style kiln); clay had to be transported from many miles away (sometimes as far afield as Devon); and the tourist season (when the market came to Leach, rather than vice versa) lasted at most for six weeks – and that was in a *good* summer. But, undaunted, Bernard Leach and Shoji Hamada – both of whom believed passionately in the preparation of both clays and glazes from local, natural sources (complete with impurities) by the simplest of methods – attempted to bring together, in their bowls and jugs, the Japanese sensitivity to shape and brushwork with the down-to-earth vigour of traditional (often medieval) English slipware. At first, they concentrated on the making of *raku* and stoneware they had studied in Japan, but, after a series of visits to other potteries (for there *were* others) and local museums, they began to introduce slip-decorated lead-glazed earthenware in the traditional English style. The

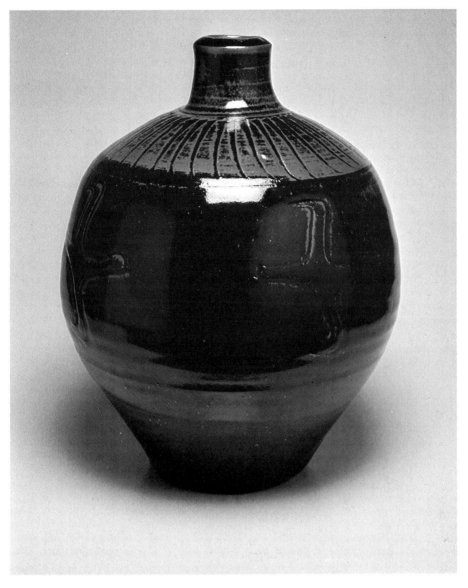

Stoneware vase by Bernard Leach (c.1960). Height 33.5 cm.

delicate *raku*-glazed wares did not, unfortunately, prove adaptable to English table manners.

In the 1920s, Leach and Hamada had to discover many of their techniques (and much of their physics and chemistry) for themselves. For example, they re-discovered, by sheer trial and error, the technique of how to apply combed decoration onto a biscuited mould. Eventually, their unusual synthesis of East and West was successful (and to a lesser extent predictable) enough for them to introduce aspects of it to Japan.

But, whatever the myth may say, the St Ives pottery was not a commercial success in the 1920s. Losses in the kiln were often up to 20 per cent, and it was rare for more than 10 per cent of all pots to be up to Bond Street standards. By the late 1920s, the pottery was showing a dismal profit of about £30 per annum. It was Leach's associates in Japan who helped to save the 'studio' by arranging selling exhibitions and sending back all the proceeds. While William Staite Murray, the head of pottery at the Royal College of Art, was marketing *his* pots in Bond Street (under the label of 'abstract art' and with titles to match) for anything up to £100 a time, you could buy a complete tiled fireplace by Leach for £27 10 shillings. And yet, Leach was convinced that 'the solution to the underlying problems of craftsmanship, or at any rate those which presented themselves most forcibly, were not likely to be discovered in the expensive precincts of Bond Street' (quoted in Barley Roscoe, 'Only connect' in *Crafts*, Sept–Oct. 1982, p. 39).

It was only in the 1950s that Leach's work came to be sold, and to some extent to be produced, as the work of a major artist. Throughout the inter-war period, the position of Leach's work in the market remained ambiguous. He rejected 'Bond Street', but always stressed that St Ives was based as 'the economics of the studio and not of the workshop'.

A combination of factors rescued the St Ives pottery: the generosity of Leonard and Dorothy Elmhurst, which enabled Leach to open a small pottery near Dartington Hall in 1933 and, subsequently, to research and write *A Potter's Book*, which earned steady royalties, and the introduction of a mechanical pugwheel and an oil-fired kiln for the production of a range of cheap and functional standardware (decorated plates, cups and saucers and so on) under the SI seal – which sold for shillings rather than pounds, and which produced uniformly reliable results. At first, Bernard Leach was not happy with this development, introduced by his son David: but when he saw

Part of a tea-set by Bernard Leach (1950s). Porcelain with celadon glaze.

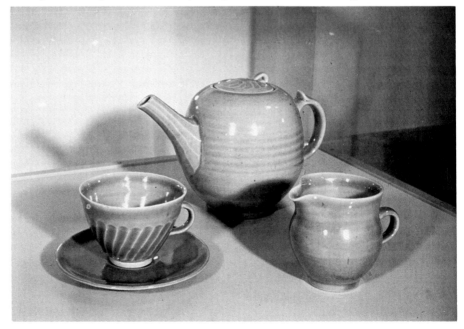

the quality of the results (and realised that the standardware could, in time, make the finer pieces possible), he adjusted to it. Parts of the first chapter of *A Potter's Book* (but only parts) seem to have been written in this spirit of rapprochement.

After the war, when there was a sudden demand for non-white pottery, the SI standardware began to sell very well indeed, as (at a different level of the market) did the more personal products of the St Ives pottery – notably the stoneware jugs, bottles and jars for which Leach himself became famous (and which today command fabulous prices at auction). Where these were concerned, throughout the 1950s, Leach continued the Japanese practice of developing a decorative motif on different shapes or bodies over an extended period of time: examples range from bird's nests, leaping fish, or other forms from the natural world, to apparently abstract brush drawings (colour pl. 8).

The legacy which Bernard Leach left to the 1960s and 1970s generation of potters was an ambiguous one. As we have seen, he did much to re-vitalise the concept of the 'artist-craftsman' (and to see it enshrined in the work of the Crafts Centre and the Crafts Council) and to publicise 'the studio' as a unit for producing craft-work. And, ironically for someone who professed to believe in 'the unknown craftsman', he made the name 'Leach' and the impressed seal 'BL' synonymous – in the public eye – with studio pottery. But, as the art college took over from the bohemian environment of the artist as *the* place from which 'artist–craftspeople' characteristically emerged, and as the 'Leach style' degenerated into browne muggs, there was a strong reaction among craftspeople against both his work and his philosophical defence of it. The catalogue of the ICA exhibition *Fast Forward: New Directions in British Ceramics* (1985) rightly concluded:

Leach's influence and achievements cannot be underestimated, but his very success has created tensions for subsequent generations. Distortions have arisen in the urgency of some potters' hostility towards the Leach phenomenon which are as debilitating to English pottery as those created by people trying to imitate Leach.

Of Bernard Leach's first British students, Michael Cardew produced traditional English slipware at the Winchcombe Pottery in the inter-war years, before spending long periods between 1942 and 1965 in the Gold Coast, West Africa, and in Nigeria, teaching pottery and producing African-inspired pieces including coiled pots (colour pl. 9). Katherine Pleydell-Bouverie concentrated on producing experimental glaze-effects on stoneware pottery, with the aid of her gardener, a small army of woodmen, and a wood-fired kiln, at her family home in Coleshill, Berkshire. And Richard Batterham, who worked in the Leach pottery for two years in the mid 1950s, continues to produce domestic stoneware (bottles, dishes and boxes) which represents a genuine development of the Leach tradition: 'pots', as he puts it, 'to enrich rather than to adorn life'.

But most of the 'Craftsman's Art' people have defined themselves in opposition to all aspects of the St Ives phenomenon (except, of course, the new status accorded to 'the artist–craftsman'). The Leach pottery was rural, they are urban; Leach dug his own clay, they prefer theirs to arrive on the doorstep in polythene bags; Leach derived his imagery from Japanese and

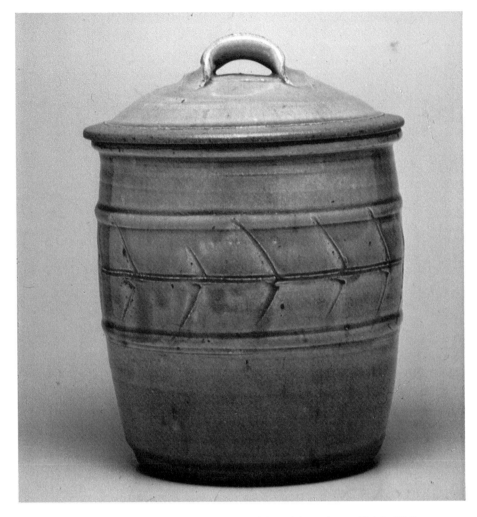

Jar with cover by Richard Batterham (1978). Ash and iron glazes. Height 22.2 cm.

Korean ceramics, they seem to prefer American and European abstract painting; Leach attempted to regenerate 'the English tradition', they emphatically reject what they style 'traditionalism'; Leach cut loose from 'Bond Street' (at least in the inter-war period), they aren't so squeamish; most of all, Leach claimed that there was no beauty without usefulness (even if it meant re-defining what 'usefulness' was), they are concerned, in the words of the ceramicist Alison Britton, 'with the outer limits of function'.

This strong reaction, which has happened since the 1960s, has inevitably led to a re-interpretation of the long-term significance of Bernard Leach (although, as Barley Roscoe has pointed out, 'the strength of the reaction is equal to and therefore indicative of the force of the Leach tradition itself'). The potter John Maltby, writing at a time (1986) when that tradition has too often become 'anachronistic, debilitated . . . tired and trivial', believes that

Leach *was* a bad craftsman when measured by any pre-industrial standard. His kiln was an extremely unsophisticated instrument compared to its industrial counterpart; his preferred wheel was a kick-wheel, although powered wheels were reliable. His skills were inevitably under-developed and certainly inexact – yet he made the finest and liveliest pots of this century.

('The Leach tradition', in *Crafts*, May–June 1985, p. 52)

William Newland, a successful potter and teacher whose work represented a rare alternative to the St Ives tradition in the 1950s and 1960s, agrees that Leach was the key potter in Britain up to the era of 'The Craftsman's Art', but adds:

I think he suffered from a crisis of identity. Remember he knew nothing of English pottery when he returned from Japan in 1920. He only knew Korean and Japanese ware and the unsophisticated peasant country pot . . . Leach reverted in his middle period to Korean brush-work, Cardew to African ware. Both, I think, suffered indecision about roots. . . . He and Cardew closed their eyes to contemporary life and art. . . . Ironically I believe both Leach and Cardew would have been masters of slipware had they opened themselves to new ideas and been influenced by the art of the times.

('The modern potter's art', in *Fast Forward* catalogue, ICA, 1985, p. 42)

It seems to be generally agreed, among practising potters and ceramicists of all persuasions, that Bernard Leach *was* responsible for one important insight which, by implication, was to change the English 'artist-potter's' entire approach to his or her work: 'a conception of the pot as a whole' – including the relationship between clay body and glaze, between what the card-carrying modernists called 'form and function'. This was, of course, the traditional way of assessing finished pots in Japan. The insight has been challenged by the 'Craftsman's Art' generation (some of whom specialise in a disjunction between 'form and function'), but it was a crucial one – so crucial that for nearly half a century after Bernard Leach first articulated it, it went without saying, and it is still the basis for the teaching of ceramics at many art schools.

The craftsman's artist

In the tenth anniversary issue of *Crafts* magazine, published by the Crafts Council in April 1983, several well-known artist–craftspeople (as they had come to be called) were asked 'which books have influenced your thinking and work during the last ten years?' Amongst the many replies, the writings of John Ruskin, William Morris, C.R. Ashbee, George Sturt, Bernard Leach and David Pye were not mentioned once. Instead, the furniture designer and maker Fred Baier (whose reply was the first to be quoted) wrote:

I'm not a great reader of books, especially not ones without pictures . . . As far as books and work, the first one that springs to mind is Groucho Marx's *Letters* . . . At college we were spoon-fed Nikolaus Pevsner and Herbert Read but they never really got to me. One that did was *The Principles of Art* by R.G. Collingwood. I remember enjoying the Collingwood.

For the generation which had been at art college, or had just left art college, when the 'Objects USA' exhibition was touring Britain, and when the 'Craftsman's Art' show opened at the Victoria and Albert Museum (both in 1973), the 'brown and grey' aesthetic of the latter-day inheritors of the Arts and Crafts tradition was of little interest – except, perhaps, as the subject of the occasional ironic reference; and that tradition's emphasis on skill – as a statement about the 'de-skilling' tendency which seemed to be turning the industrial worker into 'a mere cog in a machine' in society at large – was there to be rejected, or at least pushed to one side, as an unnecessary obstacle to aesthetic experiment. The crafts weren't a *solace* any more – they simply provided a 'language' (to use the then fashionable terminology of structuralism) through which young artists could express themselves. Bernard Leach may have turned the 'artist–craftsman' into a heroic figure, but his emphasis on the *morality* of that project had still left the 'artist–craftsman' as a second-class citizen, where the fine arts were concerned. The 'Craftsman's Art' people, who were the products of craft and applied art departments in urban art colleges of the late 1960s and early 1970s, and who had no wish to decamp to Cornwall after they left – wanted to be taken seriously as artists as well as craftspeople.

The 'action-crafts' of 1950s America (which had abandoned the traditional values of good practice, to emphasise craft as abstract art) and the 'funk-crafts' of 1960s west coast America (which had been allied to the pop art movement, with a shared interest in the imagery of mass culture) had introduced the concept of an avant garde into the crafts for the first time, and, as a result, had decisively blurred the boundaries between the 'fine artist' and 'the craftsman'. The artists (such as Peter Voulkos and Robert Arneson who moved into the craft world in the 1950s and 1960s) seemed to be free from (or ignorant of) the holy writ which said 'there is no beauty without utility'. The west coast craftspeople who moved into the art world at the same time, with their ceramic Mickey Mouses and their funky versions of everyday objects, were probably aware of William Morris and the Arts and Crafts (or rather, of a hippie version which made the bizarre connections between Morris and Zen Buddhism), but they weren't going to allow that to restrict the aesthetic possibilities which were open to them. And in any case it wasn't their tradition. The commonsense folk definitions of 'craft' (as virtuoso skill) and 'art' (as self-expression) were beginning to distract from the appreciation of modern work – such as the sculptural furniture of Wendell Castle. The 'Objects USA' which resulted from this radical re-definition were dismissed by Michael Cardew as 'Rubbish USA'.

Illustrations of this work circulated in Britain at a time when developments in the fine art world – notably conceptualism and minimalism – had created a new space in the galleries for the artist-craftsman to inhabit (as Misha Black's lecture 'Craft: Art or Design?' had suggested). The consequence was, in the words of one critic, 'a paradoxical renaissance':

The 1970s saw the upthrust of a second Art and Crafts movement, which was very different from its predecessor. There were a number of reasons for this revival. One was the fact that pop art's self-identification with mass-consumerism began to seem unattractive, whether or not it was tinged with irony, in a world where the environment was increasingly at risk from industrial processes. At the same time, there began to appear a hunger for physical virtuosity in the handling of materials, something which many artists were no longer happy to provide. The result was a renewed fascination with the figure of the artist-craftsman, who replaced the Pop painter or sculptor as a fashionable culture-hero.

(Edward Lucie-Smith, *The Story of Crafts*, p. 274)

In Britain, it wasn't so much a question of fine artists choosing to express themselves through a range of new media – like Picasso making his paintings on ceramic bodies – it was more a question of craftspeople turning their objects into critical and expressive statements, with a new emphasis on sculptural form and on decoration which didn't 'fit the form'. And a question it undoubtedly was. Fred Baier's choice of Collingwood's *Principles of Art* (1938) as an influential text was very significant, since it was Collingwood who in 1938 had tried to define the boundaries between 'what I shall call craft' and 'art proper' in a philosophically defensible way – from the point of view of the artist. For Collingwood, writing in the wake of T.S. Eliot's *The Waste Land*, there was a prevailing misconception which encouraged 'people who write about art today to think that it is some kind of craft: this is the main error against which modern aesthetic theory must fight'. This misconception he labelled 'the technical theory of art' – a theory which implied that art activity had something to do with 'the power to produce a preconceived result by means of consciously controlled action', and it only succeeded in confusing 'what I shall call craft' with 'art proper': 'a technician is made, but an artist is born'. If the 'theory of art' continued to lay so much stress on *mere* craft technique, Collingwood concluded, 'it is no more to be

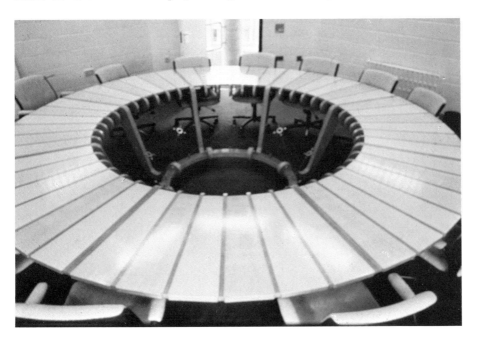

Conference table by Fred Baier (1979). Birch and spruce plywood veneered with natural sycamore; legs and base-ring in scarlet. Diameter 3.75 m, height 72 cm.

called art criticism, or aesthetic theory, than the annual strictures in *The Tailor and Cutter* on the ways in which Academy portrait painters represent coats and trousers'. The words 'artist' and 'artisan' may have had the same linguistic origins, but that is where all similarity ended.

So it is not surprising that an artist–craftsman who emerged in the 1970s, such as Fred Baier, admitted to 'enjoying the Collingwood' in preference to Pevsner's *Pioneers of the Modern Movement* and Read's *Art and Industry* (both of which were, at one level, moral tracts about design). Baier's own statements about his furniture (pieces such as the extraordinary Tartan Chair and the Whatnot in wood) shared many of the same or similar assumptions about 'the technical theory of art':

For me it is not the making that is the driving force. The only reason I make is because I can't afford to pay anyone who is sufficiently good to do it without worrying myself to death. Colour is one of my prime concerns . . .

Where the young artists of the 'Craftman's Art' generation were concerned, the 'rules' which had been taught in craft or design faculties of post-Coldstream art colleges in the late 1960s and early 1970s – that 'less was more', that 'the pattern should fit the form', and above all (following Leach and Cardew) that 'there was no beauty without utility' – were *all* open to question. And the crafts rapidly seemed to be moving through the personal philosophy of Bernard Leach, via modernism, to post-modernism in the space of one decade. The ceramacist Jacqui Poncelet, for example, started her career by making bone china pots in moulds, and, after visiting New York, gradually developed towards the production of angular ceramic sculptures which resembled brightly coloured crustacea or serpents (colour pl. 11): at first, her work functioned as a 'comment' on the craft world which surrounded her (complete with references to Brecht and Robbe-Grillet), but by the mid 1980s it was being exhibited as sculpture on the floors and walls of fine art galleries. At this point, she stopped referring to herself as a 'craftsperson' at all:

the only limitation is your own imagination. People shouldn't be concerned about 'how are they made?' when they see an exhibition of my work. They should be concerned about the *ideas* . . .

Alison Britton – who also approaches her material as something that arrives on the doorstep in a polythene bag, rather than something which should be dug out of mother earth in the West Country – refers to the clay 'as background and as canvas: all I need is something that holds together'. Unlike Jacqui Poncelet, she has continued to produce pieces which are vessels and containers, but has moved on from 'pictorial pottery' to three-dimensional shapes which increasingly resemble multi-plane abstract paintings:

Being a vessel is not very demanding. Once the functional requirements of 'holding' are fulfilled, there is still plenty of room for interpretation and variety of outer form. I and my peers continue to hang around on the fringes of making useable things because it is tantalising to try and take up the slack in so many different ways.

('Sèvres with Krazy Kat', in *Crafts*, March–April 1983, p. 20)

The most successful of the young ceramicists who continued to 'hang around on the fringes of making usable things' has been Elizabeth Fritsch –

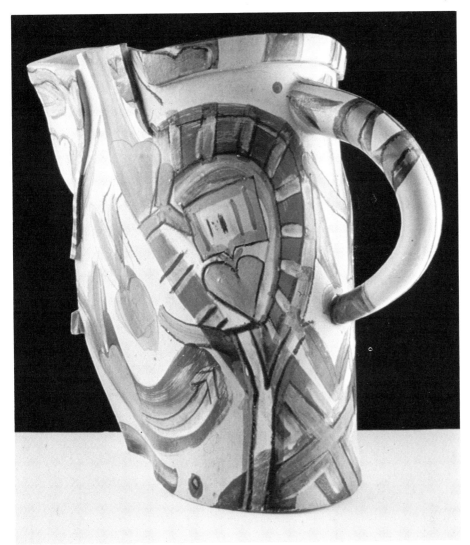

Flared jug by Alison Britton. Pink, white and green. Height 36 cm.

whose austere hand-built pots, with matt finish and coloured fresco effects, seem to owe a great deal to the work of her tutor at the Royal College of Art: the sculptor and studio potter Hans Coper: and his friend and associate the Viennese potter Lucie Rie (who settled in London just before the Second World War; colour pl. 10). If Elizabeth Fritsch makes reference to a craft tradition, it is not to the Anglo-Oriental tradition of Leach and Hamada, but to these two artist–craftspeople from Europe whose work (as one critic has put it) 'had no nostalgic undertones of folk art; the style was that of someone conscious of modern architecture'. But when she is describing her decorative sources, Fritsch is equally likely to talk about alternative systems of thought – such as the labyrinths of Jorge Luis Borges and the complexities of modern music (which she was originally trained to perform, at the Royal Academy of Music, on harp and piano):

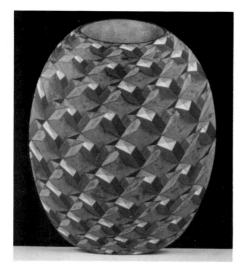

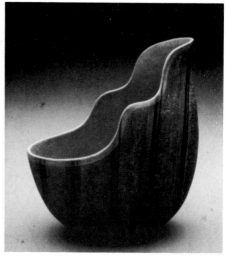

Elizabeth Fritsch, Quantum Pocket (Death and the Compass) *(1984–5)*. *Handbuilt stoneware, painted with slips.*

Elizabeth Fritsch, handbuilt stoneware with painted slip decoration (1973).

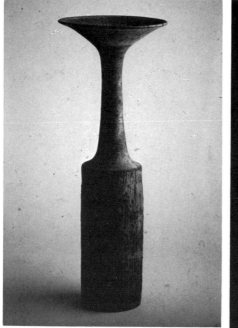

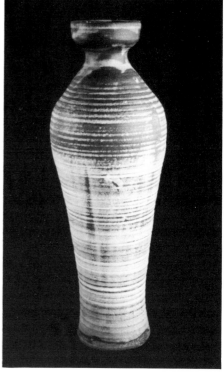

Stoneware bottle by Lucie Rie (1938). Grey and brown. Height 39.6 cm.

Anubis stonewarg jar by William Staite Murray (1938). Buff glaze breaking to red-brown over ribbing. Height 19.25 cm.

Because of Hans Coper's pots (and also because of his friend Lucie Rie's work) I saw the possibilities of combining music with clay, of combining the airborne with the earthbound, of combining the ancient auras with those of the twentieth century.

('Hans Coper', in *Crafts*, Jan.–Feb. 1982, p. 35)

It is significant that the artist who has most influenced her pots (for Hans Coper was not considered an 'artist' by the exhibition-going public until the late 1970s) dates from the Italian Renaissance – a time when the roles of 'artist' and 'craftsman' were still inseparable:

The work of Piero della Francesca is undoubtedly my highest, if unattainable ideal in respect of colour and clarity; air and light; the unity of geometry and precision in painting. There is also in the frescoes the combination of the stoniness of the materials with the airborne softness of the colours which I find very moving. He used colour in a most musical, rhythmic, atmospheric way, above all the celestial blues, the colour of heaven . . . I'd say that he above all artists gives the feeling that Space is like Silence; form like music.

(quoted in Edward Lucie-Smith. *The Story of Craft*, 1981, pp. 279–80)

By the early 1980s, it wasn't unusual to hear (at private views of craft exhibitions, or in intense seminars on the subject 'are you a craftsperson or not?') conversational gambits such as 'I make small sculptural pieces in non-precious metals which subvert the traditional values and meaning of jewellery'. With the almost simultaneous appearance of ceramic sculpture, fine art textiles, also known as soft art or fibre art, re-defined jewellery, art blacksmithing of the 'new iron age' and wooden sculptures bearing the message 'do not sit on this', the critics, the collectors, the grant-giving institutions and a high proportion of the 'journeyman craftsmen' surveyed by *Working in Crafts* were becoming thoroughly confused. Was the work of the craft avant-garde to be interpreted as sculpture? Did it have to be 'useful' to count as craftwork? Could it be both useful and sculptural at the same time? If it was sculpture, could the work hold its own in galleries devoted to fine art? Or did it depend for its meaning on being exhibited within the confines of the craft world? Were the categories 'art' and 'craft' – and their complex histories since Renaissance times – distorting our response to craft exhibitions? It was all very well to 'lay bare the device' (in the Brechtian language of the day), but as a prelude to what . . . ?

The time was ripe for the craft world (insofar as the Crafts Council still represented it) to take stock of itself, with another major exhibition devoted to the craftsman's art. On this occasion, instead of a national call for exhibits to be selected by the Crafts Advisory Committee, the exhibition would be selected by some of the makers themselves. It was called 'The Maker's Eye', and, in the words of the Crafts Council's energetic director throughout 'the paradoxical renaissance', Victor Margrie:

Each of the fourteen selectors was invited to define the idea of craft in terms of his or her personal experience . . . The diversity of their choices is an accurate comment on the position the crafts hold today in the spectrum of the visual arts, embracing not only objects which draw their inspiration from the historical crafts, but those which look also towards fine art and design.

In the event, David Pye selected, among many other pieces, a block smoothing plane, a leather saddle, a child's high chair in wood by Richard La

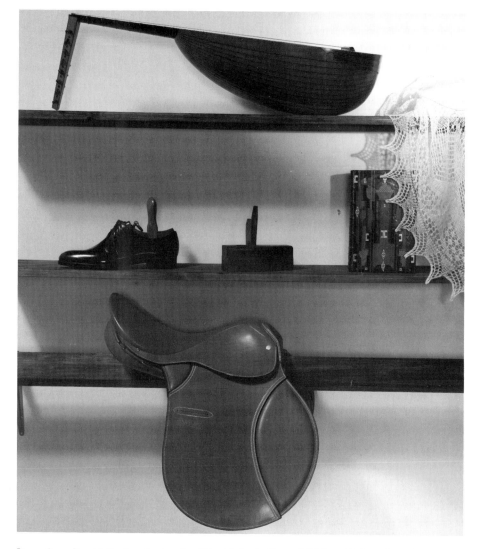

Items from David Pye's selection for The Maker's Eye exhibition (1982). Lute by
Stephen Gottlieb; brogue shoes by John Lobb Ltd; traditional toothing plane
(anonymous); domino set in Indian rosewood box by Desmond Ryan; Shetland lace shawl
by Elizabeth Gray; leather saddle by George Parker & Sons.

Trobe Bateman, a red, orange and pink woven rug by Peter Collingwood, a
pair of Lobb's brogue shoes with trees, a Lucie Rie bowl and a length of
fabric by Marianne Straub. Michael Cardew selected, among many other
pieces, vases and bottles by Katherine Pleydell-Bouverie (most of them
dating from the 1930s), bowls by the teacher of studio potters Norah Braden
(again from the mid 1930s), two decorated dishes by Bernard Leach – one
featuring an oriental landscape, the other a griffin design – and a Pilgrim dish
dating from the very end of Leach's career, a stoneware piece called *Wheel of
Life* and made by William Staite Murray in 1939, and, to bring the story up
to date, some bowls by the contemporary studio potter Richard Batterham.

Alison Britton selected, among many other pieces, an elegant black
bottle/sculpture by Hans Coper (who had also been *her* tutor), an Elizabeth
Fritsch pot with fresco-like spiral grey bands, two vessels by the wheel-potter
Wally Keeler, a 'comma' shaped bowl with abstract decoration by Jacqui
Poncelet – as well as still life paintings by Ben Nicholson and Bernard
Myers.

In other words, the three main traditions of contemporary British
craftwork – the designer–craftsman tradition, the arts and crafts tradition and
the craftsman's art tradition – explicitly presented *as* traditions and selected
by some of their greatest living exponents, remained to a great extent
separate but at the same time uneasily united under the banner of 'the crafts'
(or, less controversially, 'the makers'). So 'The Maker's Eye' didn't exactly
help the critics, the collectors, the quangos and the 'journeymen–craftsmen';
it was too relativistic in conception for that. The state-of-the-craft was not
ready for a committee to legislate aesthetic standards from above. But it did
provide a showcase for the best or most characteristic of contemporary
craftsmanship, from all the main schools of practice (except, of course, the
craft shop, airport lounge and souvenir end of the spectrum). And it enabled
the selectors to state their case in an unusually articulate way. This chapter
has already quoted from the statements written for 'The Maker's Eye' by
David Pye and Michael Cardew. Alison Britton's statement is worth quoting
here, since it succinctly captures the atmosphere surrounding the 'return to
the crafts' (or should that be 'turn to the crafts'?) of the 1970s and 1980s:

My work may in the future be seen to have belonged to a 'group', a hypothetical
group of artist–craftspeople, having certain trains of thought in common, whether or
not these have been articulated or brought to the surface. I would say that this group
is concerned with the outer limits of function; where function, or an idea of a possible
function, is crucial, but is just one ingredient in the final presence of the object, and is
not its only motivation . . . Some people will certainly feel that this represents the last
decadent throes of an artistic crafts movement of dwindling relevance, where over-
self-conscious makers turned in on themselves for want of a real sense of necessity.
But perhaps to others it will be seen as something closely in line with 'modernism' in
the other arts, in painting or literature for example. A 'modern' novel (one following
such writers as Proust and Joyce) is both made of, and about language. Some of the
objects I have chosen are similarly self-referential, that is, they perform a function,
and at the same time are drawing attention to what their own rules are about . . . In
some ways such objects stand aback and describe, or represent, themselves as well as
being. In the analogy with the novel, 'function' stands for 'story' as the central
content.

(The Maker's Eye catalogue, p. 16)

Whether the era of 'The Craftsman's Art' is the equivalent of 'modernism'
(leading to the reaction of 'post-modernism') in the fine arts, or whether it is,
in the end, simply a 'culture of doodles' which by definition can lead nowhere
(as more than one critic has suggested) is still a matter for debate. Looking
back on the 1970s and early 1980s, David Pye has said:

I think the fact that what they call 'the crafts' are edging rapidly in the direction of
abstract art, means that the process of producing them is getting much more difficult,
and I think you can often – regrettably often – see that. There's a great deal of stuff

turned out which is terribly meretricious: it looks thin, it is thin. The famous saying of W.R. Lethaby is very applicable to it: 'no art that is one man deep is very much good'. And a lot of it is, very obviously, only one man deep. It's highly *original* – but originality and nothing else is terribly easy to achieve.
('Workmanship – a word to start an argument', in RCA *Dialogue on Craft* 3, 1983)

Meanwhile, some of the finest practitioners from two out of the three main craft traditions have moved, with the development of their work, into the more established worlds of art and design. Some have been accepted on their own terms by the fine art world. Others are now producing prototypes for batch production. Others still – notably furniture-makers and craftspeople who work with glass – are beginning to form design teams with architectural practices. In these ways, 'the crafts' still seem to be playing their historical role as a means by which research (of a hit-and-miss kind) can be carried out, for others to develop. Only the studio potters have tended to stay where they are – but then, they have to as an article of faith.

The last fifteen years have been a confusing period in the history of the crafts, at many levels. There has been an atmosphere of 'work-in-progress' about them. And this has been reflected in the Polonius-like array of terms which have been chosen to describe the practitioners who have made their names since the early 1970s. As long ago as 1965, the World Crafts Council suggested a range of categories within the overall concept of 'the craftsman':

Artisan–craftsman – one who executes traditional designs or the designs of others;
Artist–craftsman or designer–craftsman – one who is capable of originating his own designs and who exhibits and sells them under his own name;
Designer in the craft field – one who knows the techniques in given media but prefers to design work for others rather than execute it himself.
(quoted in Ken Baynes, 'Designing by making', in *Design*, July 1965, p. 28)

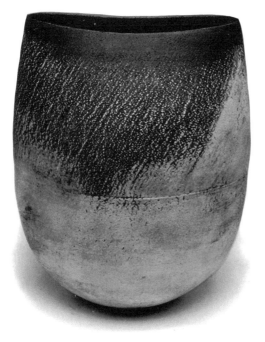

Oval vase by Hans Coper, (1972). Oxidised stoneware with iron and cobalt oxides under a matt white glaze with textured surface. Height 22 cm.

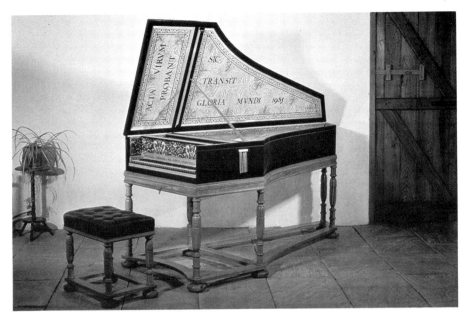

Harpsichord designed and made by M. Johnson (1985), based on Johannes Rucker's 1640 Antwerp model. Block-printed design on underside of lid.

Since then, the prefixes artist- and designer- have at one time or another been added to just about every activity in which craftsmen engage. (On the west coast of America there are even artist–plumbers.) In Britain, the basic categories appear to have been reduced to 'artist–craftsman', 'designer–craftsman' and 'journeyman–craftsman' (although David Pye still prefers the word 'workmanship' to 'craftsmanship'; many people resent the connotations of 'journeyman'; and there are fierce disputes about the relative merits of 'craftsman' and 'craftsperson' – for obvious reasons). Recently, there has been a revival of the nineteenth-century categories 'decorative artist' and 'applied artist', as a way of side-stepping the problem (by entirely missing the point). It is ironic, and rather sad, that today's craft world is in danger of ending up where it started – with the Victorian concept of the 'fine art workman'. For the era of 'The Craftsman's Art' has produced some of the most exciting work – and, as a result, some of the most stimulating debates – since the time when William Morris re-invented the 'artist–craftsman' as a figure on the landscape of art and design. And it has done so, without bringing Merrie England into the picture at all – except as the target for esoteric jokes. Despite all the confusions, many of which have taken until the late 1980s to be productive, most craftspeople today would surely agree with Tom Stoppard's Henry Carr, when he dared to take issue with Tristan Tzara in the play *Travesties*, over the vexed question 'is it Art if I say its Art . . . ?':

Don't you see you are simply asking me to accept that the word Art means whatever you wish it to mean; but I do not accept it . . .

(For helpful discussions during various stages in the preparation of this essay, thanks to Marigold Coleman (Introduction), James Noel White (the 'designer-craftsman' section), Oliver Watson and Barley Roscoe (the 'arts and craftsman' section), Martina Margetts (the 'craftsman's artist' section) and to my wife, Helen, throughout.)

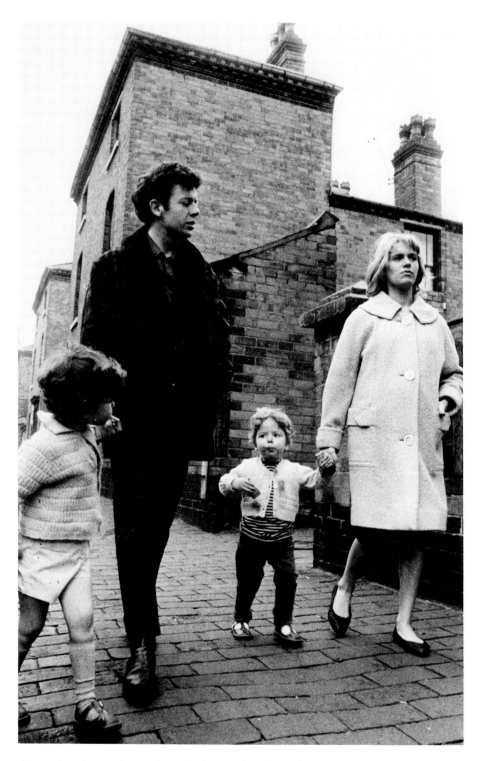

A scene from Cathy Come Home *by Jeremy Sandford; The Wednesday Play for 16 November, 1966.*

7 Literature and Drama

GILBERT PHELPS

Introduction

The political and social factors

This chapter is concerned with the latest period of a literature which for 500 years has been the richest in the world, virtually without a break. In all the previous volumes of this *Guide*, moreover, (with the exception of the first, which deals with a time when literature in English hardly existed) it is the literature which holds pride of place, or at least shares an equal eminence with one of the other arts. This undoubtedly applies to the earlier decades of our own century, when writers whom we think of as near-contemporaries were producing, out of a society with many of the characteristics of our own, and in full awareness of those elements in twentieth-century civilisation that carried the threat of breakdown and decay, some of the greatest works in our literature. It cannot be said with the same degree of conviction of the literature of the post-war period, whose overall achievement for the first time falls short of that in music, sculpture, painting and the crafts.

There have been no writers, that is, who can unhesitatingly be placed on the same high level as W.B. Yeats or T.S. Eliot among the poets, or Henry James, Joseph Conrad, E.M. Forster, Wyndham Lewis, Virginia Woolf, D.H. Lawrence and James Joyce among the novelists – or if it comes to that beside those like Ford Madox Ford, Arnold Bennett, H.G. Wells and others, who can be placed in the 'second rank' only by comparison with this great galaxy.

The gradual decline in the general level of literary attainment, signs of which were apparent in the late 1930s, in spite of the advent of important new writers, suggests – if one is to avoid the alarmist view that the great tradition of English literature is itself undergoing a process of attrition – that one of the peaks has been succeeded, as has often happened before, by a trough, though one must remember that Eliot, one of the 'great galaxy', wrote his most profound poem, *Four Quartets*, after the thirties, during the war.

Certainly there has been no slackening in the literary output or in new writers – far too many, in a chapter of this length, to do more than pick out a few who seem most aptly to illustrate the main tendencies and themes of the period. Many of these writers (including some who have had to be omitted solely for reasons of space) are interesting, provocative, and highly talented, and a few of them demand consideration of the most serious kind.

In charting the general course of the literary struggle and outlining the main tendencies and themes of the period, one broad generalisation will serve as a starting point: that all post-war English literature has been over-shadowed by a sense of social and cultural disintegration and of the ever-present threat of violence and chaos. In a revised edition of *A Short History of the World* published a month after his death in 1946, H.G. Wells wrote of the

tremendous series of events [which] had forced upon the intelligent observer the realisation that the human story has already come to an end and that *homo sapiens*, as he has been pleased to call himself, is in his present form played out . . .

There were many who shared Wells's pessimism when they contemplated the concentration camps and the holocaust, the effects of saturation bombing – and, above all, the advent of nuclear weapons which seemed indeed to spell the end of the earlier Wellsian faith in human progress to be achieved through science and technology.

It is hardly surprising that all this has entered into post-war English literature, or that many of the works dealing with it take the form of admonitory parables of the future. An obvious early instance was Aldous Huxley's *Ape and Essence* (1949), which envisages the degraded Californian survivors of an atomic holocaust bowing down to Belial – the same god worshipped by the young refugees from some global conflict (perhaps a nuclear war) who revert to savagery in William Golding's *The Lord of the Flies* (1954). Nuclear wars and the aftermath of the Bomb feature, too, in many other works: and there is little doubt that an awareness of the new potentialities for global destruction has been present in the minds of all post-war writers almost everywhere.

There have been other preoccupations of a specifically English nature. Of the moods generated by the Second World War, one was of disillusionment with the official patriotic and heroic myth, expressed over the years in a number of works from Evelyn Waugh's trilogy *Men at Arms* (1952), *Officers and Gentleman* (1955), and *Unconditional Surrender* (1961) onwards. This anti-heroic mood was, of course, closely related to the withering away of Britain's imperial power (highlighted by the Suez fiasco of 1956), with the final stages of the British Raj providing the richest imaginative seam, notably in Paul Scott's *Raj Quartet* (1966–75) and its moving coda *Staying On* (1977).

There were other political disillusionments. The left-wing idealism that had inspired many of the older writers during the 1930s had for the most part dissipated. A few, like Edward Upward, continued to explore their socialist preoccupations, though usually in modified forms. Rex Warner, whose compelling anti-capitalist allegory *The Wild Goose Chase* (1937) was more or less prescribed reading among the ardent young socialists of the

1930s, published *Men of Stones*, his novel about the concentration camps and the Civil War in Greece in 1949, but thereafter, in novels such as *The Young Caesar* (1958), *Imperial Caesar* (1960) and *Pericles the Athenian* (1963) – distinguished by their imaginative and historical insight as well as by their classical scholarship and clarity of style – he turned to the Ancient World for his subject-matter. But as Stephen Spender has commented:

With a few exceptions the writers associated with the thirties tried after 1939 to break with their political connections.

This was particularly true, Spender suggests, of W.H. Auden, 'who edited out of his work what might be termed the Thirties Connection'. After his conversion to Christianity in 1940 the left-wing elements virtually disappeared from his poetry, though Spender is right in arguing that for Auden 'Marxist materialism was the most transitory of his ideological ports of call', and that his Marxism 'dissolves into the theological, psycho-analytical and mythical idea systems of his whole work'.

It was, of course, from George Orwell, that highly individualistic and independent radical (who had clearly proclaimed his socialist beliefs in *The Road to Wigan Pier* (1937) and joined the Republican army in Spain during the Civil War, but who never joined a political party in Britain and was scathing in his criticisms of the left-wing intelligentsia including Auden), that the most sustained onslaught on Stalinist communism came, beginning in *Homage to Catalonia* (1938) and culminating in *Animal Farm* (1945), while his horrific *Nineteen Eighty-four* (1949) was directed against all kinds of dictatorship and 'thought control'.

Other writers who had not been directly involved in left-wing political activity nevertheless found that the break with the ethos of the 1930s was attended not only by a change of direction but also by a certain loss of power. Christopher Isherwood (it seems to me) is a case in point. Although in his early autobiography *Lions and Shadows* (1938) he described how his rebellion against his middle-class background and his sense of guilt at having 'missed' the Great War combined to sharpen his criticism of the existing class structure, and although he collaborated with Auden in the writing of *The Dog Beneath the Skin, or Where is Francis?* (1935) – and two other expressionist plays – which contains unequivocal left-wing pronouncements and slogans, he was never officially 'committed' as were Auden, Spender, Cecil Day Lewis and other writers belonging to the Popular Front against Fascism. It was no doubt this degree of detachment that helped Isherwood survey the pre-war Berlin scene with such compassionate objectivity in *Mr Norris Changes Trains* (1935) and *Goodbye to Berlin* (1939). At the same time these novels grew out of the tense and troubled atmosphere and concerns of the times. Isherwood's later preoccupations (yoga among them) do not carry the same creative charge, and novels like *The World in the Evening* (1954) – his first after settling in America – are not of the same quality as his novels of the 1930s.

The political temper of the first post-war generation was on the whole much more low key and sceptical (not to say cynical) than that of their predecessors in the thirties. Although many writers welcomed the advent of the Labour governments, their initial enthusiasm soon tended to wane.

Disenchantment with existing political, social and economic systems has, in consequence, been another of the motifs of post-war literature. There have, for example, been what may be called 'condition of England' novels, especially during the 'affluent sixties', with their exposure of the greed and dubious commercial practices of the times and their implication that the so-called 'social revolution' had left the centres of political or at any rate financial power untouched – well illustrated by Margaret Drabble's *The Ice Age* (1977). There has also been the growth of Marcusian, Trotskyist, Anarchist and other extreme radical views (and various combinations of them), reflected later on in the period by a new generation of political dramatists who were to rival any of their predecessors of the 1930s in the passion of their convictions. The greater social mobility and the partial breakdown of the old class structures (brought about in part by the policies of the Labour government, but also by changed economic circumstances) has provided other prominent themes, as in one of the most pungent of the earlier novels of alienation, Nigel Dennis's satirical *Cards of Identity* (1955).

At the same time there was a considerable expansion of the literature of working- or lower-middle-class life, for example in plays as diverse in background, content and approach as John Osborne's *Look Back in Anger* (1956), Arnold Wesker's *The Kitchen* (produced privately 1959; publicly 1961), Shelagh Delaney's *A Taste of Honey* (1958), John Arden's *Live Like Pigs* (1958) and Harold Pinter's *The Caretaker* (1959). In fiction, it is noticeable that the working-class heroes or anti-heroes are often either trying to climb out of their class, like Joe Lampton in John Braine's *Room at the Top* (1957); or even Alan Sillitoe's Arthur Seaton in *Saturday Night and Sunday Morning* (1958), convincingly (if not likeably) working-class, but eventually beginning to move up the social scale through marriage to a 'superior' girl and his promotion to charge-hand; or they are untypical of it, as in Stan Barstow's *Ask Me Tomorrow* (1962), whose hero aspires to be a writer – though Barstow's North Country detail and atmosphere are always convincing and authentic.

These features help to explain why it is rare to find the inner life of a working-class character within a working-class environment explored in depth. There are exceptions, as when David Storey enters fully and sympathetically into the feelings and aspirations of the hero's working-class parents in the earlier part of *Saville* (1979). But generally speaking there is little to compare with the psychological subtlety and insight of D.H. Lawrence's pre-war stories and plays about miners and their families.

More common has been the setting of professional life, notably in C.P. Snow's depiction of the clash between private and public consciences among the upper echelons of the Civil Service in his *Strangers and Brothers* sequence (1940–70), which together with Anthony Powell's *A Dance to the Music of Time* (1951–75) constitutes the outstanding post-war English examples of the long fictional sequence. University life, too, has been a characteristic setting, sometimes with predominantly satirical purpose, as in Kingsley Amis's pioneer *Lucky Jim* (1954) and David Lodge's *Small World* (sub-titled *An Academic Romance*) (1984). In other cases, as in Snow's *The Masters* (1951) and Malcolm Bradbury's *The History Man* (1975), and in a number of post-war plays, notably Tom Stoppard's zany and anarchic

Jumpers (1972), the university has been used as a microcosm of the power struggles as well as of other social and political issues in the larger world outside.

The changed attitudes towards the home and the family, accentuated by the new morality of the 'swinging sixties' and the 'permissive society' have inevitably affected the literature of the period. Conflict or a painful unease between parents and children has been one of the recurrent themes in the work of David Storey, as in his play *In Celebration* (1969) as well as in some of his fiction. Paradoxically, though, in view of the fact that her fiction is set in the enclosed world of the Edwardian country house (or its equivalent), it was Ivy Compton-Burnett who, continuing the series of novels which had begun with *Pastors and Masters* in 1925, with characteristic sardonic wit probed most deeply into the dark places of family life in novels like *Manservant and Maidservant* (1947), *Mother and Son* (1955), and *A God and His Gifts* (1963)

The cultural reaction

A corollary to the reaction against the mores of pre-war society was a rejection of most of its cultural assumptions and traditions. The main force of the protest, social as well as cultural, of the so-called Angry Young Men of the 1950s, was directed against those who, it seemed to them, constituted a still powerful though outdated literary Establishment – what Kenneth Allsop in *The Angry Decade: A Survey of the Cultural Revolt of the Fifties* (1958) called 'the old literati, the candelabra-and-wine *rentier* writers'. Amis's *Lucky Jim* – with its exposure of a certain type of academic high-browism and the cultural and social pretensions that accompany it – remains the most vigorous and effective as well as the funniest of the protests (though the comedy does not equal that of P.G. Wodehouse in ease and inventiveness).

But the Angry Young Men threw out too many babies with the bath-water. The impatience which some of them felt for the social and psychological refinements of the pre-war 'writers of sensibility' is sometimes understandable – though in fact the best of these produced some of their finest and most humane work in the first decade after the war, as with Elizabeth Bowen (a representative of the strong strain of Anglo-Irish fiction) in *The Heat of the Day* (1949) and *A World of Love* (1955); Rosamond Lehmann in *The Echoing Grove* (1953); and L.P. Hartley in *The Go-Between* (1957).

There was also, however, Amis's famous dismissal, in his review of Colin Wilson's *The Outsider* (1956) – another representative document of the period, of Kierkegaard, Nietzsche, Dostoevsky and Blake, among others, as 'those characters you thought were discredited, or had never read, or (if you were like me) had never heard of'. Moreover, in their concern not to be associated in any way with the old, genteel, concepts of 'fine writing', many of the 'Angry Young Men' adopted a relaxed style of writing, while the loose, picaresque structure favoured by the novelists was symptomatic of an emphatic rejection both of the old Jamesian concept of form and of pre-war experimentalism. Many of the poets belonging to The Movement also cultivated a free and easy colloquial style, a good example of which was John Wain's collection *A Word Carved on a Sill* (1956). Coupled with these features, the anti-foreignness illustrated by Amis's review of Wilson's *The*

Outsider was a prominent feature of the Angry Young Men phenomenon. Attachment to a wider international tradition was, in their eyes, a typical posture of the Establishment they were seeking to discredit. There is no doubt that at the time these writers represented a considerable narrowing of perspectives and a retreat into a kind of defiant 'Little England' provincialism.

The provinces and literature

Provincialism, though, has had its positive as well as its negative aspects, and regional attachments and traditions have often proved vital and creative. The landscapes, history and idiom of Northumbria, for example, permeate Basil Bunting's *Briggflatts* (1966), perhaps the finest long poem of the period and one indication of a partial revival in the 1960s of the pre-war poetic tradition of Eliot and Pound, to which he had been consistently faithful.

As far as poetry is concerned, however, the most important developments outside the London-centred groupings belong to the separate national entities within the United Kingdom. It was in 1952 that David Jones published his long, erudite, baffling but intermittently powerful poem, *The Anathemata,* which in the opinion of T.S. Eliot had affinities with the work of James Joyce, the later Ezra Pound, and with his own poetry. The 1950s also saw the publication of Dylan Thomas's *In Country Sleep* (1953), and *Collected Poems 1934–1952* (1952). Although repudiation of his kind of romanticism and impassioned poetic utterance was part of the revolt of The Movement poets, as Donald Davie pointed out it was also 'an angry reaction from the tawdry amoralism of a London Bohemia which had destroyed [him]'. Whatever the evident faults of imprecision, inflation and immaturity in Dylan Thomas's work there is little in post-war English poetry to surpass the incantatory passion and excitement of his handful of achieved poems, which include 'Fern Hill', 'The force that through the green fuse drives the flower', and the fine 'Author's Prologue' to the *Collected Poems* of 1952, all of them deriving their force from a Welsh bardic heritage little understood in England. R.S. Thomas's poetry too, is rooted not only in his experience of Welsh landscape and people, but also in Welsh religious and literary traditions.

It was also in the 1950s that the work of Hugh MacDiarmid, stretching back to the 1920s, began to be more generally known, though it was not until the publication of his *Collected Poems* (1962) that its scope and variety were fully appreciated (the *Complete Poems* appeared in 1978). MacDiarmid's aim was to revive a Scottish tradition that had been largely in abeyance since Burns – though in a thoroughly flexible and modern form. Though quite unlike Eliot, he too was keenly aware of 'the mind of Europe' and his verse absorbs a wide and cosmopolitan range of allusion and reference. Another feature of post-war Scottish poetry has been the pull exercised by the northernmost fringes of the country, partly because of their very remoteness from the cultural uncertainties of metropolitan-centred experience, partly because they offer a relatively unspoiled environment, and partly because they still retain some living links with the traditions of the past. His childhood in the Orkneys lay, for instance, behind much of the best poetry of

Edwin Muir, again little known to a wider audience until the 1950s, and recently the reputation of another younger Orcadian, George Mackay Brown has been steadily growing.

But perhaps the most striking manifestation of the continuing vitality of an independent poetic tradition has been in Ireland, both south and north, and among both Catholics and Protestants. What Yeats called 'the matter of Ireland' has provided a strong impetus and a focus. Thus in Seamus Heaney's poetry – for example in *Death of a Naturalist* (1966), *North* (1975) and *Bog Poems* (1975) – Ireland's history and prehistory, the politics of the present, childhood memories, the landscapes, the land and those who work on it, are closely integrated into a personal vision held together by a web of compelling metaphor and language. Heaney's example illustrates two important points of contrast. Like Ted Hughes (an acknowledged influence) he is fascinated by animals of all kinds and by what he called in *North* 'the slime kingdoms' of non-human existence – but unlike Hughes, his stress is rather on what man and nature share in common. The picture he presents of man in relation to his environment and his work on the land is not, however, one of alienation as it has tended to be among the more urban-centred English writers. These distinctions apply, too, in varying degrees to other Irish poets: to older ones like Austin Clarke, whose pre-war poetry only began to be properly appreciated in the 1950s: to John Montague, whose poems in *The Rough Field* (1966–9), are, to quote Seamus Heaney, 'redolent . . . of the history of his people, disinherited and dispossessed' and who introduces documentary, historical matter in the margins of many of his poems: and more recently to a vigorous group of Ulster poets like Derek Mahon, Michael Longley, Paul Muldoon and Tom Paulin.

Women writers and the influence of feminism

It would be quite wrong, of course, to treat writing by women, now or in the past, as if it belonged to a separate category, though there may be aspects of it which, in a male orientated system of values, have received insufficient attention. At the same time the marked post-war increase in the number of women writers, in all departments of literature, has been accompanied by an increased awareness of issues, particularly social and political, which have a particular relevance to women – and often, in consequence, by an extension of the human range itself both in subject-matter and point of view. The advent of women's publishing houses (notably The Women's Press and Virago) and of departments of women's studies in some of the universities, has encouraged new creative writing by women, rescued from obscurity many interesting women writers of the past, and evolved new critical approaches which throw fresh – and for men, often unexpected – light on the themes and imagery of the major women writers, from Jane Austen onwards. It was, too, the new critical perspectives thus created that were partly responsible for the rediscovery of the long neglected novels of Jean Rhys and Barbara Pym. Feminist theatrical groups, such as 'Monstrous Regiment', have also acted as a stimulus to many gifted new women playwrights and producers. Since an exploration of the social, psychological and spiritual challenges facing women in a world still dominated by dangerous masculine power-drives is more or less inescapable – many of the best women writers, like Iris Murdoch, Doris Lessing (see below. pp. 230–6) and Muriel Spark, with her consciousness and precision of style, her cool appraisal of human vagaries and self-deceptions, and her delicately restrained handling of the forces of evil and of the supernatural in novels like *Memento Mori* (1959), *The Prime of Miss Jean Brodie* (1961) and *The Girls of Slender Means* (1963), have been affected by the feminist movement, at least in the sense that the issues it raises are part of their consciousness.

The decline of passion and conviction

Generally speaking, though, positive affirmations are rare in post-war English literature. Few writers have been capable of confronting the chaos and nullity at the heart of contemporary civilisation and creating out of it something fundamentally positive and vital, as T.S. Eliot did in *The Waste Land* or *The Four Quartets*. There is at least one outstanding exception in Samuel Beckett, however, who in his novels and plays alike progressively carried nullity to its farthest limits and yet managed to wring out of it statements about the contemporary human condition that, paradoxically, are *not* ultimately defeatist or negative. It is noteworthy that some of the best English novels of the period have come from outside the United Kingdom, precisely because their authors have been caught up, whether they like it or not, in political or social situations that demand a passionate response. The most obvious example perhaps is Nadine Gordimer, who has found that, in novels like *The Conservationist* (1974) and *Burger's Daughter* (1979), she cannot avoid dealing with the situation in South Africa because, she has said, it 'has moulded the lives of the people around me . . . one might say (too often) that politics *is* character in South Africa'. But even in the case of Patrick White, a novelist of profound universal themes, the pressures of the Australian past and of the social ferment of the present provide an additional charge of energy. As for V.S. Naipaul, he has become an integral part of the English (and international) literary scene, but to a large extent it is his earlier experience of the political and social turmoil in Trinidad, combined with his sense of his lost roots in India, that have given force and purpose to his novels, as in *Guerillas* (1975) with its rendering of a universal contemporary rootlessness in which, as one of the leading characters puts it: 'Everybody wants to fight his own little war . . . everybody is a guerilla'.

What is remarkable, moreover, is that many of these novelists, like Chinua Achebe in Nigeria or like the Indians Raja Rao and R.K. Narayan, are using a language which, though their chosen literary medium, is not their mother tongue. Salman Rushdie was born and educated in this country and speaks no Indian language, but his fine novel *Midnight's Children* (1981) is an extraordinary amalgam of Dickensian richness, of the quirky circumlocutions of Laurence Sterne, of grim realism, extravagant farce, fantasy, magic, and symbolism, all attended by an exuberant verbal and stylistic inventiveness in the rendering of the multi-faceted reality of modern India.

The crisis of humanism

The emotionally tentative or negative approaches of much contemporary English literature are clearly related to the erosion of former humanistic moral values, leading frequently to scepticism as to man's right to regard himself as a moral being at all. There has been a loss of faith in the efficacy of literature either as a barrier against adverse social forces, or as a means of influencing the future. The resulting strain accounts in part for the marked preoccupation with the forces of evil, displayed at times almost as independent entities, beyond the reach of human will or choice, as in some of the novels of William Golding and William Trevor, or in the savage comedy of Joe Orton and the plays of Edward Bond, with their horrific intrusions of violence. To some extent, too, it accounts for the revival of the Gothic mode, used often comically or sardonically as a kind of containment of evil and violence, or as a means of safeguarding a precarious moral poise, as often in the novels of Angela Carter, Beryl Bainbridge and Fay Weldon. There are also Gothic elements in the novels of Iris Murdoch, combined (if not always happily) with others drawn from popular romance and melodrama: but in spite of the fact that in some of her existentialist novels, such as *A Severed Head* (1961) the behaviour of the characters conforms rather to an amoral, ritualistic, almost dance-like pattern, there is, of course, no doubting the deep ethical and philosophical concerns underlying her fiction as a whole, especially in such distinguished novels as *Bruno's Dream* (1969) and *The Sea, the Sea* (1978).

Much of the literature of the period also reflects the accelerated post-war decline in religious beliefs, though exceptions have to be made in respect of some of the professed Christian writers. The Catholic faith, for instance, of Graham Greene, Evelyn Waugh, Muriel Spark and Anthony Burgess contributes to their work, in varying degrees, a recognisable extra dimension and an underlying system of values, to some extent proof against the prevailing flux. At the same time one only has to consider the seedy, defeated Roman Catholic characters, tortured by religious doubt, in many of the novels of Graham Greene (whose unusual sense of topicality and atmosphere has remained as acute since the war as before it), for example in *The Comedians* (1966), set in the Haiti of 'Papa Doc' Duvalier and one of his most satisfying novels; or the harsh Jansenist world, obsessed with the ramifications of Original Sin, in such novels of the versatile and prolific Anthony Burgess as *A Clockwork Orange* (1962) and *The Waiting Seed* (1962), to realise that these writers, too, have been affected by the pessimism and scepticism of the age.

The formidable difficulties of making positive Christian affirmations are particularly well illustrated by the poetry of R.S. Thomas, with its austere, starkly honest grapplings with the doubts and problems of his faith (though in its quieter moods of recoil and return it can be reminiscent of George Herbert), and that of Geoffrey Hill, with its packed and impacted expression – though in both cases notably fruitful tensions are generated.

One of the obvious difficulties facing both those who strive after a transcendental dimension and those who seek a firm ethical basis of values has been the presence of a predominantly relativist philosophical background. As far as literature itself is concerned it has been the aspect of 'linguistic determinism' as expounded by various French and American formalists, structuralists and post-structuralists, that has made the most dramatic (though not necessarily the most lasting) impact. The challenge posed by the exponents of the *nouveau roman* who embodied many of the new theories in their work, arguing that 'reality' (even our innermost thoughts and desires) is in effect just another 'text', intrigued a number of English novelists of the 1960s and 70s. The most obvious example is *The French Lieutenant's Woman* (1969) by John Fowles with its frequent 'subverting' of the basic realistic 'text' and its alternative endings. A far more thoroughgoing attempt to approximate to the *nouveau roman* was Christina Brook-Rose's *Thru* (1975), a dazzling linguistic display, soaked in the influences of Roland Barthes and other post-war French linguistic-critical thinkers and novelists. The novels of B.S. Johnson, of Alan Sheridan (influenced in particular by Alain Robbe-Grillet), Alan Burns and Ann Quin afford other instances. In all these cases, talent endows the application of these methods with a genuine vitality – but in others it can result in aridity, trivialisation and the substitution of a programme in place of theme or creative originality. With other novelists it has been not so much a matter of adopting the methods of the *nouveau roman*, as a readiness to experiment or play with some of the ideas it incorporates, as with Anthony Burgess's use in *MF* (1971) of an Algonquin Indian myth cited by the French structuralist anthropologist Claude Lévi-Strauss.

With regard to literary criticism, the analyses conducted by structuralists have often been valuable in countering the simplistic view that thought is one thing and language another; in exposing repetitions, inconsistencies, evasions, contradictions and ideological bias; in correcting the over-emphasis on social, historical and biographical factors; and by directing attention to the relations between the parts of a text and the universal qualities it embodies.

On the other hand these analyses are frequently in essence specialist and technical, demanding the skills of a formal logician or a philosopher of mathematics. Many structuralists, moreover – intent on abstracting 'rules' from literature and universal elements from their studies of narrative theory – have no interest in differences of quality between narratives. This explains why so many of the literary texts they choose for their purpose are of little intrinsic merit from the literary-critical point of view. The danger of such approaches is that response to the richness and variety of literature may be stunted by the imposition of what sometimes comes close to being a new Scholasticism.

An obvious consequence of the irruption of these and subsequent schools of linguistic theory into the English literary scene has been a questioning of the whole English literary-critical tradition of the earlier part of the century, from T.S. Eliot's seminal essay 'Tradition and the individual talent' (1919) onwards. In point of fact much of what is offered by the 'new' criticism was already present within that tradition. No one, for example, could have been more insistent on the necessity of 'impersonality' in literature, or more

dismissive of the 'inner voice' (anticipating Barthes) than Eliot or Wyndham
Lewis. No one could have been more scornful of the kind of romantic
criticism that treats language as a means of giving direct access to the writer's
emotions *outside* the text than I.A. Richards in his *Principles of Literary
Criticism* (1924); while Barthes's (perfectly valid) comments on the plurality
of meaning in literature had in many respects been anticipated more than half
a century before by William Empson's *Seven Types of Ambiguity* (1930 –
never translated into French). Even more serious in its implications is the
devaluation of valuation, including the kind so consistently exemplified by
F.R. Leavis, rigorous and disciplined in its attention to the text while calling
upon the full emotional and imaginative range of the work, and rooted 'in the
creative response of individuals, who collaboratively renew and perpetuate
what they participate in – a cultural community of consciousness'.

   Not surprisingly, the challenge to the principle of evaluation has resulted
in a widespread critical confusion and instability, evident (in works of
criticism and in the review columns of newspapers and magazines alike) in
frequent shifts of opinion, rapid changes of fashion and sudden and
capricious inflations or deflations of reputations.

Escape or imaginative extension?

The critical confusion as to the validity of such terms as 'realism' and 'truth'
in literature, may also help to explain the very marked increase in fantasy
writing of all kinds. There were, of course, a number of pre-war precedents
(particularly in the field of the social and political fable). The outstanding
example, indeed – and one of the most imaginatively powerful and
intellectually challenging fictional work of the whole post-war period – really
belongs to the creative ferment of the 1920s: Wyndham Lewis's trilogy *The
Human Age*, which began with *The Childermass* in 1928, but whose two other
parts, *Monstre Gai* and *Malign Fiesta* did not appear (together with a revised
version of *The Childermass*) until 1955.

   One of the most interesting of the post-war fantasies was Mervyn Peake's
Gormenghast trilogy (*Titus Groan*, 1946; *Gormenghast*, 1950; *Titus Alone*,
1959). Although the setting of his huge rambling castle is largely that of the
traditional fairy tale, its baffling architectural ramifications, its hierarchical,
caste-ridden inhabitants ruled by a complex and antiquated protocol and a
proliferating bureaucracy, and the down-trodden natives beyond its walls,
also make it a sardonic image of a post-war Britain still clinging to dreams of
imperial power and to outworn social conventions and traditions. The overtly
Christian allegories of C.S. Lewis, usually in a somewhat tentative science-
fiction framework, and of Charles Williams, mostly expressed in a crypto-
Gothic mode, enjoyed a considerable vogue in the 1940s and 1950s. It was,
though, *The Lord of the Rings* trilogy (1954–5) by their friend and colleague
J.R.R. Tolkien which achieved a spectacular international success and a
highbrow, cult following – an indication that Tolkien was right in his long-
maintained belief that modern mankind was starving for new myths. But
although a genuine mythopoeic imagination is intermittently at work in the
trilogy, the core of the narratives is hollow, consisting of not much more than

vague assertions of the need to maintain the variety and separateness of living things against the 'darkness' that threatens them, and an ultimately comforting confrontation between the forces of good and evil.

Another form of post-war fantasy, was the 'magic realism' practised for instance (with considerable narrative verve) by Angela Carter in *The Infernal Desire Machines of Dr Hoffmann* (1972) and other novels. In most of these novels it is difficult to find any real objective correlative (to use that now unfashionable phrase) of the kind that inevitably exists in the novels of the German Herman Hesse, (with their roots in Germany's deeply troubled recent history); or in the novels of some of the modern Latin-American novelists for whom a form of magic realism is (as Gabriel García Márquez has pointed out) a natural outgrowth of the political, social, psychological and even climatic and geographical circumstances in which they live and work.

The most popular form of post-war fantasy writing has obviously been science fiction. At its lowest level it is not much more than a re-hashing of the old sensational adventure-story formulae, with Gothic additions in the shape of various grotesque life-forms, and catering for the most elementary and age-old craving for signs and wonders – though even here contemporary anxieties often break through. There are, too, science fiction works which are seriously concerned with the dilemmas of modern mankind and imbued with a genuine poetic imagination, as with some of the novels and stories of J.G. Ballard and Brian Aldiss.

If the various kinds of post-war fantasy writing are by no means always escapist, most of them bear witness to a profound dissatisfaction with the existing structures of society – and the marked increase of interest (especially among some of the poets) in primitivism, savage nature, pre-history, archaeology and mythology offers testimony of a similar kind.

Books in the market place

From one point of view post-war Britain would seem to be a highly literate nation. The production of books, aided by new technological techniques, has been one of the major growth industries. The number of new titles and reprints had in 1980 reached the record figure of 48,000. At the same time, there has been a spectacular expansion of the export trade in books, now one of the main concerns of the large publishing houses. The borrowing figures from the public libraries are equally impressive, and there is a boom in paperbacks – in 1948 little more than a side-line, by 1960 the most dynamic factor in the British publishing world. Some aspects of the changes have been necessary and valuable, but other consequences are far from desirable or promising for the future. One of the most striking of the developments of mass markets has been the introduction of a highly unstable lottery element into the dissemination of literature. Radio or television adaptations of books, for example, create a sudden massive demand. No one is likely to deplore the fact that thousands of people turn to the novels, say, of Jane Austen, Dickens or George Eliot. The rescuing of the 'safer' established works of the past, however, is basically haphazard, and liable to produce serious distortions in the literary heritage. Literary prizes have also been absorbed into the economics of the mass society. Not only the winners but the runners-up as well achieve best-sellerdom. The size of the stakes and the disproportion between the rewards of those who make the jump to the best-seller list in this way and those who *nearly* did so, make the winning of one of the major literary prizes analogous to winning the football pools, and that does not help to create the kind of climate in which important literature can flourish.

Naturally enough, publishers have set out to manufacture best-sellers to carefully researched formulae and to use new marketing techniques. Peter Benchley's *Jaws*, for example, which was one of the great sales successes of the 1970s, was accepted by the publisher on the basis of a brief outline after the film rights had been bought, so that the book was famous before it even existed. The effects of these methods upon the book market as a whole, and therefore upon literature itself, are far-reaching. The printing of vast editions of a few titles creates a serious imbalance affecting the sales of other books, which affects booksellers just as much as publishers.

The main victims of this state of affairs have been those who write these other books. Ever since 1945 there has been a sharp and steady downward trend in author's earnings. In 1966 Richard Findlater's *The Book Writers: Who are They?*, a statistical enquiry commissioned by the Society of Authors) revealed that only about one in two full-time authors earned from their writing as much as half the national average wage at the time. By 1982 the great majority had been forced to regard authorship as a part-time occupation and to make their livings by other means. It is often assumed that the Public Lending Right which, after a long battle conducted by the Society of Authors, the Writers' Guild and other campaigners, was authorised by Parliament in 1982, would improve the situation. Although it is a welcome development, in fact it substantially benefits only the members of what Findlater called 'the golden nucleus' whose books are already in wide demand (Barbara Cartland as much as, say, Graham Greene).

The poetry boom

Another phenomenon which seems at first sight to suggest that post-war British culture is in a flourishing condition has been the marked upsurge of interest in poetry. The public have bought the verse of their favourite poets to an extent unprecedented in modern times: Philip Larkin's *The Whitsun Weddings* (1964), for example, sold 70,000 copies; Ted Hughes' *Crow* (1970), 50,000; and Seamus Heaney's *North* (1975), 30,000, while John Betjeman's volumes, beginning with *Summoned by Bells* (1960) moved into the best-seller class. These are figures which rival those achieved by Scott, Byron and Tom Moore in the early nineteenth century. In addition, poetry readings and festivals have drawn big audiences, and poetry programmes on BBC radio attract many listeners. There have also been numerous poetry magazines, especially during the 1950s and early 1960s, many of them edited outside London, like Hull's *Listen* and *Wave* and Edinburgh's *Lines Review*, and although in recent years economic factors have forced many of them out of business, they still come and go, and some, like Newcastle-upon-Tyne's *Stand* (which contains criticism and prose as well as new verse) persist.

Moreover many more people are apparently writing poetry – as witness the startling scale of entries for the various annual poetry competitions, no less than 40,000 in one recent case. It would appear that the sense of almost continuous political and social crisis, the threat of nuclear warfare, and the loss of faith not only in religion but also in general ethical standards and in social and political institutions which had once seemed tested and proved, has created a mood of anxiety and impotence which has led more and more people to look to poetry to provide answers, or at least to impose some sort of order on the chaos.

There has certainly been no lack of established poets to cater for the demand. Few of these write less than decent poetry, and some of them do very much better than that. What has become rare is the production of a really solid body of poetic work, marked by variety and steady progression. With a few notable exceptions, long poems that seek to probe deeply into the contemporary human situation have become equally rare. Short poems or lyrics are the general rule, and the term 'occasional' – not necessarily in a pejorative sense – often seems the appropriate one.

At first sight the adjective is particularly applicable to Betjeman's poetry, with its tremendous popularity. Some of it is undoubtedly light verse like the famous 'Miss Joan Hunter Dunn, Miss Joan Hunter Dunn': but the pre-war suburban world which many of Betjeman's poems conjure up – with their tennis courts, vicarage garden parties, and old-style railway stations – is a far more stable and therefore comforting one than our own. At its best, the easy lyrical measures of Betjeman's poetry are the result of considerable artistic subtlety, as Auden among others observed; while the emotions with which he deals – the remembered joys and terrors of childhood, the fear of death, a hard-won religious faith, and the belief in simple pieties and virtues – sometimes have a genuine dramatic urgency and the kind of innocence that commands respect because of its complete freedom from self-conscious cleverness or intellectual faking.

This kind of appeal is in many ways a healthier phenomenon than some of the post-war trends in the popularising of poetry. One of these has been a movement towards a concept of poetry that regards it primarily as performance or group activity. Christopher Logue's frequently stimulating experiments with poetry and jazz in the 1950s pointed the way; the first considerable breakthrough was the Albert Hall reading of 1965, which Michael Horovitz, one of its organisers, described as 'a sacramental jubilee'. If the work of the 'pop' poets is often worth reading, that can hardly be said of the 'rants' of other poets – vituperatively anarchic doggerel, full of obscenities, usually accompanied by a violently aggressive and amplified musical backing. These writers challenge the traditional idea of the permanence of poetry, from a standpoint which regards considerations of quality and evaluation as the remnants of an anachronistic bourgeois and patriarchal society.

There have also been other 'aural' developments, including the 'sound' poetry of Bob Cobbing and others, who compose tape-recorded pieces, using different sound levels and speeds, together with non-human sounds or sometimes electronic effects, with results which are close to *musique concrète*, as well as various forms of 'concrete poetry' concerned with visual presentation.

To return to the part played in the poetry boom by the competitions. The general aim was the laudable one of encouraging the thousands of would-be poets in the hope of bringing hidden talent to the surface. But it is doubtful whether the methods employed to promote the Poetry Society's first national competition (in 1977) – the slogan, for instance, advertising the £1,000 winning entry as 'The Most Expensive Poem Ever Written' – is the best way of nurturing the needs of the thousands who are hoping to find in poetry a new focus of values.

Philip Larkin and Ted Hughes

Philip Larkin and Ted Hughes are perhaps the two post-war poets who most clearly illustrate the salient features and contrasts in post-war English verse. Larkin's prominence dated from the publication of his fourth collection, *The Less Deceived* in 1955, and his inclusion a year later in *New Lines*, the anthology edited by Robert Conquest which launched The Movement. To his fellow-contributors (among them Amis, Wain, Enright, Thom Gunn, and Davie) in their reaction against the 'dynamic romanticism' of Dylan Thomas, Larkin's poetry with its lucidity, scepticism, severe emotional restraint and technical accomplishment seemed the exact model of all that they stood for.

To a large extent this was a reflection of a particular temperament and life experience, combined with the decisive influence of Hardy's poetry, and of a rejection of all that seemed extraneous. The area that remains is a narrow one, dominated by a few basic themes – loss, diminution, the poignancy of the past, the pathos of thwarted expectations, loneliness, fear of old age, decay and death, change and renewal in nature – and by a mood of disenchantment, sometimes grim and savage (as in 'Sunny Prestatyn' 1964), sometimes sardonic and witty ('Naturally the Foundation will Bear Your Expenses' 1964), but more characteristically, ironic and rueful. Within his chosen area, Larkin often moves with an admirable technical control, marked by precision of language, colloquial ease, sensitive cadences and firm but subtle and unobtrusive rhyme schemes. The progression in his best poems (one might almost call it the story-line) is nearly always the same – from the concrete rendering of a specific situation or scene, through a process of scrutiny and deflation designed to guard against the intrusion of anything approaching soft-centredness, to a final retrieval of whatever small positive element is, in the poet's view, permissible. 'The Whitsun Weddings' the title-poem of his 1964 collection (which together with *The Less Deceived* contains his best work) is a particularly good example. There is the easy, almost prosy narrative opening:

> That Whitsun, I was late getting away:
> Not till about
> One twenty on the sunlit Saturday
> Did my three-quarters empty train pull out,
> All windows down, all cushions hot, all sense
> Of being in a hurry gone . . .

Then comes the sudden stir of the wedding parties gathered on the platforms, as the newly-weds board the train, on their way to London and their honeymoons. There follows the inevitable wry commentary:

> They watched the landscape, sitting side by side
> – An Odeon went past, a cooling tower,
> And someone running up to bowl – and none
> Thought of the others they would never meet,
> Or how their lives would all contain this hour.

And then, as the journey comes to an end, some small expectation of fulfilment (for the couples, that is, not for the observing poet, whose isolation forms part of the total effect) is reluctantly admitted:

> . . . this frail
> Travelling coincidence, and what it held
> Stood ready to be loosed with all the power
> That being changed can give.

The strongest emotional charge in Larkin's poetry perhaps is that at the end of 'An Arundel Tomb' (1964). The 'sharp tender shock' experienced when the observer notes that the sculptor of the stone effigies of the earl and countess has depicted them holding hands, is quickly deflated, but far more gently than usual; and in the final stanza it, too, is endowed with a kind of grace:

> Time has transfigured them into
> Untruth. The stone fidelity
> They hardly meant has come to be
> Their final blazon, and to prove
> Our almost-instinct almost true:
> What will survive of us is love.

Larkin is often at his most humanly engaged when he is dealing with the past – 'How Distant', his evocation of nineteenth-century emigrants, is another moving example. Where contemporaries are concerned, his sympathies go out most spontaneously to the old or dying. The tone of 'Ambulances', for instance, is gravely compassionate, the observations soberly and movingly apposite. For Larkin, as for Wilfred Owen, 'the poetry is in the pity'. Or perhaps one should say 'in the suffering'. That alone, Larkin implies, tells the truth. The momentary recognition of the possibility of religious feeling in 'Church Going' (1955) is a fallacy. So, too, is 'The glare of that much-mentioned brilliance, love' ('Long Songs in Age', 1964) and Larkin comments in 'Lines from a Young Lady's Photograph Album' (1955), 'when Desire takes charge, readings will grow untrue'. The same poem demonstrates, too, that memory and the art (in effect equated here with photography) that seeks to preserve it are also deceptive, and the emotional charge of the poem lies in the pain of the recognition, in the poignant final lines where the young lady's photograph, with the recollections it awakens, is seen as a vain attempt (reinforced by the ambiguity of the word 'lie') to condense:

> . . . a past that no one now can share,
> No matter whose your future; calm and dry,

It holds you like a heaven, and you lie
Unvariably lovely there,
Smaller and clearer as the years go by.

The pain that lies at the centre of many of Larkin's poems is
fundamentally his own. Although he can be deeply understanding of those
who live thwarted or restricted lives, forced to accept with whatever dignity
they can muster that the 'much-mentioned brilliance, love' will never be
theirs (it is easy to see why Larkin admired the novels of Barbara Pym), or
with people working in hard and dangerous jobs, as in his evocation of
colliers in 'The Explosion' (1974), an ongoing sympathy for other people is
not always in evidence. Often Larkin puts a distance between them and
himself – in 'The Whitsun Weddings' there is a distinct touch of hauteur as
he surveys the comical goings-on of the lower orders. His most positive and
unqualified emotions are reserved for pastoral scenes emptied both of human
beings and of himself. In 'Here' (1964) for example, the train (a natural
vantage-point for someone who remains on the inside looking out) takes him
from the crowded industrial city to a countryside finely and palpably
rendered, where:

Loneliness clarifies. Here silence stands
Like heat. Here leaves unnoticed thicken,
Hidden weeds flower, neglected waters quicken,
Luminously-peopled air ascends;
And past the poppies bluish neutral distance
Ends the land suddenly beyond a beach
Of shapes and shingle. Here is unfenced existence:
Facing the sun, untalkative, out of reach.

In these lines there is none of the pathos of loss, regret, disenchantment, and
diminution that tangling with the human condition brings. 'Loneliness
clarifies' the muddle; silence is a firm reliable presence; weeds and water are
not meddled with by man; the air is 'peopled' but not *by* people; the distance
is 'neutral'; existence is not fenced in by circumstance, free of the clatter of
human voices, distanced – the note of almost jaunty relief is unmistakable,
and conveyed with impressive compactness and economy.

In dealing with his own experience, directly or refracted through that of
others, the cool, clinical tone and, paradoxically, even the precise, economic
style, is sometimes a technique of restriction and constriction. The purpose of
some of his poems, moreover, seems to be not so much to hold emotion in
check as to evade or belittle it or to conjure it out of existence altogether.
Time after time, the same note is struck: 'all they might have done had they
been loved', 'how things ought to be' ('Home is so Sad', 1964); 'our young
unreal wishes' ('The Large Cool Store', 1964) – to read too many of these
sad disclaimers at a stretch is to experience a certain monotony, a sense of
perversely willed defeatism. In 'Afternoons' (1964) 'Summer is fading' for the
young mothers in the recreation ground:

Their beauty has thickened.
Something is pushing them
To the side of their own lives.

It is Larkin who says so: in poems like this no allowance is made for the possibility of adjustment, growth, the presence of other satisfactions or fulfilments, and certainly no hint of 'ripeness is all'.

It is difficult to resist the conclusion that much of Larkin's work is not that of a realist but of a disappointed romantic. Perhaps it was his realisation that he could not go on repeating a confrontation between 'realism' and 'romanticism', in which the latter must inevitably (for him) be the loser, that accounts for the fact that after the publication of 'High Windows' in 1974, his last and on the whole bleakest collection (though 'To the Sea' and 'How Distant' as well as 'The Explosion' are among his best poems) he wrote so little.

There is a nucleus of fully achieved poems in his work in which negation and affirmation *are* balanced in beautifully resonant language, and where Larkin shows what a strong, disciplined talent can make out of a deliberately reduced area of experience. The reduction itself, moreover, together with the sharp, precise technique, is in his best poems a valid means of preserving a core of genuineness in the midst of what he sees as the surrounding cultural and social anarchy. In this respect, Larkin is very much a poet for his time. Yet can a writer of such 'minimal affirmation' whose poetic world is one of pathos, defeat, disenchantment, and death-in-life, endured passively rather than with creative defiance, be the major poet some critics have claimed him to be, let alone one who represents a growing-point or a source of nourishment for 'hungry mouths?'.

There could hardly be a greater contrast than that between Philip Larkin and Ted Hughes, and in attempting to place such a baffling poet as the latter, the contrast itself is a helpful starting-point. Take, for instance the first two stanzas of 'Wind' (from Hughes's first volume *The Hawk in the Rain*, 1957):

> This house has been far out at sea all night,
> The woods crashing through darkness, the booming hills,
> Winds stampeding the fields under the window
> Floundering black astride and blinding wet
>
> Till day rose; then under an orange sky
> The hills had new places, and wind wielded
> Blade-light, luminous and emerald,
> Flexing like the lens of a mad eye.

The rush and thrust from those lines are in striking contrast to Larkin's careful, patient tread. It is almost as if the plethora of explosive participles and epithets – 'crashing', 'booming', 'stampeding' – was overtly meant to challenge his method. Even the more lyrical moments in the volume (as in the beautiful opening lines of 'October Dawn') possessed a marked energy and physicality. Seamus Heaney sees the importance of Hughes's poetry as residing precisely in its opposition to 'the Larkin voice', to the voices of 'literate English middle-class culture' – whereas Hughes's 'great cry and call and bawl is that English language and poetry is longer and deeper and rougher than that'. The 'great cry and call and bawl' has taken a variety of forms. It can be as rigorously controlled as anything in Larkin, impacted so to speak in order to convey a sense of the self-contained weight, heat and power of animals, as with 'The Bull Moses' and 'View of a Pig' in *Lupercal* (1960), Hughes's second volume. His fascination with the inviolable otherness of non-human creatures is reminiscent of D.H. Lawrence, one of his formative influences. Hughes's interest, however, was increasingly in wild, predatory creatures, as part of some wider cosmic mystery with which he was struggling to come to terms. This became very apparent in *Crow* (1970, rev. edn 1972) the sequence of explosive and baffling poems, sub-titled *From the Life and Songs of the Crow*. There the technique is a deliberate avoidance of verbal or rhythmic subtlety in favour of the devices of primitive oral poetry, among them repetitions, incantations, lists of cryptic riddle-like questions, runic pronouncements and the use of simple, direct adjectives and primary colours (as with the 'red, red blood' of the old ballads).

The primitivism of the technique is designed, of course, to match that of the contents. Crow, a demonic embodiment of blackness and death whose only positive quality is an unquenchable instinct for survival, emerges as a kind of primordial force, born of the inchoate raw materials of creation, savagely scornful of all later attempts to order or humanise them in myth. At the same time he is entangled with this myth-making process, but only to undermine it, contributing, for instance, his own grotesque and scabrous variations to the story of the Fall and of God's plans for the redemption of mankind through the Crucifixion:

> When God, disgusted with man,
> Turned towards heaven.
> And man, disgusted with God,
> Turned towards Eve,
> Things looked like falling apart.
>
> But Crow Crow
> Crow nailed them together,
> Nailing Heaven and earth together –
>
> So man cried, but with God's voice.
> And God bled, but with man's blood . . .

Perhaps Hughes is trying to convey the duality of light and darkness, or perhaps the inevitability of an eternal alternation of creation and destruction before which all sustaining myths and creeds must wither away into meaninglessness, leaving the continuing vitality of matter as the only 'truth'. It is not always easy to explicate satisfactorily what Hughes is getting at in *Crow*.

In the late 1950s and early 1960s Hughes had become deeply interested (like Yeats before him) in the corpus of magical literature and also in Robert Graves's *The White Goddess* (1948), and in the idea of the poet as shaman. There are certainly clues here. Hughes has said, for instance (in a 1971 interview in *London Magazine*) that the shaman '. . . can enter trance at will and go to the spirit world . . .'; and it seems that in his search for a poetic spontaneity beyond Larkin's control and rationality, Hughes is prepared to surrender himself to that kind of condition. In reading *Crow*, however, what often emerges most clearly is a passionate but baffled difficulty in coming to terms with the cruelty and destructiveness which the poems in it express, accompanied by a deep pessimism in face of the dark forces released by his shamanistic – as opposed to creative (in the Coleridgean sense) – imagination.

A lesser poet might have been driven into silence by so bleak a vision. It is a measure of Hughes's vitality that he continued the struggle to come to terms with it – for example, in *Cave Birds* (1975; rev. ed. 1978), in *Gaudete* (1977), and in the sequences *Adam and the Sacred Nine* and 'Prometheus on his Rock' in *Moortown* (1979). The latter poem contains many fine passages but, again, Hughes seems uncertain what he means his Prometheus figure to signify. Sometimes he is merely a focus for the savagery and violence, as in the passages describing the onslaughts of the vulture. Sometimes, though, Prometheus seems to be a positive and redemptive force, but at others his situation is presented as utterly futile, the symbol only of an endless martyrdom to the pitiless laws of Necessity and Nature.

Hughes is, as a rule, much more at ease with animals (leaving aside the mythical ones) than with people. The first part of *Moortown*, for example, which Hughes described as kind of 'verse farming diary', contains some of his most concentrated and successful poems; they are very different from the pastorals of Larkin, quite untouched by nostalgia, based on his own experiences as a farmer and unflinchingly realistic but without anything approaching stridency or rhetoric. Human beings, though, are often equated with animals. It is significant that he was attracted to the bloody and violent world of the first-century Roman tragedian Seneca, commenting in the preface to his masterly translation of Seneca's *Oedipus* (1969) that the protagonists 'are more primitive than aboriginals. They are spider people, scuttling among hot stones.' When human beings do appear in a more sympathetic light, as in *Remains of Elmet* (1979), what mostly interests Hughes is the contrast between the fundamental impermanence of all the frantic industrial human activity, and the continuing reality of the natural environment in which it has taken place. The contrast is beautifully captured, in spite of the vatic overtones, in 'The Trance of Light':

> The upturned face of this land
> The mad singing in the hills
> The oprophetic mouth of the rain
>
> That fell asleep
>
> Under migraine of headscarves and clatter
> Of clog-irons and looms
> And gutter-water and clog-irons
> And clog-irons and biblical texts
>
> Stretches awake, out of Revelations
> And returns to itself . . .

The vision, though, is of a land emptied of people – except insofar as they are denizens of a habitat; one of the *Elmet* poems, for instance, states that the surrounding moors: 'Are a stage for the performance of heaven, /Any audience is incidental'. All the same these poems are much less despairing, much more tranquil in tone, than most of Hughes's prophetic verse, and there are moments of muted hope as in the conclusion of 'Lumb Chimneys' with its implied possibility of some kind of regeneration that might include humanity itself: 'Before these chimneys can flower again, /They must fall into the only future, into earth.'

Hughes is a poet of continuous surprises. The unevenness and stridencies can suddenly be succeeded by passages of daring originality and power. The 'free' spontaneity and unselfconsciousness at which he aims can achieve strikingly beautiful results, as notably in *Season Songs* (1975; rev. 1976), in many of the poems intended primarily for children (like the magically atmospheric 'Full Moon and Little Frieda', written for his daughter, in *Wodwo*) and in the animal poems in *Under the North Star* (1981).

Hughes feels a special kinship with the beleaguered poets of Eastern Europe (in 1976, for example, he published a selection, brilliantly rendered into English, of the poems of the Hungarian Janos Pilinsky), no doubt because he, too, regards himself as a survivor poet, forced like them to write out of the destructive reality of the modern world. In poems like *Crow*, Hughes's response to it is basically nihilistic. On the other hand he has certainly had the courage to surrender himself to the dangerous complex of emotions that his search for some sort of meaning in the apparent chaos involves – and who else in post-war English poetry has undertaken such an ambitious and daunting task? It is always accompanied, moreover, by the 'great cry and call and bawl', which is one of pain, frustrated rage and defiance as much as it is one of defeat, and taking Hughes's kind of risks may be more conducive to poetic vitality than a cautious restraint and rationality.

Post-war drama

It has often been said that the richest and most vigorous area of post-war English literature has been its drama. There have, indeed, been so many developments that here it is only possible to discuss a few of the most outstanding, and to indicate a few of the leading practitioners.

In the immediate post-war years it looked as if the English theatre was about to return to the pre-war patterns, relying for the most part on already established playwrights – such as Priestley, Maugham, Coward and Rattigan. The only noteworthy symptom of adventurousness was the introduction of plays from France by Sartre, Cocteau and Anouilh. The only important new development was in the field of poetic drama, and in particular Eliot's attempts to apply his earlier and very sound argument – that the genre cannot succeed unless there is an organic relationship between the poetry, the action and the structure of the play – to contemporary characters and situations rather than to historical ones, as in his *Murder in the Cathedral* (1935). Eliot had started this process of adaptation in 1939 with *The Family Reunion* and continued it after the war with *The Cocktail Party* (1949), and *The Confidential Clerk* (1954). The blend of drawing-room comedy and the frameworks of classical tragedy, with religious overtones, however, was an uneasy one, and soon seemed irrelevant to the post-war world. The verse itself, moreover, failed to fulfil Eliot's purpose of making the audience feel that it was a perfectly natural talking medium, and one that would 'transfigure' ordinary life; and this became only too obvious with *The Elder Statesman* (1959), the last of his plays.

At the same time a number of young playwrights were strongly attracted to experiment in poetic drama. John Whiting's *Saint's Day* (1951), for example, was written in prose but of a very 'poetic' kind, while in a 1957 lecture he insisted that the speech of the theatre 'must be as artificial as any other form', and all his work is deeply imbued with Eliot's influence. John Arden's *Serjeant Musgrave's Dance* (1959), one of the outstanding plays of the period, contains substantial passages of rhymed verse, much of the prose is poetic, and it is permeated with the language, narrative devices and construction of the traditional ballads, as is *Armstrong's Last Goodnight* (1964), which is indebted to the Johnnie Armstrong ballad. Indirectly, too, poetic drama at that stage reinforced the English tradition of highly verbal theatre.

The first real landmark in post-war British theatre was the London production of Beckett's *Waiting for Godot*, in 1955 (produced first in Paris, 1952). After the first shocked incomprehension, the play had the effect of widening dramatic horizons, establishing continental existentialism and a non-realist mode on the English stage. Beckett's evident aversion to traditional theatrical and dramatic assumptions also had its long-term effects. *Waiting for Godot* showed that drama could be made out of *inaction*, that a climax could be dispensed with and that a play could end just as well with a whimper as a bang:

> *Vladimir*: Well? Shall we go?
> *Estragon*: Yes, let's go.
>
> *They do not move*

In subsequent plays Beckett dramatised his sense of futility and human isolation by progressively making less and less use of scenery, lighting, movement, less of the actors' personalities – and even less of their bodies: in *Endgame* (London, 1958), the characters are blind, immobilised, cowed or helpless; *Krapp's Last Tape* (London, 1958) features only one man and a tape-recorder; the main character in *Happy Days* (1961) is buried up to her neck in sand; *Act Without Words* (1967) dispenses with language; and in *Not I* (1973) nothing is visible except the actress's mouth.

The other major theatrical event of the 1950s was the arrival in London in August 1956 of Bertolt Brecht with his Berliner Ensemble, and his production at the Palace Theatre of *The Caucasian Chalk Circle*, and *Mother Courage* (which Joan Littlewood had already produced the previous year). The influence of Brecht was to prove momentous. It is, in consequence, not altogether correct to cite the production of Osborne's *Look Back in Anger* at the Royal Court Theatre in 1956 as the start of the 'new' English drama – as is often done. Osborne's play had a theatrical context. In many ways it was a muddled old-fashioned play. But it proved explosive in its effect because through the mouth of his disgruntled hero, Jimmy Porter, Osborne had brilliantly verbalised so many contemporary frustrations. In *The Entertainer* (1957), a much better constructed play, the scenes in which Archie makes the audience play a collective role as in a variety theatre followed Brecht's precept (though in fact Osborne has denied any influence) that the invisible

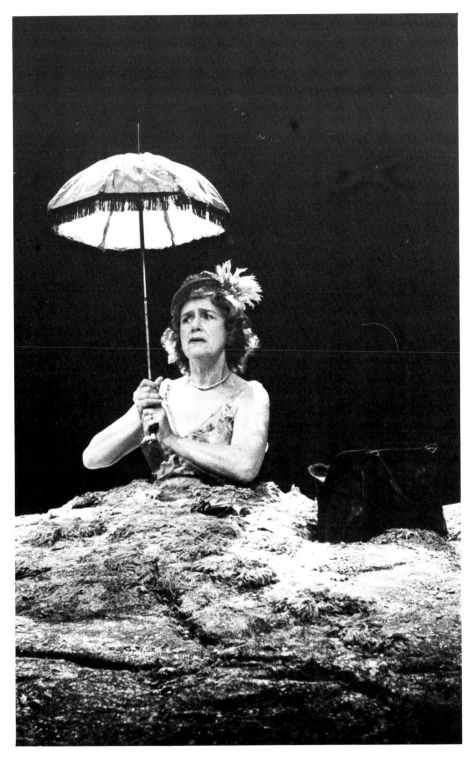

Peggy Ashcroft in Samuel Beckett's Happy Days *at the Lyttleton Theatre, March, 1976.*

'fourth wall' of traditional theatre must be removed; while the equating of the decay of the variety theatre with that of the cultural and political situation of contemporary Britain added a further Brechtian resonance. Brecht's Marxist approach to the dramatisation of history is also strongly present in Osborne's *Luther* (1961) whose hero is another rebel against a social corruption which has modern correspondences. After *Inadmissable Evidence* (1964), one of his most satisfactory plays, employing various modernist techniques – including a quasi-expressionist dream sequence, and very effective sequences of inter-woven monologues – most of Osborne's later plays reverted both structurally and theatrically to older conventions.

Of the English dramatists thrown up by the new wave, the most original was Harold Pinter. Like Beckett, who greatly influenced him, he belongs to the wider European literary scene, in that his handling of theme, character and situation has much in common with that of Kafka, Brecht, Ionesco, Adamov and Durremat. In plays like *The Birthday Party* (1958), *The Dumb Waiter* (Germany, 1959; England, 1960), *The Caretaker* (1960), and *The Homecoming* (1965) Pinter created drama of a peculiarly intense and menacing kind (even when it is at one level hysterically comic) out of the speech patterns of his characters. Many of these, it is true, are deprived, inadequate, or semi-literate, but to listen to them talking is to experience an uneasy suspicion that they are perhaps no more imprisoned within their modes of speech, impoverished in their inner lives, subject to secret longings and despairs, frantic for a safe and inalienable corner to call their own, and no more frightened of an incomprehensible and anarchic world outside than we are ourselves.

The term 'non-communication' is sometimes applied to Pinter's plays in a misleading way. His characters are capable of bursts of extraordinary volubility – Aston's speech in *The Caretaker* where he tells Davies about his experience of shock-therapy is an obvious instance. But these outbursts are essentially of the same nature as the fumblings, ramblings, stutterings, non-sequiturs and silences, and the two kinds of utterance are the two faces of the same inner sense of alienation, both of them devoted to the same end of concealing it from the other characters or from themselves and of escaping any real personal contact because it would be too painful. As Pinter himself has said:

The speech we hear is an indication of what we don't hear. It is a necessary avoidance, a violent, sly, anguished or mocking smokescreen which keeps the other in its place.

And the drama is created out of the tension and dislocation between the two. When his characters avoid communication, it is usually because they are deliberately doing so, not because they are incapable of it.

Yet in spite of the bewildering transitions in dialogue that result, the elements of fantasy in the near-schizophrenic day-dreams and nightmares of the protagonists – and in spite of the 'absurdist' label that has so often been fastened on him – in his earlier plays Pinter is basically realistic in his characterisation, in his use of language, and also in his stage sets which, in contrast to those of Beckett, carefully place his people in a recognisable social milieu.

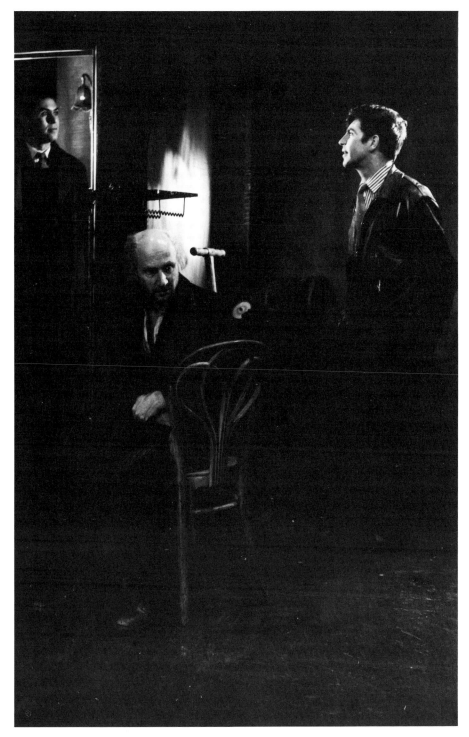

Harold Pinter's The Caretaker, *which opened at the Arts Theatre in April, 1960.*

In the late 1960s, however, Pinter entered into a more experimental and non-naturalistic phase. In his one-act plays *Landscape* and *Silence* (double bill, 1969) he drew closer to Beckett by reducing the movement to a minimum, conveying the relationships and backgrounds of the characters almost entirely by the words they speak, and making the stage setting, for the first time, neutral and generalised. Both plays are in effect dramatic poems, employing conventions similar to those of radio drama – and *Landscape*, in fact, though written for the theatre, was first broadcast (in 1968).

Pinter now applied his changed approach to full-length plays. In *Old Times* (1971) the relationships between the characters, and between their past and present situations are fluid and ambiguous. At the beginning of the play, for example, Anna is seated in a dim light at the back of the stage while Deeley and Kate are talking: although when Anna joins them in the brighter light downstage it is clear that she has overheard part of their conversation, it is *not* clear where exactly she has come *from*. She certainly hasn't made a conventional stage entrance: she might be present in her own right, but at times it seems as if she might just as well be an emanation from the others' memories of her, or even – since the identities of the two women are often blurred when Deeley is reminiscing about them – a projection of Kate herself. The uncertainties are accentuated by sudden temporal transitions into the immediate future or twenty years back to a period when Anna and Kate were secretaries sharing a flat. Sometimes, moreover, re-enactment of the past alternates with the spoken reminiscences, and at other times past and present are fused, so that the action we are watching seems to be a representation of what is happening inside the mind of one or other of the characters.

In *No Man's Land* (1975), the central situation, in which the wealthy writer Hirst is entertaining the poor poet Spooner in his grand Hampstead house, at first sight seems straightforward enough, but ambiguities about the relationship between the two men soon emerge. To begin with it appears as if they haven't met before, but later on Hirst speaks of having once seduced Spooner's wife; at another point, though, it appears as if he doesn't even recognise the guest we have seen him entertaining – at yet another he addresses him intimately with the words: 'Charles, how nice of you to drop in'.

In some respects the two one-act plays, with their Beckett-like brevity and compression, are more satisfactory expressions of Pinter's new kind of experimentalism than either *Old Times* or *No Man's Land*, which sometimes strike one as too long for the purpose Pinter had in mind. Nevertheless their disturbing but carefully controlled ambiguities generate further dramatic tensions, deeper psychological and poetic insights, and fresh resources of language.

The clearest link-figure between the new wave and later developments is Arnold Wesker. For one thing, in true Brechtian fashion, the working-class characters in Wesker's trilogy (*Chicken Soup with Barley*, 1958; *Roots*, 1959; and *I'm Talking about Jerusalem*, 1960) have their being in a specific social and political context at a crucial moment in history. *The Kitchen* (1959) and *Chips with Everything* (1962) convincingly showed how the routines of a work situation affect both the relationship of those inside it and the rhythm of their lives in general, while the anti-patriotic, anti-Establishment sequence at the end of the latter play could hardly have been more politically hard-hitting. At the same time Wesker's socialism and the cultural and educational ideas that sprang from it, though sometimes put over too didactically (especially in *Roots*) were always accompanied by an insistence on the need for a system of moral and humane values. There are continuities between Wesker's earlier and later plays, especially in *The Old Ones* (1973) which is a nostalgic return to the world of the trilogy. But still in most of the later plays, while the social and political preoccupations are still there, there is a greater concern with private pain and the inner lives of the characters, and the emphasis usually falls on family or other intimate relationships, as in *The Friends* (1970).

Wesker's kind of socialism and his methods of conveying it had little in common with the dramatists of the 'New Left', whose initial impetus was disillusionment with the Labour government which came into power in 1964, and therefore with the parliamentary system itself, regarded by them as no longer capable of fulfilling working-class aspirations or coping with the cultural decay of contemporary British society. By 1978 there were at least eighteen full-time socialist theatrical groups in operation (all of them, ironically perhaps, receiving subsidies) as well as many local ones, all devoted to the propagation of revolutionary ideas, and priding themselves on their mobility immediacy and adaptability, sometimes playing in existing theatres but just as ready to make use of makeshift venues. Later on, a number of plays by leading New Left dramatists, among them Howard Brenton, David Hare, David Edgar and Trevor Griffiths, became notable successes in the big subsidised London theatres, including the National, and to some extent in the commercial ones. In the long run only John McGrath, who in 1971 formed his 7:84 company (84 per cent of the country's wealth in the hands of 7 per cent of the population, that is) continued to resist absorption into mainstream theatre, continuing to take his revolutionary message further and further afield, especially in Scotland. But the New Left dramatists, while differing on matters of politics, ideology and strategy, were united both in their condemnation of existing society and in their reaction against the forms and aims of such predecessors as Osborne and Wesker.

By the mid-1970s a far more uncompromising form of socialist realism than anything offered by Wesker, for instance, had become the norm. That Brecht's influence continued to be important in this new phase is particularly well-illustrated by the older and already established Edward Bond. Both his *Narrow Road to the Deep North* (1968) and *The Bundle* (1977), for example, are Brechtian in their non-realistic use of Oriental history to make Marxist points, while his *Lear* (1971) adapts and modernises Shakespeare's plot in order to focus on social and political issues (turning Lear into a representative of military authoritarianism) in much the same way as Brecht did in his version of Shakespeare's *Coriolanus*. These and later plays also aimed at the Brechtian epic format. Many of Bond's juniors, too, came to regard Brecht as their mentor. Thus Brenton's *Weapons of Happiness* (1976) presents a series of scenes which are in effect separate discourses with the audience, in classic Brechtian manner; this is substantially the method, too, of his two most famous (and 'shocking') dramas, *The Churchill Play* (1975), which presents contemporary Britain as a vast concentration camp, and *The Romans in Britain* (1981) – a succession of images of colonialism with implied bearings on the particular problems caused by the English in northern Ireland.

What was rarer was any approximation to Brecht's poetry. These playwrights, in seeking to project their over-riding aim of promoting social change, have relied primarily on other means than language – and in this respect the influence of Antonin Artaud in his reaction against the dominance of language and in his emphasis on spectacle, performance, immediacy and physicality, was more apparent than that of Brecht. 'You must have plays with strong physical force', David Hare declared 'you have to find the lowest common denominator for a show', and shock-tactics of all kinds have been commonplace, the most notorious instance being the sodomising of a Briton by a Roman soldier in Brenton's *The Romans in Britain*. In other plays, on-stage murder, torture, rape and cannibalism have been presented. The aim of these acts of violence was, of course, to force audiences into participation in the underlying social and political objectives, and in the process, some powerful exposures of the corruptions of contemporary society have been enacted, sometimes in plays that have indeed been memorable theatrical spectacles. In theory at any rate, if by no means always in practice, propagandist aims take precedence over purely literary considerations. Arden, for instance, turned his back on his earlier poetic manner, collaborating in McGrath's transformation of *Serjeant Musgrave's Dance* into *Serjeant Musgrave Dances On* (1972) – which sharpens the political edge of the original, at the cost of blunting its language and dissipating its subtlety. In a discussion on 'British Playwriting in the Seventies' in 1976 David Edgar dismissed 'bourgeois, individualistic psychological values' as inimical to 'radical , alternative Marxist theatre' and asserted that human behaviour must be portrayed primarily 'as a function of their social nexus'. It is hardly surprising, in consequence, that subtlety of characterisation, too, is not always regarded as of any particular importance.

On the other hand, since some of these writers are highly talented, and possess an instinctive feel for the theatre, they often transcend their self-imposed limitations. Bond in particular, besides being a gifted and resourceful playwright, is capable of bursts of eloquence and metaphorical brilliance. David Hare has developed a growing interest in individuality as a product of the social situation, usually an enclosed one symbolising a bourgeois centre of power – an exclusive girls' school in *Slag* (1970), for example, Jesus College, Cambridge in *Teeth 'n' Smiles* (1975), and a country house in *Licking Hitler* (1978). Trevor Griffiths's *The Comedians* (1975) is a good deal more than an ideological confrontation between Waters, the retired performer on the northern circuits conducting a class of up and coming comics as a representative of a reformist liberal stance, and the abrasive Price, his most gifted pupil, as a representative of revolutionary values; though of course it is that, it is also a dramatically satisfying engagement between two human beings, involving the audience through a closely knit structure of plot and characterisation. David Edgar, the most prolific of the group has increasingly explored the relationship between politics and individual psychology, as notably in *The Jail Diary of Albie Sachs* (1978), which concentrates the whole South African political struggle into the experience of one minimally involved prisoner. Some of Edgar's later plays also present social and political issues – the womens'-consciousness movement in *Teendreams* (1979), for instance – subjectively rather than tendentiously. In recent years, in fact, there has been a shift of direction in left-wing political drama, with a recognition of the necessity for harder and more searching debate, and even of compromise, unthinkable during the 1970s. The problems of the Third World occupy more attention, as in Hare's *A Map of the World* (1983); and it is the anti-nuclear issue that has become the main focus of interest: Edgar's *Maydays* (1983) and Brenton's *The Genius* (1983) (his adaptation of Brecht's *Galileo*) both end at Greenham Common (near the US missile base).

The movement towards a concept of drama in which the written word is no longer of paramount importance – and of course there have also been many instances in which plays have in effect been the work of the director (with Joan Littlewood's *Oh What a Lovely War*, 1963, as the most obvious example), or sometimes of a whole production team – is bound to raise misgivings among those who see drama as an integral part of a literary tradition. At the same time, there can be no question that these 'political' playwrights are fulfilling the drama's traditional task of holding up a mirror to the world in which contemporary men and women have their being.

In any case, an attempt such as this to isolate a few of the most striking aspects of post-war British drama is immediately to become aware of how much vital and innovative work there has been besides – by Brendan Behan, Joe Orton, Peter Nichols, Charles Wood, N.F. Simpson, Peter Terson and Peter Barnes, to mention only a few of the omissions from a singularly crowded field. By and large, in fact, the story of British drama since 1945 does justify the assertion that it is one of the most vigorous and encouraging areas of contemporary British culture.

Radio and television drama

In discussing post-war British drama, some attention must also be given to the part played by broadcasting. The BBC Third Programme, for example, helped both Osborne and Pinter to find their individual dramatic voices at crucial points in their early careers, and in 1957 broadcast Beckett's seminal *All that Fall*. Playwrights found in radio's fluidity, rapidity of transitions, temporal telescopings, and use of interior monologue, some of the devices they needed to break out of the confines of conventional theatre. Donald McWhinnie's description of radio drama as 'an expression in voices of something which cannot be exteriorized' is a particularly apt description, for example, of the radio plays of Giles Cooper, one of the most distinctive practitioners of the genre, with an uncanny ear for verbal mannerisms and clichés.

Louis MacNeice's *The Dark Tower* (1947), which was a landmark in the history of broadcasting, came from Laurence Gilliam's Features Department which also launched Henry Reed's witty and socially percipient Hilda Tablet series (published in *Hilda Tablet and Others*, 1971). R.C. Scriven's series of autobiographical plays *The Seasons of the Blind* in the seventies also displays all the intrinsic strengths of the sound medium in evoking the intense, sensuously receptive inward world of the child within the concretely rendered context of ordinary family life. But the unique nature of radio drama is perhaps most strikingly illustrated by the case of Dylan Thomas's *Under Milk Wood* (1954). Brought into being and produced by Douglas Cleverdon, Thomas described it as 'a play for voices', and it is only as such that its somewhat baroque verbal invention fully succeeds.

Initially BBC television was mostly concerned with adaptations of existing stage plays, as the title 'Armchair Theatre' implied. Nevertheless an authentic, independent genre of television drama established itself. Two of the most successful practitioners are particularly interesting because, paradoxically perhaps, they are the most acutely aware of the effects of external pressures (including those of the mass media) on individual living. One of them was the late David Mercer, whose underlying theme was the dislocation of public and private worlds, notably in his trilogy *The Generations* (1961–3), where the threat of nuclear warfare is powerfully evoked at the level of personal and family relationships and within the consciousness of each of the individual selves concerned. The other is Dennis Potter who is deeply concerned with the struggle of the individual to achieve some sort of identity and self-respect in a society that continually narrows the area in which one can operate. In his most challenging work, and above all perhaps in *The Yellow Brick Road* (1972) and the six-play series *Pennies from Heaven* (1978), the concern centres on the invasion of this narrow area by the debilitating images of advertising, popular music and cheap entertainment – with an ironic recognition of the power of television itself to disseminate and perpetuate such images.

In many ways television drama is at its best when it comes closest to the conditions and conventions of radio, by exploring the intimacy of the small screen; by the use, for example, of close-ups with their emphasis on nuances of gesture and expression and the illusion of bringing a character right inside the viewer's room. And that means, too, that every *word* that is spoken must be carefully chosen and placed. In the outstandingly resourceful plays of both Mercer and Potter words are never mere spoken captions to the pictures but are integral to the total effect. The same is true of John Hopkins's distinguished quartet *Talking to a Stranger* (1966), which chronicles the emotional history of a divided family, generating a powerful and intimate rapport between characters and viewers, and achieving a natural fusion of word and image.

The same cannot always be said of the filmed play, which is all too often an unsatisfactory hybrid that is neither theatre, television play, nor film. There have, of course, been important exceptions. The film techniques of Jack Rosenthal, Peter Nichols and Alan Bleasdale, for instance, have created authentic and often compelling drama in which both eye and ear have been under genuine artistic control. In many ways their plays were obviously close to Jeremy Sandford's acted documentaries *Cathy Come Home* (1966), *Edna the Inebriate Woman* (1971) and other works like them, which made effective use of the flexibility of the modern film camera to gather images of the tragedies or comedies – and certainly the realities – of day-to-day living and then to organise them in the cutting room, in itself a genuine artistic process.

The fact remains that television is one of the mass media, subject like all the others to their inherent pressures, whether these take the form of the search for bigger audiences or of more direct market forces. Under these pressures the frequent recourse to ready-made formulae in television drama itself is inescapable. Only one in a thousand of unsolicited plays offered to British television is ever even considered, and as John Bowen, an experienced writer of television drama, has pointed out, producers

do not require either depth of characterization . . . or felicity of dialogue. They do require the ability . . . to manipulate familiar situations in a familiar way, and a readiness to allow one's work to be messed about in any way the producer wishes.

In such circumstances, it is surprising that a number of television plays worthy of serious consideration have managed to struggle through. With the ever-increasing, mesmeric popularity of soap operas, the cultural prospect, however, is not encouraging.

Joyce Cary, Angus Wilson and Doris Lessing

If Henry James's now unfashionable concept 'the art of the novel' were invoked in its full rigour, it is probable that since the war only the fiction of Joyce Cary would qualify. No writer could have pursued the struggle for rightness of style and form with more industry and dedication. His first novel, *Aissa Saved* (1932), had been the result of ten years of continuous reshaping and redrafting; the manuscripts of *Cock Jarvis*, left unfinished at his death (in 1957), run to nearly a million words; and many other novels were abandoned before completion. His two trilogies, the first consisting of *Herself Surprised* (1941), *To be a Pilgrim* (1942), and *The Horses Mouth* (1944); and the second of *Prisoner of Grace* (1952), *Except the Lord* (1953) and *Not Honour More* (1955), which mark the peak of his achievement, are among the most accomplished novels of the century. They are distinguished by a remarkable grasp of historical processes, of gradual change within the social structure, of the interlocking of political events with sectional interests and individual destinies, of subtle shifts in public and private morality with their accompanying changes in dress, idiom and mores – all of them conveyed in vivid and concrete detail. They are also notable for their presentation of the characters through their individual habits of thought and feeling, their Jamesian (or Joycean) elimination of author as story-teller, and their techniques of 'impersonation', the search for which was one of the main reasons for Cary's continuous writing and re-writing. Yet it must be admitted that, dying in 1957, Cary's work does not seem at the moment to have the same immediate relevance to post-war British culture as that of some of his juniors, lesser artists though most of them may be.

If comparable artistic judgements cannot be applied with the same confidence to the novels of Angus Wilson and Doris Lessing, the two other most considerable novelists since the war, they are nevertheless among the most relevant to the evolution of the contemporary British consciousness. In Wilson's case, the whole of his career has also been a continuous and highly literary search for the fictional mode that would best suit his particular gifts and responses to the rapidly changing social and political conditions of his times; and as with Henry James the action and characterisation of most of his novels revolve round a moral issue.

In his autobiography *The Wild Garden* (1963), Wilson suggested that his 'principal asset as a writer' was the gift of 'impressionistic mimicry'. It was one he first put to use in his two volumes of short stories *The Wrong Set* (1949) and *Such Darling Dodos* (1950), which brilliantly captured the manners and speech styles of the period and with them the myriad nuances of snobbery and sectional exclusiveness in British middle- and lower-middle-class society. The people in Wilson's stories find it difficult to relate to others because usually they have never found real selves, preferring to hide them behind the masks of class, convention and habit, or behind a callous egotism. Moral judgements and discriminations are implicit thoughout – Wilson is devastating, for example, in his exposure of the high-minded superiority of progressives who have no real moral basis in their own behaviour to justify it. The goal to be aimed at, the stories imply, is a maturity that proceeds from self-knowledge, but the path to it is no easy one, always liable to disruption by the dark, irrational forces of human nature, and these often take the form of macabre fantasy or sudden irruptions of violence and cruelty.

These two volumes of short stories exemplify most of Wilson's basic themes and preoccupations. Though he criticised those who called for 'a return to the great tradition of the English novel', because they were afraid of 'the new, the fresh, the experimental', it was a Dickensian type of realism that dominated Wilson's earlier novels. In both *Hemlock and After* (1952) and *Anglo-Saxon Attitudes* (1956) there is an explicit rendering of social and historical change intimately related to the destinies of the fictional characters. The personal crisis of Bernard Sands in *Hemlock and After* is also a reflection of the crisis in the political convictions which he had held as an ardent left-winger in the thirties, and in the liberal–humane philosophy behind them. Most of the political issues of the day are referred to and debated from various political points of view, ranging from Hubert Rose's Conservatism to Louie Randall's Communism. The personal moral dilemma, however, is central, and evil emerges as an independent, almost transcendental force. Quite early in the novel there are references to Sands's 'growing apprehension of evil', which comes to focus in particular on Mrs Craddock, the grossly possessive mother of the gentle Eric (Sands's lover), the procuress Mrs Curry, Hubert Rose her client, and the vicious theatrical producer Sherman Winter. Sands, though, has been only too aware of the presence of evil in himself from the moment when, witnessing the arrest of a young homosexual in Leicester Square, he had to his horror experienced a 'sadistic excitement', a 'hunter's thrill', which he felt had in effect placed him, the professed liberal-humanist, alongside 'the wielders of the knout and the rubber truncheon'. At the same time Wilson's protagonists have freedom of choice as to whether they will listen to or ignore the promptings of conscience. It is not Sands's discovery of his own homosexuality that is the source of guilt, but the growing realisation of his past hypocrisies and self-deceptions, and of his human failures in relation to his friends and family.

For Gerald Middleton, too, the elderly medieval historian of *Anglo-Saxon Attitudes*, it is the spiritual freedom that proceeds from his lengthy moral self-examination that really matters. In a sense the original fraud (the placing of a pagan fertility figure in the coffin of an Anglo-Saxon bishop, thus giving rise to all kinds of scholarly confusions and misinterpretations) is in itself of no more intrinsic importance than Sands's homosexuality. That Gerald has never allowed his suspicions of the fraud to surface for so many years is essentially a symbol for the fact that his conscience has, in many other respects as well, been lying dormant. In the course of his long drawn-out efforts to set the record straight, Gerald is also facing the truth about himself, the reasons for his original indolence, the dishonesties and evasions behind it, and far more important, the ways in which they had affected his personal relationships. The 'right to judge' is the phrase that haunts him. He learns the hard lesson that one first has to sit in judgement on oneself, a lesson that, in one form or another, underlies most of Wilson's fiction.

Although one of his finest novels, Wilson's *The Middle Age of Mrs Eliot* (1958) was still fundamentally traditional. His first tentative break into a different mode in *The Old Men at the Zoo* (1961), a fable which was still realistic in its actual treatment of an England of the future, was not as startling a new departure as it seemed at the time. If, a few years earlier, questioning the 'truth' of fiction, he had said that 'All fiction for me is a kind of magic and trickery – a confidence trick, trying to make people believe something is true that isn't . . .' he now make it clear that he had changed his mind about the pre-war experimental novelists, especially Virginia Woolf, whose influence from then on became increasingly apparent. In retrospect it can be seen that there were, in fact, modernist elements in Wilson's earlier novels. *Anglo-Saxon Attitudes* makes elaborate use of documents both in the body of the novel and in the Appendix, some of them real – as with the extracts from Bede's *History* and J.R. Green's *History of the English People* – others invented, such as the 'extracts' from *The Times*. These invented passages do not merely illustrate Wilson's gift for mimicry and pastiche, but in effect raise the kind of questions asked by the French modernists about textuality itself: the extent to which the printed word can convey the truth about human affairs.

Wilson's new phase did not properly begin until 1967 (four years after the publication of *Late Call*, perhaps the high point of his realistic mode) with the appearance of *No Laughing Matter*. It is an impressive interweaving of psychological, social and political narratives revolving round the lives of a family from just before the First World War into the sixties, and constituting one of the most successful post-war attempts in fiction to chart, analyse and embody, through the changing attitudes and activities of the characters, the social and political decline of the country itself. In his handling of this multi-faceted theme Wilson's new-found respect for Virginia Woolf's methods plays an important part: the presentation of each of the Matthews children by means of interior monologues, for example, and the transitions from one monologue to another, producing at times the effect of a kind of group consciousness, is strongly reminiscent of Woolf's *The Waves*; while the structuring of Wilson's novel, with time flowing round the fixed marks of carefully placed dates, has much in common with that of her novel *The Years*. But the most striking of Wilson's techniques in *No Laughing Matter* is his introduction of the Matthews children's playlets about their relationships with their impossible parents, nicknamed Billy Pop and The Countess, acting out their need 'to relieve their pent-up shame, distress and anger in histrionics, to heal their hurts with mimicry's homeopathic sting.'

In addition, there are pastiches of the invented literary styles of various members of the family, with specimens of Billy Pop's vapid, old-fashioned essays, of Sukey's cosily popular radio scripts, and of Margaret's novels, with their artistically dedicated struggle to break out of the inhibitions imposed by an upbringing which was indeed 'no laughing matter'. The continuous dialectic between fact and fiction is one of the sources of the novel's richness and vitality. At the same time, realist methods are not abandoned. In *No Laughing Matter* Wilson accomplished a genuine synthesis of the two, and in doing so achieved the goal his fictional novelist Margaret set herself towards the end of the novel – to create a humanist art instead of playing 'a glorified game of chess' with her characters and 'to adapt the tongue to poetry, to attune the ear to deeper music than mere mimicry.'

The synthesis of realism and modernism is not as satisfactory in *As If By Magic* (1973) and *Setting the World on Fire* (1980). In the latter, the long-drawn-out descriptions of the fictional Tothill House, the frescoes depicting Phaeton driving his chariot across the domed ceiling of the Great Hall, and the rehearsals and performance of Lully's opera on the subject, result in a structural imbalance and create a claustrophobic effect. And the details of the plot itself, especially the business of the terrorists, are handled in a curiously perfunctory manner, as if Wilson had grown weary of them. Nevertheless, Wilson's work as a whole offers one of the rare instances of a post-war writer who has faced up to the challenges posed by new critical approaches and artistic techniques, the philosophical theories underlying them, and the cultural chaos of the modern world that gave rise to them, without losing his creative vitality or his humanist values.

There is sometimes an element of sleight of hand and even downright fun in Wilson's experimentation. For Doris Lessing the issues with which she is dealing weigh on her mind too much to allow for this kind of technical playfulness. Describing Balzac, Stendhal, and particularly the great Russian novelists as 'my blood brothers', her natural, instinctive mode is that of realism: the narrative in all her novels is direct and down to earth, and when in the sixties she began to turn to more modernistic methods, one had the feeling she was doing so out of grim necessity. The charting of that necessity is in effect the story of Lessing's struggle to come to terms with her own life experience as it was enmeshed with the political, social and psychological issues and traumas of the post-war world.

Although *The Grass is Singing* (1950) had already established Lessing's reputation, the most obvious starting point is *Martha Quest* (1952) and the four novels that followed to form her *Children of Violence* sequence, which she described as 'a study of the individual conscience in its relations with the 'collective' – and this constitutes one of the major themes in her fiction. The central individual conscience in the sequence is that of Martha. At the beginning of the first novel of the quartet she is introduced in her Rhodesian setting (and with strong autobiographical overtones) as:

. . . adolescent, and therefore bound to be unhappy; British, and therefore uneasy and defensive; in the fourth decade of the twentieth century, and therefore inescapably beset with problems of race and class; female, and obliged to repudiate the shackled women of the past.

In this novel, *A Proper Marriage* (1954), and in *A Ripple from the Storm* (1958) Martha breaks free from the 'collective' represented by home and parental authority, to go and live in the Rhodesian capital. She throws herself into the life of the young white set – the close-knit, self-absorbed world of the young, fired by idealisms which are themselves essentially in-grown, is rendered, as always in Lessing's work, with extraordinary vividness and insight. Martha becomes interested in the left-wing political stance of the *New Statesman* and marries the young man with liberal ideas who introduces her to it. Later, joining a group of Communists and fellow-travellers, she falls under the spell of Anton Hesse, a refugee Communist from Hitler's Germany, 'a man in cold storage for the future', and marries him. Her growing disillusionment with this political collective, which to begin with seems to promise the perfect blending of private and public conscience, is paralleled and in effect symbolised by the deterioration of her relationship with Anton.

In *Landlocked* (1965), Martha lives through the agonising final stages of the breakdown of her second marriage and a love affair with the enigmatic Polish Jewish peasant Thomas Stern, who seems to represent in an almost mystical sense the possibility of a more highly developed human awareness. At the end of the novel, with Stern gone to fight in Israel, Martha feels herself, like the little colonial community to which she belongs, 'landlocked' – and she decides to go to London, as Lessing herself had done in 1949.

In the interval between *A Ripple from the Storm* and *Landlocked* Lessing had published *The Golden Notebook* (1962), one of the most remarkable of all post-war English novels. This interruption of the *Children of Violence* sequence was necessary to Lessing, because she found it essential to probe more deeply into the themes she had so far been exploring through the consciousness of Martha Quest, and it is the close, symbiotic relationship between the author as a thinking, feeling and suffering human being and the work itself that makes it so compelling. It was in this context, too, that the choice of techniques became a matter of urgency. The realistic approach was not abandoned. In her Preface to the 1972 edition of *The Golden Notebook*, Lessing described the 'skeleton or frame' – the five sections of *Free Women* – as 'a conventional short novel, about 60,000 words long . . . which could stand by itself'. Nothing indeed could be more conventionally realistic, even pedestrian, than the opening of the book: 'The two women were alone in the London flat', or than the words which introduce Anna's and Molly's backgrounds: 'The history of these two was as follows . . .' The non-realist methods, though, are of vital importance. Among these are the variations in style to match the different characters, and the textual arrangements of the four Notebooks which the central figure Anna Wulf keeps and which separate the sections of *Free Women*. There are, for instance, the departures from the chronological order, the sequence of newspaper extracts about world events, the passages from Anna's diary about the Communist Party meetings she attends, her sketches for short stories and novels, and so on. Also, towards the end of the Golden Notebook section, Anna's departing lover Saul Green writes down the words: 'The two women were alone in the London flat', the first in the novel which Lessing herself has already written – thereby recalling Marcel Proust's narrator, who on the last pages of *A la recherche du temps perdu* (1922–32) begins the novel Proust has already written.

In a 1962 interview, Lessing, while insisting that 'the old-fashioned novel' was not dead, pointed out that in the confused and anarchic contemporary world its methods were not always adequate. It is to demonstrate as much that *Free Women* is deliberately composed *as* an old-fashioned novel, and then interspersed with the frequently formless and chaotic material of the Black, Red, Yellow and Blue Notebooks – exactly the kind of material that could not be contained within the old forms. Her 'major aim', Lessing explained in the 1972 Preface, was 'to shape a book which would make its own comment, a wordless statement: to talk through the way it is shaped'. This of course is another way of saying that Anna's experiences themselves could not be encompassed within the bounds of traditional realism; hence her writer's block and her contempt for her first (commercially highly successful) novel which she knows was not a truthful transposition of these experiences into fiction.

Many of them, whether conveyed through *Free Women* or through the Notebooks, are in effect a deeper and more radical examination and assessment of those of Martha Quest in the first three novels of *Children of Violence*. Anna herself has lived in Salisbury, Rhodesia, between 1939 and 1945, and the spell of the Communist 'collective' in that distant setting is re-created with great power and beauty (as always when Lessing is writing about Africa). Anna's more mature commitment to the Communist collective in London is also explored in considerable detail, as she performs all kinds of humdrum and uncongenial tasks for the Party, watches members who had once been eager young idealists degenerating into rigid and desiccated officials, and gradually becomes aware of the ruthlessness, evasions and hypocrisies of Communism in practice. Anna's decision to leave the Party and the comradeship it affords – at a human as well as a political level – is one of the most painful of the many crises that beset her; and Anna's attitude towards this phase of her life is close to Lessing's own. In Anna's case, the immediate effect of the loss of the political collective is a further assault on her mental stability. Her nerves are left raw and exposed. All the horrors of violence, social injustice, famine, war, and above all the ever-present threat of nuclear holocaust bear down on her more relentlessly than ever. When, in a trance-like state she watches her African experiences unrolling like a film, she recalls the great cloud of butterflies which had once hovered round the Mashopi hotel and sees it as:

a white flower opening slowly, under the deep steamy blue sky. Then a feeling of menace came into us, and we knew we had suffered a trick of light, had been deluded. We were looking at the explosion of a hydrogen bomb . . .

Lessing has described artists as 'the traditional interpreters of dreams and nightmares' – and in *The Golden Notebook* she shows Anna as their victim.

An essential constituent of her sufferings proceeds from the apparent hopelessness of her struggle to become a 'free' woman in a society still fixed in outworn patriarchal patterns – to which she herself still finds herself unconsciously contributing. In conversation with her friend Molly, she says:

I am always amazed in myself and in other women at the strength of our need to bolster men up . . . Women have this instinctive need to build a man up as a man . . . I suppose this is because real men become fewer and fewer.

And a little later she comments: 'What's the use of being free if they are not?' To see these remarks as points scored in the sex war, though, would be to miss the point altogether. What Anna is groping towards is the possibility of a new human condition growing out of the present chaos, of which the destructive imbalance in the relationships between the sexes is a part and a symptom. Thus in one of her sessions with her psychoanalyst (whom Anna and Molly call Mother Sugar) she insists that when she has a vision of 'a life that isn't full of hatred and fear and envy and competition every minute of the night and the day', she doesn't want to be told that this is merely 'the old dream of the golden age brought up to date', because today she feels that the dream is 'a million times more powerful because its possible, just as total destruction is possible. Probably *because* both are possible . . .' In the light of this possibility, the sex war becomes almost an irrelevance. It is significant, moreover, that in the Golden Notebook itself, which is intended to bring together and resolve the intellectual and psychic splintering represented by the other four Notebooks, the breakdown – seen, in spite of all its pain and horror, as a necessary process on the way to self-healing and new life – is shared between a man and a woman. As Lessing says in her Preface:

Anna and Saul Green the American . . . 'breakdown' into each other, into other people, break through the false patterns they have made of their pasts, the patterns and formulas they have made to shore up themselves and each other, dissolve . . .

The theme of mental breakdown and the kind of healing and insight it can bring was developed further in *The Four-gated City* (1969), the last of the *Children of Violence* sequence. Here Martha (now in London) finds herself intermittent mistress to her employer; nurse and companion to his wife Lynda, who is suffering from a serious mental illness; and substitute mother to the two Coldridge sons, Paul and Francis – in exactly the kind of tangled emotional situation, the same old woman's self-sacrificial trap that she had run away from Rhodesia to escape. To her surprise it is through her contact with the sick Lynda and her twilight world that she at last begins to glimpse the possibilities of a deeper kind of understanding, on an altogether different plane, the other side of madness. When she herself also begins 'to see visions and hear voices' she is at one and the same time terrified and grateful, realising that they are not merely 'symptoms' but may also be communications from deeper layers of the human consciousness that have hitherto been stifled.

The novel now takes a leap into a future in which the nightmare of nuclear disaster has actually arrived. Martha, who has escaped to an island off the coast of northern Scotland, is one of the survivors, and towards the end of her life she realises that a few of the children born after the catastrophe can 'see' and 'hear' things denied to ordinary people, able to communicate with each other by telepathy and apparently to look into the future. She feels they are beings who have somehow included the troubled history of the century 'in themselves and transcended it' and that 'they are our guardians'. The collective against which the individual rebels in this last book of the sequence is therefore the whole of modern human society – the product of 'the children of violence'. From them as a whole, it is implied, nothing can be expected, although certain individuals at the cost of intense suffering and perhaps madness may catch intimations of an altogether different future. In the main, though, salvation can only be looked for in some new human adaptation, an entirely new generation which has learned to cultivate or revive areas of the mind long forgotten or repressed.

The Four-Gated City obviously marks the beginning of Lessing's interest in a new kind of material, and a new fictional mode in which to express it, that culminated in her space-fiction series *Canopus in Argos: Archives* (1979–82). It is obvious, too, from her short preface to *Re. Colonised Planet 5: Shikasta* (1979), the first of the four novels, that she enjoyed the 'sense of exhilaration that comes from being set free into a larger scope, with more capacious possibilities and themes', and that she saw the whole phenomenon of science fiction as a welcome 'breaking of the bonds of the realistic novel', and an exciting symptom of the human mind 'being forced to expand'. Thus Lessing's ventures into space fiction are a species of myth-making whereby she could examine the themes of her earlier work in a wider perspective, freed from the immediate pressures of personality. A realisation that the identification between herself and her characters was becoming too painfully close and claustrophobic was perhaps one of the reasons that led her into the new mode. Another was that the myth-making lent itself particularly well to a broader examination of the relationship between the sexes and to a greater emphasis, already foreshadowed in *The Four-Gated City* (Lynda Coldridge in fact reappears in *Shikasta* as an agent of the benevolent galactic empire Canopus), on the special powers of women.

The three galactic empires of Lessing's sequence are all subject to the 'Plan'. What that may be it is impossible to say, but it is obvious that Canopus comes closest to fulfilling its mysterious intentions – and Canopus has reached its eminence by a near-perfect fusion of male and female principles, in which the powers associated specifically with women have received full scope. Pre-eminent among these powers is that of love, the main constituent of 'the rich and vigorous air' which Canopus had once supplied in abundance to Shikasta, in the happy days before 'the Catastrophe'. The

Canopeans have also developed to the highest degree the kind of feminine mental powers – still secretly cherished on Shikasta (which is of course our own benighted planet) by a few women, persecuted by men as witches. The Canopeans can see into the future, they communicate by means of telepathy, and their emissaries use mental powers to do their travelling. By contrast, those of Sirius, the neighbouring galactic empire, several stages behind Canopus in its development, employ space-ships and other forms of 'masculine' science and technology, and conduct their civilising 'experiments' on Shikasta in a traditional masculine and neo-colonial manner. These experiments, though prompted by self-interest, are benevolent in practice. Those inspired by Shammat, the evil planet are, however, entirely inhuman, dictated by an emotionless masculine intellectual curiosity, or by a desire to perfect weapons of destruction. One of the prominent symptoms of Shikasta's progressive deterioration moreover, is the decline in the status of women – as Ambien II, the top-ranking Sirian woman official (in *The Sirian Experiments*, 1981) finds in the course of her various missions to Shikasta (the action in the books is spread over millennia). On the last of these she can no longer assume the Shikastan forms of queen or female official, as she had done previously, but must resort to those of servant or courtesan – and she comments: 'the females of this culture were truly enslaved'.

In these books Lessing is nowhere suggesting that women are ipso facto superior to men – only that women have powers which the human race has so far undervalued to its cost. Moreover, in *The Marriages Between Zones Three, Four and Five* (1980), it is made clear that the gentle, indulgent and infinitely beguiling Zone Three, ruled by its queen Al'ith, no more represents the solution to the human dilemma than the archetypal male Zone Four, hierarchic, disciplined and inflexible under its warrior king Ben Ata. The marriage between Al'ith and Ben Ata symbolises a blending of feminine and masculine elements to the benefit of both Zones, though there is a further step (perhaps with sexual as well as cultural implications) when Ben Ata is ordered to leave Al'ith and marry the savage queen of the equally savage and backward Zone Five – while Al'ith, after her return to her own now much altered country, eventually enters some other unspecified region which transcends all the others.

The gradually developing love between Al'ith and Ben Ata is very different from the stormy and mutually hurtful relationships between men and women in Lessing's earlier novels, but it is accomplished with humour (a rare quality in her work) and not at all on the level of fantasy. In all these space fiction novels, fable is continually set in dramatic opposition to reality. In *Shikasta*, for instance, there are long narrative passages set in contemporary times and with contemporary backgrounds, some of them in Africa and London, which might have come from one of her earlier realistic novels; while many of the issues she dealt with in them – colonialism, left-wing politics, the Bomb, personal relationships and others – recur. In entering her new mode of space-fiction Lessing had not entirely abandoned the earlier one, and she returned to it without any sense of strain or discontinuity in *The Good Terrorist* (1985), the only too realistic portrait of a group of young terrorists, 'mothered' by the thirty-six year old drudge Alice, who lavishes her thwarted love on her equally lost brood and, with a terrible irony, gives them the domestic stability from which to perpetrate their outrages against a hated society. It is a powerful and disturbing presentation of a new and utterly negative 'collective', peopled by the present-day 'children of violence'.

The most lasting impression created by a reading of Lessing's work is that she has not only confronted the most painful issues of the contemporary world and striven to understand them more thoroughly and courageously than any other post-war novelist, but also that in the process she has taken the brunt of them upon herself with all the personal suffering that entails.

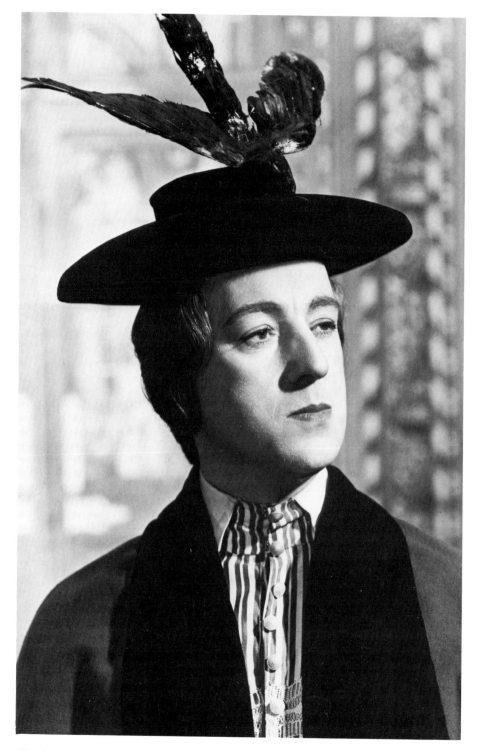

Alec Guinness as Lady Agatha in the Ealing comedy Kind Hearts and Coronets *(1949)*.

8 Film

NEIL SINYARD

Quality British cinema since the War has tended to be a struggle for supremacy and critical respect between two factions: the realists and the dreamers. The realists have taken fewer risks and have shown a gift for skilful literary adaptations that have enhanced the respectability of popular cinema. They have adhered to the three Rs of prestige national cinema: realism, rationalism and restraint, which have not only established the key of their emotional range but also their visual style. The dreamers have courted controversy by electing a very different set of priorities: an accent on style over subject-matter, a flair for full-blooded fantasy over dour documentary.

Each faction has its own attractions and disadvantages, and one can see these in a variety of examples of the immediate post-war period. The flamboyance of a Gainsborough costume drama like *The Wicked Lady* (1945) shows the spirit of the dreamer reduced to relatively mundane melodrama. Yet in a film like Michael Powell and Emeric Pressburger's *Black Narcissus* (1947), a dream-like drama of sexual hysteria in a convent, the visual majesty is overwhelming. 'You either ignore it, or you give in to it,' says one of the nuns about their physical and emotional situation. It is a statement that also applies to audiences of the film: if they 'give in' to the film's colour, tempo, and elemental emotions, the experience can be as intoxicating as a reading of *Wuthering Heights*. The realist tradition has similar highs and lows. It can veer between the plodding sincerity of Basil Dearden's earnest, unexciting *The Blue Lamp* (1949) and the imperishable suspense of Carol Reed's *The Third Man* (1949), in which Graham Greene's screenplay charts a story of evil exploitation and betrayed friendships against an expressive background of decadent, divided post-war Vienna.

David Lean

Of the British film-makers who consolidated their reputations immediately after 1945, no director has been alternately more deified and downgraded than David Lean. The only British film-maker to have won two directing

Oscars, for *The Bridge on the River Kwai* (1957) and *Lawrence of Arabia* (1962), Lean has been held up as a representative of tasteful cinema craftsmanship and impeccable story-telling that have been an acknowledged influence on Hollywood directors as far apart as Billy Wilder and Steven Spielberg. Yet for many critics, Lean has also been the cinema's archetype of academic impersonality, whose tastefulness is exceeded only by his absence of passion or style, and who is heavily dependent on his writers and literary sources. Thus he makes scrupulous, safe adaptations of, for example, Noël Coward's *Blithe Spirit* (1945), Charles Dickens's *Great Expectations* (1946) and *Oliver Twist* (1948) and E.M. Forster's *A Passage to India* (1984), and draws on the structural skills of writer Robert Bolt for the dramatic substance of *Lawrence of Arabia*, *Dr Zhivago* (1965) and *Ryan's Daughter* (1970). Yet the intriguing thing about Lean's films is the very personal way in which they show the unexpected struggle between repression and romanticism that beats in the hearts of the British bourgeoisie. No film exhibits this better than Lean's masterpiece *Brief Encounter* (1945).

Based on Noël Coward's one-act play, *Still Life*, *Brief Encounter* tells a seemingly simple story of a middle-class housewife Laura (Celia Johnson) who briefly encounters a doctor Alec (Trevor Howard) at a railway station when he helps her remove a piece of grit from her eye. From this inauspicious beginning, they fall in love, but both are married and eventually Alec takes a job in Johannesburg and Laura returns to her husband. On the surface it is the quintessential British realist film: low-key, restrained, and an index of the repressed national character – a love story in which nothing actually happens. The performances of Celia Johnson and Trevor Howard are a model of the kind of delicate decorum that seethes with, yet eventually smothers, more volatile desires. For many it exemplifies what is most exasperating about British cinema, and even the national character: the awkwardness in dealing with emotion, the yielding to the pressures of conformity. Yet there is a lot of the dreamer as well as the realist in Lean, and *Brief Encounter* is by no means as simple as it seems.

The ostensible realism of the film is quite deceptive. The comic love affair in the station buffet between Stanley Holloway and Joyce Carey is not realistic background but ironic counterpoint, mocking the anguished love affair at the centre of the film. Milford Junction Station is not a realistic backdrop but a highly stylised setting which encapsulates a whole variety of key emotions in the film – routine, isolation, the scream of emotional pain, the sweep of adulterous passion.

If Lean were merely celebrating middle-class inhibition which has been the traditional way of discussing *Brief Encounter*, there are two aspects of the film that are quite incomprehensible: the use of Rachmaninov's music, and the heroine's narration. Far from signalling restraint, these devices deliberately intensify the passion under the surface. It is particularly important to remember that the events of the film are seen through Laura's eyes. Her internal monologue becomes an unwitting self-portrait that begins to reveal another side to this seemingly ordinary, respectable housewife. Romantic imagination is the quality above all others that is emphasised about her. She loves reading romantic fiction, goes to romantic films, and loves romantic

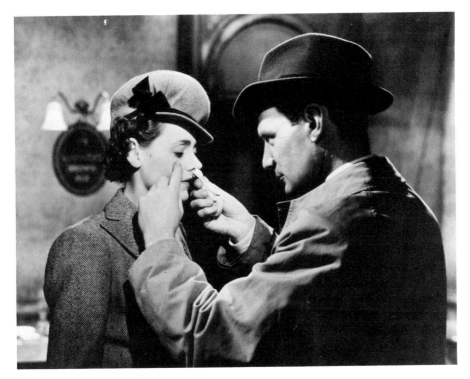

Trevor Howard and Celia Johnson in David Lean's Brief Encounter *(1945)*.

music, in contrast to her husband (Cyril Raymond) who at one stage has to turn down the music on the radio and hence modify his wife's internal rhapsodising. She knows romantic poetry, and the one time she can help her husband with his *Times* crossword puzzle is the moment when he is unable to complete a quotation from Keats: the missing word, which Laura supplies, is 'romance'. It is this word, in fact, which triggers off Laura's reverie: for her husband the word is only 'something – in seven letters.' It fits in with delirium, he says.

Delirium is a surprisingly common state of mind of Lean's protagonists – one thinks of Pip's fever in *Great Expectations*, Colonel Nicholson's delusions in *Bridge on the River Kwai*, Fleda's hallucinations in the Marabar Caves in *A Passage to India*. *Brief Encounter* has less the outlines of surface realism than of subjective reverie, with the suspicion that this grand romance could all be a dream anyway. Laura is swept along by a passionate nature so twisted by convention and constraint that it can only express itself through an accompanying guilt and shame. One can almost see Laura as an English Anna Karenina, but within typically English restraints that fall short of Anna's abandonment: unlike Tolstoy's heroine, she *almost* has an affair, *almost* deserts her children, *almost* throws herself under a train. 'Whatever your dream was – it wasn't a very happy one, was it?' says her husband towards the end. Indeed it was not: it has undermined the very structure of Laura's existence.

On the surface, *Brief Encounter* might appear a sensitive suburban drama about the morbidity and moral obligation of being English. But beneath the surface, *Brief Encounter* seems almost a subversive film, a desolating commentary on the sterility of bourgeois life that gives rise to the frustrated longings of a Laura and her desire for romantic escape. Lean always stayed within the bounds of the middle-class experience and emotions he knew and trusted, but his greatness as a director comes probably from his ambivalence towards the emotional temperateness that goes with being English and his understanding of the vitality as well as the danger of the romantic dream.

Ealing Studios and Alexander Mackendrick

There might not seem to be much that links the work of David Lean and that of Ealing Studios in the forties. After all, Lean was an individualist whilst Ealing prided itself on its team spirit, nurtured under the benevolent paternalism of Michael Balcon. Indeed, when one thinks of Ealing, one thinks of a kind of shared excellence between actors like Alec Guinness and Stanley Holloway, writers like T.E.B. Clarke (*The Blue Lamp, The Lavender Hill Mob*) and William Rose (*The Maggie, The Ladykillers*) and cameramen like Douglas Slocombe (*Kind Hearts and Coronets, The Man in the White Suit*). Yet there is a certain continuity of tone and spirit between Lean and Ealing at this time: a preference for realism, middle-class values, and a desire to project an image of the British character. But the differences are more significant, particularly the difference in tone between Lean's sobriety and Ealing's urbanity. Henry Cornelius's *Passport to Pimlico* (1949) might satirise British bureaucracy, and Charles Crichton's *The Lavender Hill Mob* (1951) might take the law for a ride but, in both cases, the tone is one of affectionate whimsy rather than any kind of critical anger.

Nevertheless, there were two directors in the Ealing stable who took a more quizzical attitude to the studio's celebration of the endearing quaintness of the English character. Robert Hamer's *Kind Hearts and Coronets* (1949) is a black comedy of murder and revenge that delights through the polished prose of its writing, the perfect poise of its performances, and its mordant observation of sexual indiscretion and social snobbery. More consistent than Hamer was Alexander Mackendrick. His four Ealing comedies – *Whisky Galore* (1949), *The Man in the White Suit* (1951), *The Maggie* (1954), and *The Ladykillers* (1955) – are all quite exceptional. Their originality stems from their status as 'problem comedies', films of cruelty and cunning as well as charm that end ambivalently and which deny any kind of comfortable audience identification.

Mackendrick's own favourite is *The Man in the White Suit*, about a secluded Cambridge scientist Sidney Stratton (Alec Guinness) who invents a fabric that will not wear out. This might be of benefit to the customer but it is ruinous to both industry and workforce, and unions and management unite in their attempt to stop Sidney from making his discovery known. It is the typical Ealing saga of an innocent at large in an experienced world ('You're not even born yet', Sidney is told) and almost bringing it down.

Sidney's innocence is highlighted by his white suit, which makes him, he thinks, a 'knight in shining armour'. By contrast, the other workers are dressed in neutral grey, whilst the employers wear funereal black. In a sense, these signify Mackendrick's moral shadings of the basic situation. Sidney's white signifies his innocent idealism but also his naive unworldliness; the greyness of the workers is a comment on their routine lives and their pragmatic values for survival; the dark-suited employers are personifications of sleek privilege, and not averse to a spot of sexual blackmail when other attempts to persuade Sidney to give up his invention have failed. The company head, Sir John (Ernest Thesiger) is a wheezing asthmatic who seems to have strayed in from a horror film, first glimpsed in shadow in the back of his limousine with only his 'dead hand of monopoly' visible in the shot. As it happens, Sidney's suit turns out not to be indestructible. He is dismissed, and the impression is given that working relations will return very much to what they were. Nevertheless, Sidney's experience provides the basis for an unusually incisive study of industrial relations as well as a brilliant comedy about failures in communication.

It might not be too fanciful, in fact, to see *The Man in the White Suit* as an allegory of the film industry in general and of Ealing in particular. One suspects a strong identification between Mackendrick and Sidney Stratton. Stratton is not averse to diverting business funds for his own uses if he feels he is on to something important: similarly, Mackendrick was not averse to

A scene from the Ealing comedy The Man in the White Suit *(1951) with Michael Gough (left), Howard Marion-Crawford (right), Cecil Parker, and Ernest Thesiger (centre).*

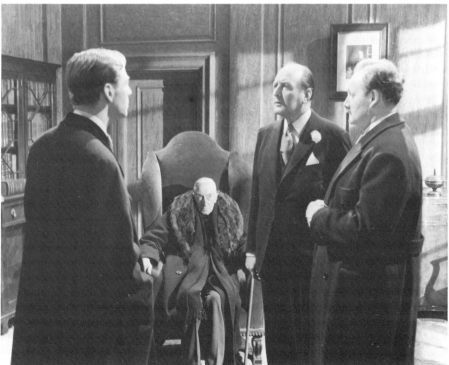

stretching rehearsal time and shooting schedules to achieve his ends. Both
Sidney and Mackendrick are perfectionists in industries given over to profit.
Both of them are not simply trying to invent and market a product: they wish
to produce something permanent from their labours. Both have to
accommodate themselves to an industrial structure which will humour them
up to a point but basically want a return on their investment. In that sense
the textile plant of Birnley Mills in *The Man in the White Suit* is not that
different from Ealing itself: indeed, Cecil Parker as the head of the firm, Mr
Birnley, bears a striking physical resemblance to Michael Balcon. *The Man in
the White Suit* is thus a debate on the fate of individualism within a
capitalistic framework, whether that framework is the textile or the film
industry. Read in that way, the ending of the film is quite complex. Although
Mackendrick was still to make three more films for Ealing – *Mandy* (1952),
The Maggie and *The Ladykillers* – the fate of Sidney seems to anticipate his:
he will soon be departing through the company gates. On the one hand, it is
a daring and defiant departure, for Sidney is having another idea and
Mackendrick has got his eyes on Hollywood. Yet just as Sidney's
inventiveness has been squashed in *The Man in the White Suit*, so
Mackendrick's radicalism has been contained within Ealing boundaries, and
the film is finally a pessimistic allegory of the artist.

Mackendrick left Ealing after making that most bizarre and brilliant of
British film comedies, *The Ladykillers*, and indeed the days of Ealing Studios
as a force in the British film industry were numbered. Its tasteful bourgeois
comedies were soon to seem tame in comparison with the upcoming *Carry
On* series at the end of the fifties, which infused British film comedy with the
coarseness of the picture postcard. As a studio with a distinctive style, Ealing
was also to be upstaged in public esteem by Hammer. With films like *The
Quatermass Experiment* (1955) and *Dracula* (1958), Hammer brought
extravagance and red-blooded fantasy into the British film.

Most significantly perhaps, the British society that Ealing films had
celebrated was fast becoming an anachronism. The rebellious voices of John
Osborne in *Look Back in Anger*, Arnold Wesker in *The Kitchen* and Shelagh
Delaney in *A Taste of Honey* were being heard in the theatre. In the novel, a
new sub-Lawrentian group of writers like John Braine (*Room at the Top*),
Alan Sillitoe (*Saturday Night and Sunday Morning*) and Stan Barstow (*A
Kind of Loving*) were achieving enormous popularity with their earthy and
outspoken portrayals of working-class life. All of these works were to be
turned into films in the next few years. Politically the Macmillan period was
fading into the Wilson years, and the films reflected that, with an emphasis
on empirical rather than imperialist themes. Around the corner was the film
era of L-shaped rooms and disgruntled long-distance runners, the period
promiscuity of Tom Jones (in Tony Richardson's 1963 Oscar-winning film of
the Fielding novel) and the sexual athleticism of Sean Connery's James Bond:
in short, the short-lived explosion of Swingin' London and permissive
Britain.

Several eminent British directors made major films about British society in
the 1960s. John Schlesinger directed *Darling* (1965); Lindsay Anderson made
This Sporting Life (1962) and *If* (1968). Yet it is possible to argue that the

most perceptive films about this era in Britain were made by two emigré Americans, Richard Lester and Joseph Losey. In such Lester films as *A Hard Day's Night* (1964), *The Knack* (1965), *How I Won the War* (1967) and *The Bed-Sitting Room* (1969), one can chart the shift of a whole nation's mood, from bouncy iconoclasm to weary cynicism. Joseph Losey's films of the period are equally incisive anatomies of British society but aesthetically even more ambitious.

Joseph Losey

His career in America abruptly halted by his being blacklisted during the McCarthy era, Losey had come to England in the fifties with the reputation for making visually striking melodramas about socially explosive themes. During the decade this flair was to be revealed in films such as *Time Without Pity* (1956), *Blind Date* (1959) and *The Criminal* (1960), where tawdry thriller material is transformed by striking insights into British class and character. But Losey's most prestigious work was to come through his association with two men: the actor Dirk Bogarde, with whom he worked on five films, including *The Servant* (1963), *King and Country* (1964) and *Accident* (1967); and the writer, Harold Pinter, with whom he worked on three (*The Servant*, *Accident* and the 1971 adaptation of L.P. Hartley's *The Go-Between*). Bogarde's acting subtlety and Pinter's elliptical eloquence were to provide a perfect foil to the probing lucidity of Losey's camera. These are all remarkable films, challenging the hypocrisies they see implicit in class attitudes and social institutions. They are also conspicuously adult films, penetrating and pessimistic studies of the frailty of relationships and humanity's tragically limited capacity for self-knowledge. Perhaps the best of them is *Accident*.

Based on the novel by Nicholas Mosley, *Accident* is basically a character study of a middle-aged Oxford philosophy don, Stephen (Dirk Bogarde) who is subliminally aware of being at the crossroads of his life – in terms of his marriage, his career, his future. The accident of the title is a car crash that kills one of his students, William (Michael York) who has been driving to see him with his fiancée, Anna (Jacqueline Sassard). The accident takes place at the beginning of the film and in flashback we learn of the emotional complications that have been gathering, notably Stephen's secret desire for Anna and his discovery that she is having an affair with his best friend and academic rival, Charley (Stanley Baker). The accident seems somehow an inevitable outcome for wary and deceitful characters who are on an emotional collision course.

The role of women in *Accident* is secondary. Anna is merely a catalyst for the action: Stephen's wife Rosalind (Vivien Merchant) is simply the voice of good sense. Mainly *Accident* is an ironic, sometimes humorous and sometimes horrifying study of the conflict of male egos, where Stephen feels intimidated by William's youthful vitality and threatened by Charley's media popularity and sexual success. The film is also an analysis of the split between intellect and emotion, where characters know their own minds but not their own

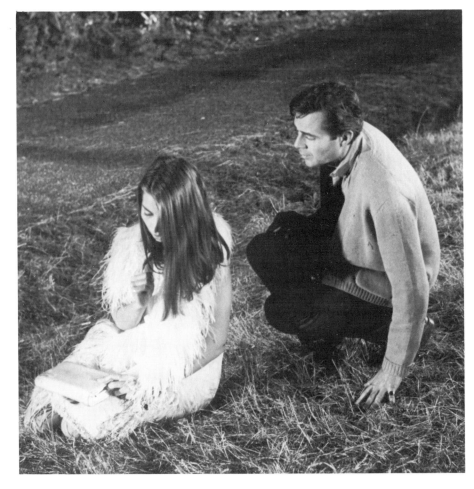

Dirk Bogard and Jacqueline Sassard in Joseph Losey's Accident *(1967).*

hearts. Losey described it as a film about a kind of moral bankruptcy, an indictment of an intelligentsia who have every resource of civilisation and who can pontificate grandly about large philosophical questions without having any idea of how to cope with their own lives.

The maturity of the themes is one of the principal pleasures of *Accident*, but equally pleasurable is the way in which the film is done. Both Pinter's dialogue and Losey's direction are masterly in the way they imply a tension and horror lurking beneath the seeming innocence of the words. Nothing is underlined, and yet every detail – Rosalind's conspicuously unoccupied chair during the antics of the tennis match, the brutal way Anna pulls down the spider's web, Stephen's touching of the rocking horse after he has discovered Charley and Anna in the bedroom – is pregnant with meaning. One sequence, where all the major characters gather at Stephen's home for a leisurely Sunday lunch that stretches into a drunken Sunday supper, is one of the most precisely plotted of modern cinema. Another sequence, where Stephen's mind seems to be collapsing two separate conversations into one –

one with his wife, one with Charley's wife – shows a complete mastery of intricate film form. As a study of middle-aged crisis, of marriage and infidelity, the barrenness of so-called civilised behaviour and the tension between the surface order of English life and its underlying passion, *Accident* has a surprising amount in common with *Brief Encounter*. Yet the difference between the two films is equally significant. Lean's classical craftsmanship is the art that conceals art. Losey's stylisation is more self-conscious, a deliberate attempt to raise the reputation of British film by emulating the method and achievement of acknowledged European masters like Michelangelo Antonioni and Alain Resnais. It could have seemed impossibly pretentious, but *Accident* has the gleaming intelligence to justify such pretensions.

Unfortunately, despite critical esteem, Losey's most ambitious English films were not commercially successful. He was to leave the country in the 1970s and make films in France, returning to England to direct his final film before his death in 1984, an elegiac and affecting adaptation of Nell Dunn's play, *Steaming* (1984). Losey's disillusionment at the end of the sixties was symptomatic of a more general crisis in the British film industry. By then, the film boom was over, and the Americans were withdrawing investment from the British cinema. The seventies was to be a decade marked more by individual eccentricity than by studio continuity. A number of distinctive talents did succeed in making unusual films – one thinks of Ken Loach's *Kes* (1969) and the Bill Douglas trilogy (*My Childhood*, 1972; *My Ain Folk*, 1974; *My Way Home*, 1978) – but these tended to be films of a specialised appeal for a very limited audience. Other talented directors, like John Boorman (*Deliverance*, 1972), found the horizons much broader in America. But one British-based director began at this time to make an international reputation: Nicolas Roeg.

Nicolas Roeg

Like David Lean, for whom he had worked on the second-unit of *Lawrence of Arabia* and *Dr Zhivago*, Nicolas Roeg is a child of the British film industry. He had begun as a clapper-boy and worked his way up to cameraman, photographing some of the most visually distinguished films of the sixties, including Francois Truffaut's *Fahrenheit 451* (1966) and Richard Lester's *Petulia* (1968). Roeg's own directing debut, sharing the director's credit with Donald Cammell, was on *Performance* (1970), a remarkable study of the disintegration of the sixties' egalitarian dream into drugs and anarchy. His subsequent films have not betrayed that promise. The originality of the style – the striking use of slow motion, fragmented narratives, subliminal images – has been matched by a similar boldness of theme and material. Films like *Walkabout* (1971), *Don't Look Now* (1973), *The Man Who Fell to Earth* (1976) and *Bad Timing* (1980) are glimpses into another psychic world, afforded to leading characters of moral conservatism and emotional vulnerability who will either be liberated or destroyed by this exciting, yet dangerous vision. The furious emotions and fervent sexuality of Roeg's films give one the impression of a cinematic D.H. Lawrence.

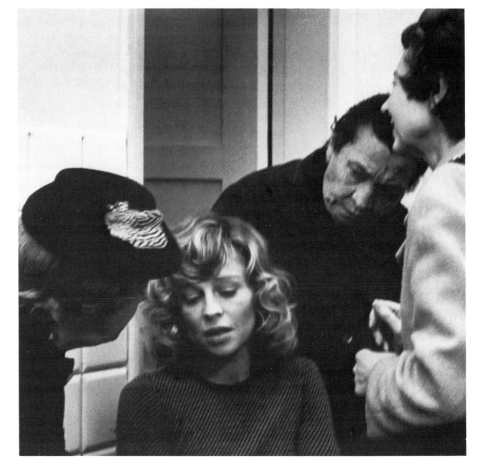

*Julie Christie with the 'weird sisters' (Celia Matania, left, and Hilary Mason, right) in
Nicolas Roeg's* Don't Look Now *(1973). COURTESY OF PARAMOUNT
PICTURES CORPORATION.*

Roeg's most popular film to date is his adaptation of the Daphne du
Maurier short story, *Don't Look Now*, and it is still his best, a psychological
thriller worthy of Hitchcock. Horror breaks into a normal Sunday afternoon
of a married couple, John Baxter (Donald Sutherland) and his wife Laura
(Julie Christie) when their daughter is accidentally drowned in a nearby
pond. The drowning is shown in a chilling opening sequence, made all the
more uneasy by brilliant montage which makes clear that the husband has a
premonition of the disaster before it happens. During a stay in Venice, in
which Baxter is restoring the mosaics of an old church, Laura comes into
contact with two weird sisters, one of whom is blind but who claims to have
second sight. She tells Laura that John also has the gift but that he is in
terrible danger if he stays in Venice. The tension this creates within the
marriage is intensified by a series of mysterious murders taking place in
Venice, and by John's recurrent vision of a mysterious hooded figure in red
that reminds him of his dead daughter and who was first glimpsed on a slide
Baxter was inspecting immediately before the drowning.

Roeg's film can be compared to Losey's *Accident*. As in the Losey film, there are audacious jumps between present and future, as time seems to collapse in confusion inside the hero's head, and an opening tragic accident that scatters people's lives into disarray. It is also interesting to compare Roeg's vision of Venice in *Don't Look Now* with that of Losey's in *Eve* (1962), where it is a city of baroque decadence, and David Lean's in *Summer Madness* (1955), where it is the city of summery romance. Roeg's Venice is the 'abhorrent, green slippery city' of D.H. Lawrence's poem, 'Pomegranates'. Venice is a protagonist in this film, a city that is stagnant and submerging (the motifs of drowning and hidden depths are crucial in the film) and a city in peril, like the hero.

Conclusions

There is an important tradition of British cinema to which *Don't Look Now* belongs, and that is the tradition of the horror film. It shares a number of characteristics and themes with stylish predecessors. Like the Ealing compendium *Dead of Night* (1945), it has the theme of 'I've been here before'. Like Michael Powell's notorious yet remarkable film, *Peeping Tom* (1959), it is about watching and voyeurism; and like Jack Clayton's *The Innocents* (1961), a subtle adaptation of Henry James's *The Turn of the Screw*, it involves threats to innocence and the death of children. *Don't Look Now* is the most distinguished of this list, but its context is important, for the horror film has made a significant contribution to British film culture, highlighting and emphasising elements that are not associated with British film at all.

The first of these is colour. Classic British film has tended to come in shades of grey: documentary in the thirties; David Lean, Carol Reed and Olivier's *Hamlet* in the forties; Ealing comedy, Free Cinema, the New Wave of the sixties. The emotions are grey too: subdued, controlled, ironical, repressed. But Powell and Pressburger's films, the horror rhapsodies of Hammer, the rich brews of Roeg come in colour, which gives a powerful emotional coating to the films. They pump blood into the pale cheeks of British cinema. Like Hitchcock, Roeg uses colour sensually in his films. This is the other important element which the British horror film infuses into the national cinema: sensuality. Indeed, one could say that passion generally comes under the guise of horror in British films: sexuality and fear are curiously linked. It was mentioned before that the greatest love story in British cinema is Lean's *Brief Encounter*, in which nothing happens. It is a curious coincidence that Laura in *Don't Look Now* (who also has the same name as Lean's heroine) meets the two sisters in exactly the same way as Celia Johnson meets Trevor Howard in *Brief Encounter* (grit in the eye). What the meeting leads to is not frustration, as in the Lean film, but a liberation of feeling in the heroine and the most passionate and beautiful love scene in British cinema. *Don't Look Now* is, in many ways, a defiant repudiation of the David Lean tradition. It is full-blooded, violent, unrestrained. It shows the limits of rationalism and civilisation. In heart-stopping sequences like the opening tragedy, the love scene, the scene in the

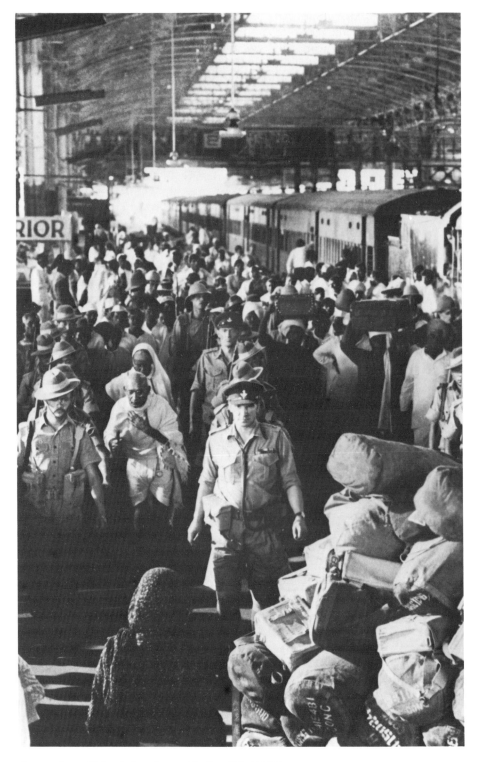

A scene from Richard Attenborough's Gandhi *(1982)*.

church where Baxter almost falls to his death, our own visual perceptions are manipulated by montage and memorably shaken and enlarged.

In a way, Lean and Roeg represent the two extremes of British film artistry: between a tasteful, restrained, literary sensibility on the one side, and fire, poetry and passion on the other. Moving into the 1980s, one can see how each of the traditions is being maintained. The Oscar-winning productions of David Puttnam and Richard Attenborough, namely *Chariots of Fire* (1981) and *Gandhi* (1982), are squarely in the David Lean tradition. Alternatively, films like Neil Jordan's reinterpretation of the Red Riding Hood myth in terms of adolescent sexuality, *The Company of Wolves* (1984), or Terry Gilliam's *Brazil* (1985), a hallucinatory alignment of the worlds of Monty Python and George Orwell, are closer to the mad poetry of Nicolas Roeg. There is an equally significant group of idiosyncratic directors in between, of course. It is heartening to see the Mackendrick legacy live on in the wry comedies of Bill Forsyth (*Local Hero, Comfort and Joy*) and to feel something of Losey's brand of intelligence and humanism in the work of Michael Radford (*Another Time Another Place*, 1984).

It should be said that British film-makers have had a lot stacked against them over the years. Successive governments have given no encouragement in the form of substantial subsidies; audiences have continued to decline; the quality of British television has provided severe competition; and the monopolistic distribution system has perpetually squeezed out the more experimental, unconventional film-maker, like Stephen Frears, Mike Leigh or Peter Greenaway. It should also be said that British film has never really been afforded much intellectual prestige in its own country. Film educationalists were very slow even to acknowledge, let alone seriously examine, the richness of their own film culture. Happily, that situation has changed in recent years, and it is no longer possible to argue that British film is strong on acting and verbal substance but short on visual style. David Lean, Alexander Mackendrick, Joseph Losey and Nicolas Roeg are only some of the major directors who have attempted to catch on celluloid the collective unconscious of the British people, and who have made our post-war national cinema one of the richest and most rewarding to study.

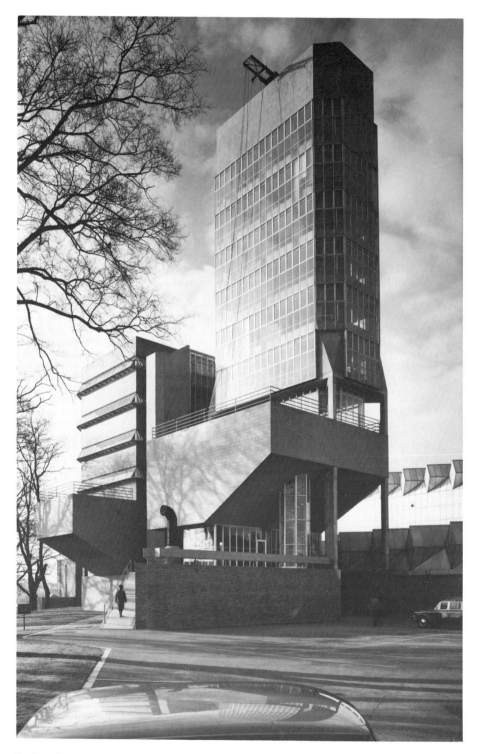

Engineering Building, University of Leicester (1959–63). James Stirling and James Gowan.

9 Architecture

JOSEPH RYKWERT

Introduction

When peace broke out in 1945, physical reconstruction was everybody's priority. About half a million dwellings were lost: there were vast mounds of rubble in all the major cities, but especially in London and the industrial Midlands. 'London pride', a weed also rightly called 'none-too-pretty', flourished on the ruins and was hymned by Noel Coward. Reconstruction inevitably implied planning of course. Planning was seen as the business of civil servants and economists, but also of architects – who became the specialists, the technicians of the rebuilding of the country.

Architects had gone into the planning business long before the War. In fact post-war rebuilding was – in a sense – the physical realisation of the reconstruction which the planners of the thirties already considered essential. A number of planners and architects made independent proposals, of which the most radical perhaps was the MARS Group plan for London, prepared by young architects just before the war, though not published until 1942. Although the proposal for a London grouped round an east–west spinal parkway, with eight 'fingers' opening to the south and north was ignored in the official reconstruction schemes, it represented the ideas of the most important group of architects who were to be involved in the business after the war.

Reconstruction was also planned under official patronage: in the year of Munich the government of Neville Chamberlain appointed a Royal Commission chaired by Sir Anderson Montagu-Barlow, to consider the distribution of industrial population. Although it did not make very firm recommendations, the minority report demanded a central planning authority and the building of satellite towns. In 1943 a new ministry of Town and Country Planning was created to implement such a policy.

Local government was dragged into the act. Lord Reith, from the Ministry of Works, appointed Sir Patrick Abercrombie, the doyen of British town planners, to prepare a plan for the London County Council with the Council's own architect, J.H. Forshaw, which was published in 1943, and extended (in his name alone) over a much larger area for the new Ministry of Planning and other authorities a year later. Both plans contained specific architectural projects, involving (particularly in the first report) high slab-blocks surrounded by lower buildings, flats, shops, terraced and semi-detached houses, of the kind which were to typify British building in the fifties and sixties – as well as definite proposals, such as the development of an entertainment–cultural centre on the south bank of the river round Waterloo bridge, which was in fact carried out. Both versions recommended decentralising the capital and reinforcing the peripheral districts, the 'neighbourhoods' and set the tone of much post-war planning. Moreover, the structuring of London by a series of ring-roads, crossed by radial arteries, made a kind of spider's web in which relatively traffic-free 'precincts' remained enmeshed, even after both types of roads became motorways.

The planners did not have it all their own way. Some of the older architects looked to Sir Edwin Lutyens, and his plan for the City of London. This report was revised as an 'academic' plan, in the worst sense of the word, in 1942. Lutyens, whose death in 1944 left the 'old guard' without an obvious leader after the War, was a 'classicist', but the senior 'gothicist' Sir Giles Gilbert Scott – whose Liverpool Cathedral, the winning design in a competition of 1904, was still building when he died in 1960 – was active: he had in fact compromised his 'gothicism' by a certain 'modernism' during the thirties: Battersea Power Station (1932/4) and Waterloo Bridge (1937/42) were often quoted as examples of tradition (at least, traditional materials) adapted to modern function.

Of the 'moderns', the most important had been involved in the MARS group and its plan. Maxwell Fry, who had designed Impington Village College in Cambridgeshire with Walter Gropius, and F.R.S. Yorke, who had worked in partnership with a contemporary, Frederick Gibberd, as well as another well-known refugee from Hungary (via Germany), Marcel Breuer, were best known: Yorke perhaps better for books than buildings. Two *émigrés* were also well-established: Ernö Goldfinger (a Hungarian who reached London via Paris and the studio of the great French architect Auguste Perret) and Berthold Lubetkin, a Russian who also reached London via Paris and had been the animating presence in what was perhaps the most interesting pre-war architectural office, Tecton. The office of Connell, Ward and Lucas was to have a lasting but covert role. Colin Lucas, a New Zealander, who had worked at the Building Research Station – a government establishment which was to regulate building matters in the immediate post-war period almost despotically – moved to the London County Council architects' office in 1951.

Many younger architects had, like Lucas, seen war service in some government agency or been involved in quasi-military activities: camouflage, fortifications, munitions factories. The moment the Blitz started, in spring 1940, the re-housing of the bombed-out became an urgent problem, and parts of the munitions industry were harnessed early on to the production of 'temporary' – which proved to be very long-lasting – prefabricated bungalows, of which five variants were manufactured. The very tight planning of these single-storey homes became something of an obsession with

British post-war house-builders, and while it produced some very sensible planning reforms and building regulations, it also led to excesses: the unquestioning acceptance of the two-up, two-down house type as a staple of post-war building, and the conviction of planners that they could foresee every detail of the future use of a house – as if it would never change – from the placing of the cat's basket to that of the cottage piano in the front parlour. These planning types, given wide publicity through government manuals, were also perpetuated by various extensions of wartime manufacturing techniques into the building industry – the part-prefabricated house which Frederick Gibberd designed for the British Iron and Steel Federation is an example.

The morale of British architects was high: they had the confidence of the country, they would 'build the future'. This attitude was certainly seconded by both main political parties and by the Civil Service. In spite of the austerity programme which was instituted by the first post-war Labour administration, rebuilding and new building was the economic priority.

Planning New Towns

Only two years after the official end of hostilities, in 1947, the policy advocated in the wartime reports and plans was incorporated into the New Towns Act which set up the first institutional corporations under which these towns were to develop independently, free of external restrictions (see chapter 5 on 'The New Towns'). By 1950 eight New Towns had been planned and were building round London, and six more further west and north. They were emphatically conceived as full towns – much as the earlier garden towns had been – and their industrial potential given active encouragement (in the shape of subsidies and tax remissions) by central government. Success was slow, partly because industrialists did not share the planners' faith, but none the less the New Towns grew steadily. Everything was done to avoid the character of the dormitory suburb. The main public spaces were conceived as 'precincts' isolated from traffic, and 'neighbourhoods' were also designed in such a way that through traffic was excluded altogether; each of them, composed of low-rise, and on the whole, low-density housing, centred on a public building, school, church or shopping area which was to act as a focus for the community, a kind of planning developed thirty years earlier in the USA by Clarence Perry, though it had its origin in the garden cities. In the USA another planner, Clarence Stein, had systematically separated pedestrians and automobiles in his plan for Radburn in New Jersey – the place gave its name to that kind of planning. The notion of a traffic-free enclave was also important in the many town plans (Glasgow, including 'greater' Glasgow, Bath, Hull, Plymouth) which Abercrombie, and another, younger planner, Thomas Sharp (Exeter) prepared at the end of the War. It has remained a near-obsessive concern of planners and architects. And in fact there is a close parallel between the 'precincts', which Abercrombie had proposed in his two London plans (and which were included only sporadically within the proposed road-mesh) and the 'neighbourhoods' planted on near-virgin ground in the new towns.

The urban character of these new towns depended not only on the presence of industry, but also on public space and public buildings. While it was generally agreed that the new towns offered an acceptable standard of amenity and fair employment prospects, no great claims have ever been made for their architecture. The buildings were designed in part by corporation offices, and in part by independent architects. This pattern of patronage was characteristic of the period after 1945.

Prefabrication and CLASP

Though building by public agencies became so important, buildings of a public nature were pushed into second place in the immediate post-war period. Town-halls, even when badly bombed, could be patched up or given temporary additions, while the new emphasis on schooling up to the late teens, as well as the rapidly rising birth-rate, required an immediate response from local government, which was expected to provide the school buildings for this new influx. While some local authorities were still relying on pre-war procedures and techniques, others, notably the small home county of Hertfordshire, attempted a long-term and adventurous policy. An alliance between the very enterprising county educational officer, John Newsom and the county architect, C.H. Aslin, produced a programme for the building of prefabricated metal-framed schools, which was to become a model for several other counties, notably Nottinghamshire, though none achieved the refinement and accomplishment of later Hertfordshire examples such as those designed by Bruce Martin. With time this approach was seen as a matter of national importance and a co-ordination of the various schemes was undertaken under the aegis of the Ministry of Education, Stirrat Johnson-Marshall, who had been much involved in the development of the Hertfordshire schools, became architect to the ministry in 1948. Heavily industrialised, the metal-framed, prefabricated school building system came to be known as CLASP (Consortium of Local Authorities Special Programme; there was also a further improved version, SCOLA). It became the admiration of the world and remained the norm of school-building for over a decade. For a while CLASP was even considered a viable export, and attempts were made to re-calibrate the system, which had been set up in imperial measurements, to the metric's system. One or two govenments (notably the Mexican) attempted, not wholly successfully, to emulate the British example. In later years it was adapted to larger buildings, most extensively for one of the earliest of the new universities, at York.

Housing in London

The replacement and improvement of housing stock was however the most obvious and pressing architectural task, and London, one of the largest of the world cities as well as one of the most bombed, became a workshop in which

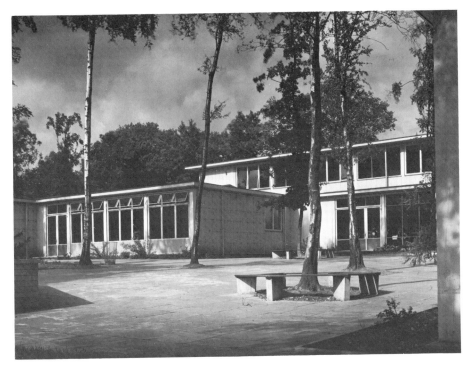

Pentley Park School, Welwyn Garden City, Hertfordshire (1955–6). Hertfordshire County Architects' Office.

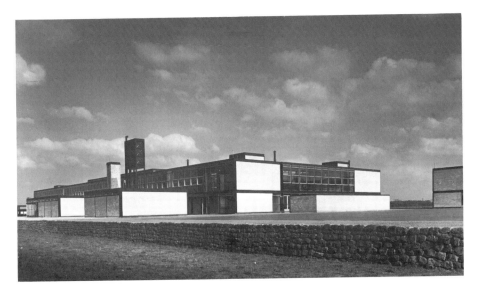

Hunstanton Secondary School, Norfolk (1954). Peter and Alison Smithson.

many ways of coping with the task were tried. The County Council office became the natural centre of all this activity, and consequently architects from all over the country and later the world gravitated to it. At the end of the War the younger designers were mostly concerned to evolve a 'popular' architecture. Some were doctrinaire left-wingers who were looking for an architectural equivalent of Stalinist social-realism and saw the only possible precedent for this in nineteenth-century working-class housing such as the Peabody building estates; while others saw a quite different kind of popular architecture based on late thirties and wartime Swedish housing practice, where the office of the Co-operative Association provided a model for emulation, both of the work and the organisation. The brick-faced high-rises with wood-slatted balconies, the wood-framed double windows, the banks of flower-boxes which agreeably domesticated the flat roofs seemed to make point blocks palatable. It was a manner practised by a number of talented Swedish architects with more or less success; their English emulators called this the 'New Empiricism'.

The first important housing scheme in London was the result of a competition run by the Westminster City Council for the terrain between Lupus Street and the Thames (now known as Churchill Gardens) in 1946. The winning scheme, by Philip Powell and Hidalgo Moya adapted the 'new empiricist' look to the larger scale and the industrial materials of post-war Britain: and by that transformation robbed the manner of some of its charm. But the scheme was much refined and hardened over a decade of design, and the preservation of older buildings within the scheme was unusual and welcome.

The demand for housing and the stiff pre-war organisation meant that the Council offices did not immediately go into a new kind of production. But in 1949, as a result of some sharp criticism (primarily by J.M. Richards, of whom more below) and the appointment of a new head to the housing section, there was rapid change. Under the command of Colin Lucas, the first new estate was built quickly in Putney (Ackroyden) and work was begun on the very much larger piece of land at Alton East, in Roehampton (which is the subject of a separate chapter: see pp. 279–87). It is very difficult to assess individual contributions in the planning of these collective enterprises. Alton East was commanded by Rosemary Stjernstedt, Alton West by Colin Lucas again. But the neo-empiricist ethos was promoted by an informal group of which Oliver Cox (who worked at Ackroyden and Alton East) was a member, as was his future partner Graeme Shankland – they were later to establish a highly successful planning practice which was responsible for such projects as the evisceration of Liverpool – as well as Michael Ventris, who is now remembered for his decipherment of Cretan linear-B script rather than for his architectural activities. The Alton West estate was designed by a different group, from which another practice emerged: William Howell, John Killick and John Partridge; it was much more forthrightly 'modern', both in the detail of the buildings and in the planning: higher point blocks were faced with concrete panels surfaced with pebbly aggregate, and larger areas of glass were introduced. Meanwhile (in 1952) another group built an emulation of Le Corbusier's slab-block, the *Unité d'Habitation de Grandeur*

Conforme (which was going up in Marseilles, 1946–52,) at Bentham Road, Hackney. Five slabs in a rather thinner version of the Bentham Road block were sited to look over the great expanse of the deer-park at Richmond and therefore approached closest to the condition of the slab-block overlooking parkland which Le Corbusier advocated. The form was adopted by the LCC office on other sites also, and increasingly emasculated by other public and private architects (the first essay in emulation was the most interesting).

There were always differences between the British emulations and the French model. Le Corbusier conceived the block as two-sided, the flats being connected by an internal street every third storey, while a shopping centre ran through the middle height of the block, and the roof had a nursery school and an open-air theatre. The British blocks were one-sided, the flats entered from access galleries, the roofs (with the honourable exception of Bentham Road) used for lift-machinery and water tanks. They could not achieve the chunky plasticity of Corbusier. They were always thinner, a little blood- (and certainly colour-) less. They were usually part of a mixed development, and among the terraces and semi-detached houses lost the dignity which they could maintain when hovering on their pilotis over grassland – as they did at Roehampton. Members of the LCC were miffed when the French film-maker François Truffaut selected Roehampton as the site of his bookless society for *Fahrenheit 451*, a film based on a Malcolm Bradbury novel.

Festival and fifties

The austerity programme, originally formulated by Sir Stafford Cripps, Clement Attlee's President of the Board of Trade and Chancellor of the Exchequer from 1945 to 1950, effectively dampened any private excesses in expenditure and curbed government spending on matters not considered essential. Some of his government colleagues were nevertheless determined to put a fillip into reconstruction. During the war government propaganda had led to the employment of the best graphic designers by the Ministry of Information. The wartime government had also sponsored initiatives such as 'austerity' furniture and clothes which put the work of some of the best British designers within the economic reach of everyman. The first major post-war display of this reservoir of talent was a government (Board of Trade) sponsored exhibition, 'Britain Can Make It' at the Victoria and Albert Museum in 1946, which was of course intended to show Britain as a leader in designed goods, primarily for export, but also included a series of interiors, some quite luxurious, showing the work of the best of the 'modern' architects and designers working for hypothetical, but carefully specified 'clients'. Their real chance for display, however, came five years later in 1951, when the centenary of the Crystal Palace was officially celebrated with a 'Festival of Britain'. (See chapter 11 on Industrial Design.) This was considered so important that a cabinet minister, Herbert Morrison, was detailed to look after it. Shows were designed in Glasgow and Belfast, a pleasure garden opened in Battersea, as well as a 'live architecture' exhibition (a model settlement in fact) designed by Frederick Gibberd in Dockland; but the main show was a many-pavilioned exhibition on the South Bank of the Thames, where Abercrombie had originally planned his cultural/amusement centre. That piece of planning turned out to have been valuable.

The Festival itself included an important offering by the LCC office (where Leslie Martin, chief architect of one of the railway companies, but well-known for his avant-garde association, had meanwhile succeeded Robert Matthew) – a permanent concert hall, now the Royal Festival Hall, which became (with the Albert Hall) London's principal auditorium. It was planned by a team whose most important member perhaps was Peter Moro, a German-born but very naturalised architect, whose later work was to include a number of theatres, and who was responsible for much of the very influential interior detailing.

The boxy and rather dour exterior sheltered an interior where polished marble, brass, and fine hardwoods appeared for the first time in post-war building, and moreover in a context which was uncompromisingly 'modern', even if rather heavily, and rather prissily, patterned. The patterning was one of the efforts to invent a new, 'modern', ornament – a curious will-o'-the-wisp which obsessed a number of architects at that time. In the course of the following two decades the site attracted the National Theatre, the National Film Theatre, the Hayward Gallery, and other concert halls: Forshaw and Abercrombie's 'cultural centre' of 1943 was realised twenty years later, even if the riverside development between Southwark and County Hall has a very different complexion from their forecast.

In 1951 the Festival Hall was surrounded by the exhibition pavilions. Most of the designers of the exhibition belonged to the pre-war 'modernist' group and were 'conducted' by Hugh Casson (later President of the Royal Academy), who had originally been involved in the MARS Group exhibition of 1937–8. Its centrepiece was the Dome of Discovery, a vast steel-and-

The South Bank Arts Complex, London, (1951–3).

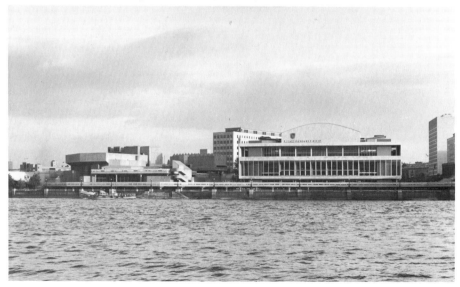

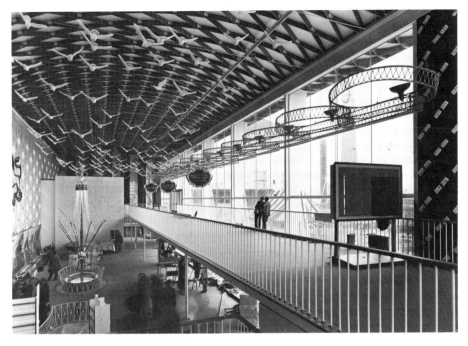

The Festival of Britain, interior of the Lion and Unicorn Building (1951).

aluminium shell supported on thin steel frames. Near it, the 'vertical feature' of the exhibition (another design commission won in a competition by Philip Powell and Hidalgo Moya) was a thin cigar-shaped object balanced on three counterpoised steel struts which provided the perfect phallic symbol for the age of contraception. In spite of the excitement of the run-up and of the exhibition, none of the buildings were architecturally outstanding: what created the most striking impression was the generous but sensible use of the exterior spaces and the lively quality of the main features (such as the entrance pavilions and the general offices), as well as the furnishings provided by the Festival office. These furnishings were widely emulated and copied, but they were rather fragile, and the fashion which they started was short-lived. Their rarity value made them worth collecting by 1980.

The aim, and to a great extent the success, of the exhibition was to celebrate the century's achievement, show the world that Britain could indeed 'make it', and persuade the British that present or future modernity was not as glum as austerity had led them to believe: that it was as authentically British as Paxton's glass-and-iron Palace; and that it provided the proper model for all future development.

The ethos which the Festival enshrined was broadcast by the most important periodical of the time, the *Architectural Review*. Hugh Casson was part of the editorial team, with the German historian Nikolaus Pevsner (an independent critic), James Richards, Gordon Cullen (a very prolific and skilful draughtsman) and Hugh de Cronyn Hastings, the proprietor. Pevsner's contribution is perhaps more important than is usually realised; he examined the roots of the 'functional' tradition in early industrial Britain and

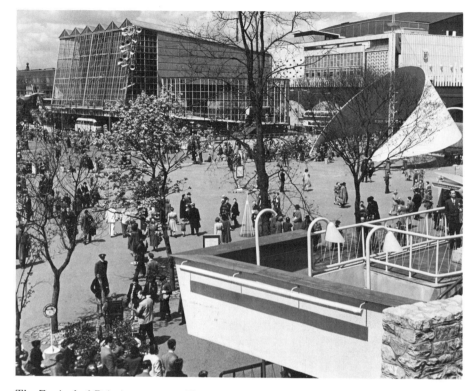

The Festival of Britain, entry pavilions (1951). Festival of Britain Office.

explored the implications of picturesque planning theory as formulated in the late eighteenth and early nineteenth centuries by gardeners and architects. Pevsner's teaching confirmed the lessons of the Festival. Cullen was able to translate it into a great many sketch projects for real as well as imaginary sites, which in their insistence on such details as spindly metalwork, artfully varied surface materials as well as an episodic, anecdotal use of colour influenced the commercial and municipal architecture of succeeding decades. No other publication or teaching institution had a comparable influence, particularly on the younger architects who were filling the expanding local authority offices.

Two other competitions at that time had important consequences. The first was for the rebuilding of the only British cathedral which had been destroyed by bombing: the vast, upgraded fifteenth-century parish church of St Michael, Coventry. As a major industrial centre Coventry was one of the most bombed of British cities. The rebuilding of the Cathedral was backed by all appropriate institutions. The winning scheme by Basil Spence (who had also taken part in the Festival of Britain) used the ruins of the medieval church as a forecourt, and struck a stylistic note which exactly suited the moment: a camped-up version of modernity which owed very little to the best of pre-war British architecture. Yet it was the first major public building to go up in a British city since the War and excited curiosity and sympathy, as work continued for the whole decade.

Many of the most notable British artists contributed to the building. The patronal statue by the entrance was one of Epstein's last, though far from his best works. The stained glass windows were by a number of artists of whom John Piper is the best known; and the foreseeably unfortunate acoustic effects of the Cathedral had a fortunate by-product: the vast tapestry (said to be the largest in the world) designed by Graham Sutherland but made in France, which was hung behind the high altar – the only echo in England of the somewhat artificial but very enthusiastically received revival of the old craft of tapestry weaving in France.

Among the unsuccessful competitors for Coventry Cathedral were a young couple from County Durham, Peter and Alison Smithson. Although not awarded any prize or mention, their spectacularly presented project was given a great deal of publicity. Their main cathedral space was sheltered under a single hyperbolic–paraboloid concrete shell; the outer buildings owed a great deal to the early work of the German-American, Mies van der Rohe. About the same time they won another competition, for a secondary school at Hunstanton in Norfolk: an austere and again a Miesian building, though now echoing his later work at the Illinois Institute of Technology in Chicago – rectangular blocks outlined by steel stanchions, with walls of glass or brick both outside and in. It was a polemical counter to the cosiness of the neo-empiricists, and the user-friendly elegance of the Hertfordshire schools. By the time of the next competition scheme, for a large housing project in Golden Lane in the City of London, they had chosen their banner and were known as the 'Brutalists', a modern 'British' movement, though it owed its name largely to Le Corbusier's extensive use of concrete cast in unplaned wood shuttering (whose grain and shape it moulded) and which he called *béton brut*. The doctrine of the movement included the use of unadulterated industrial materials and a dogmatic attachment to the notion of the image in architecture. It focused much protest against the tinselly and picturesque style of the Festival of Britain and the *Architectural Review*, as well as the gentilities of the new Empiricism. But although the Smithsons recruited the very talented sculptor Eduardo Paolozzi for a while, and maintained contact with other artists (notably Richard Hamilton), the movement never seems to have taken off. Their only self-confessed follower outside the British Isles was the Italian Vittoriano Vigano; his Istituto Marchiondi in Milan is the one Brutalist building abroad. In 1962 the Smithsons were commissioned to design a sumptuous office complex for *The Economist* in St James' in London and although there and in the later very ambitious projects for Sheffield University and central Berlin they raised a number of interesting issues about city pattern, yet the very absence of a definite grammar or image, of a definite taste, condemned the 'movement' to a certain sterility. Perhaps the moment for such movements in architecture had passed.

The Golden Lane competition was won by another young partnership, Chamberlin, Powell and Bon, whose later extension of it into the Barbican has created one of the most expensive bits of urban blight in Europe. Notable in that competition was the last essay in British social realism, a re-vamping of a Viennese-type housing block in a Peabody, Victorian almshouse style. But it came too late. Only months after the competition, Stalin died; within a year came the twentieth Party Congress, Krushchov's disavowal and the end of social-realism. It changed the fate of public housing in Great Britain, since many members of local government offices, which had grown enormously, were left-wingers, even Communist sympathisers. At one point the LCC was employing 2,000 architects, which made it one of the world's largest architectural practices, if not the very largest.

But the volume of work was too big to be accommodated even by them. Two new offices of importance were engaged in housing for both public and private clients: Lyons, Israel and Ellis, which became something of a nursery for the best architects of the next generation – their work included the Engineering and Science building of the London Polytechnic, outbuildings for the Old Vic theatre, as well as a number of housing schemes – and Darbourne and Darke, who made a small sensation with a housing scheme in Lillington Road, Pimlico (1961). Of the older architects, Ernö Goldfinger built Alexander Fleming House at the Elephant and Castle in two phases (1959, 1963) and a vast housing block in Poplar (1965). Although Maxwell Fry did some housing in South London and some building for Liverpool University, he was working mostly outside this country – in Africa and India – where he and his wife, Jane Drew, were commissioned to plan and design the new capital of Punjab at Chandigarh. Their decision to involve Le Corbusier in that enterprise led to the creation of what may well be the most important single complex of buildings put up since 1945.

The office of Tecton split into two separate practices: the borough of Finsbury went to Lubetkin and Tecton, while the Hallfield estate in Paddington project, whose slab blocks are laid out at forty-five degrees to the prevailing road pattern, so making a rather sharp intrusion into the urban texture of London, was taken by Lasdun and Drake. Lubetkin's major

Cluster residential block, Bethnal Green, London (1952–5). Denys Lasdun.

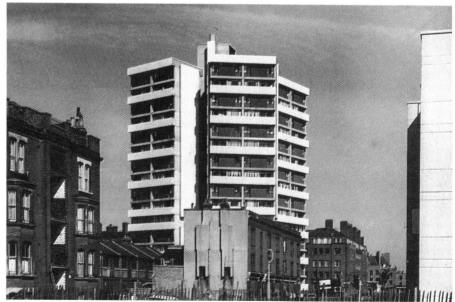

commission after the War was the planning of the New Town of Peterlee in County Durham; his disappointment there led to his retiring from architecture in 1950.

Denys Lasdun began to experiment with a new housing form, the cluster block, at Bethnal Green in London in 1952–5; a central core of services and access galleries connected short but high slabs of maisonettes – which gave a much more 'neighbourly' feel to the buildings than the more usual access-gallery slab-block. Although organised vertically, Lasdun's management of the horizontal planes gave the cluster a remarkably harmonious physiognomy.

The National Theatre, London.

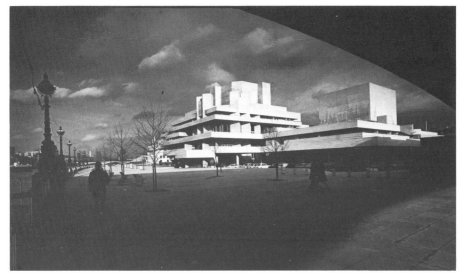

Interior of the Olivier Theatre, part of the National Theatre, London.

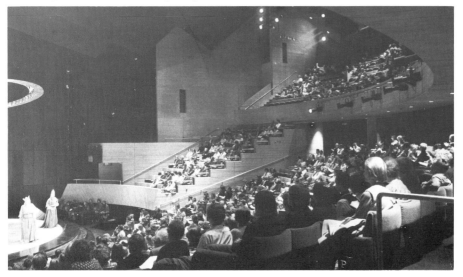

Unfortunately it proved to be difficult to justify economically. Apart from Lubetkin, Lasdun was the most interesting British architect to develop the heritage of Le Corbusier in the next generation, and two prominent buildings of his, the Royal College of Surgeons (1960) and the National Theatre (1967), show him developing further the metaphor of building as an extension, an analogue of the earth – in its horizontality and its layered structure.

Two houses which Le Corbusier put up outside Paris for the Jaoul famly in 1952/3 were to have a great influence in Britain. Simple rectangles in plan, the floors and roofs were shallow barrel vaults supported on concrete framing members. The infill walls were of unrendered brick and the deliberately coarse surface texture had something of the 'brutality' associated with concrete buildings at the time. The combination of shallow concrete vault and brick infill attracted a number of British architects; in particular Basil Spence based the buildings of his biggest commission after Coventry Cathedral, the new University of Sussex outside Brighton, on the Jaoul prototype.

The development of universities

Founded in 1958 cosy Sussex was a translation of medieval cloisters into a modified Jaoul house modernity. Sussex was in fact the first of the new universities but others were to follow. Not only did new universities have to be built, but old ones had to be expanded to accommodate the swelling number of qualified university entrants in the next generation. A committee under Lord Robbins planned the expansion of the old universities and the provision of entirely new ones, organised, like Sussex, on the campus principle, outside urban centres. Their combination of industrial plant, housing and representational building (since universities are the last of our institutions in which a good measure of ceremonial is expected and practised) provided a kind of condensed analogue, an experimental model, of the city.

As it happened, all of these universities were to be the work of independent practices: Lasdun was responsible for East Anglia, outside Norwich – the only one with a linear plan, a deliberately urban building with working, teaching and common rooms disposed along a spine; the old office of F.R.S. Yorke (Yorke had died by then), Rosenberg and Mardall did a standard industrial job for the University of Warwick, near Coventry; while Peter Shepheard and Gabriel Epstein did the new University at Lancaster. Robert Matthew, late of the LCC and by then Professor of Architecture at Edinburgh, was responsible for the new University of Stirling; and his London office, commanded by Stirrat Johnson-Marshall, for the Universities of York and Bath. York was the one major project in which the CLASP system of prefabrication which had been developed for schools was adapted to a much larger and inevitably more stately programme. It certainly showed the system's versatility, though it also implied later maintenance problems. The low silhouette of the building and the decentralised, collegiate organisation meant that covered walkways (a notoriously difficult formal

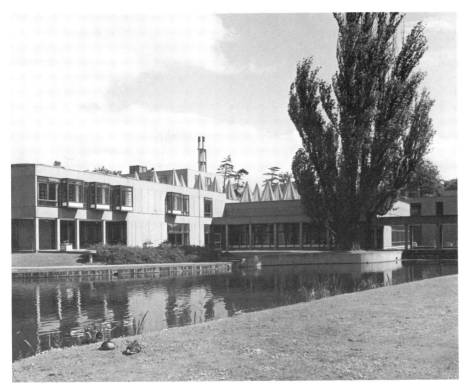

Derwent College, Univerity of York (1961–8). Robert Matthew and Stirrat Johnson-Marshall.

element) assumed a disproportionate importance in the configuration. The most troubled and fraught of all, the University of Essex outside Colchester, went to a post-war practice, the Architects' Co-Operative (now Co-Partnership), who had done the one notable British factory, at Waen Pond, near Brynmawr in S.E. Wales in the early fifties). They inverted the usual urban relationship: they filled the valley which ran through the centre of the site with work and teaching rooms, and imposed a near continuous platform over them; the students were accommodated in fourteen-storey point blocks on either side of the valley. This rather capricious inversion was blamed for the severity of student problems in 1968–9, though other factors must have been equally influential.

The sixties opened with a new type of building dominant – the universities, in which housing had a secondary function, and whose laboratories were often near-monumental industrial pavilions. In fact no industrial building of the post-war period quite achieved the grandeur of some of the earlier examples: not only the grimy 'satanic mills' of the nineteenth century, but of more recent examples, like Sir E. Owen Williams' Boots factory at Nottingham, which was one of the showpieces of the thirties. There were many reasons for this. The almost exclusive concentration on housing in the wake of the War coincided with the shrinking of British industrial potential; and much earlier, there was both a feeling of powerlessness before the vast scale of new industrial installations (oil refineries, generating stations) and a lack of public pride in industrial achievement. This was not an exclusively British, but a world-wide phenomenon. In no country are industrial buildings important architectural monuments after about 1930.

University buildings modify this picture in Britain, but only marginally. Perhaps the single most impressive one is the semi-industrial engineering laboratory which James Stirling and James Gowan designed for the University of Leicester. These two architects started their career more conventionally with a very skilful adaptation of the Jaoul formula to a block of flats at Ham Common, in South London. The Leicester building gave them international fame. It established their particular way with historical context. References to Wright, to Corbusier and to the Russian Constructivists are welded with great sculptural virtuosity: the harsh contrast of the office tower to the horizontal, milky-glazed, angularly lighted laboratories was startling. Stirling, who was to become the better-known of the two, did two more academic buildings in a similar manner: the Florey Building for Queen's College, Oxford (1971) and the Faculty of History for the University of Cambridge (1967). This last was developed on the curious notion imposed by the university's programme, that the theft of library books was the faculty's principal problem. Stirling created an atrium shaped as a quarter-cone therefore, which would allow one librarian to control the whole space, while making its volume, to which the inner passages open, into the unifying element of the building. Given the limitation imposed upon him, Stirling did manage to wield the disparate elements of the building into a powerful, even aggressive unity and deserved better, whatever the physical shortcomings, than to act merely as a focus for anti-modern philistinism.

Problems of scale and density

The great volume of post-war building created its own leeway. The building of the universities led to a reconsideration of the New Towns policy. Cumbernauld outside Glasgow was planned about 1955 as a new kind of New Town, which would avoid the miscalculations about traffic that flawed the first series. The city centre was the most innovative element: an isolated, linear castle-like block straddling a main supply road (which skirted the edge of the town); internally, ten levels of streets and stairs interconnect parking and a multiplicity of shops, workshops and small flatted factories, the whole crowned with a crest of penthouses. There is something heroic, but also slightly absurd about this vast complex, which stands, separated from acres of low-rise housing, by a moat of green fields.

At Hook in Hampshire a New Town was designed by a group seconded from the LCC, led by Oliver Cox and Graeme Shankland. They had set themselves to deal with it in a new way; the residential areas were planned on a kind of inverted Radburn scheme, with the houses facing onto the streets and the gardens making a soft core to the block, while the centre, where a number of high-rise buildings were to rise, was on a platform which sheltered the circulation and parking, providing the 'piazzas' for town life – a traffic-free, urban pedestrian area, detached from the ground. But the scheme, published in 1961, was still-born, for financial and organisational reasons.

These two projects, together with the University of Essex, illustrate a whole series of new problems. It had become obvious that current urban structures could not deal adequately with the by-products of new technology, nor with the rapid and growing increase of urban motor traffic, which was clogging all roads. A worried Ministry of Transport commissioned a report which was to recommend drastic measures. Headed by Colin Buchanan (whose name has remained attached to the enterprise), it published *Traffic in Towns* in 1963. It suggested improvements to public transport, and multi-level traffic arteries between traffic-free 'neighbourhoods'. There followed a decade of confusion and the piecemeal adaptation of a few of the Committee's recommendations.

The growth in the scale of buildings, and the consequent lengthening of access roads were also cause for concern. The largest urban housing estate before the war had been the Quarry Hill flats in Leeds, but they were positively dinky in scale when compared to the Hyde Park and Park Hill developments in Sheffield, though all over the country minor versions of that giant, which dominated its city and provided the climax of all high-rise low-density housing, were being built about the same time.

Parkhill and Hyde Park developments, Sheffield (1955–65). Sheffield City Architects' Office.

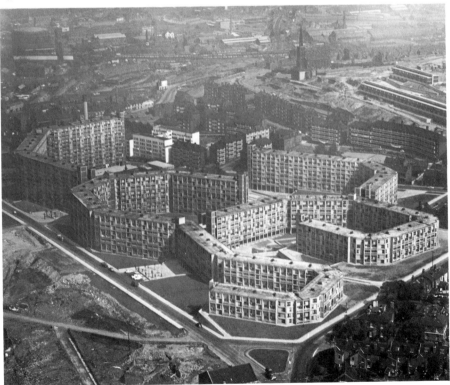

In the early sixties too, as a result of the relaxing of structural regulations and the introduction of office development permits on an industrial model (by a Labour administration!), tall speculative rental buildings grew up first in London, then in larger cities. The tallest building in Britain to date, the fifty-storey National Westminster Tower in the City of London, was designed by Colonel Richard Seifert, who had by then one of the largest practices in the country: but not the very largest. That dubious honour belonged for a while to John Poulson, whose doings were unexpectedly exposed when his undertaking collapsed under the double pressure of Income Tax inspectors and foreclosing banks. It exposed a success based on a mixture of graft and the manipulating of government regulations, and revealed the total indifference of those in authority to architectural quality.

The sixties also saw the growth of several large architectural offices (C.H. Elsom; Gollins, Melvin & Ward), much of whose work depended on property developers, and whose buildings were very much larger in volume than that of the better-known, more 'advanced' practices. Although commercial patrons could not take the sort of liberties with property lines and densities which were allowed the local authorities, nevertheless the constraints of tax structure, profit margin and zoning forced some very ingenious solutions, such as Seifert's Centre Point building on the corner of New Oxford Street and Charing Cross Road in London. However, not one high-rise building of the period is worth evaluating in a brief survey of the art of architecture in Britain at that time.

The new office buildings produced even more violent environmental pressures than the high-rise flats: between them both categories completely altered urban configuration in Britain. There was a double reaction to all this. Some saw the solution in a drastic reduction in the scale of building. A team under Leslie Martin, who had moved from the LCC to Cambridge as Professor of Architecture in 1956, worked out the implications of the relation between the heights of building and size of plot and urged the advantages of low-rise, high-density building; but this lesson took time to sink in. A much more impatient group, calling themselves Archigram, poured out a mass of drawings and polemics: the best-known being perhaps the Plug-in-City scheme of 1964. They responded visually to the 'wonders' of post-war technology and through their projects attempted to free architects from the shackles of any austere 'design' discipline by accepting the computerised plastic pleasures with uncritical enthusiasm. Their drawings – there were some other, equally adventurous practitioners of the same genre, though none more prolific – propagated an ethos which made the 'high-tech aesthetic' of the next decade possible. Archigram saw themselves as working in the same vein as some of the artists of the 'pop' tendency and they appealed to the same taste: streamlined objects, Disney-like inflations. Contemporaries of the Beatles, stills from the *Yellow Submarine* appear in their publications.

Another protagonist of the tendency, Cedric Price, planned a new university to be set in old railway stock in one of the large disused shunting yards of the north (the Potteries Think-Belt, 1960), as well as a 'Fun-Palace' conceived with the impresario, Joan Littlewood (1961). Although his visions were interesting propaganda exercises in favour of a value-free way of building, they were never translated into a graphic (and therefore architecturally plausible) language. All these projects, Price's and Archigram's, relied on elaborate assembly techniques, the use of large prefabricated metal and plastic elements as well as a computerised electronic industry – which in turn presupposed abundant and cheap energy. It was somehow assumed, though not stated, that the execution of such projects would improve the quality of life of both the builders and the buildings' inhabitants. These fantasies retained their appeal until the energy crisis provoked by the Six-Day War in the Middle East triggered a reaction which came to be associated with the writing and preaching of Ernst Schumacher ('Small is Beautiful') and Ivan Illich: that the quality of life does not depend wholly on material possession, that economic growth is not an unmixed blessing, that radical change can mean loss as well as gain and must be set against some kind of value.

One important by-product of these conflicting tendencies was the attempt to fuse the various and usually separately zoned elements of the new city: parking, housing, office-space, manufacturing and service industry, leisure, culture – into a single, unified built entity. This came to be known as a megastructure – an urban conglomeration developed in height as well as in length and breadth – a three-dimensional town. A number of designers all over Europe were experimenting with various formal devices to achieve this aim, and most of them went well beyond the economic or technical resources of even the greatest powers. The word seems to have been coined by Japanese architects. But Cumbernauld Centre (with Moshe Safdie's *Habitat* in Montreal) was often quoted as a credible prototype for the concept. Another, more modest British building can be fitted into this context: the Brunswick Centre by Leslie Martin and Patrick Hodgkinson. Like Cumbernauld, it is also a linear building with a base containing parking, but the volume makes a valley between two banks of flats, with a shopping centre, and working and communal facilities. Although the complex also includes some public spaces (a cinema, for instance) it is both smaller in scale and less demanding of attention than Cumbernauld civic centre – and it is also much more refined in detail.

Disillusion in the seventies

Megastructures were very much an exception. A substantial proportion of the dwellings built during the seventies relied on the steady adoption of large-scale prefabrication methods, some developed in Britain, others imported (notably from Scandinavia) by a number of local authority and government agencies, which promised the low-cost rapidly-erected mass-housing demanded by both Conservative and Labour administrations. However, from the early sixties onwards, there were complaints about the damp, the difficulties of weatherproofing and heating. What made these developments even more problematic was their inability to shelter a society in which vandalism had to be accepted as a permanent social phenomenon. In 1968, a small gas explosion blew out several storeys of a corner in a prefabricated high-rise block at Ronan Point in south London. This event focused the

complaints and awoke the fears of many prefabricated high-rise dwellers; it
damned the whole enterprise. Ronan Point was finally destroyed in 1986, but
increasingly a number of estates built to much higher standards of
accommodation than any of the pre-war period were declared unusable and
even pulled down. This led to much litigation and a final rejection of post-
war housing policies. Developers in central cities did not react as quickly,
however.

Inevitably, at the beginning of the seventies, the architectural profession as
a group was thrown off balance; its collective judgement, or at least the
judgement of the majority of practitioners, was popularly seen to be very
mistaken. A few younger architects began to form a line of retreat. As flat
roofs had been a dogmatic symbol in the thirties, so these architects adopted
pitched roofs as a sign of a new reaction. Throughout the decade, the office
of Robert Matthew and Stirrat Johnson-Marshall (under Andrew
Derbyshire) was working on the Hillingdon Civic Centre: a mass of double-
pitched and pyramidal roofs atop dark red-brick walls conceal the usual
bureaucratic office-landscape machine. At the same time a number of
municipal and county offices (Essex most explicitly) directed their architects
to respect the 'vernacular character' of certain localities. This even led certain
'reputable' commercial offices to adopt what looked to them like a new
winning line. The rediscovery and revaluation of the Edwardian past and its
comforts was then manifested in the fashion for Edwardian clothes, an
inordinate admiration for Edwin Lutyens, and a blank rejection of all
modernity from William Morris (even Pugin!) until their own generation,
without any allowance for quality – and in the built reality, the support of
local government housing with polychrome brick walls, small windows and
pitched roofs.

Meanwhile one of the very largest housing estates in Britain to combine
relative low-rise with high density and an uncompromising modernism, went

*Architects' drawing for Paraplegic Home, Camden
(1972). Eldred Evans and David Shaler.*

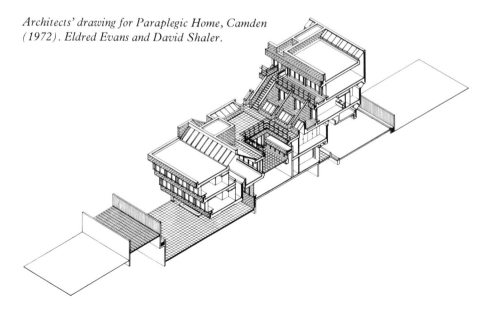

up at Alexandra Road in the borough of Camden in London. It displayed the explicit dissociation of modern architecture from high-rise and incorporated features which had proved successful in the proto-megastructures of the earlier generation. But in spite of the change in massing, it was afflicted by some of the problems which had hit the earlier high-rises. Two buildings on the edge of that estate, a home for paraplegics, and another for deprived children by Eldred Evans and David Shalev, owed more perhaps to Dutch examples of the thirties than to more recent prototypes. They were perhaps the most elegant English buildings of the decade.

The last of the New Cities, the sketch plan for which was published in 1968 and 1970, claimed to be more closely tailored to the 'ordinary Englishman's needs and requirements than its predecessors, and to provide a garden and garage to every house. Milton Keynes was to be an entirely motorised town. To avoid traffic jams and tides, work-places were dispersed round the periphery; and the 'town centre', excentrically placed, was like an American shopping mall. It was also to have its own university, though this, the Open University, which operates through radio and television, did not produce a resident community of teachers and students. Indeed, Milton Keynes has not proved to be the magnet its planners expected, and has grown more slowly than most other New Towns. (See chapter 4 on New Towns.)

However, it was founded at a turning-point in planning policy. A new interest in the eviscerated and vandalised inner city centres penetrated to government circles about the turn of the decade. This coincided with the slow-down of immigration from the old imperial lands, as well as with a decisive fall in the birth-rate. Equally the monetarist policy of the Conservative government elected in 1979 led to a growth of private investment in city centres and a cut-back both in public building and in public transport – which in turn had an inevitable effect on the life of the New Towns.

Former children's reception home, Camden, now used by the British Refugee Council.
Eldred Evans and David Shaler.

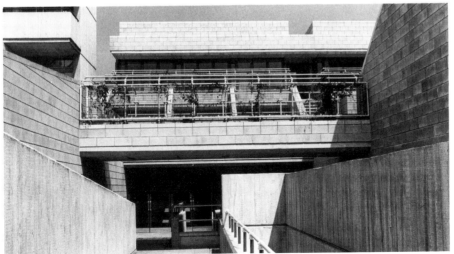

An easily identifiable tendency which came into prominence at the beginning of the seventies, usually labelled 'high-tech', was clearly dependent on the utopian visions of Archigram and their like; though when the Archigram architects began to build their first major and virtually their only work (under the aegis of the Greater London Council, which had by then replaced the LCC), the Hayward Gallery and the adjoining concert halls (1960–7), it looked to the public more like an old-style Brutalist exercise than an instalment of 'Plug-in City'. The first triumph of 'high-tech', therefore, was appropriately cosmopolitan, when Richard Rogers, an Anglo-Italian architect, teamed up with the Genoese-Parisian Renzo Piano to win the competition for the Pompidou Centre on the Plateau Beaubourg in Paris. It was to become the most popular (and perhaps also the most prestigious) gallery-museum of the seventies and eighties. Because of its dependence on a visual vocabulary developed in Britain, and because of Rogers' leading part in its conception (as well as that of London-based engineers, Ove Arup and Partners), it must be considered an export British building, the only such export up to that date apart from the CLASP schools system of twenty years earlier; and like that earlier export, it seems to produce problems of maintenance.

Norman Foster, who had originally worked in partnership with Richard Rogers, developed on analogous lines after their separation. His first building was the hangar-like Sainsbury Arts Centre at the University of East Anglia, which is a curious finial to the line of Lasdun's buildings described earlier. His other notable commission was for an insurance office building in Ipswich, which provided the first instance in Britain of the use of reflective glass (a staple of developers' buildings in the later seventies and the eighties) on a large scale.

However, the reputation which emerged as the most important in Britain during the seventies was that of James Stirling. While his earlier British buildings were bedevilled by teething troubles, their outstanding quality was recognised by a number of foreign commissions: the Academy of Science in Berlin (unexecuted) and the School of Architecture at Rice University in Austin, Texas were to lead to other work in Germany, the most important of which, the City Museum in Stuttgart, was completed in 1984, as was the extension of the Fogg Museum in Cambridge, Massachusetts. In Italy, the town library of Latina was finished in 1986, while in Britain the extension of the Tate Gallery and the new Tate installation in the Liverpool Docks belong to the second half of the eighties.

Like many other British architects, Stirling began as an emulator of Le Corbusier, and went on to develop a personal manner in the academic buildings of the sixties, absorbing and transforming other avant-garde influences, though he always remained attached to a native tradition of engineering building. In the later seventies, his work took another, almost archaeological turn. It was not antiquarian, however, but concerned with manipulating ancient fragments, much as Early Christian builders had re-used columns and cornices from classical buildings and given them new and sometimes startling meaning by setting them in unexpected contexts. In Stirling's buildings this process is clumsily explicit in the Berlin Academy of

Sciences, but was progressively refined until it becomes a virtuoso performance in the project for Columbia University (unexecuted) and the Stuttgart Museum.

While Stirling represents the architect as an individual artist, another current gained much popularity in the seventies under different names, though all of its practitioners in fact played variations on what in the United States had come to be called 'advocacy planning'. Though perhaps a contradiction in terms, the main monument of this tendency is the Byker Wall in Newcastle-upon-Tyne, a mile-and-a-half long building of varying height, with barely any windows to the north and a busy display of balconies to the south. It was the object of an elaborate consultation exercise, though the final result does look very like Ralph Erskine's other buildings in Sweden. Various housing association groups adopted more or less radical versions of the advocacy technique. It worked well where the adaptation of older buildings was concerned, but seemed less convincing in the case of new buildings, perhaps inevitably. The most important figure in this movement, John Turner, has worked in Latin America, in India and Africa and is perhaps the most respected 'authority' on dweller-built housing. His studies of the *barrios* of Peruvian towns are perhaps the most important contributions he has made; they are based on a much more thoroughgoing understanding of the place of building in society than most of the 'advocacy planning' propaganda.

The eighties

There were, therefore, three tendencies round which architectural opinion clustered at the beginning of the decade. Advocacy designers were flourishing, mostly in urban communities. The increasing disillusion with fifties and sixties mass-housing, particularly with high-rises, and the steadily growing number of such schemes abandoned (and even demolished) persuaded local authorities forcefully of the wisdom and relative economy of supporting housing associations and similar enterprises. This was certainly of benefit to many citizens. However, since these bodies took a neutral attitude to the architects' contribution to their workings, critical attention tended to concentrate on other, more spectacular trends. Of these, 'high-tech' continued to be represented primarily by Norman Foster and Richard Rogers. Norman Foster's Hong Kong and Shanghai Bank is the most prominent building on the territory's waterside: it will probably – with its vast atrium and grey enamelled walls – turn out to be the most dour, if also the most accomplished exercise in the genre. Foster was the obvious candidate to design the new headquarters for the BBC in the west end of London: but almost immediately the project fell to government spending cuts.

Rogers, who after Beaubourg did a number of domestic and industrial buildings, was commissioned to design the new headquarters for Lloyd's of London, the Vatican of insurance. That building is also conceived round an American-style atrium, which Rogers, rather surprisingly, enclosed in *rétro*, Paxton-style glazing. In so far as 'high-tech' is a movement, its tenets –

display of the services on the exterior, and reliance on industrial production to provide the 'expressive' detail, remain unmodified.

The third trend is difficult to qualify: the modish label 'post-modern' has been applied to some of its principal figures, and rejected by many of them. Indeed, the trouble with that label is that it has become a blanket term to describe the period after 1960 or thereabouts when stylistic preferences seemed to come adrift from any critical standards. It could therefore equally well include the 'high-tech' tendency. However, it is more usually attached to an amorphous group of designers who distinguish themselves by their often ambivalent attitude to traditional materials and a more sympathetic view of the past than that of the modernists. Unlike 'high-tech', it has attracted some sympathy from 'advocacy' designers. Many architects recognised the violence of the shift in their social position since the sixties. This change was due only partly to the several disappointments of their clients listed earlier. Even within the profession there was a tacit recognition of the intellectual and formal poverty of a design method geared either to the positive fulfilment of (often misconceived) social needs or to the streamlining of the process of industrial manufacture.

The most urgent need was for some rational consideration of the social and visual *context* of a building and the specific *internal* rules of architecture; or put another way, to identify what distinguishes architecture from other kinds of building. While most would agree that unreflective, mindlessly optimistic modernity was dead and gone, some (like Stirling – to take the most conspicuous example) consider their work as coming out of, as a continuation and an understanding of what was best in the modern movement. Yet others interpret the *post* of post-modern to mean *anti*, and call for a return to some specific past period ('Georgian' or 'Arts and Crafts') without any reference to the intervening century or two. In the fifties and sixties the leading architects had professed a conviction that any interest in the buildings of the past was a purely private affair, irrelevant to their current concerns. Many of the next generation have in common a belief that architecture has some autonomous discipline, independent of social considerations or matters of building technique.

This, of course, could only be rediscovered by some reference to history; and a new interest in history is concurrent with a revival of interest in architectural theory – which has resulted in a flood of publications on the subject, as well as a proliferation of courses on it in schools of architecture all over the country. The epicentre of this activity is the Architectural Association School in London, one of the largest and oldest schools of architecture in Britain. About half (if not more) of the architects mentioned here were trained at the AA, and its cosmopolitan staff and student body have made it one of the best in the world.

Two *causes célèbres* occupied a great deal of public attention in the first years of the eighties. The first was the projected extension of the National Gallery in London on a conspicuous site (on the north-west corner of Trafalgar Square) adjoining the much-loved (though not particularly distinguished) late Georgian/William IV (1834–8) building by William Wilkins. After a series of competitions and the personal intervention of the

Prince of Wales, an American architect (devoted, according to his own words, to the concept of 'the decorated shed') was appointed.

The other episode came at the culmination of a long campaign by a developer to acquire an important tract of land at the centre of the City of London, next to its Mansion House. His personal devotion to a certain kind of modern architecture had prompted him (even before all the land had been bought) to commission the design for a huge open square and a tall office block from the German-American architect, Mies van der Rohe, a scheme which seemed unobjectionable to the City fathers when it was mooted in the sixties. However, its final publication and the impending start of site-work provoked such public outcry that the scheme was withdrawn and Stirling was commissioned by the developer to produce an alternative project.

In spite of all this flurry of activity, 'quality' architecture remains a minority matter, particularly since the architectural patronage of local authorities has been drastically reduced. The judgement of quality in building remains an individual matter and no consensus of opinion, not even of the broadest kind, can obtain: though most people would agree that when the art of architecture is being discussed, it is 'quality' architecture only that is meant.

However, it is notable that a revival of interest in the art of the fifties began in the early eighties – first in New York – and had moved by 1985 to London and Paris. Younger architects have also shown an interest in the more 'advanced' work of that period. The centenaries of Mies van der Rohe and Le Corbusier were celebrated with large and comprehensive exhibitions in 1986–7 and it remains to be seen whether this revival, like many of the others, is a passing fashion or whether it augurs a revaluation of the deeper concerns of the modernists.

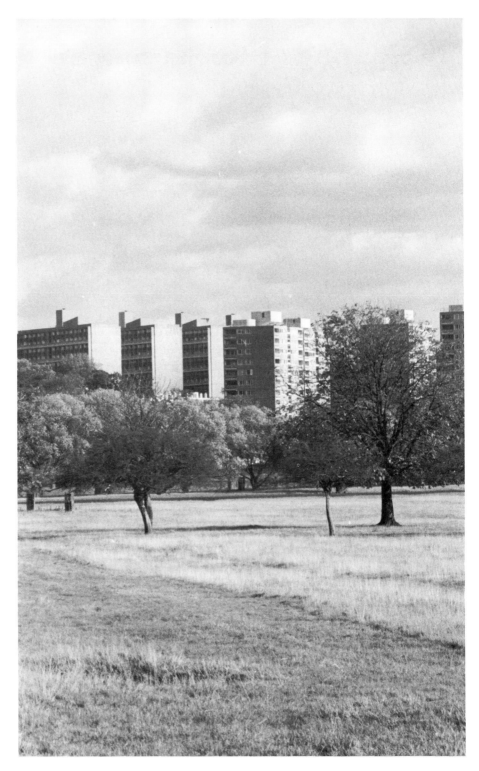

Alton West (1954–8) seen from Richmond Park.

10 Housing at Roehampton

SIMON PEPPER

The London County Council's Roehampton housing was a group of projects built throughout the 1950s in well wooded surroundings on the fringes of Putney Heath and Richmond Park. Alton East (1952–5) and Alton West (1954–8) occupied the extensive grounds of four eighteenth-century mansions near old Roehampton Village. Ackroydon (1951–4), on a smaller site near Wimbledon Tennis club, served as the prototype for the mixture of high and low rise housing which was to make Roehampton the showpiece for post-war British public housing architecture. Tower blocks rose from the trees to give spectacular views across London's south-west suburbs, while lower blocks of maisonettes, terraced houses and old people's bungalows enjoyed more intimate bosky settings. The whole ensemble came closer than perhaps any other post-war project to the humane vision of the 'Vertical Garden City'.

Its target population of nearly 10,000 made Roehampton much the largest of the LCC developments planned to meet the post-war housing shortage. Indeed, construction at Roehampton would constitute some two-thirds of the county council's housebuilding programme during the early 1950s. There was of course some local opposition to the wholesale movement into desirable suburbs of working-class tenants, but this was blunted by widespread acceptance of the council's obligation to provide extra accommodation. The most serious criticism was concentrated on the lack of local employment, the poor public transport links with central London, and on the unacceptable architectural character of the first scheme prepared for the site.

This had been designed in 1947 and 1948 by the staff of the LCC's Director of Housing and Valuer who, in the post-war emergency, had been given overall responsibility for land acquisition, building, letting and housing management. In fairness it should be added that the Valuer operated under strict committee instructions to employ only slightly modified pre-war flat plans for the four-, five-, and six-storey blocks that formed much of the first Roehampton scheme. To save as many trees as possible, the Valuer incorporated some eight-storey blocks with lifts, similar to four experimental blocks then under construction on the council's Woodberry Down estate in

Hackney. A few two-storey houses were also included, giving a variety of low, medium and high rise buildings which was known in LCC circles as 'mixed development'. As an attempt to break away from the monotony of pre-war estates – which tended to be composed entirely either of walk-up tenement flats or the ubiquitous garden suburb cottages – the scheme was admirable. But its execution was uninspired. Not surprisingly, the critics directed their fire at the taller flats which were described by one outraged correspondent in the *Wandsworth Borough News* as 'raw, red rectangles, eight stories high, jostling at varying degrees with their lesser brethren'. To *The Times* leader writer they were 'unimaginative barrack-like blocks'.

Controversy over the shape of London's largest post-war project played an important part in the decision taken late in 1949 to return responsibility for housing design to the County Council's recently appointed Superintending Architect, Robert Matthew. As chief officers, Sir Robert Matthew and his successors, Sir Leslie Martin and Sir Hubert Bennett, are often credited with the design of Roehampton. They always insisted on sharing credit with Whitfield Lewis, who headed the Housing Division, and with the design teams responsible for the different phases. Indeed, the ethic of teamwork was a notable feature of the reconstituted LCC Architects Department, which employed experienced designers as well as many newly qualified architects who were destined to make their mark.

The architects' plans for the prototype Ackroydon estate were unveiled in November 1950. Just over 2,000 people would eventually be housed on a 23 acre site that extended from Wimbledon Park Side to Princes Way, and included over 400 mature trees as well as 3 large Victorian houses which would be incorporated into the scheme. Most of the new housing at Ackroydon was not in high rise blocks. By 1954 the completed estate contained 436 dwellings, including 16 houses, 106 maisonettes in four-storey staircase access blocks, and 314 flats of which 182 were in three-, four- and five-storey blocks – again without lifts. The remaining 132 flats were in three eleven-storey and one eight-storey towers, described by the LCC as 'point blocks'.

With 3 flats on each floor, clustered around the lift and staircase lobby, the T-shaped point blocks fitted easily into small clearings. Their irregular plan, plus the use of a variety of surface finishes, window openings, projecting balconies and canopies made them interesting focal points on the site. The lay press, of course, were much taken by their height and immediately dubbed them 'London's First Skyscrapers'. The real achievement of the Ackroydon design team, however, was to preserve so much of the mature landscape in a high density scheme of 100 persons per acre, while breaking so completely from the rigidities of pre-war housing layout. In these terms, 'mixed development' was highly successful.

It was less impressive as a new form of accommodation. Apart from those living in ground floor flats or maisonettes and the handful of houses, the scheme provided accommodation off the ground, without benefit of lifts. The point block flats were all two-bedroom units, which meant that families with children would inevitably be housed far from the ground. Another problem was the high cost of the eleven-storey point blocks, which came in at roughly

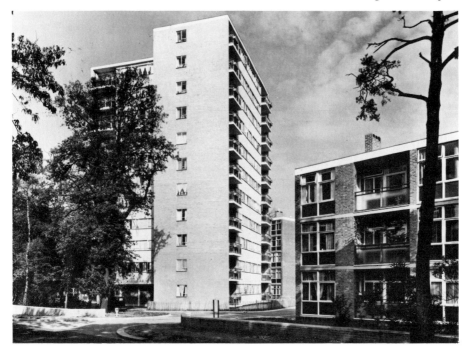

Ackroydon: London's first skyscrapers. T-plan point blocks in the prototype scheme of mixed development.

twice the unit cost of the experimental eight-storey flats at Woodberry Down (previously much the most expensive units constructed by the LCC). This lesson had only been partly digested when the next phase of development was embarked upon.

Alton East was developed between 1952 and 1955, a rather larger scheme of 744 dwellings on 28 acres between Portsmouth Road and Roehampton Lane. Here too the point blocks were sited in gaps between the trees and, with their small areas of foundations, lent themselves very well to the sharply undulating terrain. To reduce unit costs a fourth flat was added to each floor, which made better use of the lifts and gave the blocks a somewhat squarer plan (thus avoiding the excessive external wall areas of the earlier T-shaped versions). Cost savings were very necessary here because almost sixty per cent of the Alton East accommodation was provided in the point blocks. But the relaxed atmosphere of mixed development was retained. Commentators remarked on the informal architectural language of the point blocks, with their brick skins, small recessions and projections, balconies with ribbed 'Festival of Britain' panels and timber planting boxes. The lower blocks of maisonettes and the small number of terraced houses were also handled in a self-consciously domestic style, with pitched roofs, broken eaves lines, panels of timber cladding, and windows of different sizes treated as holes in the predominantly brick walls. In Pevsner's words, it was 'Architecture at ease'.

On the 100 acres of rolling, park-land at Alton West a very different approach was adopted for the 1,867 dwellings built between 1954 and 1958.

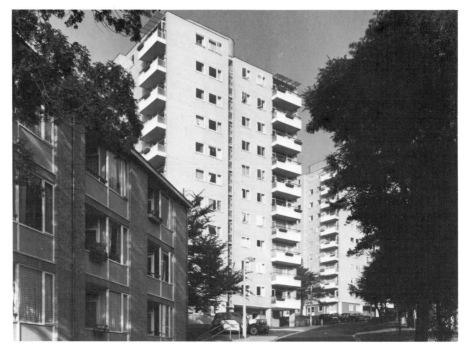

Alton East: sixty per cent of accommodation during this phase was provided in eleven-storey point blocks.

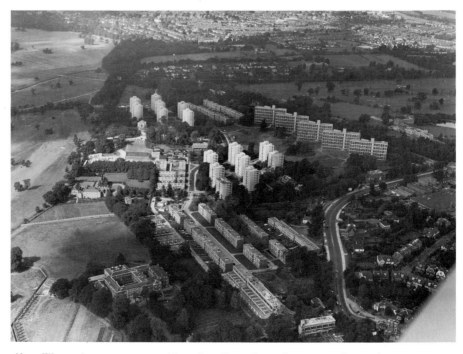

Alton West: picturesque composition of medium-rise maisonettes and town houses (foreground), point blocks (centre), and slab blocks (background, right) in parkland setting.

All the basic elements of mixed development remained, but the point blocks, maisonettes and low rise houses were now disposed in quite separate groups. At the junction of Alton East and West, close to old Roehampton village, the only 'civic space' was established around the shopping parade, community centre and branch library. Elsewhere large masses of housing were arranged in the landscape, not rigidly, but quite deliberately in a way that reminded many observers of the calculated 'picturesque' quality of eighteenth-century English design.

The fifteen point blocks were now clustered formally in two staggered groups; the blocks themselves were tightly planned within rectangular shere-faced skins made from a limited range of standardised precast concrete panels. The imagery of 'Modern' industrialised construction carried over into the lower blocks, all of them now equipped with flat roofs broken only by tank rooms and vent pipes. No doubt it was the hard-edged quality of the later phases of Roehampton that commended the scheme to the makers of the film *Fahrenheit 451*. But the Bravest part of this New World was the group of five eleven-storey slab-blocks that marched across the upper slopes of Downshire Fields, the large area of open grassland at the centre of Alton West.

Alton West: slab blocks containing two-floor maisonettes.

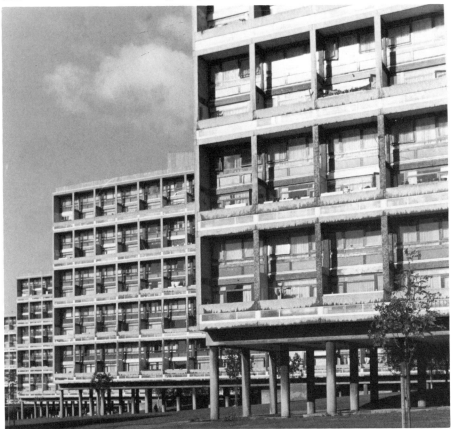

This latest addition to the repertoire of mixed development was directly inspired by the writings of Le Corbusier, and the first of the Swiss-French architect's *Unités d'Habitations* to reach completion at Marseilles in 1952. Housing some 1,600 people in a self-contained residential unit with its own shops, cafes and library, as well as a rooftop kindergarten and recreation area, the Corbusian block was raised on short stilts (or piloti) to allow free pedestrian and vehicular movement through an urban parkland setting. It was enormously influential to the post-war generation of British architects. In May 1951 the *Architectural Review* published a discussion of the still incomplete Unité amongst staff of the LCC's Housing Division, many of whom had returned from their Marseilles 'pilgrimage' convinced they had seen the ideal building block for the reconstruction of Britain's cities. None of the Unité-inspired LCC blocks built at Bentham Road in Hackney, the Loughborough estate in Brixton, or at Alton West could match the facilities of Corbusier's first project. However, the LCC architects were able to incorporate into their own designs Corbusier's piloti, and a modified version of the two-storey narrow-fronted maisonette units which can be seen expressed so clearly in the pattern of columns and balconies on the slab-block façades.

Each of the main levels contained fifteen maisonettes, which made efficient use of the centrally located lifts and helped to bring unit costs below the obstinately high figures of the point blocks. The access gallery was set into the block to give shelter, and passed only kitchen windows and front doors (a

Le Corbusier: montage of the Marseilles Unité d'Habitation *showing the piloti, the interlocking maisonettes, and sculptural shapes of the roof-top recreation area.*

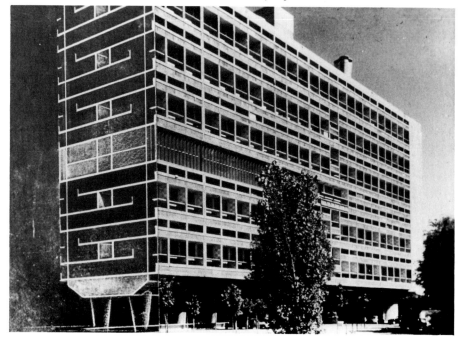

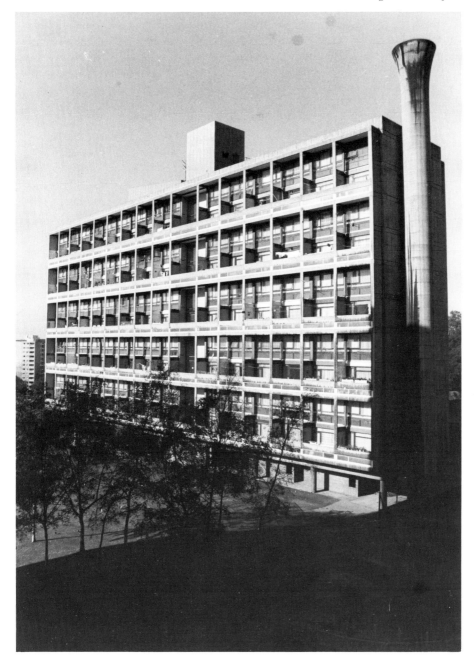

Alton West: eleven-storey slab block with boiler house chimney.

much more private arrangement than in pre-war gallery-access flats, where passers-by could often look into bedroom windows). The entrance lobby provided a pram parking area, overlooked from the kitchen through a glazed screen. The kitchen itself was fitted with a U-shaped run of worktop, incorporating a sink and drainer, with space for the tenant's own cooker, washing machine and fridge. For those without a fridge, a ventilated larder was provided (and each block contained a launderette for those without a washing machine). These kitchens marked a breakthrough in low-income domestic provision, for those in pre-war council flats often contained a bath, while in cottages the kitchen functions were frequently split between the main living room with its solid fuel range, and the small scullery where the sink and wash copper were located. The fully equipped working kitchen – for years the preserve of the servantless middle classes – had now reached the council tenant. From it a hatch served the dining end of the living room, while at the 'lounge' end picture windows opened onto a balcony running the full twelve foot width of the unit, and rising two complete floor levels. Upstairs the bathroom and WC were located off the central landing and ventilated mechanically. This arrangement allowed the windows of the two bedrooms to extend the full distance between party walls. Central heating radiator units were located beneath each window. These were supplied from a district heating circuit serving all of Alton West from a boiler house beneath one of the slab-blocks.

LCC dwellings were let unfurnished, so probably very few of the interiors would have matched the fifties elegance of the show flats, with their

Living room interior of a slab block show unit, Alton West.

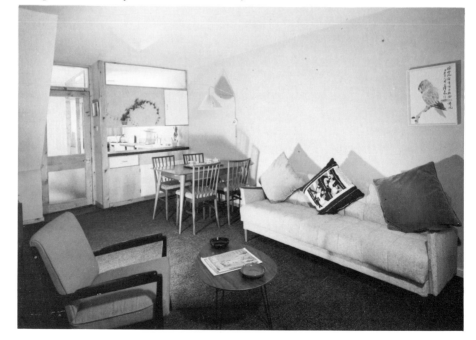

Scandinavian-inspired natural finish door frames and dining suite, plain carpets and wallpapers, and the low, straight lines of the sofa and not-so-easy chair. In terms of space, servicing, and quality of planning, however, the LCC's tenants enjoyed standards matching anything provided by the private sector beneath the 'luxury' class. This has to be kept in mind when pondering the legacy of these and other seminal high rise projects.

High rise housing has not been Britain's greatest post-war success story. The cost problems of high building were never to be solved. It is now probably the most controversial aspect of modern architecture, and has acquired a notoriety out of all proportion to the number of dwellings actually built during the fifties and sixties in blocks high enough to demand lift access. Roehampton certainly played a part in establishing what is now recognised in this country to be a form of housing suitable only for the higher income groups, who can choose where they live, and are not therefore compelled to bring up young families far from the ground in blocks which have always demanded a higher standard of servicing, maintenance and policing than local authorities are able to provide. Few of the schemes that followed Roehampton benefited from the care lavished on it by idealistic designers who sincerely believed that they had found the El Dorado of the Modern Movement, a sensitive architectural formula for mass housing in an eighteenth-century landscape.

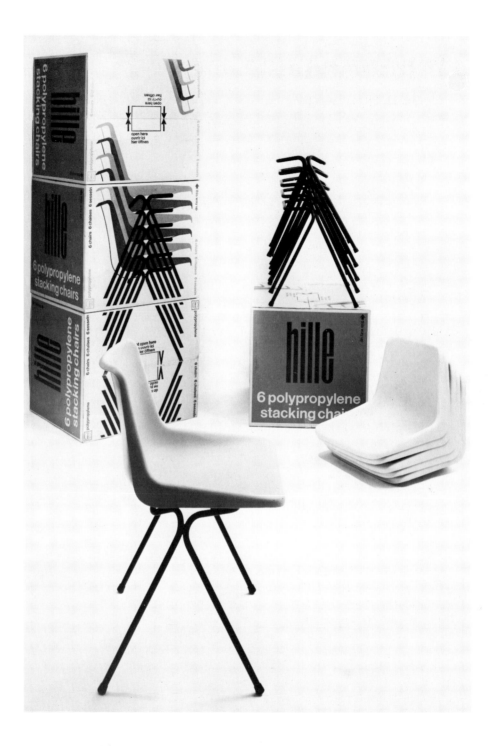

Polypropylene stacking chairs designed by Robin Day in 1963; packaging designed by Ivan Dodd.

11 Industrial Design

JOHN HESKETT

Introduction

The surroundings inhabited by most people in modern Britain, and the facilities they provide, whether at home, work or school, on the street, in transportation systems, or pursuing leisure and recreational activities, are overwhelmingly man-made. The extent of human intervention in creating environments has been constantly accelerating since the Industrial Revolution, accompanied by sweeping changes in power sources, production and materials technology, commercial organisation and government policies. The vast range of machines, artefacts and implements readily available as a consequence of these changes have transformed material standards of living and expectations, and simultaneously, social conceptions and standards.

The objects of everyday life are therefore not simply the result of technological and commercial impulses, intended to satisfy utilitarian needs, but are also capable of expressive values. Since 1945 the task of giving form to manufactured articles has become increasingly specialised in the role of industrial designer, sometimes concentrating on one particular area of production, such as furniture, or automobile design, often ranging across a multiplicity of materials and products. In addition, in the past and still to a considerable extent today, forms have been created by people with a large variety of backgrounds, artists and craftsmen, architects, engineers, draughtsmen and pattern-makers, amongst others. Such serial- or mass-produced designs, because of their ubiquity, and the frequent need for compromise in meeting varying demands, can rarely approach the unique intensity or expressive complexity of an individual work of art. Nevertheless, collectively, they constitute a significant expression of contemporary popular culture, both for those who create these multifarious objects and those who use them in their daily lives.

Before the Second World War the term 'Industrial Design' was rarely used. Its origins lie in two main strands of development, stemming from the very different disciplines of art and engineering. The first was widely characterised as 'Decorative Art' or 'Applied Art' in the nineteenth century, but later came to be generally known, in the inter-war years, as 'Industrial Art'. A common element, despite the variations of terminology, was a conviction that the values of art could be more widely disseminated and the standards of products improved by the application of artistic principles to the form of manufactured goods. This belief evolved predominantly in industries with a long heritage of artistic participation, such as ceramics and glassware, metalwares and furniture. At best, where there was a genuine recognition of artists' contributions by a company, it could be highly successful. The Wedgwood company, for example, still maintained its long traditions of employing consultants in the 1930s with excellent products designed by Keith Murray. However, there was a danger that without an effective integration of an artist-consultant into the overall process of design and production, designs could result that, although artistically viable, were unsuitable for production or market demands.

The second strand of development evolved out of the transition from technical crafts into engineering, where although mechanical or structural function might have been of primary concern, there was also a belief that 'if it works right, it should look right'. In other words, quality should be perceptible. Some of the finest results of this belief can be seen in collections such as those of the Science Museum in London and the National Railway Museum at York. In the 1930s the tradition was still strong, one of the best examples being R.J. Mitchell's Supermarine Spitfire. The recollections of pilots who flew it in the war have constantly emphasised not only the superb performance of the aircraft, but also the belief that it was a thing of beauty. Indeed, the aircraft assumed a powerful iconic role in the popular imagination, a symbol of resistance against the might of Germany when Britain stood alone in the war.

Despite many fine achievements emanating from both the artistic and engineering traditions, however, each remained limited in scope, based on the work and conviction of individuals and organisations and lacking a firm basis in a wider recognition in British industry and society. Indeed, in 1937 Nikolaus Pevsner wrote: 'When I say that 90 per cent of British industrial art is devoid of any aesthetic merit I am not exaggerating.'

Yet in the inter-war years many efforts on several levels had sought to remedy this situation. In 1919 the Ministry of Reconstruction had emphasised the role of industrial art in re-entering markets neglected in the war years. In 1932 the government had established a Committee for Art and Industry to promote design in industry, commerce and education. Private bodies such as the Design and Industries Association, founded in 1915, had proselytised the values of design through exhibitions, publications and meetings. Journals such as *Art and Industry* and the publications of writers such as Herbert Read, John Gloag, Nikolaus Pevsner and Anthony Bertram had all advocated not only the commercial value of improved design, but its essential role in developing a new industrial culture widely accessible to the whole population. Perhaps most crucially, there were a number of private companies and public corporations which established a strong commitment to design. All these endeavours, however, had but marginal effect. In too many sectors of British industry there was considerable resistance to new ideas.

The imperatives of war brought many changes after 1939. Victory in the Battle of Britain in the summer of 1940 owed as much to tactics as any innate superiority of British aircraft. Elsewhere a depressing run of defeats revealed grievous faults in the design and quality of equipment. Much was achieved in British industry in a very short time, for example developing a capacity to produce and use aluminium for a vast range of purposes, or applying techniques of wood lamination to provide strong lightweight structures for aircraft, such as the de Havilland Mosquito, or for high-speed motor torpedo boats.

There was also a significant initiative in domestic design, caused by the diversion of furniture production to the war effort and the restricted imports of timber available, which created a shortage of furniture for the civilian population. Public anger at profiteering by manufacturers, and the plight of families who had been bombed-out, created a need for some form of emergency provision. A 'Utility Scheme' to control the supply, quality and price of clothing had been established in 1941, which in 1942 was extended to furniture. Production under this scheme was limited to licensed producers, who could only manufacture twenty specified articles at strictly controlled prices, for sale only to those with a defined need. The problem was to ensure the most efficient use of scarce materials to maintain standards of quality, and it was in this respect that design proved the key. For each item of approved furniture, only a standard design selected by an Advisory Committee to the

Wartime utility furniture.

Board of Trade was to be manufactured. The Committee's Chairman was Charles Tennyson, an industrialist active on the Council for Art and Industry, and its membership included Gordon Russell, furniture designer and manufacturer, John Gloag, consultant and writer on industrial design, and Elizabeth Denby, an expert on low-cost housing and equipment. Within six weeks of their first meeting, a team of invited designers presented drawings and one month later prototypes of selected designs were available for inspection. After another month, in October 1942, they went on view to the public and were in production and available to the public on the first day of 1943, along with Utility ceramic wares and cooking utensils.

The majority of designs were by two High Wycombe, highly experienced furniture designers, Edwin Clinch and H.T. Cutler. Their designs were simple and sturdy, well-made with frames of solid timber and easily manufactured by the inexperienced workers employed in wartime. Since plywood was unavailable, panels were constructed of veneered hardboard, which led to some deprecatory comments about 'cardboard furniture'. However, it satisfied a great need in difficult times.

In June 1944, a Design Panel was established under Gordon Russell to advise on alternative designs within the scheme, particularly using new techniques and materials, in anticipation of the war soon ending. When it did, and the new Labour government took office, it was decided to continue the Utility scheme to provide for post-war needs. Under the Design Panel's auspices the range was widened and restrictions on purchase were gradually relaxed. The scheme finally ended in 1952 after the Conservatives returned to power.

The originators of the scheme had much to look back on with satisfaction. Edwin Clinch asserted that 'Furniture never went back to what it was like before the war – thank God.' Gordon Russell wrote with characteristic understatement: 'I felt that to raise the whole standard of furniture for the mass of the people was not a bad war job.' Certainly, Utility designs were a vast improvement on the array of poorly made revivalist styles generally available for the popular market before the war. However, for a public starved of fantasy, and for designers like David Joel returning from war service, the degree of control necessary to sustain the Utility programme became increasingly intolerable. Joel wrote bitterly of the restrictions which hampered his efforts to re-start production of his own designs on a small-scale and the title of his book, *Furniture Design Set Free*, aptly summarised his reaction to the abolition of the Utility Scheme.

Industrial design since the Second World War

The Council of Industrial Design

For many of the Labour ministers who served in the wartime coalition and later under Attlee, however, such as Hugh Dalton, Sir Stafford Cripps, Aneurin Bevan and George Strauss, control could ensure fairness for all, emphasising the needs of consumers rather than producers, whilst good standards of modern design could serve as a visible symbol of socialist achievement. Dalton, the minister responsible for introducing Utility furniture in the war, believed it could establish standards of taste for simple, well-made designs in the post-war period. Improved design was thus seen as an integral element in the political vision of higher general standards of well-being the Labour party hoped to create. In a futher practical initiative to this end, Dalton was also responsible for establishing a new body, the Council of Industrial Design, in December 1944, with the purpose of promoting 'by all practicable means the improvement of design in the products of British industry'. His successor as President of the Board of Trade in the post-war Labour government, Sir Stafford Cripps, was no less committed to design. One of Cripps' first acts on taking office was to notify the CoID that he wanted a major exhibition of British goods organised with all speed. The intention was to provide a tangible image of the better future that lay ahead.

It rapidly became clear, however, that the range of British goods available was strictly limited, since industry was in the difficult transitional period of converting from wartime to peacetime production. The progress was not simple, for new materials and processes had been widely introduced and new skills learnt. To return to pre-war routines was impracticable, and time was needed to adapt to new possibilities. It was therefore decided that a major purpose of this exhibition would be to stimulate both manufacturers and public with ideas about what could be produced. This more speculative approach involved a risk that little might be forthcoming, which, together with the continuing drabness of Britain after years of austerity, led the chief designer of the exhibition, James Gardner, to opt for a bright, colourful display so that 'in fact there was plenty to look at even if no exhibits came'.

This was indeed a possibility, for the CoID adopted a policy that exhibits should be selected by panels it nominated and not by manufacturers. Its minutes stated: 'Maintenance of high standards is the over-riding consideration and selection committees should not feel bound to choose enough goods to fill the given space if that means a lowering of standards.' It was a brave and high-minded decision, but the missionary spirit which imbued the CoID at that time could also lead it to ignore zealously any point of view but its own, as another minute demonstrated:

The Council has no intention of organising an exhibition of 'best sellers'; the purpose of the exhibition is to give a lead to manufacturers, retailers and the public alike, and the judgement of the market is itself something which is capable of education and development.

The site eventually agreed for the exhibition was the Victoria and Albert Museum, and Cripps' diversion of London's total glass supplies for two months to repair its bomb-damaged glass-roofs was a powerful inducement in the decision. Under the title of 'Britain Can Make It', the exhibition was opened by King George VI on 24 September 1946. The layout was planned on a general sequence which began with the themes 'From War to Peace' and 'New Materials', through a sequence showing the potential of design in various environments, such as homes and schools, in product groups such as clothing and domestic appliances, and activities such as sport and leisure. It culminated in a section emphasising the role of the CoID and industrial design in creating the new post-war world.

Central to all the sections was a concern to educate the public, whose knowledge of design was assumed to be limited. A major educational section was entitled 'What Industrial Design Means', using the theme 'The Birth of an Eggcup', devised by Misha Black to give the public a step-by-step instruction into the processes of industrial design. The public were then given the opportunity of voting for items considered good design. Although the majority of goods on show were either prototypes or for export only, which led to the exhibition being dubbed 'Britain Can't Have It' in the press, it was highly popular with a public starved of colour and novelty, with almost one and a half million visitors.

Sadly, for the home population, the promise of the exhibition remained unfulfilled for several years in an economy bankrupted by the war effort and requiring rigid controls on home consumption in order to rebuild export markets. This brought forced changes in the design awareness of many companies as they struggled to come to terms with overseas markets and differing tastes, particularly in the lucrative American market where, for example in the field of ceramics, simpler, non-decorative forms influenced by Scandinavian products meant abandoning the quaint configurations and floral decoration which had long been the hallmark of British taste. At home too American influence began to penetrate, as in the built-in kitchens of prefabricated houses imported from the USA, which revolutionised concepts of this part of the home, and, in a more diffuse sense, with the images of Hollywood films dominating in the British cinema.

The atmosphere of austerity and making-do was broken in 1951, however, with another major exhibition, the Festival of Britain, in which, again, the CoID played a leading organisational role. Originally conceived as an international exhibition to celebrate the centenary of the Great Exhibition of 1851, it was pared down for economic reasons to a national celebration to recovery from the war. The influence of the CoID was apparent on many levels, in the appointment of architects and designers for specific tasks, in the selection of exhibits, in the furnishing of model homes for the 'Living Architecture' exhibition on the Lansbury Estate in London's East End. There were also two specific projects relating to design.

In 1949 a conference had been organised by the Society of Industrial Artists to explore the visual potential of new scientific methods, at which Dr Kathleen Lonsdale had shown slides of crystallography structures, suggesting they might be appropriate for pattern designs. The idea was taken up by Mark Hartland Thomas of the CoID, who formed a Festival Pattern Group to exploit possibilities of creating new forms. Not only crystallography, but microscopic organisms and bacterial forms and atomic, molecular models were also used for textile, wallpaper and ceramic patterns. This deliberate attempt to create a self-conscious Festival style had some success but only of limited duration.

The second project by the CoID was the assembly of what was first known as the Stock List, a collection of selected designs in all categories of production which could be referred to by potential overseas buyers visiting

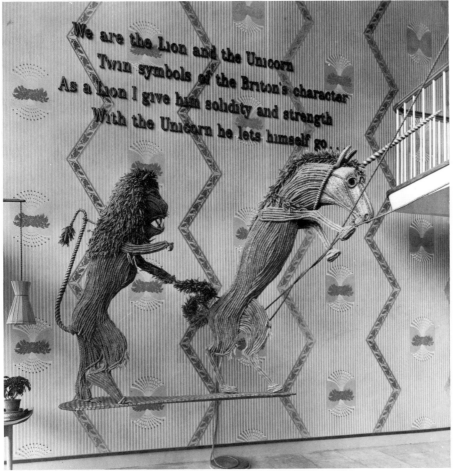

We are the Lion and the Unicorn
Twin symbols of the Briton's character
As a Lion I give him solidity and strength
With the Unicorn he lets himself go...

Lion and Unicorn models designed and made by Fred Mizen for the Festival of Britain (1951).

the Festival and wanting a survey of what was best in any market sector. It later became a permanent collection under the title of the Design Review.

If the Festival can be seen in retrospect as the culmination of the wartime capacity for co-operation and improvisation on projects of national importance, it also looked forward in important respects to a world beyond the drabness of the austerity years. Though hardly pioneering in any original sense, the Festival introduced the British public to a concept of modernity in design, to new forms, materials and practices, above all, to a use of bright, bold colour, that was avidly adopted in all aspects of design. Certain characteristics emerged which were at first collectively designated the 'Festival style', but more generally, simply as 'Contemporary'.

The Festival coincided with a change of government as the Conservatives were returned to power and began the process of dismantling the restrictions of the austerity period. The new policy induced a consumer boom that went on for some fifteen years in a rising curve of expectation. The over-riding emphasis on exports under the post-war Labour government ended, which meant that the need to use design to explore new concepts appropriate to overseas markets was less apparent. If British industry has since become uncompetitive in this respect, the turning point can be identified as the early 1950s with the retreat to the known, comfortable and in many respects undemanding values of a rapidly expanding and prosperous home market.

'Contemporary' style was the first indication of that new prosperity. In furniture and other structures it came to mean planes and surfaces, often of an organic curving shape, supported by slender means such as metal rods. Chairs of all kinds displayed legs that tapered and were angled outwards. Patterns in textiles and coverings were generally of abstract rather than naturalistic forms, again combining organic shape with spikey, linear forms. Many of the materials developed in the war years such as laminates and pressed boards, plastics and aluminium were applied with new paints and dyes and synthetic fabrics and surfacing to produce what at the time was regarded as a striking image of novelty and even of daring.

In retrospect, it can be seen that in many ways 'Contemporary' was not very innovatory, since many of its features could be found in pre-war

Nesting chair designed by Ernest Race in 1960. The steel rod frame was white and the springs were covered in red, blue, yellow and grey plastic.

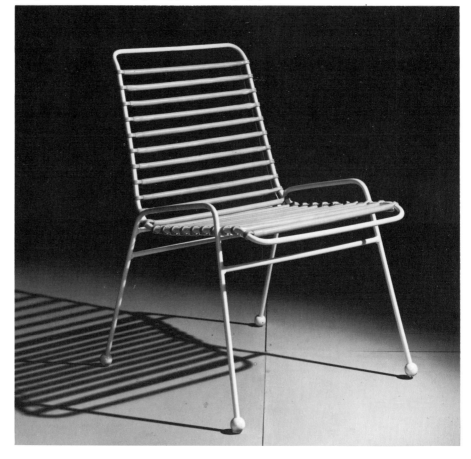

European design. In furniture production, for example, German and Scandinavian designs before 1939 anticipated 'Contemporary' in many respects. The fine arts also had a powerful influence, the organic forms of Henry Moore or the curving linearity of Ben Nicholson in the 1930s suddenly finding their way after the interruption of the war years into a popular vocabulary.

If colour was the most immediate stimulus provided by 'Contemporary', with its bright primary hues and stark contrasts, there was also a change of long-term consequence in the concept of structure. The use of manufactured timber sheet and light-metal meant that strong, lightweight furniture could be mass-produced and challenge older concepts of solidity and massiveness as an indicator of strength and durability. This change was epitomised for many visitors to the Festival of Britain by the chairs designed for it by Ernest Race, which were key objects of 'Contemporary'. The 'Springbok' was constructed of mild steel rod, stove-enamelled to prevent corrosion, with PVC-covered springs stretched across the frame to provide seat and back. They could be used indoors or outside, were stackable and light. The balls at the end of the thin legs were a sensible solution to the problem of a thin rod pressing on vulnerable surfaces or jamming in interstices; but they were also reminiscent of atomic models with their circle and line patterns. More than anything this motif later typified 'Contemporary', with the balls often in bright primary colours.

A second chair designed by Race for the Festival was the 'Antelope', again of welded and white stove-enamelled rod, but this time with a plywood seat sprayed in primary colours. The techniques used by Race in both chairs had been evolved and refined since 1946, but the Festival provided a spectacular platform for his ideas which had a tremendous impact and became very popular.

However, if the Festival stimulated a concept of design that sought to embody the values of new technology and modernity, it also marked the inception of a counter-current. Some aspects of it were characterised by a self-indulgent nostalgia, expressed in a turn towards a romanticised view of the past, as in the Agriculture and Country Pavilion on the South Bank. The Battersea Pleasure Gardens was an important locus of this tendency, deliberately intended as a contrast to the more serious concerns of the Festival as a whole, at which one of the greatest attractions was Rowland Emmett's 'Far Twittering and Oyster Creek Railway', based on cartoons in *Punch*. It was wildly eccentric, freely using a range of old decorative forms such as brass mouldings and fretted barge-boards, and was an enormous popular success. The post-Festival period was therefore characterised both by a range of new developments, and a return of ornamented historical forms, with the latter being the greatest in quantity.

There were, however, significant efforts on a commercial level to popularise new ideas. The range of furniture known as 'G-Plan' introduced by the firm of E.H. Gomme and Sons was mass-produced to provide soundly designed and manufactured goods at prices accessible to a large proportion of the population. It was simple, relying on good proportion and material finish rather than any added decoration, and by being based on a system-concept of matching and interchangeable pieces, enabled any home to be furnished according to the needs of the users. A logical consequence of the use of manufactured boards, widely adopted in furniture production in the 1950s, was that it was most suitable for cutting in rectangular sections and assembling into box-like units. The standardisation of these units on a three-dimensional modular pattern was also exploited to provide built-in and unit furniture. By such means, a limited range of components could be flexibly adapted to meet a vast variety of needs. The 'Extend' system of furniture by D. Meredew Ltd was one of the best-designed and most flexible systems of its kind in the 1950s.

There were also many significant developments in textile design after 1951. Lucienne Day's design 'Calyx' for Heal and Son shown at the Festival is an excellent example, composed of abstracted natural forms which cleverly created an impression of asymmetry within the grid of printing repeats (colour pl. 13). Another very typical pattern of the time was Marianne Straub's 'Helmsley', based on the molecular structure of nylon, which she developed as a furnishing fabric for Warner and Sons.

Carpet design predominantly reverted at this time to traditional forms or freely used naturalistic motifs, but in wallpaper patterns there were many interesting innovations. John Line had commissioned several artists to produce screen-printed patterns, including Lucienne Day, Jacqueline Groag and John Minton, which were issued in 1951. Their designs were set

'Extend' unit furniture by D. Meredew Ltd, 1955.

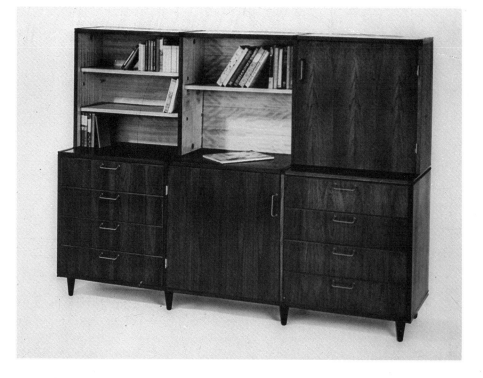

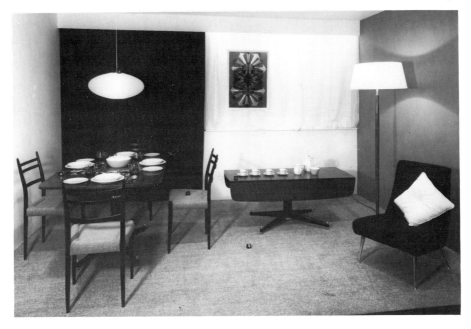

G-Plan furniture made by E. Gomme Ltd at the Design Centre, 1959–60.

alongside plainer and less expensive matching papers, which created a fashion for the stronger design on featured walls or areas, complemented by the simpler papers on other walls.

The ending of restrictions in 1952 on ceramic production for the home market also meant a return to decorative forms, of floral sprays and natural motifs, scalloped or angular surfaces and gold borders. However, David Queensberry developed a notable range of tableware for Crown Staffordshire which relied upon simpler forms and patterns. There were also a number of attempts to introduce new plastics such as melamine into the production of tableware, though its tactile qualities were very different to ceramic products and limited its acceptance.

In the 1950s, innovative products were stoutly supported and publicised by the CoID. Its position as arbiter of taste in all matters concerned with design had seemingly been confirmed by its role in the Festival of Britain and through its journal *Design*, first published in 1948, it was able to advocate its views and present a wide range of work which epitomised its ideals. Its Director from 1947 to 1959 was Gordon Russell, who had a tremendous influence in forming the character and role of the CoID as an institution. Russell had grown up in the Cotswolds, a heartland of the Arts and Crafts movement, but although respecting many aspects of its achievements, he differed emphatically on the subject of mechanisction. 'The hatred of all machines so loudly proclaimed by the Arts and Crafts movement was something I could never share', he wrote in his autobiography, 'but I hated to see wonderful machines badly directed.' In furniture made by his own company for a limited market, also in the mass-production radio cases it manufactured for Murphy before the war, and in the direction of the Utility programme in which Russell was a decisive figure, he sought to emphasise designing for mechanised production which creatively exploited the nature and potential of machines. The tools applied in any area of design were ultimately unimportant for Russell, however; what mattered was an uncompromising adherence to standards of quality. Just as there were standards of honesty, in driving, or in housing, he emphasised, so there should be standards in design. His concept of 'good design' was, on one level, eminently practical, emphasising production techniques, appropriate materials and the purpose of an object, and summarised in two questions: does it work? and, does it look right? He believed in the commercial importance of a design, but also in its capacity to bring pleasing, well-made products within everyone's reach to enhance their lives. The public had to develop critical standards, however, if design was to be effective, based on a permanent improvement of standards rather than short term opportunism.

Under Russell's Directorship of the CoID the idea of a permanent showpiece for British design was realised with the opening in 1956 of the Design Centre in London. It was intended as a permanent home for the Design Review, by now a huge collection of photographs, samples and information on designs chosen by CoID Selection Committees, and for permanent and rotating exhibitions of British goods. In its first twelve months over 700,000 people visited the Centre, and it even featured in one of BBC Television's most popular programmes 'The Grove Family', a series about a suburban London home, when an episode was dedicated to a visit by the family to the Design Centre, with an appropriate discussion of 'good design' woven into the script. In 1957 the Design Centre Award scheme was established to select outstanding achievements each year in design. A broad range of achievement was recognised in 1959 with the Design Centre label, a distinctive mark which companies could attach to their products, acknowledging it had been exhibited at the Design Centre. It was later extended to any product selected for the Design Review.

With Russell as Director, the CoID became an extensive organisation, and it undoubtedly played a considerable role in publicising the work of many companies and designers and improving public awareness of the role of design. Although Russell strenuously rejected any concept of design dictatorship (he saw the CoID's role as one of persuasion and example) there was a problem in that the standards the organisation sought to promulgate were manifested in a simple and often austere aesthetic believed to embody enduring values. Such qualities, however, were not inevitably relevant to the realities of the market-place. In the 1950s, the growth in disposable income was accompanied by visible affluence, consumerism-based changing fashion, ostentation in many respects, built-in obsolescence and disposability, all of which ran counter to the values of the CoID. There was at times a somewhat condescending denigration of what its representatives called 'Borax', or the deliberate styling of products to meet market tastes. This was regarded as a cosmetic marketing device imported from America and a denial of 'good design'. The fact was, however, that neither the British economy, nor British public taste, was susceptible to a common set of values as advocated by the CoID. As austerity changed to increasing affluence, so a plurality of influences became clearly evident, some drawing on imports from other countries as the economy was progressively de-regulated.

This did not necessarily contradict the position of the CoID, as evidenced by the growing imports from Scandinavia, such as Orrefors glassware from Sweden or Arabia ceramics from Finland, and other well-designed and skilfully manufactured products which stocked the numerous 'craft' shops that sprang up in the 1950s to cater for a more sophisticated middle-class clientele. The contrast with influences from America, particularly on a growing youth culture enjoying a new economic independence, was, however, stark. Films such as *The Young Ones* starring Marlon Brando, the impact of rock music associated with Elvis Presley, Chuck Berry and Jerry Lee Lewis, and the imagery of science fiction typical of the more colourful reaches of American design, epitomised in the juke-box, combined to create a thriving sub-culture in Britain among many of the young. Another, very different, strand of imported imagery came from Europe, particularly Italy, with icons such as the chrome-plated Gaggia espresso machines which were the centre-pieces of the coffee bars that mushroomed in the late 1950s, and the Vespa and Lambretta motor-scooters which provided an inexpensive means of transport for many young people.

An interesting contrast with the standpoint of the CoID in the 1950s was provided by the annual exhibitions and yearbooks of the 'Ideal Home' organised by the *Daily Mail*. Although in some respects overlapping with the concerns of the CoID, the exhibitions mirrored a wider range of taste that encompassed traditional designs, and, in particular, indicated a fascination with new domestic concepts in areas such as the kitchen. Built-in units and appliances and continuous working surfaces effected a total transformation from the early utilitarian patterns to a more stylish concept of living/working area. Above all, the range of domestic appliances to which people could realistically aspire, such as vacuum cleaners, televisions, refrigerators and washing-machines, brought a new dimension to the consumer economy.

The Independent Group

This tendency was also evident in a powerful intellectual challenge to the purist aesthetics of what was seen as an older, outmoded generation. Its focal point was the Independent Group, comprising artists, designers and critics, based on the Institute of Contemporary Arts in London, which collectively celebrated the popular mass-media and consumer culture. One of its most prominent figures was the artist Richard Hamilton who utilised the imagery of popular magazines, advertisements, television imagery and consumer products in witty prints and paintings. In 1959, Hamilton gave a lecture at the ICA entitled 'The Design Image of the 'Fifties', which explored the ideas of mass-production, consumption and marketing that were commonplace in the USA, as the basis for an aesthetic relevant, as he saw it, to modern society. It was later printed in *Design* magazine, with dark editorial warnings against American manipulative techniques that threatened 'a form of economic totalitarianism not greatly dissimilar from Orwell's terrifying prophecy'.

The Independent Group's main spokesman on architecture and design, however, was Reyner Banham, who had worked as an aircraft engineer before studying the history of art, and who in numerous articles and lectures waxed lyrical in praise of 'Detroit Tin' and the space-age imagery of American cars in the mid-1950s, as a polemical antithesis to the proclaimed certainties of the CoID design 'establishment'. Although Banham had not at that time visited America, and the phase of fins and other exotic forms had ended around 1957, he argued that these cars were 'the product of science and free aesthetic fancy'. Some years later, he stated:

The case we wanted to make was simply that Detroit styling should at least be looked at, before it was dismissed as trash . . . those of us who were prepared to make a case for Borax and for American styling would claim that we were properly immersed in the subject matter and 'them up there' were not.

Basically, the Independent Group argued that mass art was, like it or not, the popular culture of the age, its universality a strength if only one were able, and willing, to understand it. The ideas of the Group gave a vital impetus, moreover, to a younger generation of designers who had matured in the post-austerity years and were seeking a means of expressing their perception of the modern world.

The most dramatic outcome of their search for new forms and meanings was the pop culture of the mid-1960s. Based on values which raised the ephemeral and disposable to an article of faith, it too was transitory and soon discarded. If it raised television and print media to major forms of expression in modern life, and enjoyed a fleeting notoriety through them, it ended by being exploited and abandoned. In that, there was an appropriate symmetry in its rise and fall. It was essentially localised, the Kings Road and Carnaby Street in London being the main locations with a few out-stations. Yet it was a genuinely open phenomenon, providing access and recognition to talent from whatever it came. Although it became lost in a blind alley of drug-induced fancy in its later stages, probably its major achievement was to break through the barriers of social stratification still existing in British society and create a real sense of validity for many aspects of popular culture.

Specific expressions of pop in three-dimensional design were few, printed ephemera such as posters and record covers being a more natural vehicle for it. There were attempts to create disposable furniture, however, such as Peter Murdoch's Child's Chair of 1964 in laminated paperboard coated with polyethylene, and a series of tables and chairs designated Tom-a-tom by Bernard Holdaway. Produced in 1966, this was made from enamelled hardboard. However, such products had a limited life and were comparatively expensive in a market where veneered chipboard offered an impression, at least, of durability. Perhaps the most apt expression of pop was the ephemeral range of trinkets and memorabilia produced for and sold to the innumerable tourists who sustained Carnaby Street and similar locations in their brief boom years.

Even the CoID, however, could not remain totally impervious to what its next Director, Sir Paul Reilly, called 'The Challenge of Pop'. In an article published in 1967 in *Architectural Review*, he conceded that the values

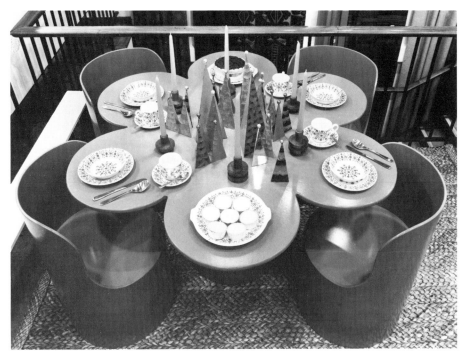

Clover-leaf table and Tomoton chairs by Bernard Holdaway at the Design Centre, 1966.

promulgated by the organisation a decade earlier were no longer entirely valid, and recognised a shift 'from attachment to permanent universal values to acceptance that a design may be valid at a given time for a given purpose to a given group of people in a given set of circumstances . . .'.

Generally, a new freedom to experiment and challenge accepted practice became apparent by the mid-1960s, though often struggling to obtain wide public acceptance. The ideas of the Archigram group for an architectural environment based on flexibility and rapid change were paralleled by Max Clendinning in his Maxima range for Race Furniture. This consisted of a range of basic structural elements, capable of assembly into different formats to support chairs, settees and tables. It was a well-executed idea, but the gulf between the theory informing it and the public's preparedness to accept it was too great.

A similar gulf was evident in the use of plastics, a material considered in pop theory to epitomise modernity. From Italy there was a brilliant succession of designs in this material, but it was more slowly adopted in Britain. Among the better work produced was Robin Day's Polyprop chair for Hille (see page 288) first produced in 1963 and later refined, and David Powell's Nova tableware range which won the Duke of Edinburgh's Prize for Elegant Design in 1968.

Although the 1960s are indelibly associated with pop, there were in fact other strands of development emphasising totally different values. The period was also important for the emergence of a new generation of designer–craftsmen who, in part, at least turned their attention to serial or mass-production. Robert Welch produced some excellent designs for Old Hall Tableware in stainless steel, particularly the Alveston range of tea-set and cutlery. Gerald Benney designed cutlery also in stainless steel for Viners that was totally machine-produced without hand-finishing. David Mellor similarly designed two ranges for use in public canteens that were excellently adapted to machine-processes. Welch and Mellor later established their own production facilities to ensure the standards of quality they considered necessary. Also in the field of glassware, then dominated by German and Scandinavian imports, designers were responsible for establishing new glassworks at Kings Lynn, Dartington and Caithness, which rapidly established a reputation for quality work.

Design in industry

There were changes at the CoID too, in response to demands that it include capital equipment, machine tools and vehicles within its remit, reflected in a new annual award in this area instituted in 1967. In 1972 it was renamed the Design Council as a reflection of its wider range of concerns. In fact, the most successful aspects of its work were thereafter probably achieved in detailed contacts with companies, advising on beneficial links between design in all its aspects.

The work of the Design Council was made more difficult in the 1970s, however, by the continual decline in British industry's effectiveness in the face of foreign competition. Whole sectors of manufacture began to crumble,

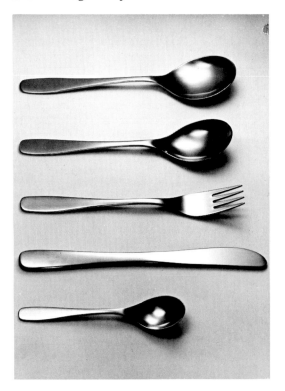

Stainless steel cutlery designed by David Mellor in 1963 for use in Civil Service restaurants and canteens, and also available to hospitals; Design Council Award winner.

and even the home market was in some cases wholly taken over by imported products. The motor-cycle industry in Britain, the world's largest in the 1950s, barely existed any longer by 1975. Whole fields of consumer electrical equipment were similarly decimated, and vehicle imports continually increased. The reasons were complex and go far beyond the scope of this chapter. What did become evident was that this industrial decline bore no correlation to the design talent nurtured in Britain, which was beginning to establish a world-wide reputation and was in continual demand. Where quality was available on the British market, it was frequently supplied from abroad, ironically often under the direction of British designers. This situation was highlighted by a Design Council exhibition in late 1981 entitled 'Designed in Britain – Made Abroad'. The lack of design awareness in British industry, moreover, was despite the fact that for nearly forty years, Britain had possessed in the CoID/Design Council, an organisation which, in its scale, organisation and funding, was the envy of its competitors.

For the first time since the post-war Labour administration, there was direct governmental intervention to try and remedy the situation. In 1982, the Prime Minister, Margaret Thatcher, held a seminar at 10 Downing Street to which representatives of government, industry, design practice and education, and the Design Council were invited. A series of initiatives followed, including the 'Design for Profit' campaign, providing funds for the employment of consultant designers in companies, measures to improve managements' awareness of design, and to relate education more closely to industrial and commercial needs. Such initiatives require time and a continuing commitment for their realisation, however, and it is too early to assess their effect.

Whatever the deficiences of design awareness in British industry, it has not been for a lack of competent practitioners. Since the war, a range of design consultancies has emerged that are second to none. This particular form of design practice evolved in the United States in the inter-war years, an adaptation of advertising consultancies, which gathered together a group of specialists to offer a collective service beyond the means of all but the largest corporations. The success of Walter Dorwin Teague, Raymond Loewy, Harold van Doren, Henry Dreyfuss and many others provided a pattern for emulation.

A powerful and consistent advocate of this form of practice was F.A. Mercer, editor of the monthly journal *Art and Industry*, a companion journal to *The Studio*. Towards the end of the war, Mercer began to look ahead to the problems of peacetime and advocated the expansion of the design profession on the American model, featuring articles by leading practitioners from that country on the role of their consultancies. For Mercer, there was little point in argument about the question 'Aesthetics or Commerce?', or whether a designer should be committed to raising public taste or increased sales. Without an emphasis on production and sales, he pointed out, firms would go out of business, but there was no reason why commercial success should not be compatible with ethical values and a raising of public taste. Consultancies, by ensuring a necessary degree of independence for designers could, according to Mercer, secure the maintenance of standards in all respects, on a basis of mutual understanding and partnership with manufacturers.

A similar argument was put forward by John Gloag, a prominent practitioner and advocate of industrial design before the war, who also pointed to the American example where industrial design was 'accepted by the business community as normal and necessary'. Both Mercer and Gloag emphasised the technical and marketing expertise that was necessary if designers were to communicate effectively with businessmen, who were generally suspicious of 'artists', to enable the creative aspects of design to be realised.

The first British consultancy on the American pattern had, in fact, been founded in 1942 by Herbert Read who acted as its chairman. The practical direction of the Design Research Unit, as it was known, was led by Milner Gray and Misha Black, two pioneers of British design practice in the 1930s. Both the range of expertise at DRU and the lack of awareness in industry meant, however, that the majority of its work was initially in the field of graphic design, especially 'house styles' in advertising and packaging, and interior design. Nevertheless, it was highly successful and rapidly expanded on the basis of extensive commissions for Courage, the brewers, Dunlop, Ilford, British Overseas Airways and P and O Lines.

In the post-war years several other consultancies emerged such as Sir William Crawford and Partners, Hulme Chadwick, who designed aircraft interiors and later was consultant to Wilkinson Sword, James Gardner, who had designed the 'Britain Can Make It' exhibition and the Battersea Pleasure Gardens, and went on to complete commissions as diverse as interiors for the Vickers Viscount aircraft, a Mississippi steam-boat, and the overall design supervision of interiors for the liner, Queen Elizabeth II.

A consultancy that made the breakthrough into specialising in industrial design was founded by David Ogle in 1954. Early commissions included a solid-fuel burner for Allied Ironfounders and, one of the best product-designs of that period, the Bush TR82 portable radio, which used a finely moulded plastic casing and controls of great simplicity and effectiveness. Its founder was killed in a car crash in 1962, but under the direction of Tom Karen, who succeeded him, Ogle have continuously grown and extended their expertise. Projects in the 1960s included further work for Bush, Electrolux and another iron-foundry, Carrons. The company had begun work on transport design in 1959 and, increasingly, began to specialise in this field, with work on projects such as the Reliant Scimitar GTE car, the Raleigh Chopper bicycle, coaches for Plaxtons and a trans-continental sleeper-car for long distance trucks for Coventry Motor Panels. In 1974, separate divisions were established for transport and product design with additional facilities being developed for prototype and model-making, and for research into materials applications, such as the use of Triplex glass to give areas of visibility in car bodies, and the use of crash-test dummies in safety testing. In the standard of services it offers, in its ability to attract the right talents and provide them with the responsibility and resources they need, Ogle have become one of the most respected design organisations of their kind in the world.

Other highly regarded industrial designers who developed their own consultancies in the 1950s were Douglas Scott, Jack Howe and Martin Rowlands. More than anything else, they established a platform of competence and confidence on which their successors could build.

Many consultancies continued to evolve, however, from origins as graphic design specialists. Wolf Olins emerged to develop an international clientele in the field of corporate design, encompassing every aspect of a company's visual presentation. Minale Tattersfield, founded in 1964, followed a broadly similar path, as did James Pilditch's Allied International Designers.

One of the most successful consultancies in Britain, Pentagram, was formed in 1972 by a merger of a major graphic design consultancy, Crosby Fletcher Forbes Kurlansky, and that of the industrial designer, Kenneth Grange. The latter's career is in many respects a paradigm of development in his discipline since the end of the war. At that time Grange was completing his secondary education at Willesden School of Arts and Crafts. There followed a wide variety of work in a series of design and architectural offices until in 1958 he obtained commissions from Kodak for their small 44A Camera and from Venner Limited for a parking meter. His practice began to grow substantially, however, after designing the Kenwood Chef kitchen machine in 1961, which remained in production until 1975. Further commissions followed from Kodak – for example, the Instamatic camera of 1968 – Ronson and Wilkinson Sword, amongst many others. Another key point in his career, however, was an invitation in 1965 to design sewing machines for a Japanese company, Maruzen of Osaka, which developed into a long-standing relationship, with Grange designing an extensive range of products. Maruzen's major client was the giant American department store chain, Sears Roebuck, and success in that context firmly established Grange's international reputation. The merger to form Pentagram in 1972 therefore came on an upward curve of success and provided a context of additional skills and expertise. The extent of his work has continued to be broad and varied, from the cab of British Rail's High-Speed train, to washing machines for Bendix, pens for Parker and disposable razors for Wilkinson Sword. Grange has the ability to reconcile technical and commercial requirements,

Kodak camera designed by Kenneth Grange in 1966, and made in plastic-coated steel, aluminium and brass with black, silver and chrome finish.

Kenwood Chef, designed by Kenneth Grange.

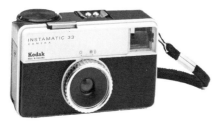

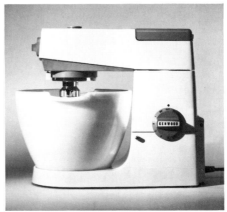

often of a detailed and complex nature, with a fine sense of form and detail. Essential to an understanding of his work is his stress on the value of a strong creative spirit in design, which can be enhanced by effective teamwork, and a belief that the public deserve the best quality attainable:

There is a lot of nonsense talked about fitness for purpose, which implies that products should be stripped of everything superfluous to their function. I submit that this is not enough. Part of the purpose of every product is to give pleasure and that . . . is one of the designer's key contributions.

The excellent relationships Grange has enjoyed with many managers in companies is testament to the latters' vital role in any design process. The development of design consultancies would indeed have been impossible without a recognition of the importance of design within many industrial and commercial organisations. Before the war, London Transport had gained an enviable reputation in this respect under the guidance of its vice-chairman, Frank Pick. After the war, it continued to employ some of the best talent available, with figures such as Douglas Scott, Misha Black, Jack Howe and Christian Barman designing buses and bus-shelters and signs. In 1963 it established the London Transport Design Panel to provide continuous advice, which was incorporated in major projects such as the Victoria and Jubilee Lines completed in 1971 and 1979 respectively.

Other major transport organisations followed the example set by London Transport. In 1945, British Overseas Airways Corporation established its Design Committee to ensure a co-ordinated design policy in all aspects of its operations. Basic to its considerations was a commitment to present an image of the best of British design to the world. This led to commissions for standardised crockery and cutlery in co-operation with a number of firms, with designs by N.G.R. Poynton and Kenneth Holmes emphasising common

London Transport Routemaster buses, designed by Scott in 1965.

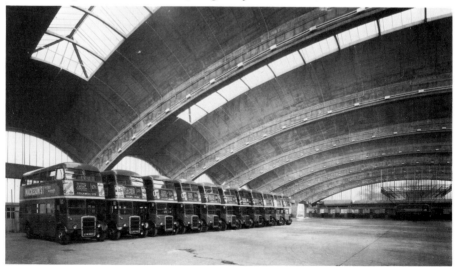

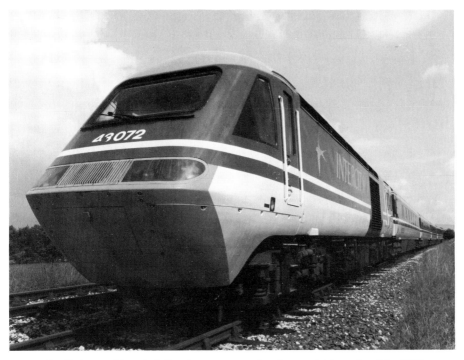

British Rail's 'Inter-City 125' diesel passenger train; first model introduced in 1976.

components in production and the need for stacking and storage in confined spaces. Aircraft interiors were also the subject of other commissions, and the Design Research Unit was responsible for the new Heathrow headquarters opened in 1955.

When the railway system was nationalised in 1948, a continuing problem was in reconciling the long-established traditions of the constituent companies. In 1956, the British Railways Design Panel was established to provide a new co-ordinated image, by using outside consultants together with its own designers and engineers. The DRU again figured prominently in some early work on a new generation of diesel locomotives, the D2000 series, for Western Region with Misha Black and J. Beresford Evans as consulting designers, and a new range of waiting-room furniture was commissioned from Robin Day. A major achievement was a new corporate identity programme under the direction of Milner Gray, also of DRU, which was launched in 1964 and encompassed every aspect of British Railways' visual appearance and communications. It was an outstanding success and has served as a model for direct imitation in many other countries. Unfortunately, this excellence of design has not always been matched by a similar quality of service on BR, and such a gulf between image and reality can be self-defeating.

In the private sector, many companies also established their own in-house design teams. The electrical industry early recognised the role of appearance as a marketing device in what, in the 1950s and '60s, became a highly competitive market. Companies such as HMV, Marconi, Ecko and Hoover brought a new, smooth style to the forms of domestic appliances in this period. The effectiveness of in-house designers depended heavily, however, on their relationships with other specialists and their status within company hierarchies.

The major automobile manufacturers also began to establish their own design teams as an extension of their basic engineering expertise in this period. However, the development of a world market in motor vehicles and the tendency for the industry to group into ever-larger multi-national concerns, has made it increasingly difficult to speak of design in this area in purely national terms. Already by 1962, the most successful car in Britain for the next two decades, the Ford Cortina, was styled under the direction of a Canadian for a European market. By the early 1980s, General Motors were designing in terms of a 'world-car' concept of a limited range of standard types, with local variations such as Vauxhall's Cavalier and Astra, adapted to the British market. This kind of trend is complicated by the fact that British designers frequently work for major international competitors, recently, for example, playing leading roles in companies such as Citröen, Audi and Olivetti.

Although there had undoubtedly been a considerable expansion in the design awareness of some British companies, and their employment of design expertise, the overall pattern would seem to indicate that too little attention has been paid to this factor compared with other leading industrial countries. Even where design expertise is valued, it may not be enough, without high levels of performance in fields such as research, production, marketing and general management. The collapse of two companies in the early 1980s with a long record of design excellence, Old Hall Ltd, producers of holloware and cutlery, and Hornsea Pottery, indicate clearly that design alone cannot secure viability.

The difficulties of establishing effective mutual communication between designers and management was already being identified in the 1960s as an obstacle in many companies. A remedy attempted by Michael Farr, a former editor of *Design* magazine, was to establish an agency specialising in managing design projects, as an intermediary between industry and designer. More recently, however, greater attention is being paid to educating management to understand the language, concepts and potential of design, and conversely, of educating designers to understand the nature of the commercial context in which they work.

Some designers have also shown a considerable capacity in managerial and entrepreneurial skills. David Mellor not only produces his own cutlery in Sheffield, but has opened shops selling domestic equipment and artefacts that accord with his concept of quality. Laura Ashley began producing printed fabrics at home and developed a multi-million pound business, encompassing the entire process from design through production to retail sales of textiles, wallpapers and other domestic items. They were based on highly popular adaptations of traditional and country forms and patterns.

The most remarkable success in this respect, however, has been Terence

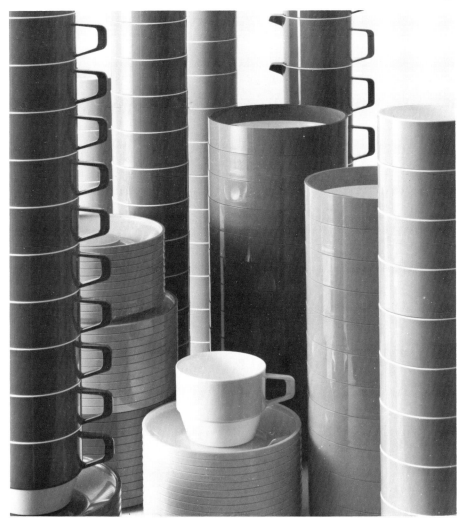

'Nova' plastic tableware designed by David Powell for Ecko Plastics Ltd in 1965; white and blue, mushroom, yellow and red.

Conran. Trained as a textile designer, Conran formed his own design company in 1955 and nine years later opened his first Habitat retail store in London in 1964, selling furniture and domestic goods. It was by any standards a spectacular success, expanding by 1985 to forty-two stores in Britain, and establishing a basis for amalgamations and takeovers that have made Conran one of the most successful entrepreneurs of the age. He established his own design consultancy, Conran Associates, in 1971, which provides services to his own holdings, but has also grown into a large organisation providing designs for other companies across a broad spectrum. The Crayonne range of compatible bathroom fittings using high quality mouldings for Airfix Plastics in the mid-1970s was an outstanding early product success.

Conran's influence has also been considerable through a series of books he has written on domestic design and furnishings, which has perhaps inevitably led to the acquisition of a publishing house. In addition, the Conran Foundation he endowed established the first exhibition centre for design in 1982. Initially housed in the Boilerhouse, a basement area of the Victoria and Albert Museum, it is intended to move to purpose-built premises near Tower Bridge in 1988, providing a centre of information and exhibits for practitioners and the public. Inevitably, the Midas-touch Conran has shown, and the range of activities in which he is involved, have aroused controversy and resentment. However, he has probably done more than anyone else, or any other agency, to bring design and its importance into the consciousness of the British public.

With the expansion of design practice, both numerically and in its scope, an increasing concern has been to establish its role on a more formal basis. Since the war, the Society of Industrial Artists has sought to escape the fanciful bohemian connotations attached to design in the minds of industrialists, by defining a more professional code of practice, and seeking incorporation similar to that accorded architects. In 1965 it was renamed the Society of Industrial Artists and Designers, but neither the change of title nor its efforts to obtain public recognition have succeeded in realising its aims. It was significant that when Mrs Thatcher held her seminar in 1982, the SIAD was not represented. It is doubtful, moreover, whether formal professional status would help designers without a fundamental and extensive change of attitude in large areas of British industry. If that can be achieved, and designers can prove their worth, such trappings of status may even be unnecessary.

Training the designer

In education, however, there has been a tremendous expansion. In 1945 no formal structure of industrial design education existed in Britain. In an

Habitat store in the Fulham Road, London, 1966.

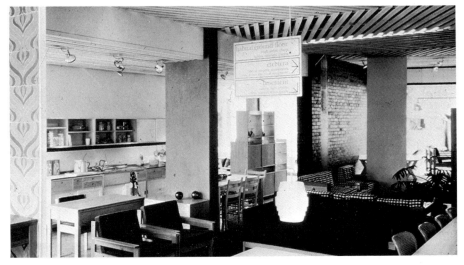

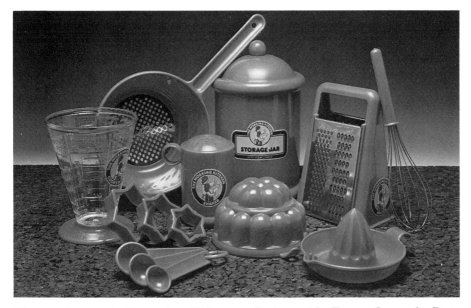

'Crayonne' range of polypropylene kitchen utensils, designed by Terence Conran for Boots and Timothy Whites.

article in 'Design '46', the catalogue of the 'Britain Can Make It' exhibition, Professor Robin Darwin noted that the names of designers could be found alongside those of manufacturers in the exhibition, with the hope they would be accorded recognition. He emphasised: 'The man who designs a refrigerator or a sewing machine may be quite a different sort of person from the designer of, say, a wallpaper, and he will need a different training.' Darwin looked to a pattern combining the sensitivity of art with the technical proficiency of production engineering. Later as Rector of the Royal College of Art, he was instrumental in establishing specialist courses in Industrial Design under Misha Black, an experienced practitioner and an outstanding teacher. Black's impact on his students, who were to form an elite corps in the succeeding years in the expansion both of practice and education, was to be one of the most formative influences on the emergence of design.

The RCA courses were postgraduate and stimulated the development of undergraduate courses in institutions across the country. By the 1960s, three year degree-level courses were widely available in a range of both general and specialist departments. They were generally located in colleges of art and, although the creative benefit of being located with other artistic disciplines is often stressed, there have been problems in overcoming the arts and crafts legacy of antipathy to industry. Many such colleges were incorporated with colleges of technology in the polytechnics established from 1968 onwards. In the best of these institutions, this has meant retaining links with the freer, more speculative influences of, for example, painting and sculpture, whilst forging links with other disciplines such as engineering and business studies. In comparative terms, Britain has the most extensive system of design education in the world, and at its highest standard, is as good as any. Yet design education too is bedevilled with the problem of status, being almost totally absent in the university sector, and therefore considered in many respects less valid than older established disciplines.

The aesthetics of engineering design

The problems faced by industrial designers in gaining acceptance have also been endured by engineers, and for a much longer period, despite a tradition that has created some of the most significant forms and structures of the last two centuries. These often display qualities of a high creative order, going far beyond the requirements of utilitarian function. The de Havilland Comet, for example, which entered service in 1952, was the culmination of a long-line of fine aircraft by that company, its sheer lines establishing a new aesthetic for jet-powered aircraft in the post-war years. More recently, the Anglo-French Concorde has provided controversy on many levels, but there is little dispute over its powerful and dramatic form.

In automobile design some British companies adopted the American practice of styling after the war, with Austin, for example, using Raymond Loewy's office for its first post-war ranges, but later employing the Italian Pininfarina. It was engineers, however, who produced the most dramatic innovations. Sir William Lyon's Jaguar company produced a succession of

Display of British-made kitchen ware at the Victoria and Albert Museum's 'Britain Can Make It' exhibition (1946).

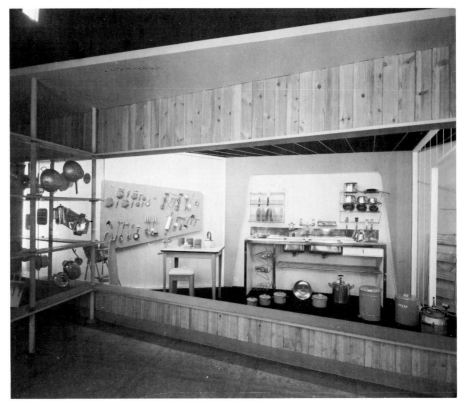

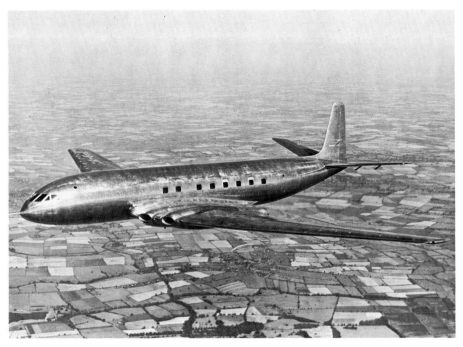

Prototype of the 'Comet' jet-propelled air-liner, made by de Havilland Aircraft Co and first flown in 1949.

thoroughbreds, their E-type sports car representing a sleek, powerful image of quality and luxury. At the other end of the spectrum, Alex Issigonis produced two classics. His Morris 1000 was one of the most comfortable and reliable small cars of the 1950s, and has since become a cult object. In terms of apprearance, its modest flowing curves were pleasing though undramatic. Compared to its major competitor, the German Volkswagen, it was quiet and spacious. Yet there the comparison ends. The Morris 1000 was designed for quiet British country roads; it simply was not robust enough in key areas such as shock-absorbers and lacked the back-up service needed to succeed abroad. It demonstrated simultaneously the continuing vitality of so much of the British design tradition, and its greatest weakness in commercial terms, namely, an insularity that frequently rendered it incapable of understanding conditions other than its own.

A similar contradiction existed in what was Issigonis' greatest achievement, his Mini car of 1959. It was conceptually and technically a genuinely revolutionary vehicle, and in Britain came to epitomise a whole trend in fashion in the 1960s. Yet although enormously popular, it could not be produced in quantities or at a cost that translated the vehicle's astonishing status into profit. The days were rapidly approaching, moreover, when the principle of building soundly engineered cars was in itself not enough. A fiercely competitive world market demanded greater sophistication and consistency. Sadly, when British Leyland at last came to take automobile design seriously, its management were still incapable of exploiting superb ideas. With his concept of the Range Rover, David Bache, the head of BL's

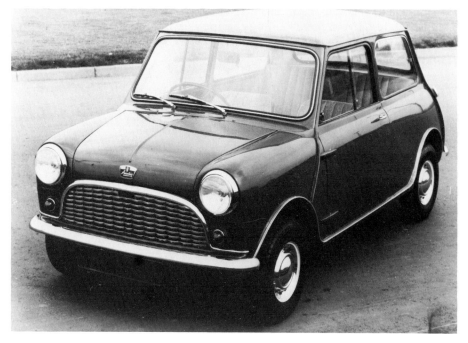

Austin Mini Cooper Mk II, designed by Alex Issigonis.

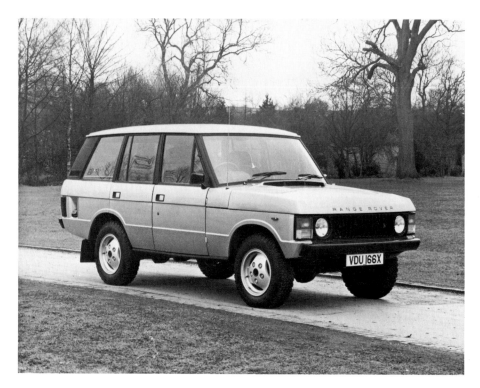

Range Rover (four-door), designed by David Bache for British Leyland, 1982.

design team, achieved an elegant vehicle combining the best of the new industrial design and the older engineering disciplines. It was never produced in quantities capable of meeting demand, however, and soon overseas competition produced their own versions.

On a more optimistic note, the combination of engineering and aesthetics can, in the right context, be highly vigorous and successful. The firm of JCB Excavators in Staffordshire, for example, produces a range of heavy construction machinery that has won a string of design awards. Their founder, Joseph Bamford, established in the post-war years an ethos for the company emphasising continual innovation, quality production and a sensitivity to appearance in every aspect of his company's activities. Machines such as an articulated wheel-loader may seem an unlikely subject for a discussion on aesthetics; however, if it is built and performs well, a detailed attention to its visual appearance becomes an expression of a range of other

Leyland 'Roadrunner' truck.

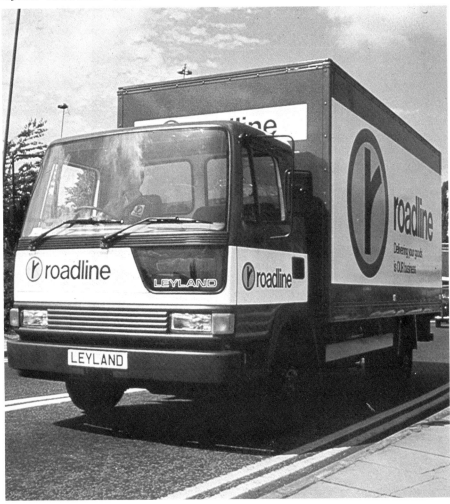

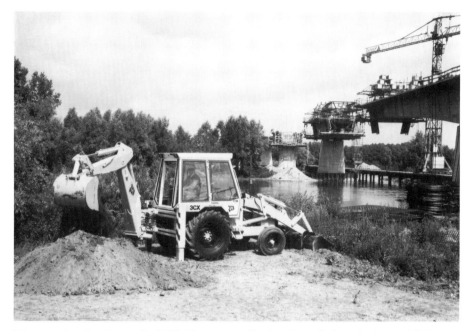

Digger designed and made by JCB Excavators; Design Council Award winner, 1984.

qualities. It will assuredly not sell on the basis of visual quality alone, but as an integral aspect of a process which emphasises quality of products as an expression of quality in life and work, it can have a value that does not deny, but neither is it constrained by, the demands of commercialism.

The idea that culture may be compatible with industry is one that has yet to take widespread root in British society. It is frequently confined to the notion of patronage for established institutions in the realm of 'high' art, as part of a company's image. That concept of image, or corporate identity, is in itself revealing, depending too often on a superficial application of design as an afterthought, usually with short term gain in mind. What is more relevant is the concept advocated by Mary Mullin of corporate character, in which every aspect of an organisation's structure and behaviour, and their manifestation in visual form, can be regarded as evidence of the values on which it is based. Without a sense of ethical purpose, design can deteriorate into an exercise in opportunistic deception for a cynical public. As an integral element of a context in which humane values predominate, however, industrial design is capable of helping to generate, on an extensive scale, that heightened sensitivity and pleasure in shared creativity which is necessary for any broadly-based culture.

Part III
Appendix: Further Reading and Reference

ALAN MUNTON

Contents

Introduction

The bibliography that follows is intended as a guide to further reading. The guidance is of two kinds. Firstly, the general reader is directed towards introductory books and to articles of particular interest. Where standard works exist, these are indicated in the annotations. The addresses of institutions which deal with particular arts are given, together with an outline of their activities and publications. Secondly, an attempt has been made to include material that will allow readers to research particular fields more deeply. The period dealt with in this volume is, from the critical point of view, still in a state of process and change. In practice, very few 'standard works' exist in any of the arts for this period. For this reason, the following listings also give the basic materials from which an assessment might be built. In a number of areas – ballet, music, painting and literature in particular – an attempt has been made to indicate the individual works out of which the art itself is made up. This may open up the possibility of further critical discussion.

In the practical arts, such as the crafts, industrial design and painting and drawing, the intention has been to direct the reader towards books which illustrate the objects produced. This has often meant reference to exhibition catalogues. These are not always easy to find, though in most cases the institutions which publish them – such as the Crafts Council or the Victoria and Albert Museum – will have copies. The inter-library loan system, used through public libraries or academic institutions, should produce a copy of any item in the following bibliography. No book on how to carry out the practical arts is included, except in one outstanding instance in the crafts, where practice transformed the field of weaving.

During this period all the arts in Britain have been variously influenced by developments in Africa, the Americas, Asia and Europe. In order to keep the bibliography to a reasonable length, all books constituting such influences have been omitted. This is not an intellectually defensible decision; but where these influences exist they are described by the authors of the essays on particular arts. Where a British author has written a significant work introducing such influences to a home audience, this has been included.

The place of publication for almost all the entries in this bibliography is London. Only if a work is published in a foreign country is the place of publication given. The name of the publisher is always omitted, but the annotations indicate the source of exhibition catalogues. The full subtitle of books is given, because such information is almost always useful (and is more useful than the publisher's name).

The most valuable bibliographical aid for the arts in general is the quarterly *British Humanities Index* (1962 to date; previously *The Subject Index to Periodicals*). This lists articles in journals, magazines and newspapers. The journals reviewed could be more wide-ranging: neither *Crafts* nor *Design* is included, for example; but there is nevertheless a multitude of relevant headings.

Excluded from the following listings are all dictionaries referring to particular arts, and all general reference books. Historical surveys of particular areas with a final chapter on the modern period are also excluded.

I The Cultural and Social Setting

The 1940s

The best accounts of the social and political aspects of the war years are Paul Addison's *The Road to 1945* (1975) and Angus Calder's *The People's War* (1969), both of which have very full bibliographies. Robert Hewison's *Under Siege: Literary Life in London 1939–1945* (1977) ranges wider than its subtitle suggests, and has a detailed list of sources, as does his *In Anger: Culture in the Cold War 1945–60* (1981). Arthur Marwick's *British Society since 1945* (1982) is a cultural as well as an historical survey.

A selection from *Picture Post* (weekly, 1 October 1938 to 1 June 1957) has been published as *'Picture Post': 1938–1950* (1984). The Communist Party cultural journal *Our Time* (1941–9), edited by Edgell Rickword, was reprinted in 1976.

HISTORY, DIARIES, MEMOIRS AND FICTION

Addison, P., *The Road to 1945: British Politics and the Second World War* (1975)

Brittain, V., *England's Hour* (1941)

Calder, A., *The People's War: Britain 1939–1945* (1969)

Calvocoressi, P. and Wint, G., *Total War* (1972)

Costello, J., *Love, Sex and War: Changing Values 1939–45* (1985)

Fitzgibbon, C., *The Blitz* (1957) [*The Winter of the Bombs* in USA (1958)]

Graves, C., *Londoner's Life* (1942) [diary August 1941–July 1942]
  Off the Record (1942) [diary November 1940–August 1941]
  Pride of the Morning (1945) [diary November 1943–December 1944]

Green, H., *Caught* (1943) [novel]

Hanley, J., *No Directions* (1943) [Blitz novel]

Henrey, Mrs Robert, *London Under Fire 1940–1945* (1969) [diary]

Hodson, J.L., *Before Daybreak* (1941) [diary March–June 1941]
  Home Front (1944) [diary April 1942–March 1943]
  The Way Things Are (1947) [diary May 1945–February 1947]

Hopkins, H., *The New Look: a Social History of the Forties and Fifties in Britain* (1963) [bibl.]

Lewis, P., *A People's War* (1986)

Longmate, N. (ed.), *Home Front: an Anthology of Personal Experience 1938–1945* (1981)

Nicolson, H., *Diaries and Letters 1939–1945*, N. Nicolson (ed.) (1967)

Orwell, G., 'War-time diaries' in S. Orwell and I. Angus (ed.), *The Collected Essays, Journalism and Letters of George Orwell: Volume II: My Country Right or Left 1940–1943* (1968, repr. 1970) [the whole collection is important]

Pelling, H., *Britain and the Second World War* (1970) [bibl.]

Waugh, E., *Put Out More Flags* (1942) [novel of 1939–40]
  The Sword of Honour Trilogy (1964) comprising *Men at Arms* (1952), *Officers and Gentlemen* (1955), *Unconditional Surrender* (1961)

CULTURE IN WARTIME

Davin, D., *Closing Times* (1975) [memoir of writers, 1940s and 1950s]

Dean, B., *The Theatre at War* (1956) [history of ENSA]

Grundy, B., *That Man: A Memory of Tommy Handley* (1976) [ITMA; see Worsley, F.]

Leavis, F.R., *Mass Civilisation and Minority Culture* (1931)

Lynn, V., *Vocal Refrain: an Autobiography* (1975)

Maclaren-Ross, J., *Memoirs of the Forties* (1965) [literary life]

Priestley, J.B., *Postscripts* (1940) [the radio broadcasts]

Wilson, Edmund, *Europe Without Baedeker: Sketches Among the Ruins of Italy, Greece and England* (1948, repr. 1986) [Britain in 1946]

Worsley, F., *Itma 1939–1948* (1948) [radio show]

The 1950s

Addison, P., *Now the War Is Over: a Social History of Britain 1945–51* (1985)

Allsop, K., *The Angry Decade: a Survey of the Cultural Revolt of the Nineteen-fifties* (1958)

Amis, K., *Lucky Jim* (1954) [novel]

Braine, J., *Room at the Top* (1957) [novel]

Driver, C., *The Disarmers: a Study in Protest* (1964) [Campaign for Nuclear Disarmament]

Everett, P., *You'll Never be 16 Again* (1986) [history of teenager]

Heron, L. (ed.), *Truth, Dare or Promise: Girls Growing up in the Fifties* (1985)

Hopkins, H., *The New Look: a Social History of the Forties and Fifties in Britain* (1963) [bibl.]

Johnson, B.S. (ed.), *All Bull: the National Servicemen* (1973) [memories]

MacInnes, C., *City of Spades* (1950, repr. 1986); *Absolute Beginners* (1959, repr. 1986); *Mr Love and Justice* (1960, repr. 1986) [novels]
  England, Half English (1961, repr. 1986) [essays]
Muir, E., 'The Horses', *Collected Poems* (1963), pp. 246–7
Orwell, G., *Nineteen Eighty-Four* (1949) [novel]
Osborne, J., *Look Back in Anger* (1957) [play]
Tippett, M., *Moving into Aquarius* (1959, repr. 1974) [essays]

The 1960s

Blythe, R., *Akenfield: Portrait of an English Village* (1969)
Bond, E., *Saved* (1966) [play]
Booker, C., *The Neophiliacs* (1969) [new hedonism]
Burgess, A., *A Clockwork Orange* (1962) [novel]
Carter, A., 'Notes for a theory of sixties style', in P. Barker (ed.), *Arts in Society* (1977)
Cockburn, A., and Blackburn, R. (ed.), *Student Power: Problems, Diagnosis, Action* (1969) [essays on higher education, student revolt, culture]
Cooper, D. (ed.), *The Dialectics of Liberation* (1968) [conference]
Hewison, R., *Too Much: Art and Society in the Sixties 1960–1975* (1986) [important survey; bibl.]
Levin, B., *The Pendulum Years: Britain and the Sixties* (1970) [journalism]
Melly, G., *Revolt into Style: the Pop Arts in Britain* (1970)
Private Eye (fortnightly, 1961 to date) [satire, political revelation]
Sampson, A., *Anatomy of Britain* (1962), rev. as *The New Anatomy of Britain* (1971); cont. as *The Changing Anatomy of Britain* (1982, rev. 1983)
Walter, A. (ed.), *Come Together: the Years of Gay Liberation* (1980)
Widgery, D. (ed.), *The Left in Britain 1956–1968* (1976)
Young, W., *The Profumo Affair* (1963)

The Arts Council

Baldry, H., *The Case for the Arts* (1982)
Braden, S., *Artists and People* (1978)
Harris, J.S., *Government Patronage of the Arts in Great Britain* (1970)
Hutchison, R., *The Politics of the Arts Council* (1982)
Minahan, J., *The Nationalisation of the Arts* (1977)
Osborne, C., *Giving It Away: Memoirs of an Uncivil Servant* (1986) [literature director]
Redcliffe-Maude, Lord, *Support for the Arts in England and Wales: a Report to the Calouste Gulbenkian Foundation* (1976)
Shaw, Sir R., *The Arts and the People* (1987)
White, Eric W., *The Arts Council of Great Britain* (1975) [personal history]

Broadcasting

Programmes can be heard at the British Library Institute of Recorded Sound, 29 Exhibition Road, London SW7. The BBC Sound Archives are for BBC use only, but researchers are admitted in exceptional cases. The most useful single bibliography is Gavin Higgens (ed.), *British Broadcasting 1922–1982: a Select and Annotated Bibliography* (BBC Data Publications, 1983).

The history of the BBC is being written by Asa Briggs; four volumes have appeared: *The History of Broadcasting in the United Kingdom, Vol. I: The Birth of Broadcasting* (1961) [1922–1927]; *Vol. II: The Golden Age of Wireless* (1965) [1927–1939]; *Vol. III: The War of Words* (1970) [1939–1945]; *Vol. IV: Sound and Vision* (1978) [1945–1955]. Briggs' *The BBC: the First Fifty Years* (1985) abbreviates the four published volumes, with new material on recent developments. The two most important recent reports on broadcasting are *The Report of the Committee on Broadcasting 1960* (Pilkington report, 1962), and the *Report of the Committee on the Future of Broadcasting* (Annan report, 1977).

Alvarado, M. and Stewart, J., *Made for Television: Euston Films Limited* (1985) [*The Sweeney, Minder*]
Bakewell, J. and Garnham, N., *The New Priesthood: British Television Today* (1970)
Frost, D. and Sherrin, N. (ed.), *That Was The Week That Was* (1963) [scripts]
Goldie, G.W., *Facing the Nation: Television and Politics 1936–1976* (1977)
Halloran, J., Elliott, P., Murdock, G., *Demonstrations and Communication: a Case Study* (1970)
Lynn, J. and Jay, A., *The Complete Yes Minister: the Diaries of a Cabinet Minister* (1984) [TV series as fiction]
Postman, N., *Amusing Ourselves to Death: Public Discourse in the Age of Showbusiness* (1986)
Schlesinger, P., *Putting 'Reality' Together: BBC News* (1978)

Williams, R., *Television: Technology and Cultural Form* (1974)

Wilson, H.H., *Pressure Group: the Campaign for Commercial Television in England* (1961)

Campaigning

Bailey, R., *The Squatters* (1973)

Pym, B., *Pressure Groups and the Permissive Society* (1974)

Tracey, M., *Whitehouse* (1979) [biography of Mary Whitehouse]

Culture/cultural studies

Anderson, P., 'Components of the national culture' in A. Cockburn and R. Blackburn (ed.), *Student Power* (1969), pp. 214–84

Cohen, S., *Folk Devils and Moral Panics: the Creation of the Mods and Rockers* (1972)

Hall, S. and Whannell, P., *Popular Culture* (1964)

Hebdige, D., *Subculture: the Meaning of Style* (1979) [bibl.]

Hoggart, R., *The Uses of Literacy* (1957) [seminal work]

Laing, S., *Representations of Working Class Life 1957–1964* (1986)

Neville, R., *Play Power* (1970) [underground culture]

New Left Review (bi-monthly, 1960 to date) [internationalist political debate]

Nuttall, J., *Bomb Culture* (1968) [British underground]

Snow, C.P., *The Two Cultures and the Scientific Revolution* (1959)

Universities and Left Review (1957–9) [continued as *New Left Review*]

Williams, R., *Culture and Society 1780–1950* (1958) [major study]
  The Long Revolution (1961) [Pt III: 'Britain in the 1960s']

Willis, P.E., *Profane Culture* (1978) [bikers, hippies]

Young, M. and Willmott, P., *Family and Kinship in East London* (1957, rev. 1962 and 1986)

Culture of ethnic groups

Cashmore, E.E., *Rastaman* (1979)

Greater London Arts, *in the Eye of the Needle: Report of the Independent Inquiry into Greater London Arts* 1986)

Hebdige, D., *Cut 'N' Mix: Culture, Identity and Caribbean Music* (1987) [Jamaica, Britain]

Johnson, L.K., 'Jamaican rebel music', *Race and Class* **17** (1976)

Khan, N., *The Arts Britain Ignores: the Arts of Ethnic Minorities in England* (1976)

The Eye of the Needle: inquiry into Greater London Arts

Education

The Black Papers: Cox, C.B. and Dyson, A.E. (ed.), *Fight for Education* [1969] *The Crisis in Education* [1969]; *Goodbye Mr Short* (1970) [nos. 1–3 repr. 1971]; Cox, C.B. and Boyson, R. (ed.), *Black Paper 1975 and 1977*

Harris, D., *Openness and Closure in Distance Education* (1987) [Open University]

The Hornsey Affair (1969) [Hornsey College of Art dispute]

Illich, I.D., *Deschooling Society* (1971)

Jackson, B. and Marsden, D. (ed.), *Education and the Working Class: some General Themes* (1962, rev. 1966)

Pedley, R., *The Comprehensive School* (1963)

Perry, W., *Open University: a Personal Account* (1976)

Peters, R.S., 'Education as initiation' in R.A. Archambault (ed.), *Philosophical Analysis and Education* (1965), 87–111

Thompson, E.P. (ed.), *Warwick University Ltd: Industry, Management and the Universities* (1970)

Universities Quarterly (1945–86) [culture, education and society]

Willis, P.E., *Learning to Labour: how Working Class Kids Get Working Class Jobs* (1977) [bibl.]

Young, M., *The Rise of the Meritocracy: 1870–1933* (1959)

Feminism/Women's Liberation Movement

Feminist Review (3 p.a., 1979 to date) [socialist feminist]

m/f: a Feminist Journal (1978–86)

Spare Rib (1972 to date) [popular monthly]

Women's Review (monthly, 1985 to date)

Barrett, M., *Women's Oppression Today: Problems in Marxist Feminist Analysis* (1980)

Bryan, B., Dadzie S. and Scafe, S. *The Heart of the Race: Black Women's Lives in Britain* (1985)

Campbell, B., *Wigan Pier Revisited: Poverty and Politics in the Eighties* (1984) [working-class England in 1982]

Feminist Review (ed.), *Waged Work* (1986) [essays from *Feminist Review*]

Greer, G., *The Female Eunuch* (1970)
[once-influential study]
The London Women's Handbook (1986)
[GLC Women's Committee: women's
issues, organisations; media and arts
section]
Mitchell, J., *Woman's Estate* (1971, rev.
1986) [origins of WLM]
*Women: the Longest Revolution: Essays on
Feminism, Literature and Psychoanalysis*
(1984) [reprints 'Women: the Longest
Revolution' from *NLR*, 1966)]
Oakley, A., *Subject Women* (1981)
Rowbotham, S., *Woman's Consciousness,
Man's World* (1973, repr. 1986)
[influential study]
Segal, L., *Is the Future Female? Troubled
Thoughts on Contemporary Feminism*
(1987)

Mass-Observation

Broad, R. and Fleming, S. (ed.), *Nella
Last's War* (1981) [war from Barrow-
in-Furness]
Calder, A., and Sheridan, D. (ed.), *Speak
for Yourself: a Mass-Observation
anthology, 1937–49* (1984) [appendix
describes M-O Archive at University
of Sussex]
Harrisson, T., *Britain Revisited* (1961) [lists
M-O publications/projects 1937–59]
Living Through the Blitz (1960)
Sheridan, D. (ed.), *Among You Taking
Notes . . . the Wartime Diary of Naomi
Mitchison 1939–1945* (1985)

Penguin Books

Morpurgo, J.E., *Allen Lane: King Penguin:
a Biography* (1979)
Rolph, C.H. (ed.), *The Trial of 'Lady
Chatterley'* (1961)
Williams, W.E., *The Penguin Story
MCMXXXV–MCMLVI* (1956)
[catalogue 1935–56]

The Press

Baistow, T., *Fourth Rate Estate: an
Anatomy of Fleet Street* (1985)
Cudlipp, H., *Publish and be Damned* (1953)
[autobiography]
Hetherington, A., *News, Newspapers and
Television* (1985) [bibl.]
Seymour-Ure, C., *The Press, Politics and
the Public: an Essay on the Role of the
National Press in the British Political
System* (1968)
Williams, F., *Dangerous Estate: the
Anatomy of Newspapers* (1957)

Punk and after

Coon, C., *1988: The New Wave Punk Rock
Explosion* (1977, repr. 1982)
The Face (Monthly, 1983 to date) [style]
Hill, Dave, *Designer Boys and Material
Girls: Manufacturing the Eighties' Pop
Dream* (1986)
Rimmer, D., *Like Punk Never Happened:
Culture Club and the New Pop* (1985)
Widgery, D., *Beating Time* (1986) [history
of Rock Against Racism]

Religion

*Faith in the City: a Call for Action by
Church and Nation* (1985) report of
Archbishop of Canterbury's
Commission on Urban Priority Areas]
Robinson, J., *Honest to God* (1963)

Video

The Independent Video and Film-makers'
Association (IFVA) is at 79 Wardour
Street, London W1V 3PH. *Independent
Video* (monthly, 1981–7, retitled
Independent Media) is the only magazine
wholly devoted to video.

Representative videos (not music)
include: 'Calling the Shots' (dir.
M. Wilcox, 1984); 'Carry Greenham
Home', (dir. B. Kidron and A. Richardson,
1982); 'Coal Not Dole: the Miners' Tapes'
(Platform Films, 1985); 'Framed Youth'
(Lesbian and Gay Video Project/Converse
Pictures, 1983); 'Street Warriors' (Ceddo,
1985).
Laing, D., 'Music video: industrial product,
cultural form', *Screen* **26**, 2
(March–April 1985), 78–83
Wollen, P., 'Ways of thinking about music
video (and post-modernism)', *Critical
Quarterly* **28**, 1–2 (Spring-Summer
1986), 167–70

II   Architecture

Magazines and journals

The Architect ran from 1869 to 1978. The
RIBA Journal of the Royal Institute
of British Architects, first appeared in 1879,
and was retitled *The Architect* (monthly) in
1986. *The Architects' Journal* (weekly, 1895
to date) covers all topics and in addition has
a technical emphasis; *Architectural
Association Quarterly* appeared from 1969 to
1982. *Architectural Design* (monthly, 1948
to date); the related *AD Profiles* are
published with the journal and numbered
separately. *Architectural Review* (monthly,

1896 to date) has an emphasis on modernism and immediate developments; *Building Design* (weekly, 1970 to date); *Casabella* (English /Italian, monthly, 1928 to date); *Domus* (monthly, 1928 to date); *Lotus International* (English /Italian, quarterly, 1963 to date); *Zodiac* (biennial, 1959 to date).

General

Auger, B., *The Architect and the Computer* (1972)

Banham, R., *Age of the Masters: a Personal View of Modern Architecture* (1962, rev. 1975) [international; several British buildings]
  The Architecture of the Well-Tempered Environment (1969, rev. 1984) [architecture, environment, technology]

Benevolo, L., *History of Modern Architecture vol. I: The Tradition of Modern Architecture; vol. II: The Modern Movement* (3rd rev. Italian edn 1966, trans. 1971([internat. bibl. in Vol. II]

Boesiger, W. (ed.), *Le Corbusier* (1972) [selection from Complete Works; see next entry]
  Le Corbusier: the Complete Architectural Works (8 vols., 1929–70) [Maison Jaoul in vols. V, VI; Chandigarh vols. V-VIII; Marseilles Unité d'Habitation vols. V, VI]

Emanuel, M. (ed.), *Contemporary Architects* (1980) [a massive reference work, international in scope]

Frampton, K., *Modern Architecture: a Critical History* (1980) [introductory; international bibl.]

Hitchcock, Henry-Russell, *Architecture: Nineteenth and Twentieth Centuries* (1958) [Pelican History of Art; bibl.]

Hitchcock, H.-R. and Johnson, P., *The International Style* (1966) [first pub. as *The International Style: Architecture Since 1922* (1932); influential study]

Jencks, C., *Current Architecture* (1982) [pub. in USA as *Architecture Today*; biogs. of architects discussed]
  The Language of Post-Modern Architecture (1977, rev. 1984) [influential study]

Jencks, C., and Baird, G., (ed.), *Meaning in Architecture* (1900) [essays by editors, Banham, Frampton, Rykwert and others]

Kron, J. and Slesin, S., *High-Tech: The Industrial Style and Source Book for the Home* (1979, NY 1978)

Lasdun, D. (ed.), *Architecture in an Age of Scepticism: a Practitioner's Anthology* (1984)

Le Corbusier: Architect of the Century (1987) [Arts Council /Hayward exhibition]

Le Corbusier, *Towards a New Architecture* (1927, new edn 1946, repr. 1976). [first pub. as *Vers une Architecture* (1923)]

Rowe, C., *The Mathematics of the Ideal Villa and Other Essays* (1976)

Venturi, R., *Complexity and Contradiction in Architecture* (1966, rev. 1977, repr. 1983) [theory and works by Venturi and partners 1957–66]

Vogt, A.M., *Architektur 1940–1980* (Frankfurt, 1980) [in German]

Watkin, D., *Morality and Architecture: the Development of a Theme in Architectural History and Theory from the Gothic Revival to the Modern Movement* (1977) [critique of Le Corbusier, Herbert Read, Pevsner]

Alternative architecture

Archigram 1–9 (annually, 1961–9) [journal which gave its name to the group]

'Archigram Group, London: a chronological survey', *Architectural Design* **35** (November 1965), 559–73 [drawings, plans, buildings 1958–65; see Cook, P.]

Banham, R., *Megastructure: Urban Futures of the Recent Past* (1976)

Burns, J., *Arthropods: New Design Futures* (1972)

Cook, P., *21 Years: 21 Ideas* (1985) [drawings, incl. Plug-in City; see Archigram]

Dahinden, J., *Urban Structures for the Future* (1972)

Dickson, D., *Alternative Technology and the Politics of Technical Change* (1974)

Rudofsky, B., *Architecture without Architects: a Short Introduction to Non-Pedigreed Architecture* (1964, repr. 1981) [influential study of 'anonymous architecture']

Rykwert, J., *The Necessity of Artifice: Ideas in Architecture* (1982)

Schumacher, E.F., *Small is Beautiful: a Study of Economics as if People Mattered* (1973)

British architecture

CONTEXT

Esher, L., *A Broken Wave: the Rebuilding of England 1940–1980* (1981)

Landau, R., *New Directions in British Architecture* (1969)

Lyall, S., *The State of British Architecture* (1980) [critical guide to 1970s]

MacEwen, M., *Crisis in Architecture* (1974)
[informed attack on architects and
RIBA]

Marriott, O., *The Property Boom* (1967)

Saint, A., *The Image of the Architect* (1983)
[ch. 7, 'The architect as entrepreneur'
for Poulson, Seifert and RIBA policy]

Tomkinson, M. and Gillard, M., *Nothing to
Declare: the Political Corruptions of
John Poulson* (1980)

WORKS

Architectural Design **56**, 4 (1986) [three
London projects, including Grand
Buildings, Trafalgar Square]

British Architecture 1984, AD Profile 52,
published with *Architectural Design* **54**,
3–4 (1984) [recent work]

*British Architects: Continuity, Crossroads,
Crisis, AD Profile* 33, published with
Architectural Design **51**, 3–4 (1981)
[recent work]

Fry, M., *Fine Building* (1944) [views of
MARS group member]

Opher, P. and Bird, C., *Architecture and
Urban Design in Six British New Towns*
(1981) [Milton Keynes, Cumbernauld,
Irvine, East Kilbride, Runcorn,
Warrington]

Osborn, F.J. and Whittick, A., *New Towns:
Their Origins, Achievements and
Progress* (1963, 3rd edn 1977)

Sudjic, D., *Norman Foster, Richard Rogers,
James Stirling: New Directions in
British Architecture* (1986) [lists
projects; bibl.]

Practitioners/architectural practices

Ove Arup

Brawne, M., *Arup Associates: the Biography
of an Architectural Practice* (1983) [lists
projects 1953–83]

Ralph Erskine

Futagawa, Y. (ed.), 'Ralph Erskine: Byker
redevelopment, Byker area of
Newcastle upon Tyne, England
1969–82', *GA* (*Global Architecture*) **55**
(1980) [photographs]

Norman Foster/Foster Associates

Banham, R. (intro.), *Foster Associates* (1979)
[selected projects 1963–79]

'Hongkong + Shanghai Bank', *Architectural Review* **179**, 1070 (April 1986)
[special number on this building]

Denys Lasdun

Drake and Lasdun, 'Cluster blocks at
Bethnal Green, London', *Architectural
Design* **26** (April 1956), 125–7

'Flats at Paddington', *Architectural
Review* **116**, 695 (November 1954),
309–18 [Hallfield estate; see also
comment by R. Banham, 'Facade',
302–7]

Lasdun, D., *A Language and a Theme: the
Architecture of Denys Lasdun and
Partners* (1976)

Richard Rogers

Appleyard, B., *Richard Rogers: a Biography*
(1986)

Cole, B.C. and Rogers, R.E. (eds.), *Richard
Rogers and Architects* (1985) [guide to
projects 1961–84]

Futagawa, Y. (ed.), 'Piano and Rogers
Architects Ove Arup Engineers Centre
Beaubourg, Paris, France 1972–7', *GA*
(*Global Architecture*) **44** (1977)
[photographs]

'Lloyd's of London Building', *Architectural
Review* **180**, 1076 (October 1986)
[special number on this building]

Alison and Peter Smithson

Banham, R., *The New Brutalism* (1966)

Pawley, M., 'Hunstanton School',
Architects' Journal **179** (23 May, 1984,
39–42)

'Secondary School at Hunstanton',
Architects' Journal **118** (10 September
1953), 323–8

'Secondary School At Hunstanton,
Norfolk', *Architects' Journal* **120** (16
September 1954), 341–52

Smithson, A. and P., *Urban Structuring*
(1967)

'Banham's bumper book on brutalism',
Architects' Journal **144**, 26 (28
December 1966), 1590–1 [rev. of
Banham's *New Brutalism*, correcting
many errors]

Basil Spence

Richards, J.M., 'Coventry', *Architectural
Review* **111**, 661 (January 1952), 3–7
[discussion of Coventry Cathedral
design]

Spence, B., *Phoenix at Coventry: the
Building of a Cathedral* (1962)

Spence, B. and Snoek, H., *Out of the Ashes:
a Progress Through Coventry Cathedral*
(1963) [annotated photographic record]

James Stirling

Hamlyn, R. (ed.), *The Clore Gallery: an
Illustrated Account of the New Building
for the Turner Collection* (1987)

Jacobus, J. (intro.), *James Stirling:
Buildings and Projects 1950–1974*
(1975) [bibl.]

'The National Gallery', *AD Profile* 63,
published with *Architectural Design* **56**
1–2 (1986) [five rejected designs,
including Stirling's]

Rowe, C. (intro.), *James Stirling: Buildings and Projects* (1984)

Stirling Gold, AD Profile 29, published with *Architectural Design* **50**, 7–8 (1980) [buildings and projects 1950–80]

Zardini, M. (ed.), *James Stirling, Michael Wilford and Associates: La Nuova Galleria di Stato a Stoccarda* (1985) [Neue Staatsgalerie, Stuttgart; supplement to *Casabella*, Sept. 1985, in Italian; essays, plans]

Other practices:

An interim report on the work of Darbourne and Darke (1977) [RIBA exhibition catalogue]; Ernö Goldfinger, 'Office buildings at Elephant and Castle, London', *Architectural Design* **29** (October 1959), 419–20; 'Recent work by Lyons, Israel, Ellis and Partners', *Architectural Design* **36** (October 1966), 498–515; Powell and Moya, 'Flats at Gospel Oak', *Architectural Review* **116**, 694 (October 1954), 219–22; 'Flats at Pimlico: Section Two', *Architectural Review* **116**, 692 (August 1954), 79–83; 'Flats at Pimlico London', *Architectural Review* **110**, 658 (October 1951), 242–7; 'The work of Yorke, Rosenberg, Mardall', *Architectural Design* **36** (June 1966), 276–85 [works 1947–66]

Schools and urban housing

Cherry, G.E. and Penny, L., *Holford: a Study in Architecture, Planning and Civic Design* (1986)

Dunleavy, P., *The Politics of Mass Housing in Britain 1945–1975: a Study of Corporate Power and Professional Influence in the Welfare State* (1981)

Edwards, A.M., *The Design of Suburbia: a Critical Study in Environmental History* (1981)

Maclure, S., *Educational Development and School Building: Aspects of Public Policy 1945–73* (1984) [bibl.]

Ravetz, A., *Remaking Cities: Contradictions of the Recent Urban Environment* (1980) [bibl.]

Saint, A., *Towards a Social Architecture: the Role of School Building in Post-war England* (1987)

Scoffham, E.R., *The Shape of British Housing* (1984)

University buildings

Birks, T., *Building the New Universities* (1972) [Sussex, York, East Anglia, Kent, Essex, Warwick, Lancaster]

Brawne, M. (ed.), 'The New Universities', *Architectural Review* **147**, 878 (April 1970) [special number]

University Planning and Design: a Symposium (1967) [AA paper no. 3; including architects' briefs, plans; bibl.]

Donat, J., 'Living in Universities', *Architectural Design* **36** (December 1966), 590–632 [including Essex, York]

Mullins, W. and Allen, P., *Student Housing: Architectural and Social Aspects* (1971) [universities, polytechnics, colleges of education; bibl.]

III   Ballet

Ballet is usually approached through particular ballets and their choreographers, rather than through the work of individual dancers. The most comprehensive descriptions of ballets are given in Cyril Beaumont's *Complete Book of Ballets* (1937), which is arranged chronologically by choreographer and has 1,100 pages. Various supplements and revisions appeared down to 1955, and these are listed below. Descriptions of ballets since 1955 can be found in Peter Brinson and Clement Crisp's *Ballet for All* (1970), and in John Percival, *Modern Ballet* (1970).

Magazines and journals

The Dancing Times, (monthly, 1894 to date) describes current performances in Britain, and activity in America. *Dance and Dancers* (1950–80, resumed in 1981) also appears monthly. *Dance Theatre Journal* (quarterly, 1983 to date), concentrates on modern dance. *Ballet Today* ran from 1946 to 1970. *The Ballet Annual*, ed. A. Haskell, appeared between 1947 and 1964, and a selection was published as *Ballet Decade*, ed. Haskell, in 1956.

Ballet in Britain

Beaumont, Cyril W., *Complete Book of Ballets: a Guide to the Principal Ballets of the Nineteenth and Twentieth Centuries* (1937, rev. 1949). Supplemented as follows: *Supplement to Complete Book of Ballets* (1942) [adds ballets of 1937–41]; *Complete Book of Ballets* (repr. with additions, 1951); *Ballets of Today: being a Second Supplement to the Complete Book of Ballets* (1954); *Ballets Past and Present: being a Third Supplement to the Complete Book of Ballets* (1955).

Brinson, P. (ed.), *The Ballet in Britain* (1962)

Brinson, P., and Crisp, C., (comps.), *Ballet for All* (1971) [synopses of ballets, including 52 by British choreographers]

Buckle, R., *Buckle at the Ballet: Selected Criticism* (1980) [years 1950–75]

Hall, F., *An Anatomy of Ballet* (1953)
  Modern English Ballet: an Interpretation (1950)
  The World of Ballet and Dance (1972) [with photos by M. Davis]

Haskell, A.L., *Ballet: a Complete Guide to Appreciation* (1955)

Kerensky, O., *Ballet Scene* (1970)

Noble, P. (ed.), *British Ballet* (1950) [essays, reference, bibl.]

Percival, J., *Modern Ballet* (1970) [introduction to 1960s]

van Praagh, P., and Brinson, P., *The Choreographic Art: an Outline of its principles and craft* (1963) [bibl.]

White, J.W. (ed.), *Twentieth Century Ballet in Britain* (1985)

Winter, M.H., *The Pre-Romantic Ballet* (1974) [international bibl.]

Ballet companies

Marie Rambert Dancers/Ballet Club/Ballet Rambert

Clarke, M., *Dancers of Mercury: the Story of Ballet Rambert* (1962) [productions 1926–61]

Crisp, C., Sainsbury, A., Williams, P. (ed.), *Ballet Rambert 50 Years and On* (1981) [revises *50 Years of Ballet Rambert: 1926–1976* (1976)]

Rambert, M., *Quicksilver: the Autobiography of Marie Rambert* (1972)

Vic-Wells Ballet/Sadler's Wells Ballet/Royal Ballet

Beaumont, C.W., *The Sadler's Wells Ballet: a Detailed Account of Works in the Permanent Repertory with Critical Notes* (1946)

Bland, A., *The Royal Ballet: the First 50 Years* (1980) [years 1931–80]

Clarke, M., *The Sadler's Wells Ballet: a History and an Appreciation* (1955) [productions 1928–55]

de Valois, N., *Step by Step: the Formation of an Establishment* (1977) [Royal Ballet]

Lawson, J., *Makers of English Ballet. No. 1: Choreography and Ninette de Valois* (1947)

Manchester, P.W., *Vic-Wells: A Ballet Progress* (1942) [1931–41]

Neatby, K., *Ninette de Valois and the Vic-Wells Ballet* (1934)

Diaghilev Ballet/London Festival Ballet/Scottish Ballet/other companies

Beaumont, C.W., *The Diaghilev Ballet in London: a Personal Record* (1940, 3rd edn 1951)

Buckle, R., *Diaghilev* (1979, repr. 1984)

Franks, A.H., *Ballet: a Decade of Endeavour* (1955) [Festival Ballet]

Gillard, D., *Beryl Gray: a Biography* (1977) [Festival Ballet]

Goodwin, N., *A Ballet for Scotland: the First Ten Years of The Scottish Ballet* (1979)

Haskell, A., *Diaghileff: his Artistic and Private Life* (1935, repr. 1955)

White, J.W. (ed.), *Twentieth-Century Dance in Britain: a History of Major Dance Companies in Britain* (1985) [Ballet Rambert, London Festival Ballet, London Contemporary Dance Theatre, and others]

Choreographers

Austin, R., *Birth of a Ballet* (1976) [Christopher Bruce's *Black Angels* for Ballet Rambert]

Coton, A.V., *The New Ballet: Kurt Joos and his Work* (1946)

de Valois, N., *Come Dance With Me: a Memoir, 1898–1956* (1957, repr. 1973)
  Invitation to the Ballet (1937) [repertory ballet]

Dominic, Z., and Gilbert, J.S., *Frederick Ashton: a Choreographer and his Ballets* (1971)

Ralph, R., *The Life and Works of John Weaver: an Account of his Life, Writings and Theatrical Productions* (1985) [complete publications]

Terry, W., *The King's Ballet Master* (1979) [Bournonville and *La Sylphide*]

Thorpe, E., *Kenneth MacMillan: the Man and the Ballets* (1985)

Vaughan, D., *Frederick Ashton and his Ballets* (1977) [major study; synopses, bibl.]

Choreology

Benesh, R. and J., *Reading Dance: the Birth of Choreology* (1977, repr. 1983)

McGuinness-Scott, J., *Movement Study and Benesh Movement Notation: an Introduction to Applications in Dance, Medicine, Anthropology, and Other Studies* (1983)

Dancers

Bland, A., *Fonteyn and Nureyev: the Story of a Partnership* (1979)
Dolin, A., *Friends and Memories* (1982)
    Last Words: a Final Autobiography (1985)
Fonteyn, M., *Autobiography* (1975)
Markova, A., *Markova Remembers* (1986)
Money, K., *The Art of Margot Fonteyn* (1966) [photographs]
Newman, B., *Antoinette Sibley: Reflections of a Ballerina* (1986)
Sexton, C., *Peggy van Praagh: a Life of Dance* (1986)

Reference

Very detailed information on ballet in the twentieth century can be found in Cyril W. Beaumont's *A Bibliography of the Dance Collection of Doris Niles and Serge Leslie*, part III (1974), and part IV (1981). F.S. Forrester, *Ballet in England: A Bibliography and Survey c.1700–June 1966* (1968) is also very detailed.

IV   The Crafts

The Crafts Council, at 12 Waterloo Place, London SW1Y 4AU, holds exhibitions and its library has an index of over 400 selected makers. There is a collection of over 25,000 slides of recent craft work, mostly by those on the index; these are available for loan. The Crafts Council (known as the Crafts Advisory Committee from its foundation in 1971 to 1979) publishes the journal *Crafts* (bi-monthly, 1973 to date). An illustrated catalogue of the Council's purchases has been published as *The Crafts Council Collection 1972–1985* (1985).

Magazines and journals

Ceramic Review (bi-monthly, 1970 to date) covers British work. The Crafts Council publishes *Crafts* (bi-monthly, 1973 to date), the major source for debates about contemporary craftsmanship and for detailed studies of working craftspeople in the 'craftsman's art' tradition.

General

Birks, Tony, *Art of the Modern Potter* (1967, rev. 1976, 1982)
Black, Misha, 'Craft: art or design?', in A. Blake (ed.), *The Black Papers on Design: Selected Writings of the Late Sir Misha Black* (1983), pp. 215–24 [talk, 13 April 1976]

Bruce, A. and Filmer, P., *Working in Crafts: an Independent Socio-Economic Study of Craftsmen and Women in England and Wales* (1983) [major survey of lives, economics, education, pleasures and difficulties, and attitudes of craftspeople; statistics; review of research]
Cameron, E., and Lewis, P., *Potters on Pottery* (1976) [interviews with Caiger-Smith, Michael Cardew, Casson, David Leach, etc.]
Collingwood, R.G., *The Principles of Art* (1938)
Digby, G.W., *The Work of the Modern Potter in England* (1952) [work by Leach, Rie, Coper, etc.]
Dormer, P. and Turner, R., *The New Jewelry: Trends and Traditions* (1985) [bibl.]
Farleigh, J., *The Creative Craftsman* (1950)
    Fifteen Craftsmen on Their Craft (1945)
Field, D., *Projects in Wood* (1985) [working methods today]
Forty, A., *Objects of Desire: Design and Society 1750–1980* (1986) [significance of design in British culture]
Frayling, C., *The Schoolmaster and the Wheelwrights* (1983) [inaugural lecture at Royal College of Art, on craft and history]
Frayling, C. and Snowdon, H., 'Perspectives on craft in the twentieth century' [series of articles in *Crafts*, Jan.–Dec. 1982]
Gloag, John, *The English Tradition in Design* (1947)
Lane, P., *Studio Ceramics* (1983) [Coper]
Lucie-Smith, E., *The Story of Craft: the Craftsman's Role in Society* (1981)
    The World of the Makers (1975)
MacCarthy, F., *All Things Bright and Beautiful: Design in Britain 1830 to Today* (1972); rev. as *A History of British Design 1830–1970* (1979) [major survey; bibl.]
Makers: an Illustrated Guide to the Work of 300 artist-craftspeople (1980) [Crafts Council]
Moody, E., *Modern Furniture* (1966) [survey of this century]
Peters, A., *Cabinetmaking: the Professional Approach* (1984) [history, theory and practice, in Cotswold tradition]
Pirsig, R.M., *Zen and the Art of Motorcycle Maintenance* (1974)
Pye, D., *The Nature and Aesthetics of Design* (1978)
    The Nature and Art of Workmanship (1968)

Robertson, S., *Craft and Contemporary Culture* (1961)

Rose, M., *Artist Potters in England* (1955, rev. 1970) [work by Leach, Rie, Coper, etc.]

Sehumacher, E.F., *Small is Beautiful: a Study of Economics as if People Mattered* (1973)

Sutton, A., *British Craft Textiles* (1985)

Turner, R., *Contemporary Jewelry: a Critical Assessment 1945–1975* (1976)

Wiener, M.J., *English Culture and the Decline of the Industrial Spirit 1850–1980* (1981)

Arts and Crafts tradition

Crawford, A., *C.R. Ashbee* (1985)

Fairclough, O., and Leary, E., *Textiles by William Morris and Morris & Co., 1861–1940* (1981) [Birmingham Museums and Art Gallery exhibition catalogue]

Morris, William, *Collected Works*, May Morris (ed.), 1910–15, 24 vols. [Morris's lectures and essays on design are largely in vol. XXII]

Pye, D., *The Nature and Art of Workmanship* (1968) [includes discussion of Ruskin, 'Critique of "On the nature of Gothic"']

Thompson, E.P., *William Morris: Romantic to Revolutionary* (1955, rev. 1977)

Watkinson, R., *William Morris as Designer* (1967, repr. 1979)

William Morris and Kelmscott (1981) [Design Council; essays on furniture, textiles, decorative arts]

William Morris Today (1984) [Institute of Contemporary Arts; essays on contemporary significance of Morris' life and work]

Exhibitions

Exhibition catalogues are followed by the name of the exhibiting gallery.

Aspects of Jewellery (1973) [Aberdeen Art Gallery]

Black Eyes and Lemonade (1951) [Whitechapel Gallery]

Britain Can Make It (1946) [Victoria and Albert Museum; see section VII below, *Design '46* and Sparke, P.]

Britton, A., *Alison Britton Ceramics* (1979) [Crafts Council]

Catalogue of an Exhibition of Victorian and Edwardian Decorative Arts (1952) [Victoria and Albert Museum]

Hughes, R. and Rowe, M., *The Colouring, Bronzing and Patination of Metals: a Manual for the Fine Metalworker and Sculptor* (1983) [also Crafts Council, 1982]

The Craftsman's Art (1973) [Victoria and Albert Museum / Crafts Advisory Committee]

Designingly Making (1965) [Design Council; work by Collingwood, Mellor and others; see *Design*, July 1965]

Fabric and Form: New Textile Art from Britain (1982) [Arts Council]

Fast Forward: New Directions in British Ceramics (1985) [Institute of Contemporary Arts; ceramics by Svend Bayer, Alison Britton, Elizabeth Fritsch, Wally Keeler, William Newland, Jacqui Poncelet, Janice Tchalenko, and others; statements by Britton and Newland]

Jewellery Redefined (1982) [British Crafts Centre]

The Maker's Eye (1981) [Crafts Council; statements by Alison Britton, Michael Cardew, John Makepeace, David Pye and others]

Making Good (1981) [South East Arts; statements by Fred Baier and others; essays by P. Sparke and S. Bayley]

Masterpiece: a Jubilee Exhibition of Crafts (1977) [Crafts Advisory Committee: metalwork and jewelry, pottery, textiles]

Les Métiers de l'Art (1980) [major catalogue from Musée des arts décoratifs, Paris]

New Glass (1981) [Victoria and Albert Museum]

Objects: USA (1973) [major visual survey of American artist-craftsmen; orig. Smithsonian Institute, Washington, DC, 1969, shown Edinburgh and Birmingham, 1973; catalogue by Lee Nordness (1970)]

Poncelet, J., *Jacqui Poncelet: New Ceramics* (1981) [Crafts Council]

Quilting, Patchwork and Appliqué 1700–1982 (1983) [Crafts Council]

Rothschild, H. (intro.), *British Potters* (1971) [Kettle's Yard, Cambridge]

Straub, M. (ed.), *Textiles Today* (1981) [Kettle's Yard, Cambridge]

Towards a New Iron Age (1982) [Victoria and Albert Museum]

Practitioners

Michael Cardew (potter, 1901–83)

Cardew, M., *Pioneer Pottery* (1969) [techniques for the practising potter; Nigerian experience; illus., bibl.]

Clark, G., *Michael Cardew* (1978)

Houston, J. (ed.), *Michael Cardew: a
Collection of Essays* (1976) [essays by J.
Houston, Ray Finch, Katherine
Pleydell Bouverie, Cardew]
Peter Collingwood (weaver, b.1922)
Collingwood, P., *The Techniques of Rug
Weaving* (1968) [bibl.]
  *The Techniques of Sprang: Plaiting on
  Stretched threads* (1974) [bibl.]
Hans Coper (potter, 1920–81)
Birks, T., *Hans Coper* (1983) [bibl.]
Lucie Rie and Hans Coper (1985) [Fischer
Fine Art exhibition catalogue]
Lucie Rie – Hans Coper (1967) [Boymans
Museum, Rotterdam, exhibition
catalogue]
Spielmann, H., *Lucie Rie–Hans Coper
Keramik* (1972) [Hamburg, exhibition
catalogue]
Kaffe Fassett (knitting designer, b.1937)
Fassett, K., *Glorious Knitting* (1985)
[patterns]
Bernard Leach (potter, 1887–1979)
Hogben, C., *The Art of Bernard Leach*
(1978)
Houston, J. (intro.), *The Art of Bernard
Leach* (1977) [Victoria and Albert
Museum retrospective]
Leach, B., *Beyond East and West: Memoirs,
Portraits and Essays* (1978, repr. 1985)
  A Potter's Book (1940, 2nd rev. edn
  1945, fourteen impressions; 3rd rev.
  edn 1976)
  A Potter's Work (1967) [source for
  illustrations of Leach's work]
Yanagi, S., *Bernard Leach* (Tokyo, 1966)
[book designed by Hiromu Hara,
contributions by Hamada and Yanagi]
John Makepeace (furniture designer,
b.1939)
Makepeace, J., 'The growing significance
of craftsmanship' in *Crafts Conference
for Teachers* (1982), 1–10 [Crafts
Council]
Roscoe, B., *A Guide to the Collections:
Holbourne of Mestrie Museum and
Crafts Study Centre* (1980) [Crafts
Study Centre retrospective, Bath]
Lucie Rie (potter, b.1902)
Digby, G.W. (intro.), *Lucie Rie: a
Retrospective Exhibition of Earthenware,
Stoneware and Porcelain 1926–1967*
(1967) [Arts Council]
Houston, J. (ed.), *Lucie Rie: a Survey of her
Life and Work* (1981) [Crafts Council
retrospective; essays]
Lucie Rie and Hans Coper (1985) [Fischer
Fine Art]
Lucie Rie–Hans Coper (1967) [Boymans
Museum, Rotterdam]

Gordon Russell (furniture designer,
design and craft administrator, 1892–1976)
Baynes, K. and K., *Gordon Russell* (1980)
[bibl.]
Naylor, G., *A History of Gordon Russell
Limited* (1976) [pub. by the company]
Russell, G., *Designer's Trade:
Autobiography* (1965)
  Looking at Furniture (1964) [on early and
  contemporary furniture]
Reynolds Stone (lettering designer,
1909–79)
Stone, R. (intro.), *Reynolds Stone:
Engravings* (1977) [includes lettering]
Robert Welch (silversmith, b.1929)
Forbes, C. (ed.), *Robert Welch: Design in a
Cotswold Workshop* (1973)
Welch, R., *Hand and Machine* (1986)
[illustrates work as designer and
silversmith]

V   Film

The British Film Institute library at 127
Charing Cross Road, London WC2H 0EA,
has a large reference collection, a collection
of scripts, and television material. BFI
Publishing, at 81 Dean Street, London
W1V 6AA, publishes the *British National
Film and Video Catalogue* (annually, 1963 to
date, video included from 1984), which
records all films and video-cassettes made
available for non-theatrical loan.

  The Macmillan Film Bibliography, edited
by G. Rehrauer (1982), is a two-volume
fully-annotated listing of books about film.
It has a bias towards US publications, but
all the important British material can be
found there.

Magazines and journals

The BFI's *Monthly Film Bulletin* (1934 to
date) describes and reviews every feature
film released in Britain, and gives full
production credits. The articles and reviews
in *Sight and Sound* (quarterly, 1932 to date)
are essential reading. David Wilson has
edited *Sight and Sound: a fiftieth
anniversary selection* (1982), reprinting
articles 1934–82. *Screen* (bi-monthly, 1959
to date) is published by the Society for
Education in Film and Television and has
been the major British journal of film
theory since 1971. In 1982 *Screen*
incorporated *Screen Education* (1968–81,
various titles from 1950). The influential
Penguin Film Review (nos. 1–9, 1946–9) was
reprinted in 1977.

British cinema: general works

Armes, R., *A Critical History of the British Cinema* (1978) [bibl.]

Auty, M. and Roddick, N. (ed.), *British Cinema Now* (1984)

Barr, C. (ed.), *All Our Yesterdays: 90 Years of British Cinema* (1986)

Betts, E., *The Film Business: a History of British Cinema 1896–1972* (1973) [general history; bibl.]

'British Cinema', *Screen* **26**, 1 (January–February 1985) [special number; essays]

Curran, J. and Porter, V., *British Cinema History* (1983) [film industry, structures, ideology; outstanding bibl.]

Dickinson, M. and Street, S., *Cinema and State: the Film Industry and the British Government 1927–84* (1985)

Durgnat, R., *A Mirror for England: British Movies from Austerity to Affluence* (1970) [a popular history 1945–58; filmographical index, bibl.]

Gifford, D., *British Cinema: an Illustrated Guide and Index to 5,000 Films* (1968)
    The British Film Catalogue 1895–1970 (1973)
    The Illustrated Who's Who in British Films (1978)

Park, J., *Learning to Dream: the New British Cinema* (1984)

Perry, G., *The Great British Picture Show* (1974, rev. 1985) [from earliest days to 1985]

Quinlan, D., *British Sound Films: the Studio Years 1928–1959* (1984) [films listed by title]

Rhode, E., *A History of the Cinema* (1976)

Richards, J. and Aldgate, A., *Best of British: Cinema and Society 1930–1970* (1983)

Rotha, P., *The Film Till Now* (1930, rev. 1949)
    Rotha on the Film: a Selection of Writings about the Cinema (1958)

Sussex, E., *The Rise and Fall of British Documentary* (1975)

Walker, A., *Hollywood, England: the British Film Industry in the Sixties* (1974)
    National Heroes: the British Film Industry in the Seventies (1985)

Walker, John, *The Once and Future Film: British Cinema in the Seventies and Eighties* (1985)

Warren, P., *The British Film Collection 1896–1984: a History of the British Cinema in Pictures* (1984)

Wilson, D. (ed.), *Sight and Sound: a Fiftieth Anniversary Selection* (1982) [articles 1934–82]

Film-makers

BOOKS

Anderegg, M.A., *David Lean* (1984) [filmography; bibl.]

Baxter, J., *Ken Russell: an Appalling Talent* (1974) [filmography]

Brown, G., *Launder and Gilliatt* (1977) [lengthy filmography]

Christie, I., *Arrows of Desire: the Films of Michael Powell and Emeric Pressburger* (1985) [filmography; bibl.]

Christie, I. (ed.), *Powell, Pressburger and others* (1978) [essays]

Ciment, M., *Conversations with Losey* (1985) [all films except *Steaming*]
    John Boorman (1986)

Jennings, M.-L. (ed.), *Humphrey Jennings: Film-maker, Painter, Poet* (1982) [essays, filmography, bibl.]

Milne, T. (ed.), *Losey on Losey* (1967)

Powell, M., *A Life in Movies* (1986) [autobiography/film history]

Silver, A., and Ursini, J., *David Lean and his Films* (1974)

Sinyard, N., *The Films of Richard Lester* (1985) [filmography]

Wright, Basil, *The Long View* (1974, rev. 1976)

FILMS

David Lean (b.1908): *In Which We Serve* (with Noel Coward, 1942); *This Happy Breed* (1944); *Blithe Spirit* (1945); *Brief Encounter* (1945); *Great Expectations* (1946); *Oliver Twist* (1948); *The Passionate Friends* (1949); *Madeleine* (1950); *The Sound Barrier* (1952); *Hobson's Choice* (1954); *Summer Madness* (1955); *The Bridge on the River Kwai* (1957); *Lawrence of Arabia* (1962); *Dr Zhivago* (1965); *Ryan's Daughter* (1970); *A Passage to India* (1985)

Joseph Losey (1909–84): *The Boy With Green Hair* (1948); *The Lawless* (1950); *The Prowler* (1951); *M* (1951); *The Big Night* (1951); *Stranger on the Prowl* (1952); *The Sleeping Tiger* (1954); *A Man on the Beach* (1955); *The Intimate Stranger* (1956); *Time Without Pity* (1957); *The Gypsy and the Gentleman* (1957); *Blind Date* (1959); *The Criminal* (1960); *The Damned* (1961); *Eve* (1962); *The Servant* (1963); *King and Country* (1964); *Modesty Blaise* (1966); *Accident* (1967); *Boom!* (1968); *Secret Ceremony* (1968); *Figures in a Landscape* (1970); *The Go-Between*

(1971); *The Assassination of Trotsky* (1972); *A Doll's House* (1973); *The Romantic Englishwoman* (1975); *Galileo* (1976); *Mr Klein* (1976); *Les Routes du Sud* (1978); *Don Giovanni* (1980); *The Trout* (1982); *Steaming* (1984)

Alexander Mackendrick (b.1912) *Whisky Galore* (1949); *The Man in the White Suit* (1951); *Mandy* (1952); *The Maggie* (1954); *The Ladykillers* (1955); *Sweet Smell of Success* (1957); *Sammy Going South* (1963); *A High Wind in Jamaica* (1965); *Don't Make Waves* (1967)

Nicolas Roeg (b.1928): *Performance* (1970, completed 1967); *Walkabout* (1970); *Don't Look Now* (1973); *The Man Who Fell to Earth* (1976); *Bad Timing* (1979); *Eureka* (1982); *Insignificance* (1985); *Castaway* (1986)

Film studios

Aspinall, S., and Murphy, R. (ed.), *Gainsborough Melodrama* (1983) [Gainsborough Pictures in 1940s]

Barr, C., *Ealing Studios* (1977)

Perry, G., *Forever Ealing: a Celebration of the Great British Film Studio* (1981)

Movies from the Mansion: a History of Pinewood Studios (1976)

Warren, P., *Elstree, the British Hollywood* (1983)

Film theory

Ellis, J., *Visible Fictions: Cinema: Television: Video* (1982) [cinema theory extended to TV; bibl.]

Hillier, J. (ed.), *Cahiers du Cinéma vol. I: the 1950s: Neo-Realism, Hollywood, New Wave* (1985) [trans. articles 1951–9]

Cahiers du Cinéma vol. II: 1960–1968: New Wave, New Cinema, Re-evaluating Hollywood (1986) [trans. articles]

Screen Reader I: Cinema/Ideology/Politics (1977)

Screen Reader II: Cinema and Semiotics (1981) [essays repr. from *Screen* vols. XII–XIV, 1971–3]

Williams, C. (ed.), *Realism and the Cinema: a Reader* (1980)

Reference

Halliwell, L., (comp.), *The Filmgoer's Companion*, 8th edn (1985)

Halliwell's Film Guide, 6th edn (1987)

VI   Housing at Roehampton

Documents relating to the various phases of the LCC Roehampton development can be found in the *Minutes and Presented Papers* of the LCC Housing Committee, held at the Greater London Record Office.

'Flats at Putney Heath', *Architectural Review* **116** (October 1954), 222–5 [the Ackroydon Estate design]

'Housing at Priory Lane, Roehampton, London SW15', *Architectural Design* **29** (January 1959), 7–21

Jackson, Anthony, *The Politics of Architecture: a History of Modern Architecture in Britain* (1970) [excellent general background]

'Le Corbusier's Unité d'Habitation', *Architectural Review* **109** (May 1951), 293–300 [report of LCC Housing Division seminar]

'Living in Cities', *Architectural Association Journal* **69** (July–August 1953), 52–62 [report of Architectural Association forum]

Pevsner, N., 'Roehampton: LCC Housing and the Picturesque Tradition', *Architectural Review* **126** (July 1959), 21–35

Architects

The senior architects and team members responsible for the principal phases of the Roehampton development were: Robert Matthew, Leslie Martin and Hubert Bennett (superintending architects of the LCC), H.J. Whitfield Lewis (principal housing architect), Michael Powell and later Kenneth Campbell (assistant housing architect). The Ackroydon design team included H.G. Gillett (architect in charge), A.W.C. Barr, E. Moholi, A.P. Roach, J. Partridge and C.A. Lucas (who is said to have been chiefly responsible for the first tower block). The Alton East Team was headed at different times by M.C.L. Powell, A.W.C. Barr, O.J. Cox and Mrs R.S. Stjernstedt. J.N. Wall, H.P. Harrison, A.R. Garrod, J. Partridge, B. Adams, H. Gravenson and P. Nevil worked on the team. Architects in charge of Alton West included C. Lucas, M.C.L. Powell and K. Campbell. The Alton West Team until 1959 included J.A. Partridge, W.G. Howell, J.A.W. Killick, S.F. Amis, J.R. Galley, R. Stout and G.F. Bailey. (These lists are compiled from the authorised credits published in the journal articles listed above; it goes without saying that many others were involved.)

VII   Industrial Design

The scholarly bibliography for design of all kinds is *A Bibliography of Design in Britain 1851–1970* by Anthony J. Coulson (1979). For the general reader there is an extensive bibliography in Fiona MacCarthy's *British Design Since 1880* (1982), which lists exhibition catalogues and describes the major British design collections.

The Design Council, at 28 Haymarket, London SW1Y 4SU exhibits objects that it considers well-designed. The *Design Index* (originally *Design Review*), is an important collection of 35,000 slides and other visual records which may be consulted, borrowed or bought. The Design Council publishes *Design* (monthly, 1949 to date). *Design Selection* (bi-monthly, 1985 to date) illustrates approved products for the general consumer. The Design Council also publishes books, conference papers and reports, many too technical to be listed here. An Educational Publications unit was established in 1986.

The study of recent design has been encouraged by the exhibitions of the Boilerhouse Project, set up by the Conran Foundation. Twenty-three exhibitions took place at the Victoria and Albert Museum during 1982–6. The Boilerhouse Project will resume at Butler's Wharf Business Centre, Curlew Street, London SE1 in late 1988 or early 1989, with exhibitions at other locations in the interim period.

All the following books, journals and magazines are illustrated; significant bibliographies are noted. Exhibition catalogues give the name of the exhibiting gallery.

Magazines and journals

Architectural Design (monthly, 1948 to date); *Architectural Review* (monthly, 1896 to date); *Art and Industry* (1936–58); *Auto & Design* (bi-monthly, Italian/English, 1979 to date) is devoted to car design; *Blueprint* (monthly, 1983 to date) is a topical magazine dealing with design of all kinds; *Design* (monthly, 1949 to date) is essential reading as the journal of the Design Centre; *Design for Today* (1933–6) was the journal of the Design and Industries Association; *Design Studies* (quarterly, 1979 to date); *The Designer* (1966 to date) is the journal of the Society of Industrial Artists and Designers (SIAD)

General

EARLY STUDIES AND SURVEYS

Bertram, A., *Design* (1938) [introductory; bibl.]

   The House: a Machine for Living in (1935)

Carrington, N., *Design and a Changing Civilisation* (1935, repr. as *Design in Civilisation* 1947)

Council for Art and Industry, *The Working Class Home: its Furnishing and Equipment* (1937) [report by Frank Pick and others]

Pevsner, N., *An Enquiry Into Industrial Art in England* (1937) [early outstanding research]

Read, H., *Art and Industry* (1934, 4th rev. edn 1956, repr. 1966) [the origin of discussion of industrial design]

SINCE 1940

Anscombe, I., *A Woman's Touch: Women in Design from 1860 to the Present Day* (1984) [bibl.]

Banham, M. and Hillier, B., (ed.), *A Tonic to the Nation: the Festival of Britain 1951* (1976) [essays and sceptical recollections]

Banham, R., *Theory and Design in the First Machine Age* (1960, repr. 1983) [standard work]

Baynes, K., *Industrial Design and the Community* (1967)

Carrington, N., *Industrial Design in Britain* (1976) [from Arts and Crafts Movement to end of Second World War]

Farr, M., *Design in British Industry: a Mid-Century Survey* (1955) [describes much of the work mentioned in the essay 'Industrial Design']

Forty, A., *Objects of Desire: Design and Society 1750–1980* (1986) [significance of design in British culture]

Gloag, J., *Industrial Art Explained* (1934, rev. 1946)

   Plastics and Industrial Design (1945)

Gloag, J. and Wornum, G., *House Out of Factory* (1946) [prefabricated houses]

Haresnape, B., *British Rail 1948–1983: a Journey by Design* (2nd edn, 1983)

Heskett, J., *Industrial Design* (1980) [bibl.]

Jankel, A. and Morton, R., *Creative Computer Graphics* (1984)

Jones, J.C., *Design Methods: Seeds of Human Futures* (1970, rev. 1980) [influential 'design methods' theory of 1970s]

   Essays in Design (1984) [essays 1971–81]

Katz, S., *Classic Plastics: from Bakelite to High-Tech* (1984)

Plastics: Designs and Materials (1978) [history of design uses of materials]

Lucie-Smith, E., *A History of Industrial Design* (1983) [introductory; bibl.]

MacCarthy, F., *All Things Bright and Beautiful: Design in Britain 1830 to Today* (1972); rev. as *A History of British Design 1830-Today* (1979) [major survey; bibl.]

British Design Since 1880: a visual History (1982) [valuable survey; bibl.]

Papanek, V., *Design for the Real World* (1972) [multi-disciplinary bibl.]

Pevsner, N., *Pioneers of Modern Design from William Morris to Walter Gropius* (1960, rev. 1975) [first published as *Pioneers of the Modern Movement* (1936)]

The Sources of Modern Architecture and Design (1968) [European and US origins]

Studies in Art, Architecture and Design vol. 2: Victorian and After (1968, repr. 1982) [essays on Gordon Russell, Frank Pick, and Design and Industries Association]

Potter, N., *What is a Designer: things. places. messages* [*sic*] (1969, rev. 1980)

Sudjic, D., *Cult Objects: the Complete Guide to Having it All* (1985) [social meanings of design]

Woodham, J., *The Industrial Designer and the Public* (1983) [bibl.]

Boilerhouse project

Art and Industry: a Century of Design in the Products you Use (1982)

The Car (1985)

The Car Programme: 52 Weeks to Job One, or how they Designed the Ford Sierra (1982)

14:24 British Youth Culture (1986) [music, clothes, bikes; bibl.]

Design Council/Council of Industrial Design

For a full list of Design Council and CoID publications to 1970, see Coulson, A.J., *A Bibliography of Design in Britain 1850-1970* (1979), pp. 26-30

Archer, L. Bruce, *Systematic Method for Designers* (1965)

Bayley, S., *In Good Shape: Style in Industrial Products 1900-1960* (1979) [international survey]

Britain Can Make It (1946) [Victoria and Albert Museum; see *Design '46* and Sparke, P., *Did Britain Make It?* (1986)]

Contract Furniture from Design Index (1964) [typical guidance of the period]

Design '46: Survey of British Industrial Design as Displayed at the "Britain Can Make It" Exhibition (1946) [see *Britain Can Make It* and Sparke, P. (1986)]

Designed in Britain – Made Abroad (1981) [Design Council exhibition catalogue]

Enterprise Scotland 1947: a Pictorial Record (1947) [Scottish Committee of the CoID exhibition]

Furnishing to Fit the Family (1947) [typical CoID pamphlet: there were many others]

Hamilton, N. (ed.), *From Spitfire to Microchip: Studies in the History of Design from 1945* (1985) [essays on Independent Group, London Underground, typography]

Russell, G., 'Focus on British design', *Design* **121** (January 1959), 20–5 [intro. to special number surveying design 1949–59]

(intro.), *Design in the Festival: Illustrating a Selection of Well-Designed British Goods in Production in the Festival Year 1951* (1951) [articles and illustrations]

Sparke, P. (ed.), *Did Britain Make It? British Design in Context 1946–86* (1986) [essays, interviews; reconsiders 'Britain Can Make It' exhibition of 1946]

50 Years of the DIA (1975) [Design and Industries Association exhibition]

Pop

Banham, R., *Design by Choice* (1981) [part two collects articles and essays on popular culture; Banham bibl. 1952–78]

Barker, P. (ed.), *Arts in Society* (1977) [essays from *New Society* by Reyner Banham, Angela Carter and others]

Hamilton, R., 'Persuading Image', *Design* **134** (February 1960), 28–32 [editorial, p. 25; replies by Reyner Banham, Misha Black and others appeared as 'Persuading Image: a symposium', *Design* **138** (June 1960), 54–7]

Reilly, P., 'The challenge of pop', *Architectural Review* **142**, 848 (October 1967), 255–7

Practitioners

Coulson (see headnote) lists the work of recent designers under 'Areas of design activity'.

Adamczewski, F., 'The point about weaving', *Design* **307** (July 1974), 58–61 [Archie Brennan and Edinburgh Tapestry Co.]

Best, A. and Brutton, M., 'Utility', *Design* **309** (September 1974), 62–71 [interviews]

Blake, A. (ed.), *The Black Papers on Design: Selected Writings of the late Misha Black* (1983)

Blake, J. and A., *The Practical Idealists: a History of Design Research Unit* (1969)

Conran, T., *The Kitchen Book* (1977)
Terence Conran's New House Book (1985)

Conway, H., *Ernest Race* (1982) [Design Council; bibl.]

Farrelly, E.M., 'Neville Brody', *Architectural Review* **180**, 1074 (August 1986), 28–32 [graphic design]

Frey, G., *The Modern Chair: 1850 to Today* (1970) [international bibl.]

Gorb, P. (ed.), *Living by Design: the Partners of Pentagram* (1978) [essays]

Grange, K., *Kenneth Grange at the Boilerhouse: an Exhibition of British Product Design* (1983)

Gray, M., Ray, P., Black, M., *et al.*, 'SIAD: the first forty years', *The Designer* (October 1970), 4–6 [notes by originators]

Habitat Catalogue (annually, 1965 to date) [contents are regarded as design statement; see Conran, T., and Phillips, B.]

Heppenstall, D.W., *Contemporary Furniture Designs* (1960) [characteristic of period]

Moody, E., *Modern Furniture* (1966) [survey of this century]

Phillips, B., *Conran and the Habitat Story* (1984) [from 1952 to 1984]

Pilditch, J., *Talk About Design* (1976) [talks and articles, 1950s to 1970s]

Pilditch, J. and Scott, D., *The Business of Product Design* (1965)

Radice, B., *Memphis: Research, Experiences, Results, Failures and Successes of New Design* (1985) [Memphis design group]

Read, H. (ed.), *The Practice of Design* (1946) [essays by members of the Design Research Unit (DRU)]

Russell, G., *Designer's Trade: Autobiography of Gordon Russell* (1968)

Sparke, P., *Furniture* (1986) [survey of twentieth century]

Utility: *CC41: Utility Furniture and Fashion 1941–1951* (1974) [Geffrye Museum; chronology, bibl.]

Welch, R., *Hand and Machine* (1986) [work as designer and silversmith; book designed by Pentagram]

Woudhuysen, J., 'Not a leg left to stand on', *Blueprint* **26** (April 1986), 32–3 [state of British furniture design]

VIII   Literature

The bibliographical source for books, articles and theses on English literature is the *Annual Bibliography of English Language and Literature* (annually, 1920 to date), published by the Modern Humanities Research Association. This can be supplemented by the *British Humanities Index* (quarterly, 1962 to date, formerly *The Subject Index to Periodicals*, 1915–61). A list of works by individual authors can be found in the bibliographical Appendix to *The Present: volume VIII of The New Pelican Guide to English Literature*, ed. B. Ford (1983).

A complete list of works is given for those authors prominently discussed in the chapter on Literature.

Fiction: magazines and journals

The major fiction journal is *Granta* (new series, 1973 to date); *The Fiction Magazine* appeared quarterly from 1982. Fiction is also published or reviewed in *Critical Quarterly* (1959 to date, fiction supplement from 1986), *Encounter* (monthly, 1953 to date), *The London Magazine* (monthly, 1954 to date), *The London Review of Books* (fortnightly, 1979 to date).

Fiction: general

Bergonzi, B., *The Situation of the Novel* (1970)

Bradbury, M. (ed.), *The Novel Today: Contemporary Writers on Modern Fiction* (1977) [Murdoch, Fowles, Lessing; bibl.]

Bradbury, M. and Palmer, D. (ed.), *The Contemporary English Novel* (1979)

Firchow, P. (ed.), *The Writer's Place: Interviews on the Contemporary Literary Situation in Britain* (1974)

Haffenden, J., *Novelists in Interview* (1985)

Hayman, R., *The Novel Today, 1967–1975* (1976)

Kermode, F., *Continuities* (1968)
Modern Essays (1971)

Lodge, D., *The Novelist at the Crossroads and Other Essays on Fiction and Criticism* (1971)

Maschler, T. (ed.), *Declaration* (1957) [Lessing, C. Wilson, Osborne, Tynan]

Raban, J., *The Technique of Modern Fiction* (1968)

Rabinovitz, R., *The Reaction Against Experiment in the English Novel 1950–1960* (1967) [Amis, Wilson, Snow; bibl.]

Sutherland, J.A., *Fiction and the Fiction Industry* (1978)

Symons, J., *Bloody Murder from the Detective Story to the Crime Novel: a History* (1972, rev. 1985)

Literary prizes

The two major annual prizes for fiction and biography are the Booker Prize, worth £15,000 and administered by the Book Trust (formerly The National Book League); and the Whitbread Prizes, the major prize worth £20,000, administered by the Booksellers' Association. The Booker winners, with date of award, have been: P.H. Newby, *Something to Answer For* (1969); Bernice Rubens, *The Elected Member* (1970); V.S. Naipaul, *In a Free State* (1971); John Berger, *G* (1972); J.G. Farrell, *The Siege of Krishnapur* (1973); Nadine Gordimer, *The Conservationist* and Stanley Middleton, *Holiday* (1974); Ruth Prawer Jhabvala, *Heat and Dust* (1975); David Storey, *Saville* (1976); Paul Scott, *Staying On* (1977); Iris Murdoch, *The Sea, the Sea* (1978); Penelope Fitzgerald, *Offshore* (1979); William Golding, *Rites of Passage* (1980); Salman Rushdie, *Midnight's Children* (1981); Thomas Keneally, *Schindler's Ark* (1982); J.M. Coetzee, *Life and Times of Michael K* (1983); Anita Brookner, *Hotel du Lac* (1984); Keri Hulme, *The Bone People* (1985); Kingsley Amis, *The Old Devils* (1986); Penelope Lively, *Moon Tiger* (1987).

Science fiction

The collection of the Science Fiction Foundation is at the library of the North-East London Polytechnic, Dagenham, Essex.

Aldiss, B.W. and Wingrove, D., *Trillion Year Spree: the History of Science Fiction* (1986) [revises Aldiss's *Billion Year Spree* (1973)]

Greenland, C., *The Entropy Exhibition: Michael Moorcock and the British 'New Wave' in Science Fiction* (1983)

Parrinder, P., *Science Fiction: its Criticism and Teaching* (1980)

Parrinder, P. (ed.), *Science Fiction: a Critical Guide* (1979) [bibl. essays]

Stableford, B., *Scientific Romance in Britain 1890–1950* (1985)

Novelists

Joyce Cary (1888–1957) fiction: *Aissa Saved* (1932); *An American Visitor* (1933); *The African Witch* (1936); *Castle Corner* (1938); *Mister Johnson* (1939); *Charley Is My Darling* (1940);

A House of Children (1941); *Herself Surprised* (1941); *To Be a Pilgrim* (1942); *The Horse's Mouth* (1944, ed. A. Wright 1957); *The Moonlight* (1946); *A Fearful Joy* (1949); second trilogy: *Prisoner of Grace* (1952); *Except the Lord* (1953); *Not Honour More* (1955); first trilogy: *Herself Surprised, To Be a Pilgrim, The Horse's Mouth* (USA, 1958); *The Captive and the Free* (1959); *Spring Song and other Stories* (1960); interview: 'Joyce Cary' in *Writers at Work: the 'Paris Review' Interviews, First Series*, ed. M. Cowley (1958, repr. 1977), 51–67

Critical works:

Cook, C., *Joyce Cary: Liberal Principles* (1981)

Echeruo, M.J.C., *Joyce Cary and the Dimensions of Order* (1978)

Wright, A., *Joyce Cary: a Preface to his Novels* (1958)

William Golding (b.1911) complete fiction: *Lord of the Flies* (1954); *The Inheritors* (1955); *Pincher Martin* (1956); *Free Fall* (1959); *The Spire* (1964); *The Pyramid* (1967); *The Scorpion God: three short novels* (1971); *Darkness Visible* (1979); *Rites of Passage* (1980); *The Paper Men* (1984); *Close Quarters* (1987); drama: *The Brass Butterfly* (1958, USA 1962); essays: *The Hot Gates and other occasional pieces* (1965); *A Moving Target* (1982); travel: *An Egyptian Journal* (1985)

Critical works:

Kinkead-Weekes, M. and Gregor, I., *William Golding: a Critical Study* (1967, rev. 1984)

Carey, J. (ed.), *William Golding: the Man and his Books* (1986)

Doris Lessing (b.1919) complete fiction: novels: *The Grass is Singing* (1950); *Children of Violence* sequence – Bk I *Martha Quest* (1952), Bk II *A Proper Marriage* (1954), Bk III *A Ripple from the Storm*, (1958), Bk IV *Landlocked* (1965), Bk V *The Four-Gated City* (1969); *Retreat to Innocence* (1956); *The Golden Notebook* (1962); *Briefing for a Descent into Hell* (1971); *The Summer Before the Dark* (1973); *Memoirs of a Survivor* (1974); *Canopus in Argos: Archives* series – Re: *Colonised Planet 5: Shikasta* (1979), *The Marriages Between Zones Three, Four, and Five* (1980), *The Sirian Experiments* (1981), *The Making of the Representative for Planet 8* (1982), *The Sentimental*

Agents in the Volyen Empire (1983); as Jane Somers, *The Diary of a Good Neighbour* (1983), *If the Old Could . . .* (1984), repr. together as *The Diaries of Jane Somers* (1984); *The Good Terrorist* (1985). Short stories: *This Was the Old Chief's Country* (1951); *Five Short Novels* (1953); *The Habit of Loving* (1957); *A Man and Two Women* (1963); *Winter in July* (1966); *The Black Madonna* (1966); *African Stories* (1964); *The Story of a Non-Marrying Man and other Stories* (1972); *This Was the Old Chief's Country: Collected African Stories* vol. I (1973); *The Sun Between Their Feet: Collected African Stories* vol. II (1973); *To Room Nineteen: Collected Stories* vol. I (1978); *The Temptation of Jack Orkney: Collected Stories* vol. II (1978). Plays: 'Each His Own Wilderness' in E.M. Browne (ed.), *New English Dramatists* [1] (1959); *Play With a Tiger* (1962). Poems: *Fourteen Poems* (1959).
Autobiographical: 'The Small Personal Voice', in *Declaration*, ed. T. Maschler (1957); *Going Home* (1957, rev. 1968); *In Pursuit of the English: a Documentary* (1960); *The Wind Blows Away Our Words* (1987) [Afghanistan]
Critical works:
Sage, L. *Doris Lessing* (1983)
Taylor, J. (ed.),
Notebooks/Memoirs/Archives: Reading and Rereading Doris Lessing (1982) [bibl.]
Thorpe, M., *Doris Lessing's Africa* (1978)
Muriel Spark (b.1918) complete fiction:
The Comforters (1957); *The Go-Away Bird, with other stories* (1958); *Robinson* (1958); *Memento Mori* (1959); *The Bachelors* (1960); *The Ballad of Peckham Rye* (1960); *Voices at Play: Stories and Ear-pieces* (1961); *The Prime of Miss Jean Brodie* (1961); *The Girls of Slender Means* (1963); *The Mandelbaum Gate* (1965); *Collected Stories I* (1967); *The Public Image* (1968); *The Driver's Seat* (1970); *Not to Disturb* (1971); *The Hothouse by the East River* (1973); *The Abbess of Crewe* (1974); *The Takeover* (1976); *Territorial Rights* (1979); *Loitering with Intent* (1981); *Bang-bang You're Dead and Other Stories* (1981); *The Only Problem* (1984)
Critical works:
Kemp, P. *Muriel Spark* (1974)
Bold, A. (ed.), *Muriel Spark: an Odd Capacity for Vision* (1985)

Angus Wilson (b.1913) complete fiction:
The Wrong Set and Other Stories (1949); *Such Darling Dodos and Other Stories* (1950); *Hemlock and After* (1952); *Anglo-Saxon Attitudes* (1956); *A Bit Off the Map and Other Stories* (1957); *The Middle Age of Mrs Eliot* (1958); *The Old Men at the Zoo* (1961); *Late Call* (1964); *No Laughing Matter* (1967); *As If By Magic* (1973); *Setting the World on Fire* (1980); other: *The Mulberry Bush: a Play* (1956); *The Wild Garden: or Speaking of Writing* (1963); K. McSweeney (ed.), *Angus Wilson: Diversity and Depth in Fiction: Selected Critical Writings* (1983); *Reflections in a Writer's Eye* (1986)
Critical work: Faulkner, P., *Angus Wilson: Mimic and Moralist* (1980)

Poetry magazines

The two major poetry journals are: *Poetry Review* (quarterly, 1909 to date), the journal of the Poetry Society, 21 Earl's Court Square, London SW5; and *PN Review* (bi-monthly, 1976 to date) which began as *Poetry Nation* (1–6, 1973–6). *Agenda* (quarterly, 1959 to date) features special issues on British poetry; *Stand* (quarterly, 1952 to date). *The Review* (1–15, 1962–7) was an influential little magazine.

Poetry anthologies

Alvarez, A., (ed.), *The New Poetry* 1962, rev. 1966 [influential anthology]
Conquest, R. (ed.), *New Lines* (1956); *New Lines 2* (1963)
Enright, D.J. (ed.), *The Oxford Book of Contemporary Verse 1945–1980* (1980) [mainly British]
Garlick, R. and Mathias, R. (ed.), *Anglo-Welsh Poetry 1480–1980* (1984)
Horovitz, M. (ed.), *Children of Albion: Poetry of the Underground in Britain* (1969) [alternative anthology]
Larkin, P., (ed.), *The Oxford Book of Twentieth Century English Verse* (1973, rev. 1974)
Liverpool Poets: *Penguin Modern Poets 10: the Mersey Sound* (1967, rev. 1974, repr. 1983) [Adrian Henri, Roger McGough, Brian Patten]
Lucie-Smith, E. (ed.), *British Poetry since 1945* (1970, rev. 1985) [introductory]
Morrison, B. and Motion, A. (ed.), *Penguin Book of Contemporary British Poetry* (1982) [read with Schmidt, 1983]
Muldoon, P. (ed.), *The Faber Book of Contemporary Irish Poetry* (1986)

Robson, J. (ed.), *The Young British Poets* (1971)

Schmidt, M. (ed.), *Eleven British Poets: an Anthology* (1980) [R.S. Thomas, Sisson, Davie, Jennings, Tomlinson, Hill, Heaney]

Poetry: general

Barker, J. (comp.), *The Poetry Library of the Arts Council of Great Britain: Short-title Catalogue* (6th edn, 1981)

Bedient, C., *Eight Contemporary Poets* (1974) [including Tomlinson, Davie, Hughes, Kinsella]

Davie, D., *Thomas Hardy and British Poetry* (1973)

Deane, S., *Celtic Revivals: Essays in Modern Irish Literature 1880–1980* (1985) [Heaney, Mahon]

Haffenden, J. (ed.), *Viewpoints: Poets in Conversation* (1981) [Heaney, Hill, Larkin]

Hamilton, I. (ed.), *The Modern Poet: Essays from 'The Review'* (1968)

Jones, P. and Schmidt, M. (ed.), *British Poetry since 1970: a Critical Survey* (1980) [excellent bibl., based on Arts Council Poetry Library]

Lucas, J., *Modern Poetry from Hardy to Hughes: a Critical Survey* (1986)

Morrison, B., *The Movement: English Poetry and Fiction of the 1950s* (1980) [Larkin, Amis, Davie, Jennings, Wain; bibl.]

Penguin Modern Poets nos. 1–27 (1962–79) [each volume selects from the work of three writers; excellent introduction to the period]

Schmidt, M., *An Introduction to Fifty Modern British Poets* (1979) [short essays]

Schmidt, M. (ed.), *Some Contemporary Poets of Britain and Ireland: an Anthology* (1983) [read with Morrison and Motion, 1982]

Thwaite, A., *Poetry Today: a Critical Guide to British Poetry 1960–1984* (1985)

Trotter, D., *The Making of the Reader: Language and Subjectivity in Modern American, English and Irish Poetry* (1984)

Young, A., *Dada and After: Extremist Modernism and English Literature* (1981) [recent poetry]

Poets

Seamus Heaney (b.1939) complete collected poetry: *Death of a Naturalist* (1966); *Door into the Dark* (1969); *Wintering Out* (1972); *North* (1975); *Selected Poems 1965–1975* (1980); *Field Work* (1979); *Station Island* (1984); *The Haw Lantern* (1987); translation: *Sweeney Astray* (1983); prose: *Preoccupations: Selected Prose 1968–1978* (1980)

Critical works:

Morrison, B., *Seamus Heaney* (1982) (1982) [introductory; bibl.]

Ted Hughes (b.1930) complete collected poetry: *The Hawk in the Rain* (1957); *Lupercal* (1960); *Recklings* (1966); *Wodwo* (1967); *Crow: from the Life and Songs of the Crow* (1970, USA 1971 with additional poems); *Selected Poems 1957–1967* (1972, USA 1973); *Prometheus on his Crag* (1973); *Season Songs* (1976, USA 1975); *Cave Birds* (1975 [limited edn], 1978, USA 1979); *Gaudete* (1977); *Orts* (1978); *Moortown Elegies* (1978); *Adam and the Sacred Nine* (1979); *Remains of Elmet* (1979); *Moortown* (1979, USA 1980); *Selected Poems 1957–81* (1982). *Under the North Star* (1981, rev. 1985); *River: Poems* (1983). For children: *Meet my Folks!* (1961); *The Iron Man* (1968); *What is the Truth? A Farmyard Fable for the Young* (fiction, 1984); *Collected Poems for Children 1961–1983* (1985); *Flowers and Insects* (1986); *Ffangs the Vampire Bat and the Kiss of Truth* (1986). For schools: *Poetry in the Making* (1967); translation: *Seneca's Oedipus* (1969)

Critical works:

Gifford, T. and Roberts, N., *Ted Hughes: a Critical Study* (1981)

Sagar, K., *The Art of Ted Hughes* (1975, rev. 1978) [rev. bibl.1980]

Philip Larkin (1922–85) complete collected poetry: *The North Ship* (1945, rev. 1966); *XX Poems* (1950); *The Less Deceived* (1955, USA 1960, repr. 1974); *The Whitsun Weddings* (1964, repr. 1971); *High Windows* (1974); *Aubade* (USA 1980); fiction: *Jill* (1946, repr. 1964, 1985, USA 1976); *A Girl in Winter* (1947, USA 1962, repr. 1965, 1975, USA 1976); jazz criticism: *All What Jazz* (1970, USA 1985); various: *Required Writing: Miscellaneous Pieces 1955–1982* (1983)

Critical works:

Bloomfield, B.C. *Philip Larkin: a Bibliography 1933–1976* (1979)

Kuby, L., *Philip Larkin: an Uncommon Poet for the Common Man* (1974)

Morton, A., *Philip Larkin* (1982) [introductory; bibl.]

Thwaite, A. (ed.), *Larkin at Sixty* (1982) [essays]

Theatre: magazines

Gambit: International Theatre Review (quarterly, 1959 to date) publishes plays and criticism; *Plays and Players* (monthly, 1953 to date); *Theatre Research International* (3 p.a., 1975 to date, *Theatre Research* from 1958).

Theatre: general

Ansorge, P., *Disrupting the Spectacle: Five Years of Experimental and Fringe Theatre in Britain* (1975)

Arden, J., *To Present the Pretence: Essays on the Theatre and its Public* (1977)

Bigsby, C.W.E. (ed.), *Contemporary English Drama* (1981) [essays]

Brook, P., *The Empty Space* (1968) [influential director's views]

Bull, J., *New British Political Dramatists* (1984) [Brenton, Hare, Griffiths, Edgar; bibl.]

Callow, S., *Being an Actor* (1984) [working with playwrights]

Davison, P., *Contemporary Drama and the Popular Dramatic Tradition in England* (1982) [music hall; bibl.]

Elsom, J., *Post-War British Theatre* (1976, rev. 1979)

Itzin, C., *Stages in the Revolution: Political Theatre in Britain Since 1968* (1980)

Marowitz, C., *Confessions of a Counterfeit Critic* (1973) [reviews]

Nightingale, B., *An Introduction to Fifty Modern British Plays* (1982) [short essays]

Pike, F. (ed.), *Ah! Mischief: the Writer and Television* (1982) [essays by Edgar, Griffiths, Hare]

Roberts, P., *The Royal Court Theatre 1965–1972* (1986)

Taylor, J.R., *Anger and After: a Guide to the New British Drama* (1962, rev. 1969, repr. 1977) [50s, Royal Court, Theatre Workshop, provinces, radio and TV, experimental]

The Second Wave: British Drama of the Sixties (1971, rev. bibl. 1978) [Mercer, Bond, Stoppard, Orton, Storey; bibl.]

Trussler, S. (ed.), *New Theatre Voices of the Seventies* (1981)

Worth, K.J., *Revolutions in Modern English Drama* (1972) [bibl.]

Theatre: playwrights

Plays are selectively listed, unless otherwise indicated. Dates given are of first book publication, not of production.

John Arden (b.1930)

Gray, F., *John Arden* (1982); Hunt, A., *Arden: a Study of his Plays* (1974)

Edward Bond (b.1934) major plays: *The Pope's Wedding* (perf. 1962, pub. 1971); *Saved* (1966); *Early Morning* (1968); *Narrow Road to the Deep North* (1968); *Lear* (1972, repr. 1983); *The Sea* (1973); *Bingo: Scenes of Money and Death* (1974); *The Fool: Scenes of Bread and Love* (1976); *We Come to the River* (1976); Collections: *Plays: One* (1977) – *Saved, Early Morning, The Pope's Wedding*, all rev.; *Plays: Two* (1978) – *Lear, The Sea, Narrow Road, Black Mass, Passion*, all rev.; *The Bundle* (1978); *The Woman* (1979); *The Worlds* (1980); *Restoration* (1981); *Summer* (1982); *War Plays: a Trilogy* (1985)

Critical works:

Coult, T., *The Plays of Edward Bond* (1977, rev. 1979)

Hirst, D.L., *Edward Bond* (1985)

Scharine, R., *The Plays of Edward Bond* (1976)

Joe Orton (1933–67)

Critical works:

Bigsby, C.W.E., *Joe Orton* (1982) [intro; bibl]

Lahr, J., *Prick Up Your Ears; the Biography of Joe Orton* (1978)

Lahr, J. (ed.), *The Orton Diaries* (1986)

John Osborne (b.1929) *Look Back in Anger* (1957); *The Entertainer* (1957); *Luther* (1961); *Inadmissible Evidence* (1965); *A Patriot for Me* (1966); *Time Present* and *The Hotel in Amsterdam* (1968); *West of Suez* (1971)

Critical works:

Osborne, J., *A Better Class of person; an Autobiography 1929–1956* (1981)

Trussler, S., *The Plays of John Osborne: an Assessment* (1969)

Harold Pinter (b.1930) major plays: *Plays: One* (1976), comprising *The Birthday Party, The Room, The Dumb Waiter* (1960), *A Slight Ache, A Night Out* (1961); *Plays: Two* (1978), comprising *The Caretaker* (1960), *The Collection, The Lover* (1963); *Plays: Three* (1978), including *The Homecoming* (1965), *Tea Party, The Basement* (1967), *Landscape, Silence* (1969); *Plays: Four* (1981), including *Old Times* (1971), *No Man's Land* (1975), *Betrayal* (1978); *The Hothouse* (1980); *Other Places: Family Voices, A Kind of Alaska, Victoria Station* (1982); *One for the Road* (1984); *The Players* (radio, 1985); Screenplays: *Five Screenplays* (1971); *The Proust Screenplay* (1978); *The French Lieutenant's Woman and other Screenplays* (1982). *Poems and Prose 1949–1977* (1978)

Critical works:

Almansi, G. and Henderson, S., *Harold Pinter* (1983) [introductory; bibl.]

Gale, S.H., *Harold Pinter: an Annotated Bibliography* (1978)

Thompson, D.T., *Pinter: the Player's Playwright* (1985)

Tom Stoppard (b.1937)   major plays: *Rosencrantz and Guildenstern are Dead* (1967); *Enter a Free Man* (1968); *The Real Inspector Hound* (1968); *Albert's Bridge* (radio, 1969); *After Magritte* (1971); *Jumpers* (1972); *Travesties* (1975); *Dirty Linen* and *New-Found-Land* (1976); *Every Good Boy Deserves Favour* and *Professional Foul* [TV] (1978); *Night and Day* (1978); *The Real Thing* (1982); *The Dog it was that Died and Other Plays* (1983); *Four Plays for Radio* (1984); *Squaring the Circle* (1984)

Critical works:

Corballis, R., *Stoppard: the Mystery and the Clockwork* (1984) [bibl.]

Whitaker, T.R., *Tom Stoppard* (1983)

Arnold Wesker (b.1932)   *Arnold Wesker*, vol. I (1981), comprising *Chicken Soup With Barley* (1959), *Roots* (1959), *I'm Talking About Jerusalem* (1960) [i.e., 'The Wesker Trilogy' (1960)]; vol. II (1981), comprising *The Kitchen* (1960), *The Four Seasons* (1966), *Their Very Own and Golden City* (1966); vol. III (1980), comprising *Chips With Everything* (1962), *The Friends* (1970), *The Old Ones* (1972), *Love Letters on Blue Paper* (1978); vol. IV (1980), comprising *The Journalists* (1975), *The Wedding Feast* (1977), *The Merchant* (1977, rev. 1983)

Critical works:

Leeming, G. and Trussler, S., *The Plays of Arnold Wesker: an Assessment* (1971)

Leeming, G. (ed.), *Wesker: Writers on File* (1985) [documentation]

IX   Music

All music in the modern period, including popular music, is represented in *The New Grove Dictionary of Music* (20 vols., 1980). There are substantial essays on composers active in the 1940s and 1950s, but more recent composers are not very fully described, though their works are listed. The best approach to the early part of the period is through Francis Routh's *Contemporary British Music* (1972), which deals with the years 1945–70, and has essays on twenty-one composers, electronic music and serialism. Routh's bibliography lists many magazine articles, and *New Grove* supplements these down to the late 1970s.

More recent composers can be approached through the bibliography in Paul Griffiths' *New Sounds, New Personalities* (1985). This collection of interviews can be read alongside Murray Schafer's *British Composers in Interview* (1963) to make an accessible introduction to most of the significant post-war composers. Griffiths gives very full listings of works by composers discussed in chapter 2 on Music, but not listed below.

For popular music, including rock and jazz, the best bibliographical source is the 'Booklist' in *Popular Music*, edited by Richard Middleton and David Horn (5 vols., 1981–5). Each volume contains scholarly essays and reviews.

Magazines and journals

Contact: a Journal of Contemporary Music (biannual, 1971 to date); *Melody Maker* (weekly, 1926 to date) for popular music; *Musical Times* (monthly, 1904 to date) surveys all musical activity; *Opera* (monthly, 1950 to date); *Tempo: a Quarterly Review of Modern Music* (1939 to date); *The Wire* (monthly, 1982 to date) surveys jazz and new music.

General

Foreman, L. (ed.), *British Music Now: a Guide to the Work of Younger Composers* (1975) [essays on Birtwistle, Davies, Hoddinott, Tavener; discography; bibl.]

Griffiths, P., *New Sounds, New Personalities: British Composers of the 1980s in Conversation* (1985) [twenty interviews, with appendix of compositions and recordings; bibl.]

Keller, H., *Criticism* (1987)

Mitchell, D., *The Language of Modern Music* (1963, rev. 1966)

Peacock, A. and Weir, R., *The Composer in the Market Place* (1975)

Routh, F., *Contemporary British Music* (1972) [see headnote]

Schafer, M., *British Composers in Interview* (1963) [sixteen interviews with an earlier generation; includes Lutyens, Wellesz, Searle]

Composers

Harrison Birtwhistle (b.1934)

Compositions: Tragoedia for wind quintet, harr and string quartet (1965); *Punch and Judy* (chamber opera, 1966–7); *Down by the Greenwood Side*, music theatre (1968–9); Verses for Ensembles (1968–9); *Meridian* for voices and instruments (1970–1); *The Triumph of Time* for orchestra (1971–2); *Bow Down*, music theatre (1977); *Carmen arcadiae mechanicae perpetuum* (1977); *Silbury Air* (1977); . . . *agm* . . . for sixteen voices and small orchestra (1978–9); *The Mask of Orpheus* (1973–83, perf. 1986); *Secret Theatre* for small orchestra (1984); *Earth Dances* for orchestra (1985–6).

Benjamin Britten (1913–1976)

Compositions: *Our Hunting Fathers* (1936); *On This Island* (1937); *Variations on a Theme of Frank Bridge* (1937); *'Les Illuminations* (1939); *Seven Sonnets of Michelangelo* (1940); *Sinfonia da Requiem* (1940); String Quartet no. 1 (1941); Serenade for tenor, horn and string orchestra (1943); String Quartet no. 2 (1945); *A Charm of Lullabies* (1947); *Saint Nicholas* (1948); *Spring symphony* (1949); *The Prince of the Pagodas* (1956); *Cantata Academica, Carmen Basiliense* (1959); *War Requiem* (1961); Cello Symphony (1963); *The Golden Vanity* (1966); String Quartet no. 3 (1975).

Operatic works: *Paul Bunyan* (1940–1); *Peter Grimes* (1944–5); *The Rape of Lucretia* (1946); *Albert Herring* (1947); *The Beggar's Opera* (1948); *The Little Sweep* (1949); *Billy Budd* (1951); *Gloriana* (1953); *The Turn of the Screw* (1954); *Noye's Fludde* (1958); *A Midsummer Night's Dream* (1960); *Curlew River* (1964); *The Burning Fiery Furnace* (1966); *The Prodigal Son* (1968); *Owen Wingrave* (1970); *Death in Venice* (1973).

Writings

Britten, B., *On Receiving the First Aspen Award* (1964, rev. 1978)

Bibliography

Mitchell, D. (comp.) *Benjamin Britten: a Complete Catalogue of his Published Works* (1973)

Commentaries and Criticism

Peter Grimes [and] *Gloriana* (1983) [English National Opera / The Royal Opera, Opera Guide 24; essays and explanations]

Brett, P. (comp.), *Benjamin Britten: 'Peter Grimes'* (1983) [handbook; essays, musical examples]

Evans, P., *The Music of Benjamin Britten* (1979)

Howard, P. (ed.), *Benjamin Britten: 'The Turn of the Screw'* (1983) [handbook; essays, musical examples]

Keller, H. and Mitchell, D. (ed.), *Benjamin Britten: a Commentary on his Works* (1952, repr. 1972) [catalogue, bibl.]

Kennedy, M., *Britten* (1981) [discography]

Mitchell, D., *Britten and Auden in the Thirties* (1981) [film *Night Mail*, theatre projects, *Our Hunting Fathers*, etc.]

Palmer, C. (ed.), *The Britten Companion* (1984)

White, Eric W., *Benjamin Britten: his Life and Operas* (1970, rev. 1983)

Whittall, A., *The Music of Britten and Tippett: Studies in Themes and Techniques* (1982)

Peter Maxwell Davies (b.1934)

Compositions: *Trumpet Sonata* (1955); *St Michael*: sonata for seventeen wind instruments (1957); *O magnum mysterium* (1960); Seven *In Nomine* for ten instruments (1963–4); String Quartet (1961); Second Fantasia on John Taverner's *In Nomine* for orchestra (1964); *Tavgrner* (opera, 1962–8), perf. 1972); *Revelation and Fall* for voice and large ensemble (1965–6); *Worldes Blis* for orchestra (1966–9); *Eight Songs for a Mad King* (1969); *St Thomas'Wake* (1969); *Vesalii icones* for dancer, cello and quintet (1969); Symphony no. 1 (1973–6); *Ave maris stella* for sextet (1975); *The Martyrdom of Saint Magnus*, church opera (1976); *Salome*, ballet (1978); *The Lighthouse*, chamber opera (1979); Symphony no. 2 (1980); *Image-Reflection-Shadow* for sextet (1982); Symphony no. 3 (1984); Violin Concerto (1985–6).

Commentary and Criticism

Griffiths, P., *Peter Maxwell Davies* (1982)

Pruslin, S. (ed.), *Peter Maxwell Davies: Studies from Two Decades* (1979) [articles repr. from *Tempo*]

Alexander Goehr (b.1932)

Compositions: *Fantasia* for orchestra op. 4 (1954); *Capriccio* for piano op. 6 (1957); *The Deluge* op. 7 (1957–8); *Sutter's Gond* op. 10 (1959–60); Violin Concerto op. 13 (1961–2); *Little*

Symphony op. 15 (1963); *Pastorals* for orchestra op. 19 (1965); *Arden Must Die* op. 21 (opera, 1966, perf. 1967); *Naboth's Vineyard*, music theatre op. 25 (1968); *Paraphrase* for clarinet op. 28 (1969); Symphony in One Movement op. 29 (1969–70); *Shadowplay*, music theatre op. 30 (1970); *Sonata about Jerusalem*, music theatre op. 31 (1970); *Metamorphosis/Dance* for orchestra op. 34 (1973–4); String Quartet no. 3 op. 37 (1975–6); *Babylon the Great is Fallen* for chorus and orchestra op. 40 (1979); *Deux études* for orchestra op. 43 (1981); *Behold the Sun* op. 44 (opera, 1981–4, perf. 1985).

Michael Tippett (b.1905)   Compositions: Concerto for Double String Orchestra (1938–9); *A Child of Our Time* (1939–41); *Boyhood's End* (1943); Symphony no. 1 (1944–5); *The Midsummer Marriage* (opera, 1946–52, perf. 1955); *Fantasia concertante on a Theme of Corelli* (1953); Concerto for Piano and Orchestra (1953–5); Symphony no. 2 (1956–7); *King Priam* (opera, 1958–61, perf. 1962); Concerto for Orchestra (1962–73); *The Vision of St Augustine* (1963–5); *The Knot Garden* (opera, 1966–9, perf. 1970); Symphony no. 3 (1972–2); Piano Sonata no. 3 (1972–3) *The Ice Break* (opera, 1973–6, perf. 1977); Symphony no. 4 (1976–7); Concerto for violin, viola, cello and orchestra ['Triple Concerto'] (1978–9); *The Mask of Time* (1977–82).

Writings
Bowen, M. (ed.), *Music of the Angels: Essays and Sketchbooks of Michael Tippett* (1980)
Tippett, M., *Moving into Aquarius* (1959, repr. 1974) [essays]
Commentary and Criticism
Bowen, M., *Michael Tippett* (1985)
Kemp, I., *Tippett: the Composer and his Music* (1984) [the standard work]
Kemp, I. (ed.), *Michael Tippett: a Symposium on his 60th Birthday* (1965)
Matthews, David, *Michael Tippett* (1980)
The Operas of Michael Tippett (1985) [English National Opera/The Royal Opera, Opera Guide 29]
White, Eric W., *Tippett and his Operas* (1979)
Whittall, A., *The Music of Britten and Tippett: Studies in Themes and Techniques* (1982)

Bibliography
Andrews, P., 'Sir Michael Tippett: a bibliography', *Brio* (Autumn 1978), 33–46.

Electronic music
Manning, P., *Electronic and Computer Music* (1985) [bibl., discography]

Popular music
Chambers, I., *Urban Rhythms: Pop Music and Popular Culture* (1985) [bibl.]
Cohn, Nik, *Rock from the Beginning* (1969)
Frith, S., *Sound Effects: Youth, Leisure, and the Politics of Rock* (1983) [revises *Sociology of Rock*, 1978; annotated bibl.]
Gillett, C., *The Sound of the City: the Rise of Rock and Roll* (1970, rev. 1983) [the standard history; bibl.]
Middleton, R., and Horn, D. (ed.), *Popular Music* (annual, 5 vols., 1981–5) [articles, extensive international bibl.; 3 vols. annually from 1987]
Street, J., *Rebel Rock: the Politics of Popular Music* (1986)

The Beatles (as a group, 1962–70) Albums: *Please Please me* (1963); *With the Beatles* (1963); *A Hard Day's Night* (1964); *Beatles for Sale* (1964); *Help!* (1965); *Rubber Soul* (1965); *Revolver* (1966); *Magical Mystery Tour* (1967); *Sergeant Pepper's Lonely Hearts Club Band* (1967); *Untitled* ['The White Album'] (1968); *Abbey Road* (1969); *Let it Be* (1970).

Films: *A Hard Day's Night* (1964); *Help!* (1965); *Magical Mystery Tour* (TV, 1967); *Yellow Submarine* (1968); *Let It Be* (1969).

Commentary and Criticism
Davies, H., *The Beatles: the Authorised Biography* (1968, rev. 1985) [discography]
Harry, Bill, *Paperback Writers: the History of the Beatles in Print* (1984) [annotated bibl.]
Mellers, W., *Twilight of the Gods: The Beatles in Retrospect* (1973) [discography, musical examples]

X   New Towns

Early plans and theories
Abercrombie, P., *Greater London Plan 1944* (1945) [includes Stevenage]

Town and Country Planning (1933, rev. 1943) [introductory but influential; 3rd edn, with a chapter by D. Rigby Childs describing post-war developments, 1959]

Howard, Ebenezer, *Garden Cities of Tomorrow* (1902, repr. 1946, 1965) [2nd edn of Howard's *Tomorrow: a Peaceful Path to Social Reform* (1898)]

Purdom, C.B., *The Building of Satellite Towns: a Contribution to the Study of Town Development and Regional Planning* (1925, new edn 1949) [Letchworth and Welwyn Garden City]

The Letchworth Achievement (1963)

The New Town debate

Alexander, C., 'A city is not a tree', *Design* **206** (February, 1966), 46–55

Cullingworth, J.B., *Town and Country Planning in Britain* (6th edn, 1976)

Evans, H. (ed.), *New Towns: the British Experience* (1972)

Gibberd, F., *Town Design* (1953, 5th edn 1967)

Hughes, M.R. (ed.), *The Letters of Lewis Mumford and Frederic J. Osborn: a Transatlantic Dialogue 1938–70* (1971)

Mumford, L., *The Highway and the City* (1964) [ch. 3, 'Old Forms for New Towns']

Osborn, F.J., *Green-Belt Cities* (1946)

Osborn, F.J. and Whittick, A., *New Towns: their Origins, Achievements and Progress* (1963, 3rd edn 1977)

Rodwin, L., *The British New Towns Policy* (1956)

Schaffer, F., *The New Town Story* (1970)

Self, P., *Cities in Flood: the Problems of Urban Growth* (1957, rev. 1961)

Webber, M.M., *Beyond the Industrial Age and Permissive Planning*, Centre for Environmental Studies Working Paper 18 (1968)

New Towns

Balchin, J., *First New Town: an Autobiography of the Stevenage Development Corporation 1946–1980* (1980)

Gibberd, F., *et al.*, *Harlow: the Story of a New Town* (1980)

London County Council, *The Planning of a New Town* (1961) [unexecuted plan for Hook]

Milton Keynes Development Corporation, *The Plan for Milton Keynes*, 2 vols. (1970)

Mullan, B., *Stevenage Ltd: Aspects of the Planning and Politics of Stevenage New Town* (1980) [International Library of Sociology series]

Orlans, H., *Stevenage: a Sociological Study* (1952) [published in USA as *Utopia Ltd* (1953)]

Walker, D., *The Architecture and Planning of Milton Keynes* (1982)

Official publications

Cullingworth, J.B., *Environmental Planning 1939–1969 Vol. III: New Towns Policy* (1979)

Report of Royal Commission on Distribution of Industrial Population (1940) [the Barlow Report]

Reference

Department of the Environment, *New Towns* (1976) [Bibliography series, HQ Library, DoE]

Golany, G., *New Towns Planning and Development: a World-Wide Bibliography* (1973) [Urban Land Institute Research Report, Washington DC]

XI   The Third Programme

Scripts and internal BBC papers can be consulted at the BBC Written Archives Centre, Caversham Park, Reading RG4 8TZ. These papers are subject to the thirty-year rule on disclosure. Programmes can be heard at the British Library Institute of Recorded Sound, 29 Exhibition Road, London SW7. The BBC Sound Archives are for BBC use only and external researchers are admitted only in exceptional cases. Parliament has received the *Annual Reports and Accounts of the British Broadcasting Corporation* since 1927 (accounts only for 1939–44).

The history of the BBC is being written by Asa Briggs, and four volumes have appeared. They are: *The History of Broadcasting in the United Kingdom: Vol. I: The Birth of Broadcasting* [1922–7] (1961); *Vol. II: The Golden Age of Wireless* [1927–39] (1965); *Vol. III: The War of Words* [1939–45] (1970); *Vol. IV: Sound and Vision* [1945–55] (1979). These are abbreviated in Briggs' *The BBC: The First Fifty Years* (1985), with new material on recent developments. The most useful bibliography is Gavin Higgens (ed.), *British Broadcasting 1922–1982: a Selected and Annotated Bibliography* (BBC Data Publications, 1983).

The *Radio Times* has been published weekly since 1923. The *BBC Quarterly* (1946–54) was intended for those 'professionally engaged in broadcasting and its organisation'; a selection from its articles on the Third Programme is included below.

Abraham, G., 'Plea for a Wider Musical Policy', *BBC Quarterly* **3**, 3 (October 1948), 148–53 [criticism of Third's music policy]

Bridson, D.G., *The Christmas Child* (1950) [poems from broadcast features, 1930s–40s]

Prospero and Ariel: The Rise and Fall of Radio: a Personal Recollection (1971) [by producer/writer; closure of Features described]

Bridson, D.G., 'Radio's Approach to Poetry', *BBC Quarterly* **5**, 3 (Autumn 1950), 167–72 [Third's poetry policy]

Briggs, A., *The History of Broadcasting in the United Kingdom, Vol. IV: Sound and Vision* (1979) [bibl.]

Brown, T. and Reid, A. (ed.), *Time was Away: the World of Louis MacNeice* (1974) [R.D. Smith and Dallas Bower on radio work; scripts listed]

Cooper, M., 'Educating the Musical Listener', *BBC Quarterly* **5**, 2 (Summer 1950), 72–6 [suggests improvements in music presentation]

Coulton, B., *Louis MacNeice in the BBC* (1980) [scripts listed]

Crozier, M., 'Four Radio Plays', *BBC Quarterly* **3**, 3 (October 1948), 165–70 [MacNeice, Sackville-West, Henry Reed]

Gielgud, V., 'Policy and problems of Broadcast Drama', *BBC Quarterly* **2**, 1 (April 1947), 18–23

Gilliam, L., 'Aspects of the Feature Programme', *BBC Quarterly* **2**, 2 (July 1947), 100–4

Gilliam, L. (ed.), *BBC Features* (1955) [post-war radio features]

Grisewood, H., *One Thing at a Time* (1968) [autobiography of former Controller, Third Programme]

'Response and Responsibility', *BBC Quarterly* **4**, 3 (October 1949), 165–9 [listener responsibility]

Hussey, D., 'The Third Programme and the Middle-Brow', *BBC Quarterly* **4**, 3 (October 1949), 160–4 [audience difficulties]

Lehmann, J., 'A Literary Magazine on the Air: problems and findings', *BBC Quarterly* **7**, 2 (Summer 1952), 77–82 [on 'New Soundings']

Lewis, C. Day, 'Broadcasting and Poetry', *BBC Quarterly* **5**, 1 (Spring 1950), 1–7

MacNeice, L., 'A Plea for Sound', *BBC Quarterly* **8**, 3 (Autumn 1953), 129–35 [sound versus television]

Christopher Columbus: a Radio Play (1944)

The Dark Tower and other Radio Scripts (1947) [*Dark Tower* repr. alone (1964)]

Morris, J. (ed.), *From the Third Programme: a Ten Years' Anthology* (1956)

Newman, E., 'Opera on the Air: some Reflections and Suggestions', *BBC Quarterly* **4**, 2 (July 1949), 94–7

Pritchett, V.S., 'Broadcasting about Literature', *BBC Quarterly* **2**, 2 (July 1947), 77–82

Pryce-Jones, A., 'The Third Programme: five years after', *BBC Quarterly* **6**, 3 (Autumn 1951), 136–41 [objectives reviewed]

Reith, J.C.W., *Into the Wind* (1949) [Lord Reith's autobiography]

Sackville-West, E., 'Music and the Third Programme', *BBC Quarterly* **6**, 3 (Autumn 1951), 142–6 [surveys first five years]

Silvey, R., 'The Third Programme and its Market', *BBC Quarterly* **8**, 3 (Autumn 1953), 164–8 [BBC Audience Research]

Simon, Lord, of Wythenshawe, *The BBC from Within* (1953)

Spender, S., 'Thoughts on the Broadcasting of Poetry', *BBC Quarterly* **6**, 1 (Spring 1951), 12–17 [radio poetic drama]

XII   The Visual Arts

The Tate Gallery, Millbank, London SW1P 4RG, is the major public gallery for modern art. Acquisitions from 1938 were listed in the *Annual Report* for 1954, and later buying in subsequent reports. Acquisitions were first described separately in *The Tate Gallery 1974–76: Illustrated Catalogue of Acquisitions* (1978); those for 1982–4 are described in the catalogue published in 1986. The most recent report appeared as *The Tate Gallery 1984–86: Illustrated Biennial Report* (1986). The annual Royal Academy Summer Exhibition is accompanied by an illustrated catalogue.

Magazines

A guide to current activities can be found in *Art Monthly* (1975 to date), *Artscribe International* (bimonthly, 1976 to date). *Studio International* (quarterly, 1893 to date, originally *The Studio*) is essential reading, particularly down to 1975, for British and international developments.

General

Brighton, A., and Morris, L. (ed.), *Towards Another Picture: an Anthology of Writings by Artists Working in Britain 1945–1977* (1977)

Chamot, M., Farr, D., and Butlin, M. (comp.), *Tate Gallery Catalogues: the Modern British Paintings, Drawings and Sculpture, vol. I: artists A-L* (1964); *vol. II: artists M-Z* (1965)

Cross, T., *Painting the Warmth of the Sun: St Ives Artists 1939–1975* (1984) [Nicholson, Lanyon, Heron, Wynter, etc.]

Harries, M. and S., *The War Artists* (1983) [standard work]

Hutchinson, S., *The History of the Royal Academy 1768–1986* (1968, rev. 1986)

Ironside, R., *Painting Since 1939* (1947) [short survey]

Lucie-Smith, E., *Art in the Seventies* (1980)

Morris, L., *The Story of the A.I.A.: Artists' International Association 1933–1953* (1983) [catalogue]

Munnings, Sir A., *An Artist's Life* (1950); *The Second Burst* (1951); *The Finish* (1952) [autobiography]

Rothenstein, J., *Modern English Painters*, vol. II: *Lewis to Moore* (1956, rev. 1984) [essays, biographies]

Modern English Painters, vol. III: *Wood to Hockney* (1984) [essays; biographies]

Shone, R., *The Century of Change: British Painting Since 1900* (1977)

Spalding, F., *British Art Since 1900* (1986) [survey]

Walker, J.A., *Art Since Pop* (1975)

Artists

Michael Andrews (b.1928)
Michael Andrews (1981) [Hayward]

Frank Auerbach (b.1931)
Auerbach, F., *Paintings and Drawings 1977–1985* (1986) [Venice Biennale, 1986]
Frank Auerbach (1978) [Hayward]

Francis Bacon (b.1909)
Ades, D., Forge, A., and Durham, A., *Francis Bacon* (1985) [Tate retrospective; bibl.]
Alley, R. and Rothenstein, J., *Francis Bacon* (1964) [catalogue raisonné, 1929–63]
Leiris, M., *Francis Bacon: Full Face and in Profile* (1983)
Russell, John, *Francis Bacon* (1971, rev. 1979) [introductory]
Sylvester, D., *Interviews with Francis Bacon* (1975, rev. 1980) [interviews 1962–79]

Adrian Berg (b.1929)
Fuller, P. (intro.), *Adrian Berg: Paintings 1977–1986* (1986) [Arts Council / Serpentine]

Peter Blake (b.1932)
Peter Blake (1983) [Tate; bibl.]

David Bomberg (1890–1957)
Cork, R., *David Bomberg* (1987)
Lipke, W., *David Bomberg: a Critical Study of his Life and Work* (1967)
Serota, N. and Brook, J. (ed.), *David Bomberg: the Later Years* (1979) [Whitechapel /Tate]

Arthur Boyd (b.1920)
Fuller, P., 'The Suffolk outback', *Art Monthly* **97** (June 1986), 6–11
Hoff, U., *The Art of Arthur Boyd* (1986) [bibl.]
Philipp, F., *Arthur Boyd* (1967)

Victor Burgin (b.1941)
Between (1986) [ICA; artworks with commentary]

Anthony Caro (b.1924)
Blume, D., *Anthony Caro* 5 vols. (1981–5) [catalogue raisonné of complete work to 1985]
Fried, M. (intro.), *Anthony Caro* (1969) [Hayward; bibl.]
Waldman, D., *Anthony Caro* (1982) [bibl.]

Cecil Collins (b.1908)
Collins, C., *The Vision of the Fool* (1947, rev. 1981)
Morphet, R., *The Prints of Cecil Collins* (1981) [Tate]

Robert Colquhoun (1914–62)
An Exhibition of Paintings by Robert Colquhoun 1914–1962 and Robert MacBryde 1913–1966 (1977) [Mayor Gallery]
Robert Colquhoun (1958) [Whitechapel; works 1942–58]

Alan Davie (b.1920)
Bowness, A., *Alan Davie* (1967)

Lucian Freud (b.1922)
Gowing, L., *Lucian Freud* (1982)

Elisabeth Frink (b.1930)
Frink, E. and Willder, J. (ed.), *Elisabeth Frink: Sculpture: Catalogue Raisonné* (1984) [essays by B. Robertson, S. Kent; bibl.]
Mullins, E., *The Art of Elisabeth Frink* (1972)

Gilbert and George (Gilbert, b.1943, George b.1942)
Gilbert and George: the Complete Pictures 1971–1985 (1986) [Hayward]

Lawrence Gowing (b.1918)
Lawrence Gowing (1983) [Arts Council /Serpentine; commentary by Gowing]

Peter Greenham (b.1909)
Peter Greenham: Paintings and Drawings
(1985) [Norwich/Royal Academy]
Richard Hamilton (b.1922)
Hamilton, R., *Collected Words 1953–1982*
(1982) [illus., bibl.]
Barbara Hepworth (1903–75)
Bowness, A., (ed.), *The Complete Sculpture
of Barbara Hepworth 1960–1969* (1971)
[interviews, bibl.]
Barbara Hepworth (1968) [Tate
retrospective]
*Exhibition of Works by John Constable,
Matthew Smith, Barbara Hepworth*
(1950) [Venice Biennale]
Hepworth, B., *A Pictorial Autobiography*
(1970, rev. 1978, repr. 1985)
Read, H. (intro.), *Barbara Hepworth:
Carvings and Drawings* (1952)
Patrick Heron (b.1920)
Patrick Heron (1985) [Barbican Art
Gallery]
*Patrick Heron: Recent Paintings and Selected
Earlier Canvases* (1972) [Whitechapel]
Ivon Hitchens (1893–1979)
Ivon Hitchens: a Retrospective Exhibition
(1979) [Royal Academy]
David Hockney (b.1937)
*David Hockney: Paintings, Prints and
Drawings 1960–1970* (1970)
[Whitechapel]
Hockney Paints the Stage (1983) [opera
designs; Walker Art Gallery,
Minneapolis/Hayward (1985); essays,
bibl.]
Livingstone, M., *David Hockney* (1981)
[introductory]
Stangos, N. (ed.), *David Hockney by David
Hockney* (1976)
Howard Hodgkin (b.1932)
McEwen, J. (intro.), *Howard Hodgkin:
Forty Paintings 1973–84* (1984)
[Whitechapel; bibl.]
John Hubbard (b.1931)
Fuller, P. (intro.), *John Hubbard* (1986)
[Yale Center for British Art, New
Haven, Conn.]
Allen Jones (b.1937)
*Allen Jones Retrospective of Paintings:
1957–1978: an Exhibition* (1979)
[Walker Art Gallery, Liverpool]
Ken Kiff (b.1935)
Hyman, T. and Kaplos, M. (intro.), *Ken
Kiff: Paintings 1965–1985* (1986)
[Serpentine; bibl.]
R.B. Kitaj (b.1932)
Livingstone, M., *R.B. Kitaj* (1985)
R.B. Kitaj (1982) [Kunsthalle,

Dusseldorf/Hirshhorn, Washington,
DC retrospective; bibl.]
Leon Kossoff (b.1926)
*Leon Kossoff: Paintings from a Decade
1970–1980* (1981) [Museum of Modern
Art, Oxford]
Leon Kossoff: Recent Paintings (1972)
[Whitechapel]
Peter Lanyon (1918–1964)
Causey, A., *Peter Lanyon: his Painting*
(1971)
Richard Long (b.1945)
Fuchs, R.H., *Richard Long* (1986)
L.S. Lowry (1887–1976)
Levy, M., *The Paintings of L.S. Lowry:
Oils and Watercolours* (1975)
Rohde, S., *A Private View of L.S. Lowry*
(1979) [biography]
Robert MacBryde (1913–66) [see Robert
Colquhoun]
Henry Moore (1898–1986)
Carendente, G., *Moore e Firenze* (1978)
[1972 Forte di Belvedere cat. in book
form]
Clark, K. (ed.), *Henry Moore: Drawings*
(1974) [1923–71]
Cramer, P., Grant A. and Mitchinson D.,
*Henry Moore: Catalogue of Graphic
Work 1931–1972* (1973) [catalogue
raisonné, vol. I]
*Henry Moore: Catalogue of Graphic Work
volume II: 1973–1975* (1976) [catalogue
raisonné]
*Henry Moore: Catalogue of Graphic
Work: volume III 1976–1979* (1980)
[catalogue raisonné]
Grohmann, W., *The Art of Henry Moore*
(1960, trans. 1965) [exhibitions, bibl.]
James, P. (ed.), *Henry Moore on Sculpture:
a Collection of the Sculptor's Writings
and Spoken Words* (1966) [bibl.]
Mitchinson, D., (ed.), *Henry Moore:
Unpublished Drawings* (1971)
Moore, H., *Shelter Sketchbook* ([1945], new
edn 1967)
Packer, W., *Henry Moore: an Illustrated
Biography* (1985)
Read, H. (intro.), *Sculpture and Drawings
by Henry Moore* (1948) [Venice
Biennale]
(intro.), *Henry Moore: Sculptures and
Drawings* (1944) [vol. I of series]
*Henry Moore volume II: Sculptures and
Drawings 1949–1954* (1955, entitled
'since 1948', rev. 1965)
Continued as:
Bowness, A. (ed.), *Henry Moore: Sculpture
and Drawings volume III: Sculpture
1955–64* (1965) [bibl.]

Henry Moore: Sculpture and Drawings volume IV: Sculpture 1964–73 (1977) [bibl.]

Henry Moore: Sculpture and Drawings volume V: Sculpture 1974–80 (1983) [bibl.]

Malcolm Morley (b.1931)
Compton, M. (intro.), *Malcolm Morley: Paintings 1965–1982* (1983) [Whitechapel]

Cedric Morris (1889–1982)
Morphet, R., *Cedric Morris* (1984) [Tate retrospective]

Rodrigo Moynihan (b.1910)
Rodrigo Moynihan: a Retrospective Exhibition (1978) [Royal Academy]

Sir Alfred Munnings (1878–1959)
Booth, S., *Sir Alfred Munnings 1878–1959: an Appreciation of the Artist and a Selection of his Paintings* (1978)
Sir Alfred Munnings (1878–1959): a Retrospective Exhibition (1986) [Atheneum, Manchester]
Munnings v. the Moderns (1986) [City Art Gallery, Manchester; Munnings among the modernists he opposed]

Paul Nash (1889–1946)
Causey, A., *Paul Nash* (1980) [standard work]

Neo-Romanticism
A Paradise Lost: the Neo-Romantic Imagination in Britain 1935–1955 (1987) [Barbican]

Ben Nicholson (1894–1982)
Russell, J. (intro.), *Ben Nicholson: Drawings, Paintings and Reliefs 1911–1968* (1969)

Sydney Nolan (b.1917)
Clark, K., MacInnes C. and Robertson B., *Sidney Nolan* (1961)

Eduardo Paolozzi (b.1924)
Eduardo Paolozzi: Sculpture, Drawings, Collages and Graphics (1976) [Arts Council; essays]
Konnertz, W., *Eduardo Paolozzi* (1984) [in German; bibl.]

Victor Pasmore (b.1908)
Bowness, A. and Lambertini, L. (intro.), *Victor Pasmore: with a Catalogue Raisonné of the Paintings, Constructions and Graphics 1926–1979* (1980)

John Piper (b.1903)
West, A., *John Piper* (1979)

Pop art
Amaya, M., *Pop as Art: a Survey of the New Super Realism* (1965) [Blake, Caulfield, Hockney, Jones, Peter Phillips, Richard Smith, Kitaj; bibl.]

Friedman, M., and Bowness, A., *London: the New Scene* (1965) [Walker, Minneapolis; bibl.]
Russell, J. and Gablik, S., *Pop Art Redefined* (1969)
Thompson, David, *The New Generation* (1964) [Whitechapel]

Bridget Riley (b.1931)
Riley, B., *Works 1959–1978* (1978) [British Council]

Graham Sutherland (1903–80)
Alley, R., *Graham Sutherland* (1982) [Tate Gallery retrospective; includes paintings of 1970s]
Berthoud, R., *Graham Sutherland: a Life* (1982)
Cooper, D., *The Work of Graham Sutherland* (1961) [1922–59; bibl.]
Hayes, J., *The Art of Graham Sutherland* (1980) [bibl.]
Portraits by Graham Sutherland (1977) [National Portrait Gallery]
Man, F.H., *Graham Sutherland: Das Graphische Werk 1922–1970* (1970) [catalogue raisonné]
Révai, A. (ed.), *Sutherland: Christ in Glory in the Tetramorph: the Genesis of the Great Tapestry in Coventry Cathedral* (1964) [conversations with the artist]
Tassi, R., *Graham Sutherland: Complete Graphic Work* (1978) [1922–78]
Sutherland: the Wartime Drawings (1979, trans. 1980 [bibl.]

Keith Vaughan (1912–77)
Keith Vaughan: Images of Man: Figurative Paintings 1946–1960 (1981) [Geffrye Museum]

John Walker (b.1939)
John Walker: Paintings from the Alba and Oceania Series 1979–1984 (1985) [Arts Council/Hayward]

Carel Weight (b.1908)
Carel Weight R.A.: a Retrospective Exhibition (1982) [Royal Academy]

Glyn Williams (b.1939)
Fuller, P. (intro.), *Glyn Williams* (1985) [Bernard Jacobson Gallery]

David Wynne (b.1926)
The Sculpture of David Wynne 1949–1967 (1968)
The Sculpture of David Wynne 1968–1974 (1974)

Bryan Wynter (1915–75)
Bryan Wynter 1915–1975: Paintings, Kinetics and Works on Paper (1976) [Hayward]

Critics

Berger, J., *Permanent Red: Essays in Seeing* (1960, repr. 1985)
Ways of Seeing (1972)
Clark, K., *Civilisation: a Personal View* (1969, repr. 1984)
Landscape into Art (1949, repr. 1986)
Fuller, P., *Beyond the Crisis in Art* (1980) [essays]
Images of God: the Consolations of Lost Illusions (1985)
Heron, P., *The Changing Forms of Art* (1955) [includes essays on British artists]
Lessore, H., *A Partial Testament* (1986) [essays: Auerbach, Bacon, Freud etc.]

Exhibitions

Preference is given to exhibition catalogues containing essays and bibliographies; catalogues are followed by the name of the exhibiting gallery.
Alloway, L., Bantham, R., and Lewis, D., (intro.), *TIT: This Is Tomorrow* (1956) [Whitechapel Art Gallery]
Bowness, A. (intro.), *Decade: Painting, Sculpture and Drawing in Britain 1940–49* (1972) [Whitechapel]
Bowness, A., Gowing, L., and James P., *54–64: Painting and Sculpture of a Decade* (1964 [Tate: British painting among US and European work]
British Painting 1952–1977 (1977) [Royal Academy]
Compton, S. (ed.), *British Art in the Twentieth Century: the Modern Movement and After* (1987) [Royal Academy; essays by D. Ades, A. Causey, R. Cork, C. Harrison, R. Rosenblum; bibl. painting and sculpture 1905–75]
Entre el objeto y la imagen: escultura britanica contemporanea (1986) [British Council; English texts]

Forge, A., *British Painting '74* (1974) [Hayward Gallery]
Fuller, P. (intro.), *Rocks and Flesh: an Argument for British Drawing* (1985) [Norwich School of Art Gallery]
The Hayward Annual (irregularly since 1977)
Kitaj, R.B. (intro.), *The Human Clay: an Exhibition Selected by R.B. Kitaj* (1976) [Hayward]
Morphet, R., *The Hard-Won Image: Traditional Method and Subject in Recent British art* (1984) [Tate; Coldstream, Freud, Hodgkin, Kitaj, Moynihan, etc.]
Nairne, S. and Serota, N., *British Sculpture in the Twentieth Century* (1981) [Whitechapel]
The New Generation: 1964 (1964) [Whitechapel; Caulfield, Hockney, Hoyland, Jones, Procktor, Riley, etc.]
A New Spirit in Painting (1981) [Royal Academy]
St Ives 1939–1964: Twenty-five Years of Painting, Sculpture and Pottery (1985) [Tate; memoirs, bibl.]
Seymour, A., (intro.), *The New Art* (1972) [Hayward; Flanagan, Gilbert and George, etc]
Situation (1960) [Royal Society of British Artists]
Spalding, J. (intro.), *The Forgotten Fifties* (1984) [Sheffield; Bratby, Clough, de Francia, Herman, etc.]
Transformations: the New Sculpture from Britain (1983) [British Council]
Tucker, W., *The Condition of Sculpture: a Selection of Recent Sculpture by Younger British and Foreign Artists (1975)* [Arts Council/Hayward]
When Attitudes Become Form: Live in your Head! (1969) [Institute of Contemporary Arts]
Young Contemporaries shown 1949–70, various galleries; resumed as *New Contemporaries*, 1974 to date

Sources of Illustrations

The publishers gratefully acknowledge the help of the many individuals and organizations who cannot be named in collecting the illustrations for this volume. In particular they would like to thank Carol Varley and Erica Schwarz for their help with picture research. Every effort has been made to obtain permission to use copyright materials; the publishers apologise for any errors and omissions and would welcome these being brought to their attention.

2a, 2b The Bettman Archive Inc, BBC Hulton Picture Library
48 Roger Wood, London
50 BBC Hulton Hulton Picture Library
61 Reproduced by courtesy of the Trustees of the Victoria and Albert Museum
75 Billy Raffety
80 EMI Records (U.K.)
84, 90, 92 Reproduced by courtesy of the Trustees of the Victoria and Albert Museum
94 Houston Rogers (Ballet Rambert Archive)
97 Nobby Clark
98 Michael Muller
105 By courtesy of the National Portrait Gallery, London
108 Anthony D'offay Gallery, London/Mr and Mrs John Kay
118 James Kirkman Ltd
121 COSMOPRESS, Geneva/DACS, London 1987
122 The Vicar and Churchwardens of St Matthew's Church, Northampton
126 Courtesy Marlbrough Fine Art, London
128 The Graham and Kathleen Sutherland Trust/COSMOPRESS, Geneva
129 Courtesy Marlbrough Fine Art, London
132 The Vicar and Churchwardens of St Matthew's Church, Northampton

146 The Architectural Review
151 The Architectural Press Ltd.
153 The Architectural Review
154 The Architect's Journal
156 Milton Keynes Development Corporation
158a John Donat
158b, 159 The Architect's Journal
160 Mrs P. Fraser
168 University of Bath/Holbourne Museum and Crafts Study Center
171a, Wendy Ramshaw
171b, 177, 178, 181, 182, 184, 187, 189, 190a, 190b, 190c, 190d, 192, 194 Crafts Council
195 Copyright © BBC 1966
203 Times Newspapers Limited
205 Zoë Dominic, London
238 Weintraub Entertainment Ltd
241 Stills from the film Brief Encounter by courtesy of the Rank Organisation Plc
243, 246 Weintraub Entertainment Ltd
248 Paramount Pictures Inc (Gulf and Western), New York
250 Columbia/Indo-British Films
252 The Architectural Press Ltd
257a, b The Architectural Review
260 Reproduced by kind permission of the London Residuary Body
261, 262 The Architectural Review
264 Denys Lasdun
265a The Architect's Journal
265b Denys Lasdun
267 The Architect's Journal
269 The Architectural Review
272 The Architectural Press Ltd
273 Camden Borough Council
278 Simon Pepper
281 Reproduced by kind permission of the London Residuary Body
282a, b The Architectural Press Ltd
283 Simon Pepper

Index

Major entries are shown in capital letters.
Literary works are listed under the author where
known. Page numbers of illustrations are shown
in italics.